Varieties of Capitalism and New Institutional Deals

STUDIES IN EVOLUTIONARY POLITICAL ECONOMY

Titles in the series include:

Understanding the Dynamics of a Knowledge Economy
Edited by Wilfred Dolfsma and Luc Soete

Advances in Evolutionary Institutional Economics
Edited by Hardy Hanappi and Wolfram Elsner

Varieties of Capitalism and New Institutional Deals
Edited by Wolfram Elsner and Hardy Hanappi

Varieties of Capitalism and New Institutional Deals

Regulation, Welfare and the New Economy

Edited by

Wolfram Elsner

University of Bremen, iino – Institute for Institutional and Innovation Economics, Faculty of Economics and Business Studies, Bremen, Germany

and

Hardy Hanappi

University of Technology, Institute for Mathematical Methods in Economics, Research Group Economics, Vienna, Austria

STUDIES IN EVOLUTIONARY POLITICAL ECONOMY

Edward Elgar
Cheltenham, UK • Northampton, MA, USA

Published by
Edward Elgar Publishing Limited
The Lypiatts
15 Lansdown Road
Cheltenham
Glos GL50 2JA
UK

Edward Elgar Publishing, Inc.
William Pratt House
9 Dewey Court
Northampton
Massachusetts 01060
USA

A catalogue record for this book
is available from the British Library

Library of Congress Control Number: 2008929275

ISBN 978 1 84720 473 8

Printed and bound in Great Britain by MPG Books Ltd, Bodmin, Cornwall

Contents

PART TWO: THE (WELFARE) STATE, THE NEW ECONOMY AND NEW INSTITUTIONAL DEALS

PART THREE: AN ECONOMICS FOR A NEW ECONOMY?

Contributors

Rabih Aridi is a PhD student in Management at Birkbeck.

Olivier Brette is Assistant Professor at the Institut d'Administration des Entreprises (IAE) of the University Jean Moulin Lyon 3, member of the Research Centre Magellan (I-CO-D unit) of the IAE of Lyon, and member of the Research Centre Triangle (CNRS/ENS-LSH, IEP Lyon, Univ. Lyon 2).

Charles Craypo is Emeritus Professor in Economics at the University of Notre Dame.

Charlie Dannreuther (POLIS, University of Leeds) researches the political economy of the small firm to critically explore the origins of globalisation.

Michael Dietrich is a Senior Lecturer in the Department of Economics at Sheffield University where he teaches Microeconomics and undergraduate and postgraduate Industrial Organisation. His main interests include the economics of the firm and organisation, political economy of the firm, institutional economics and firm growth and development.

Wolfram Elsner is Professor of Economics, Faculty of Economics and Business Studies, Institute for Institutional and Innovation Economics (iino), University of Bremen. He has worked outside academia as Director of the Planning Division of the Ministry of Economic Affairs of the State of Bremen and as Director of the Bremen State Economic Research Institute.

James K. Galbraith holds the Lloyd M. Bentsen Jr Chair in Government/Business Relations at the Lyndon B. Johnson School of Public Affairs, the University of Texas at Austin. He is a Senior Scholar with the Levy Economics Institute, and Chair of the Board of Economists for Peace and Security, a global network of professional economists.

Frank Gerlach is Senior Researcher at the Research Promotion Department of the Hans Böckler Stiftung, a foundation of the Federation of German Trade Unions.

Hardy Hanappi is Professor of Economics and Head of the Research Group 'Economics' at the University of Technology in Vienna. He is also Jean Monnet Professor for Political Economy of European Integration.

Edeltraud Hanappi-Egger is Professor of 'Gender and Diversity in Organizations' and Head of the Department of 'Gender and Diversity in Organizations' at the University of Economics and Business Administration in Vienna.

Frederic B. Jennings, Jr, is an economics graduate of Harvard College (BA 1968) and Stanford University (MA 1980, PhD 1985). He works as self-employed economic consultant at EconoLogistics and is president of the Center for Ecological Economic and Ethical Education (CEEEE), both in Ipswich, MA (USA).

Stefan Kesting is Senior Lecturer in Economics at the Faculty of Business at the University of Technology in Auckland.

Sue Konzelmann is Reader in Management at Birkbeck, University of London and Associate Research Fellow in the Centre for Business Research at the University of Cambridge.

Jackie Krafft is researcher at the National Centre for Scientific Research in France (CNRS) since 1995.

Kalevi Kyläheiko is Professor of Economics at Lappeenranta University of Technology. He is also Dean of Lappeenranta School of Business.

George Liagouras obtained his PhD from Université Paris VII in 1995. Since 2002 he is Assistant Professor of Economic Analysis in the Department of Financial and Management Engineering, University of the Aegean.

Robbert Maseland obtained his PhD in May 2006 and worked as a lecturer and researcher at the Economics Department of the Radboud University Nijmegen.

Caroline Mehier is member of the Research Centre STOICA of the Institut National des Sciences Appliquées (INSA) of Lyon.

Frank Moulaert is Professor of European Planning and Development at Newcastle University.

Klaus Nielsen is Professor in Social Sciences (Institutional Theory) at Roskilde University, Denmark, and Senior Lecturer in Management at Birkbeck College, University of London, UK.

Jacques Nussbaumer has studied Economics in Strasbourg and Lille and received a PhD with a thesis on the role of culture and institutions in local development.

Patrick O'Brien is Centennial Professor of Economic History at the LSE, Convenor of the Network in Global Economic History.

Phillip Anthony O'Hara is Professor of Global Political Economy at Curtin University, Perth, Australia.

Pascal Petit is CNRS Director of Research, working at CEPN (Centre d'Economie de Paris Nord), University of Paris 13, also affiliated with CEPREMAP Paris.

Jorma Sappinen is a Senior Lecturer of Economics at Lappeenranta University of Technology.

Michael Scheibenreif holds an MBA (Vienna University of Economics and Business Administration), an MA in Political Science (University of Vienna) and an MA in European Studies (College of Europe, Brugge).

Elisabeth Sundin is Professor at the Department of Management and Economics at Linköping University, Sweden. She is the Head of ENIGOS (entrepreneurship in and through the public sector) and is one of the Heads of an VINNOVA Excellence Center in Research and Innovation.

Frank Wilkinson is Emeritus Reader at Cambridge University and a Visiting Professor in Economics at Birkbeck.

Introduction and Overview

Wolfram Elsner and Hardy Hanappi

'GLOBALISATION': EMPIRE AND PERSISTENT VARIATION

The antagonistic dual international structure that prevailed after World War II facilitated glossing over the fact that real-world socio-economies are path-dependent historic-cultural complexes that cannot be neatly defined in terms of clear-cut economic models and systems. Thus, after the end of the state–socialist world system and of the corresponding antagonistic global structure in the early 1990s, it has become obvious that there has always existed, and now exists even more, a whole bundle of national and macro-regional *varieties* of culturally embedded governance structures which typically are mixes of corporate, state, 'market' and network ingredients. The 'liberalisation' of the capitalist world system that 'survived' from an equivalent antagonistic socialist world system, in spite of tendencies to uniform countries and socio-economic cultures in a monopolar world system now, may even have generated more room to manoeuvre and freedom for more varieties of capitalism to spread from the 1990s on. It appears, and in fact seems comprehensible, that the diversification of capitalism has gained even more momentum after the end of the 'cold war'. Thus, after the end of a fierce systems competition, it has become increasingly apparent that capitalist economies, like all socio-economies, are complex open systems, with different configurations of their properties, that typically will behave in different path-dependent ways, may find different responses to similar challenges and thus may persistently, and sometimes even increasingly, vary from one another.

'Globalisation', for instance, thus seems to be far from being a globally unifying process. It does not appear so far to lead to a unified 'market-based' capitalist system, despite powerful forces to globally unify production, consumption, mobility, leisure, or governance patterns; to general cultural habituation, globalised traffic and telecommunication infrastructures, trade and exchange; to an increasing degree of international mobility, and despite political-military ambitions to establish a monistic hierarchical world system, even if this were a collective system of a leading group of capitalist states (the 'international community'). Even though there are remainders of state-socialist countries with partly different behaviour on the global scene (China) and even though, on a more regional level, new forms of bottom-up socialist movements and governments have emerged (Latin America); the global system is a capitalist system dominated by corporate power, corporate global networks and varieties of 'market'-state combinations. This very capitalist system is diverse, and its variations are surprisingly persistent.

No wonder that the late 1990s saw the emergence of a debate on 'varieties of capitalisms', with typologies of capitalisms developed and an emerging deeper understanding of their complexities, institutional embeddedness and thus national path-dependencies.

After a first wave of the 'varieties' debate, this volume represents recent developments in the debate, of course with recent empirical material and case studies, but with critical reflections on, and also going beyond, the 'typological' approach of some earlier contributions. For instance, for some reason in the 'deep structure' of interactive socio-economic processes, country size may play a more central role in explaining different patterns of reaction of countries to the challenges of globalisation. Also, we shall consider the history of varieties of state formation and of institutions of economic growth. The contributions of this book also take a closer look, for instance, at the international firm as a channel for and mechanism of the international diffusion of capitalisms. They deal with diverse forms of national and international governance and regulation (including a global 'hegemony–war–terrorism structure') to interfere with ongoing processes of variation. It will be demonstrated that international capitalism goes 'from one variety to another'.

The volume is also policy-oriented in the sense that its contributions take the fact of varieties in capitalism seriously in order to explore the spaces for institutional reform, or 'new institutional deals', to reverse socio-ecological crises caused by contradictory and 'predatory' dimensions and variations of capitalism.

Standing in evolutionary–institutional traditions, the contributions of this volume even go beyond the general-system level prevailing in this field; they explore old and new 'socio-economic entities' within their old and new environments. These include the family, classes, organised labour, small businesses, industrial clusters and the states themselves, and 'new institutional deals' include the most basic and comprehensive 'social innovations' from local to global levels.

Finally, the varieties analysed and the potential spaces of 'new deals' explored are mirrored against the new aspects of the 'new economy'. Here, the volume presents contributions on what will be left of economics in the face of some of the new dimensions of the new economy. The contributions here are about the economics of fragmentation, complementarities, cumulation, the resulting new forms of coordination and longer planning horizons required, and facilitated, as well as the re-conceptualisation of information, innovation and growth, the embedding of economics in a cultural economics, and the merging of supply-side innovation with macroeconomic effective demand; thus potentially combining Neo-Schumpeterianism and Post-Keynesianism. Consequently, the book ends by considering the challenges of the new economy, asking: 'economics remains the same or does it?' Accordingly, the course of the present volume's overall argument comes full circle through (1) conceptualising an economics apt to deal with (2) the regulation of varieties of socio-economic systems, (3) under the conditions of a new economy, according to human standards and in socio-ecologically sustainable ways – perhaps better regulated varieties of new socio-economies.

The volume thus is a collection of conceptual, analytical, applied and policy-oriented evolutionary and institutional papers. It combines three interconnected fields of discussion:

(1) analysing 'varieties of capitalisms' and 'new economies',
(2) exploring rooms and strategies for comprehensive and systemic institutional and policy reforms (the 'new institutional deals'), and
(3) reconsidering economic theory itself, and further developing a more informed economics.

The book intends to contribute to a more detailed analysis of the underlying factors, transfer mechanisms, and the regulations of the economic systems' varieties (in Part One), state and policy reform, and social innovation, as comprehended in terms of institutional 'new deals' (in Part Two), and the further development of economic theory itself, in face of the challenges of diverse 'new' socio-economies (in Part Three). Let us look at this in some more detail.

VARIETIES, THEIR 'DEEP STRUCTURES' AND CHANNELS OF THEIR INTERNATIONAL DIFFUSION

Part One of the book takes off from the discussion on varieties of capitalism (spurred on by Hollingsworth and Boyer (1997), Whitley (2000), Hall and Soskice (2001), Hodgson (2001), Amable (2003), Coates (Ed.) (2005) (the latter with Albo (2005) and Hay (2005) included), among others). It addresses underlying mechanisms of the generation and regeneration, persistence and diffusion of varieties, its 'deep structure' so to speak. Those varieties are perceived and explored as path-dependent different reconfigurations of complex socio-economic systems to similar sets of 'exogenous' challenges, such as 'globalization', 'net-technologies', fragmented value-added chains, new properties of information, and ubiquitous new learning and coordination problems. This part also conceptualises the variety of firms, their organisations, cultures and strategies, and, for example, multinational firms as mechanisms of cultural diffusion along the global value-chains. Finally, it focuses on some national and international regulatory forms, particularly those of 'predatory' neo-liberal varieties, including hegemonic and violent empire forms. In all, it continues the debate on persistent variation under 'globalisation' and points out new critical factors of overall national socio-economic performance such as, for instance, its underlying institutional arrangements and population size.

'Varieties of Capitalism' – and Beyond

Stefan Kesting and Klaus Nielsen, in their chapter 'Varieties of Capitalism: Theoretical Critique and Empirical Observations', make a theoretical start referring to the current state of the discussion, particularly after Hall and Soskice (2001). But they clearly go beyond it with a more specific comparative institutional perspective. Much in line with, for example, Dore et al. (1999), Hodgson (2001), Kaufmann (2003), and Crouch (2005), they question the rough dual 'market'- vs. 'coordinated'-economies typology of Hall and Soskice, and even the very idea of typologies of capitalisms. More in-depth case studies might put into question the very concept of two 'benchmark' capitalisms that Hall and Soskice make do with. Taking path-dependent, and often contradictory and locked-in, processes of rather unique and complex national systems and cultures seriously, they argue, requires proceeding with more case studies that go beyond the general 'benchmark' cases given by the large countries (USA, Germany and so on). Their empirical cases indicate more diversity 'outside there'. Both Denmark and New Zealand, at a closer look, do not seem to contribute smoothly to Hall's and Soskice's dichotomy of varieties. Among other results of their cases one is particularly stressed: country size matters.

The Genesis of Varieties of State Forms

With Patrick O'Brien's contribution 'State Formation and the Construction and Maintenance of Institutions for Economic Growth in the West and the East, 1415–1846', the line of argument turns to a historical–genetic explanation of one of the central dimensions of capitalist varieties, that is the 'state'. In the frame of an historical analysis, O'Brien reconstructs the *diverse* pathways of state formation and state functions, sometimes even leading to quite similar levels of performance – a 'genetic' explanation of recent persistent varieties of capitalism. The chapter refers to a broad range of historical research on such varieties, such as Braudel (1981–84), Bonney (1995), Landes (1998), North (1990) and Pomeranz (2000), and of course his own extensive research in the field, explaining how the variety may have come up that exists today.

A Regulationist Analysis of Underlying Factors – 'From One Variety to Another'

In their chapter 'Contemporary Capitalisms and Internationalisation: From One Diversity to Another', Charlie Dannreuther and Pascal Petit use regulation theory to analyse the variety of capitalisms over time and geographical space, under the conditions of 'Post-Fordism' and internationalisation. Drawing on the French regulationist works on 'varieties' (for example Amable (2003), Coriat et al. (2006), and also Aoki (1994) and Esping Andersen (1990), among others), they examine the change of the underlying socio-economic and institutional relations in the labour market, in competitive and corporate systems, private–state structures, consumption cultures, financial markets, and international transactions. In this way, they 'endogenously' explain the change of the varieties of capitalism and put the somewhat mystical buzzword of 'globalisation' in its proper place within the overall system of national and international private and public regulations. They demonstrate not only persistent varieties but also the spatial *re-clustering* of types of capitalism, under conditions of the increased role of post-national forms of regulation, non-regular employment forms, de-regulated service sectors, small and medium-sized enterprise and network forms of regulation; finally demonstrating continuous transitions 'from one diversity to another'.

Varieties of Firm Cultures

Michael Dietrich and Jackie Krafft: 'Towards an Historically Relevant Economics of the Firm', elaborate on the variety of firms which can be properly seen, they argue, only from an historical viewpoint. The long-run and opportunity-based perspective on the firm draws on the traditions and 'classic' contributions of Penrose (1959), Machlup (1967), Richardson (1972), Chandler (1977) and Nelson and Winter (1982) and on more recent contributions such as Lazonick (1991), Foss (1993), Hodgson (2002),

Nooteboom (2004) and others, and on their own work. It includes the conventional 'efficiency' perspective (see Coase (1937), Williamson (1985), Langlois and Robertson (1995), Tirole (1988), and others) as a special part. The famous textbook case of 'General Motors vs. Fisher Body' is revisited to generate new perspectives on the firm, and the New Institutional Economics view at it again appears as a special case. The long-run institutional factors as stressed in an evolutionary, post-Marshallian view appear to provide a more overarching theoretical frame, that is a frame which allows for the conceptualisation of 'varieties of the firm'.

An International Transfer Mechanism: The Global Corporation

Sue Konzelmann, Frank Wilkinson, Charles Craypo and Rabih Aridi, in their chapter 'The Export of Varieties of Capitalism: The Cases of Wal-Mart and *IKEA*', also fit themselves in the 'varieties of capitalisms (and firms)' discussion (referring to, among others Appelbaum and Batt (1994), Dore (2000), Jacoby (2005), Quack et al. (1999), and also drawing on their own work). They have developed the concept of diverse national productive systems, where globally active firms with a strong home base still have their cultural roots. They then analyse the diffusion of 'varieties' along the value chains of international firms. Wal-Mart and IKEA serve here as two archetypal antagonistic corporate benchmarks. Their distinctive features and strategies are investigated in the areas of organisation, customer relations, supplier relations, employment standards, and stakeholder responsibility. The chapter concludes that varieties of capitalism 'enforce themselves on companies', which in turn transfer them globally, backwards and forwards along the value chains. 'Markets' thus turn out to be a void construction unless their embeddedness in the national productive systems are clearly elaborated.

The Predatory Variety: Intra- and International Aspects

James K. Galbraith in his chapter on 'Modern Economic Predation: War, Corporate Fraud and the Cruel Chimera of Labour Market Reform', an original invited statement for this volume, focuses on the neo-liberal variety of predatory capitalism in both its intra- and international interactive and policy dynamics. In a Veblenian stance (Veblen 1899), he contributes to the analysis of internal policies for external predation and empire, corporate fraud, labour market dismantling, and war as combined and mutually enforcing factors of this (dominant) international strategy variety. For new institutional deals and perhaps more proper policies and regulations, James Galbraith reconsiders what Keynes (for example (1991) [1933]) and John K.

Galbraith (for example 1967) – the latter of which has gained new interest just recently – have to tell us today.

A Regulationist View of the Predatory Variety: Is Hegemonic Uniformity Feasible?

Phillip Anthony O'Hara, 'A New Global Military–Terrorism–Hegemony Social Structure of Accumulation for Long-Wave Upswing?' takes a closer look at the international dimension of capitalist regulation and examines whether the new military dimension of it represents a new international 'social structure of accumulation' (SSA). He draws on both qualitative and quantitative analyses of the socio-economic effects of the new war–terrorism nexus (for example Enders et al. (1992), Frey et al. (2004), Ito and Lee (2004) and others, and extensive own work). In a regulationist perspective the chapter investigates the relations between the 'military–hegemony–terrorist structure' and its implications on stability and conflict resolution capacity, and between that capacity and socio-economic performance. At the end of his analysis of the features of the global system, the perspective appears sceptical towards both stability/resolution capacity and global economic performance. What seems crucial here in terms of 'varieties' is that the imperial unilateralism/monopolarism of a leading capitalist power, or a small group of leading powers, is in disarray not only with variation and diversity of capitalisms but also with the different and interesting emerging attempts at more peaceful multilateralism.

In all, the chapters of this part provide progress of the current understanding and discussion on varieties, with their
(1) theoretical critique and re-examination of the 'varieties' discussion so far,
(2) new national empirical cases,
(3) re-examination and regulationist analyses of the relations underlying the surface of the diversification and the re-groupings 'from one variety to another',
(4) reconsideration of the diversity of firms,
(5) a closer look at corporate international transfer mechanisms,
(6) intra- and international features of the 'predatory' variety, and
(7) analyses of the current more violent global regime of regulation.

VARIETIES OF THE 'NEW ECONOMY' AND OF THE WELFARE STATE: RECONFIGURATIONS AND 'NEW DEALS'

Part Two builds on the 'diverse capitalisms' debate in order to develop and apply analytical frames for new institutional deals and policy reforms. Particularly, it builds upon the knowledge of varieties and their dynamics, underlying structures and explaining factors, and international transfer and diffusion mechanisms (from diverse corporate to hegemonic–military) of capitalist cultures. This part of the book then explores 'rooms for manoeuvre' specifically to further develop forms of the welfare state, under the new social structures as well as financial and corporate conditions of the 'new economy' (see, for example Aglietta and Rebérioux 2005), in non-neoclassical and non-neo-liberal theoretical and conceptual frames. Therefore, it allows for the examination of spaces and corridors for appropriate, and appropriately diverse, 'new institutional deals', based on properly explored positive degrees of freedom of both analysis and action.

Reconfigurations and New Deals of Basic Socio-Economic Entities

Michael Scheibenreif and Hardy Hanappi, in their chapter 'New Deals of New Social Entities. Evolution of Old Friends: Workers – Firms – Classes – *States*', analyse the major social entities and agents shaping any variety of socio-economic and institutional systems. They start off from a dissolution of the 'old' set of entities, and the institutional structures connected with them, under conditions of a new global political economy. Particularly, they argue, globally extremely diverse households and working structures and a changed physiognomy of production units, finance and states have dramatically changed the environment for any entity and any institutional deal. The message underpins any analysis of conditions of 'new institutional deals' in terms of a change of the old players and the emergence of new ones. And some potential agents even appear only in a nascent state. For all cases discussed here, the need to reach out for new deals appears to be rather pressing.

Reconfigurations of the Family and New Deals for Biological and Socio-Economic Reproduction

Hardy Hanappi and Edeltraud Hanappi-Egger, in their contribution 'The Death of the Family? Evolution of a New Deal Between Biological and Social Reproduction', focus on a basic (both biological and social) entity.

The economic discussion implied here goes back at least as far as Malthus (1820). Referring to Longman (2004), Therborn (2004) and others, as well as their own work, the chapter shows that the biological–demographic 'deals' connected with the variety of family structures have been changing dramatically, with major biological as well as economic implications. They often strongly contrast with the given socio-economic conditions of reproduction. The family is subject to an extreme ideological shaping through ready-made and often politically generated visions of what 'a family' should be and how it should perform. This is mostly in stark contrast to the given socio-economic conditions that the majority of families have to face. The 'new deals between biological and social reproduction' that the chapter suggests cannot be dealt with purely by demographic science, nor by neoclassical economics, in face of the dynamics of the biological/socio-economic/ideological contradictions involved. In fact, the authors argue, this is a major task of an evolutionary political economy approach.

Reconfigurations and New Deals of Small Business

Elisabeth Sundin, 'Small Businesses: The Solution For What and For Whom?', (re-)explores another central entity of the new economy. The SME is also an entity that is largely ideologically overloaded, but at the same time extremely diverse and often subject to different socio-economic contradictions. Also SMEs are therefore requiring new deals. Sundin breaks her examination of the SME sector down to the different industrial sectors, investigating new trends across the sectors and beyond official statistics, calling for, among other things, a blurring of boundaries between the labour market and entrepreneurship research areas that are too often distinct. In fact, 'small organisations in themselves are not the solution to anything', the chapter argues; and an increase in the number of small or new enterprises cannot be generally interpreted as a 'good' thing or 'progressive structural change'. There may be quite different and overlapping trends at work. In fact, economies largely dominated by the power structures of big organisations in deregulated markets leave little room for a really independent development of the small business sector. Sundin's investigations are an extremely important and largely stand-alone countervailing analysis in the highly naïve, euphemistic and often straightforwardly ideological literature on the small business sector.

Relational and Spatial Reconfigurations of Industry: Clusters of Innovation

Olivier Brette and Caroline Mehier focus in their chapter 'Building on the

Micro–Meso–Macro Evolutionary Framework: The Stakes For the Analysis of Clusters of Innovation' on the field of spatial and socio-economic restructuring of industry under the conditions of 'globalisation'. They combine a neo-Schumpeterian approach to origination, diffusion, and retention of social rules at the meso-economic level, as suggested by Dopfer at al. (2004), with a Veblenian perspective of behavioural habits. This approach is applied to draft an institutional and evolutionary economic geography which in turn may help to better explore the cumulative processes taking place in knowledge-based and innovative industrial agglomerations. The paper refers to the general discussion of cumulative processes (see, for example, Nelson and Winter 1982, David 1985; Arthur 1990; Arrow 2000) and on the literature on regional clusters (see, for example, Saxenian 1990; Audretsch and Feldman 1996; Bergmann and Feser 1999; Jacobs and de Man 1996; Amin and Thrift 2000). The chapter investigates varieties and reconfigurations of regional industrial systems and thus develops a major step towards 'new deals' in innovation and regional policies.

A New Deal for Organised Labour in Innovation Policy

In another invited guest statement for this volume on 'The New Economy, Innovation Policies, and the Role of Organised Labour', Frank Gerlach addresses innovation policies from the German labour unions' point of view. Based on his own research and research sponsored by the German unions on regional and national innovation strategies, he develops pathways towards a more active role of unions in innovation policy, as an integral part of a new social cohesion strategy. The case reported here concerning the German unions' campaign 'better rather than cheaper' shows that unions can become stronger indeed in terms of membership, even in the service sectors of the new economy. They can become attractive for high-skilled employees if they stand up for shaping conditions of quality production and solid and professional manufacturing and service work, rather than ever more disembedded, 'financialist' and 'speculative' varieties of capitalism.

Comprehensive Social Innovation, Local to Global

Part Two closes with the development of a broad conception of innovation as social innovation between localities and global nets. Frank Moulaert and Jacques Nussbaumer, in 'Social Innovation between Local and Global', build bridges back to the broad understandings of technological and social, organisational and relational change as represented by M. Weber and J.A. Schumpeter. The contexts of discussion on social innovation are, and have always been, both analytical and normative. The discourse on social innovation clearly centres on the principles of 'the social', that is the interdependent, collective problems which require forms of recurrent interaction, joint learning, reciprocity, trust and solidarity as solutions. The social innovation discourses, therefore, stand much in line with 'alternatives to the logic of the market', to neo-liberal privatisations of the genuinely public realm, to 'the homogenising consequences of the capitalist economy', and to its one-sided and narrow rationality. Consequently, the knowledge required to empower social innovation and its carriers is largely shared, contextual and local knowledge. The analytical perspective of this chapter draws on a multi-disciplinary literature survey of the use of social innovation approaches in the social sciences over the last century which includes, among others, K. Polanyi (1944) and French regulationism (see, for example, Lipietz 2001). Social innovation also implies the development of a 'needs' conception and a corresponding operational body of knowledge, behavioural rules and socio-political strategies. No wonder, therefore, that this chapter closes with the desideratum of an 'epistemology of social innovation' rather than a short-sighted pragmatic set of objectives and political claims, that is, with the perspective of an epistemology of a roadmap towards 'new deals' as changes in the social relations.

VARIETIES OF CAPITALISM AND VARIETIES OF NEW DEALS: SOME IMPLICATIONS FOR ECONOMICS

Part Three of this volume addresses recent aspects of a 'new economics' which is more relevant vis-à-vis complex socio-economies, the varieties of 'new economies' and of new institutional arrangements.

Cumulative Processes and Persistent Varieties: Implications for Coordination Forms and Planning

Frederic B. Jennings: 'A New Economics of Complementarity, Increasing Returns and Planning Horizons', draws on the well-known theoretical elements of direct interdependencies, complementarity of factors, increasing returns and cumulation, which help to theoretically explain resulting persistent varieties among complex economies, as is common understanding in parts of mainstream and in evolutionary institutional economics. The chapter draws on classic sources such as Boulding (1956), M. Polanyi (1958), Bertalanffy (1968), Georgescu-Roegen (1971), Kaldor (1972), Myrdal (1978) and Simon (1982). It is also common that ideal, or institutionally 'dismantled' real, 'markets' largely fail under such complex conditions – and typically result in anything but 'efficiency' or stable equilibrium. The chapter yields surprising implications though. Particularly in the new economy, technological and organisational complementarities, under conditions of net-technologies, cumulativeness and collectivities of information, require more cooperative forms of coordination and longer planning horizons which had become core elements of evolutionary–institutional economic theory and policy conceptions anyway (the chapter here refers to Krupp (1982), Kohn (1986), and Elsner (2004), among others). This is quite consistent with the American pragmatist social valuing and economic policy-making tradition (see, for example, Tool 1979; Hayden 2006). Jennings makes the extremely important point to neatly derive a 'horizon effect' from processes based on complementarities and positive feedbacks, contrasting it with the experience that ever more fierce competition in the neo-liberally globalised economy is tending to shorten down planning horizons, both in private and public sectors (see also for example, Elsner 2003). In fact, time, process, and horizon become crucial in his 'new horizonal economics'. And the interrelation between 'complementarity' and 'horizon' works in both directions, deliberately increasing the space for planning, that is extended time horizons may strengthen complementary concerts of interest, cooperative forms, the economizing of collectivities, and with this social cohesion and ecological health. It is an economics capable of efficiently contributing to progressive and social problem solving new institutional deals.

Persistent Varieties and Cultural Economics

Also Robbert Maseland's contribution 'Taking Economics to Bed: About the Pitfalls and Possibilities for Cultural Economics' starts from the phenomenon of persistent differences of economic performance among societies which, according to a wide–spread argument, can be explained only in the frame of 'a new cultural economics'. For the broad evidence on cultures and economic performance, Maseland refers to Harrisson (1992), Diekmann (1996), Landes (1998), Guiso et al. (2006) and others. The chapter enters the history of thought to show how culture and the economy became two separate fields, specifically in mainstream economics, and takes economic sociology (see, for example, Granovetter 1985 and Smelser and Swedberg 1994), political science (see, for example, Granato et al. 1996), management studies (for example Franke et al. 1991) and different classics of socio-economics and institutional economics (for example, Polanyi 1944; North 1990) as points of reference and departure towards an integrated institutional/cultural economics. Also, more recent investigations and discussions on general trust and economic performance (for example, Knack and Keefer 1997) may serve as supporting the revitalisation of cultural economics, it is argued. Anyway, Maseland's evolutionary institutional reconstruction of a cultural economics goes beyond conceptions of 'culture as preferences' and 'culture as constraints', and instead envisages a political–economic frame: While the separation of 'culture' and 'economy' in mainstream economics is also a reflection of the social structure and values of the current society, the acknowledgment of the simultaneous, concurrent and mutually interdependent generation and change of both would require some 'embedded' economics. And reinventing both cultural economics and the economy as culture involves investigating 'new institutional deals'.

Technology Push and Macro-Demand Conditions: Keynes and Schumpeter

George Liagouras, 'Almost Everything You Would Like to Know About Technology and Growth and That You Will Never be Told by Neo-Schumpeterians' discusses shortcomings of a one-sided technology-push approach for socio-economic growth and explores potential complementarities between Neo-Schumpeterian supply-side strategies and Post-Keynesian growth and development. The chapter draws on Schmookler's (1966) seminal work about the importance of the demand–side dynamics for technology and growth. Evolutionary innovation economics along Neo-Schumpeterian lines, as a largely supply-sided development approach, is considered here as not being capable alone of generating growth and socially inclusive development without considering the interrelation between aggregate supply and demand (a classical argument, by the way, of Mirowski (1982) in an early review essay of Nelson and Winter 1982). Liagouras discusses extensive empirical evidence based on the EU *Community Innovation Survey* introduced 1992, on the interrelations of the supply and demand sides in innovation processes (here he refers to Geroski and Walters 1995; Kleinknecht 1998; Petit 2003; von Tunzelmann 2004 and others). In conclusion, this chapter warns against the 'supply-side (and 'market') optimism', even in a more 'enlightened' evolutionary variant. While evolutionary micro and innovation economics has led, in Liagouras's words, to an important scientific revolution, new institutional deals, as proclaimed in this chapter, would require 'to go beyond ... evolutionary microeconomics towards an evolutionary political economy'.

Varieties of the 'New Economy': Economics Remains the Same – Or Does It?

Finally, Jorma Sappinen and Kalevi Kyläheiko, in their chapter on

'Economics Remains the Same – Or Does It? Challenges of the New Economy', sum up on the challenges of the new significance and role of information to economic theorising. While economics' reaction to this has been slow so far, according to this argument, it should be faster to improve economics' explanatory power. The chapter delves into the specificities of information goods and net-technologies, and the 'new wine' does not appear to smoothly fit in the 'old bottles', as they coin it. The authors take a close look at microeconomics, namely consumer theory and the theory of the firm, and discuss incomplete and endogenous preferences, consumers as innovative users and even producers of information goods, reciprocity forms of exchange, and open-source forms of the generation of information products, increasing returns, path-dependency, lock-ins and resulting potential multiple equilibria (a theoretical equivalent of varieties of socio-economic systems). Mainstream textbook economics thus does not seem to be viable; however, mainstream economists still seem to remain surprisingly committed, on an abstract general level, to the core assumptions and policy recommendations of neoclassical economics, however dismantled the latter's basic assumptions and models may be (see for example, Davis 2006; Elsner 2007). Evolutionary and institutional economics, to be sure, has generated some better informed micro textbooks, both basic and advanced. This chapter cites Bowles (2004), and we might add Himmelweit et al. (2005), Goodwin et al. (2005), and perhaps Fireside et al. (2006). The overall message of this final chapter of the book is 'economic laws' do change – and so will and does economics.

CONCLUSION

Is evolutionary and institutional economics relevant and applicable? Certainly, and the present volume may serve here as a proof. The book's collection of papers is both analytically and politically significant with respect to

(1) diverse capitalist systems and diverse organisational forms, such as firm and state forms, their complexity and their underlying factors and international diffusion channels – and the persistence of these varieties, changing from one variety to another. This holds even in the face of a 'predatory' restructuring and 'uniformisation' of the state and society, predatory globalisation and powerful 'empire'-type attempts at global hegemonic unification;
(2) rooms, capacities, and varieties of systemic institutional reforms, that is

'new deals' for different socio-economic entities, such as labour, firms, classes, the state, the family and small business, with a comprehensive social innovations perspective, from local communities to global net forms. Thus the investigations presented here are practical and policy-oriented with their contributions to institutional reforms in a broad and systemic understanding;

(3) corresponding cutting-edge developments of economic theory vis-á-vis varieties of socio-economic systems, including varieties of a 'new economy', and varieties of potential 'new institutional deals' – new deals for more sustainable, more human and more effective socio-economies.

In this way, the book comes full circle, from the continuing change and variation of capitalism, and complex socio-economic systems in general, to the potential of diverse institutional arrangements and reforms, and a more relevant economics. It is the three interconnected pillars – varieties, new deals and new economics which we hope makes this collection of investigations particular in the landscape of applied economics.

REFERENCES

Aglietta, Michel and Antoine Rebérioux (2005), *Corporate Governance Adrift. A Critique of Shareholder Value*, Cheltenham, UK Northampton, MA, USA: Edward Elgar.

Albo, Greg (2005), 'Contesting the "New Capitalism"', in Coates (ed.) (2005), 63–82.

Amable, Bruno (2003), *The Diversity of Modern Capitalism*, Oxford: Oxford University Press.

Amin, Ash and Nigel Thrift (2000), 'What kind of economic theory for what kind of economic geography?', *Antipode*, 32.1, 4–9.

Aoki, Masahiko (1994), 'The contingent governance of teams: analysis of institutional complementarity', *International Economic Review*, 35.3, 657–76.

Appelbaum, Eileen and Rosemary Batt (1994), *The New American Workplace: Transforming Work Systems in the United States*, Ithaca, NY: ILR Press.

Arrow, Kenneth J. (2000), 'Increasing returns: historiographic issues and path dependence', *European Journal of the History of Economic Thought*, 7.2, 171–79.

Arthur, W. Brian (1990), '"Silicon Valley" locational clusters: when do increasing returns imply monopoly?', *Mathematical Social Science*, 19.3, 235–51.

Audretsch, David B. and Maryann P. Feldman (1996), 'Innovative clusters and the industry life-cycle', *Review of Industrial Organization*, 11.2, 253–73.

Bergman, Edward M. and Edward J. Feser (1999), *Industrial and Regional Clusters: Concepts and Comparative Applications*, Web Book in Regional Science, Regional Research Institute, West Virginia University.

Bertalanffy, Ludwig von (1968), *General System Theory: Foundations, Development, Applications*, New York: Braziller.

Bonney, Richard (ed.) (1995), *Economic Systems and State Finance*, Oxford: Oxford University Press.

Boulding, Kenneth E. (1956), *The Image: Knowledge in Life and Society*, Ann Arbor: University of Michigan Press.

Bowles, Samuel (2004), *Microeconomics: Behavior, Institutions and Evolution*, Princeton: Princeton University Press.

Braudel, Fernand (1981–84), *Civilization and Capitalism, 15th–18th Century*, 3 Vols, London: HarperCollins.

Chandler, Alfred (1977), *The Visible Hand*, Cambridge, MA: Harvard University Press.

Coase, Ronald H. (1937), 'The nature of the firm', *Economica*, 4, 386–405.

Coates (ed.) (2005), *Varieties of Capitalism, Varieties of Approaches*, Houndsmills, Basingstoke, New York: Palgrave Macmillan.

Coriat, B., P. Petit and G. Schmeder (eds.) (2006), *The Hardship of Nations: Exploring the Paths of Modern Capitalism*, Cheltenham, UK Northampton, MA, USA: Edward Elgar.

Crouch, Colin (2005), *Capitalist Diversity and Change*, Oxford: Oxford University Press.

David, Paul A. (1985), 'Clio and the economics of QWERTY', *American Economic Review*, PP, 75.2, 332–37.

Davis John B. (2006), 'The Turn in Economics: Neoclassical Dominance to Mainstream Pluralism?', *Journal of Institutional Economics*, 2.1, 1–20.

Dieckmann, Oliver (1996), 'Cultural determinants of economic growth: theory and evidence', *Journal of Cultural Economics*, 20, 297–320.

Dopfer, Kurt, John Foster and Jason Potts (2004), 'Micro–meso–macro', *Journal of Evolutionary Economics*, 14.3, 263–79.

Dore, Ronald (2000), *Stock Market Capitalism, Welfare Capitalism: Japan versus the Anglo-Saxons*, Oxford: Oxford University Press.

Dore, Ronald, William Lazonick and Mary O'Sullivan (1999), 'Varieties of capitalism in the twentieth century', *Oxford Review of Economic Policy*, 15.4, 102–20.

Elsner, Wolfram (2003), 'Global Industrial Policies', in M.R. Tool and P.D. Bush (eds), *Institutional Analysis and Economic Policy*, Boston, Dordrecht, London: Kluwer Academic Publishers, 523–47.

Elsner, Wolfram (2004), 'The "new" economy: complexity, coordination, and a hybrid governance approach', *International Journal of Social Economics*, 31.11–12, 1029–49.

Elsner, Wolfram (2007), 'Market and State', in P.A. O'Hara (ed), *International Encyclopedia of Public Policy*, Boston, Dordrecht, London: Kluwer Academic Publishers/Springer.

Enders, Walter, Todd Sandler and Gerald F. Parise (1992), 'An econometric analysis of the impact of terrorism on tourism', *Kyklos*, 45, 531–54.

Esping Andersen, G. (ed) (1990), *Welfare States in Transition – National Adaptation in Global Economies*, London: Sage.

Fireside D., Tilly C. and the Dollars & Sense Collective (eds) (2006), 'Real World Micro', Boston: *Dollars and Sense*, 13th ed.

Foss, Nicolai (1993), 'Theories of the firm: contractual and competence perspectives', *Journal of Evolutionary Economics*, 3, 126–44.

Franke, R.H., G. Hofstede and M.H. Bond (1991), 'Cultural roots of economic performance: a research note', *Strategic Management Journal*, 12, 165–73.

Frey, Bruno S; Simon Luechinger and Alois Stutzer (2004), 'Calculating Tragedy: Assessing the Costs of Terrorism', *CESifo Working Paper*, No. 1341, Zurich: Institute for Empirical Research in Economics, University of Zurich.

Galbraith, John Kenneth (1967), *The New Industrial State*, Boston: Houghton-Mifflin.

Georgescu-Roegen, Nicholas (1971), *The Entropy Law and the Economic Process*, Cambridge, MA: Harvard University Press.

Geroski, P., C.F. Walters (1995), 'Innovative activity over the business cycle', *Economic Journal*, 105.431, 916–28.

Goodwin, Neva, Julie A. Nelson and Frank Ackerman (2005), Thomas Weisskopf, *Microeconomics in Context*, Boston, New York: Houghton Mifflin.

Granato, Jim, Ronald Inglehart and David Leblang (1996), 'The effect of cultural values on economic development: theory, hypotheses, and some empirical tests', *American Journal of Political Science*, 40, 607–31.

Granovetter, Mark (1985), 'Economic action and social structure: the problem of embeddedness', *American Journal of Sociology*, 91, 481–510.

Guiso, Luigi, Paola Sapienza and Luigi Zingales (2006), 'Does culture affect economic outcomes?', *Journal of Economic Perspectives*, 20.2, 23–48.

Hall, Peter A. and David Soskice (2001), 'An Introduction to Varieties of Capitalism', in P.A. Hall and D. Soskice (eds.), *Varieties of Capitalism – The Institutional Foundations of Comparative Advantage*, Oxford: Oxford University Press, 1–68.

Harrisson, Lawrence E. (1992), *Who Prospers? How Cultural Values Shape Economic and Political Success*, New York: Harper Collins, Basic Books.

Hay, Colin (2005), 'Two Can Play at That Game ... or Can They? Varieties of Capitalism, Varieties of Institutionalism', in Coates (ed) (2005), 107–21.

Hayden, F. Gregory (2006), *Policy-Making For a Good Society. The Social Fabric Matrix Approach to Policy Analysis and Program Evaluation*, New York: Springer.

Himmelweit, Susan, Roberto Simonetti and Andrew Trigg (2005), *Microeconomics. Neoclassical and Institutionalist Perspectives on Economic Behaviour*, London: Thomson Learning 2001, repr. 2005.

Hodgson, Geoffrey M. (2001), 'The Evolution of Capitalism from the Perspective of Institutional and Evolutionary Economics', in G.M. Hodgson, M. Itoh, N. Yokokawa (eds), *Capitalism in Evolution: Global Contentions – East and West,* Cheltenham, UK Northampton, MA, USA: Edward Elgar, 63–82.

Hodgson, Geoffrey M. (2002), 'The Legal Nature of the Firm and the Myth of the Firm-Market Hybrid', *International Journal of the Economics of Business*, 9, 37–60.

Hollingsworth, Roger and Robert Boyer (1997), *Contemporary Capitalism: The Embeddedness of Institutions*, Cambridge, UK: Cambridge University Press.

Ito, Harumi and Darin Lee (2004), 'Assessing the impact of the September 11 terrorist attacks on U.S. airline demand', *Journal of Economics and Business*, 15, 22–44.

Jacobs, Dany and Ard-Pieter de Man (1996), 'Clusters, industrial policy and firm strategy: a menu approach', *Technology Analysis and Strategic Management*, 8.4, 425–37.

Jacoby, Sanford M. (2005), *The Embedded Corporation: Corporate Governance and Employment Relations in Japan and the United States*, Princeton: Princeton University Press.

Kaldor, Nicholas (1972), 'The irrelevance of equilibrium economics,' *Economic Journal*, 82, No. 327, 1237–55.

Kaufmann, Franz-Xaver (2003), *Varianten des Wohlfahrtsstaats – Der deutsche*

Sozialstaat im internationalen Vergleich, Frankfurt a.M.: Suhrkamp.
Keynes, John Maynard (1991) [1933], 'The Means to Prosperity', in J.M. Keynes, *Essays in Persuasion*, repr. New York: W.W. Norton.
Kleinknecht, Alfred (1998), 'Is labour market flexibility harmful to innovation?', *Cambridge Journal of Economics*, 22.3, 387–96.
Keefer, Philip and Stephen Knack (1997), 'Why don't poor countries catch up? A cross-national test of an institutional explanation', *Economic Inquiry*, 35.3, 590–602.
Kohn, Alfie (1986), *No Contest: The Case Against Competition*, Boston: Houghton Mifflin.
Krupp, Sherman R. (1982) [1968], 'Axioms of economics and the claim to efficiency' *Journal of Economic Issues*, 2.3, 273–82, repr. in W.J. Samuels (ed.), *The Methodology of Economic Thought: Critical Papers from the Journal of Economic Issues*, New Brunswick, NJ: Transaction Publishers.
Landes, David S. (1998), *The Wealth and Poverty of Nations: Why are Some so Rich and Some so Poor?*, London: Little, Brown and Co.
Langlois, Richard N. and Paul L. Robertson (1995), *Firms, Markets and Economic Change: A Dynamic Theory of Business Institutions*, London: Routledge.
Lazonick, William (1991), *Business Organization and the Myth of the Economy*, Cambridge: Cambridge University Press.
Lipietz, Alain (2001), *Pour le tiers secteur. L'économie sociale et solidaire: pourquoi, comment*, Paris: La Découverte.
Longman, Phillip (2004), *The Empty Cradle. How Falling Birthrates Threaten World Prosperity and What To Do About It*, New York: Basic Books.
Machlup, Fritz (1967), 'Theories of the firm: marginalist, managerial, behavioural', *American Economic Review*, 57, 1–33.
Malthus, Thomas (1820), *Principles of Political Economy*, London: John Murray.
Mirowski, Philip (1983), 'An evolutionary theory of economic change. A review article', *Journal of Economic Issues*, 17.3, 757–68.
Myrdal, Gunnar (1978), 'Institutional Economics', *Journal of Economic Issues*, 12.4, 771–83.
Nelson, Richard R. and Sidney. G. Winter (1982), *An Evolutionary Theory of Economic Change*, Cambridge, MA: Harvard University Press.
Nooteboom, Bart (2004), 'Governance and competence: how can they be combined?', *Cambridge Journal of Economics*, 28.4, 505–25.
North, Douglass (1990), *Institutions, Institutional Change and Economic Performance*, Cambridge: Cambridge University Press.
Petit, Pascal (2003), 'On growth regimes in a post-Fordist era', mimeo, paper presented at the 2003 EAEPE Conference, Maastricht, Netherlands.
Penrose, Edith T. (1959), *The Theory of the Growth of the Firm*, Oxford: Basil Blackwell.
Polanyi, Karl (1944), *The Great Transformation*, New York: Octagon Books.
Polanyi, Michael (1958), *Personal Knowledge: Toward a Post-Critical Philosophy*, Chicago: University of Chicago Press.
Pomeranz, Kenneth (2000), *The Great Divergence. China, Europe and the Making of the Modern World Economy*, Princeton: Princeton University Press.
Quack, S., G. Morgan and R. Whitley (eds) (1999), *National Capitalisms, Global Competition and Economic Performance*, Amsterdam: John Benjamins Publishing Co.
Richardson, George B. (1972), 'The organization of industry', *Economic Journal*, 82,

883–96.

Saxenian, Annalee L. (1990), 'Regional networks and the resurgence of Silicon Valley', *California Management Review*, 33.1, 89–112.

Schmookler, Jacob (1966), *Invention and Economic Growth*, Cambridge, MA: Harvard University Press.

Simon, Herbert A. (1982), *Models of Bounded Rationality*, Volumes 1–3, Cambridge, MA: MIT Press (1982–97).

Smelser, N. and R. Swedberg (eds) (1994), *Handbook of Economic Sociology*, Princeton: Princeton University Press.

Therborn, Göran (2004), *Between Sex and Power: Family in the World 1900–2000*, London: Routledge.

Tirole, Jean (1988), *Theory of Industrial Organization*, Cambridge, MA: MIT Press.

Tool, Marc R. (1979), *The Discretionary Economy. A Normative Theory of Political Economy*, Santa Monica: Goodyear Publishing Co.

Veblen, Thorstein B. (1899), *The Theory of the Leisure Class. An Economic Study in the Evolution of Institutions*, New York: Macmillan.

von Tunzelmann, Nick (2004), 'Integrating economic policy and technology policy in EU', *Revue d'Economie Industrielle*, 105, 85–104.

Whitley, Richard (2000), *Divergent Capitalisms*, Oxford: Oxford University Press.

Williamson, Oliver E. (1985), *The Economic Institutions of Capitalism: Firms, Markets and Relational Contracting*, New York: Free Press.

PART ONE

Varieties of Capitalism, Varieties of the Global Firm and Varieties of Regulation

1. Varieties of Capitalism: Theoretical Critique and Empirical Observations

Stefan Kesting and Klaus Nielsen

INTRODUCTION

There are two predominant ways of analysing the different economic and political institutions across countries and the development of such differences in the era of globalisation. Some regard the differences as temporary deviations from 'best practice' that are destined to gradually erode and disappear as an effect of the powerful harmonising process of globalisation. Others see the institutional variation across nations as sticky, path-dependent, specific distillations of historical choices which respond to the forces of globalisation in distinctly different ways and tend to persist. The second view seems to have become the consensus among scholars within comparative political economy. A growing literature stresses the empirical variety of national institutions and relates this to path-dependent trajectories of interdependent national industrial relations, welfare-state institutions, corporate governance and so on (Albert 1993; Esping-Andersen 1996; Berger and Dore 1996; Boyer and Drache 1996; Crouch and Streeck 1997; Kitchelt et al. 1999; Streeck and Yamamura 2001; Amable 2003).

Hall and Soskice (2001) have contributed a theoretical synthesis of this view that has become almost hegemonic not only within the tradition of comparative political economy but also among institutionalist scholars, in general. Their introduction to the volume *Varieties of Capitalism. The Institutional Foundation of Comparative Advantage* provides more than just an overview of the applications, case studies and specific topics covered in the book which consists of a selection of detailed analyses of OECD economies in Europe and North America. The introduction is characterised by a level of theoretical sophistication, explanatory scope, predictive ambition and clarity of argument that distinguishes it from other contemporary contributions. We generally sympathise with the approach and consider it worthwhile to relate to and further develop the framework in our own analyses of contemporary changes in capitalist economies. However we also consider the approach underdeveloped and in important respects flawed. In this chapter we will specify our theoretical critique and supplement it with a few empirical observations from New Zealand and Denmark.

We deliberately refer to Hall and Soskice as authors although the book is a collection of articles edited by them, but written mainly by other scholars. We do this because the introduction provides an inclusive theoretical framework that informs and links the book's diverse empirical evidence. Furthermore the critical arguments will focus on the introduction which one reviewer appropriately calls 'the book's flagship essay' (Dore 2003, p. 359).

After a brief introductory summary of the theoretical framework of Hall and Soskice, the chapter starts out with an overview of the main points of critique presented in the major reviews of the book and in the subsequent contributions to the literature. One of the significant contributions of Hall and Soskice is the identification of two ideal type capitalisms. The next section presents a few alternative theoretical approaches that question the very idea of typologies and argues for the distinctiveness of each single case instead. The two ideal type capitalisms seem to relate to large countries (the USA and Germany) only, whereas the specific conditions of smaller countries are left underexplored. We attempt to develop the framework by elaborating on this point and we supplement the theoretical argument with empirical observations from New Zealand and Denmark. A brief conclusion summarises and interprets the evidence.

THE THEORETICAL FRAMEWORK OF HALL AND SOSKICE

The theoretical framework of Hall and Soskice can be seen as constituted by five main elements. First, the importance of institutions is seen primarily as their capacity for structuring strategic interaction between economic actors and solving coordination problems of firms (internal relations to employers, industrial relations, vocational training and education, corporate governance and inter-firm relations), whereas others see institutions as either socialising agencies, distributors of power or pay-off matrices. Institutions have the capacity for facilitating cooperation, deliberation and information flows among actors, and solving collective action problems. Within the existing institutional framework, the strategic interaction among firms is perceived in game-theoretical terms and the outcomes are seen as equilibrium solutions to coordination problems. The outcomes of strategic interaction can be altered through institutions. In this sense, strategy follows structure, rather than the other way round.

Second, the contributions of single institutions to the firms' efforts to solve problems of coordination in these five spheres cannot be seen in isolation. There are interactions and interdependencies among institutions such that the return or efficiency of institutions is seen to be dependent on the presence of other complementary institutions. There is a tendency for complementarities between institutions located in different spheres of the political economy such that nations with particular forms of coordination in one sphere of the economy develop complementary practices in other spheres as well. These interlocking ensembles of institutions, spanning the spheres of industrial relations, the welfare state, corporate governance, training regimes and inter-firm relations, reinforce each other and imply resistance to change in one of its spheres in isolation.

Third, the approach is firm-centred in the sense that companies, rather than states and labour, are regarded as the crucial actors in capitalist economies. The conception of the firm is relational. It is 'the quality of the relationships the firm is able to establish, both internally, with its own employers, and externally, with a range of other actors that include suppliers, clients, collaborators, stakeholders, trade unions, business associations, and governments' (Hall and Soskice 2001, p. 6) that matters in relation to the efforts of firms to develop and exploit core competences and dynamic capabilities.

Fourth, institutional complementarities result in the clustering of bundles of interdependent institutions in distinct types of political economy. Hall and Soskice identify two ideal types: Liberal Market Economies (LMEs) and Coordinated Market Economies (CMEs), each with distinct institutional configurations. LMEs rely on market coordination and hierarchies within firms, whereas CMEs rely on non-market forms of coordination, networking, negotiation, collaboration. LMEs are characterised by strong managerial power inside the firm, equity-based capital markets, shareholder dominance and a stress on short-term profits, relatively limited collective bargaining, investment in general skills, dominance of external labour markets and arms-length relationships among firms. CMEs are characterised by sharing of power in the firm, bargaining relations between unions and employers, rigid internal labour markets, heavy investment in specific skills, long-term bank-based 'patient' capital, stakeholder dominance, inter-firm networks and a high degree of coordination among employers. The US represents the ideal type LME, whereas Germany represents the ideal type CME. Tendencies for movements towards the ideal types are identified with the implication that hybrids are seen as unstable and tend to move in the direction of either LMEs or CMEs.

Fifth, the competitiveness of nations is seen to be founded on comparative institutional advantage. The idea is that the institutional structures of particular economies make it advantageous for firms to engage in specific activities for which there is institutional support. For instance, whereas LMEs have a comparative institutional advantage in relation to swift adaptation processes and radical innovation, CMEs excel in continuous improvement and incremental innovation. Generally it is not possible to outline which type of capitalism performs most favourably. Each has its strength in different activities but the importance of these activities may vary over the years. Capacities for radical innovation may, for instance, be more crucial in some periods compared to capacities for incremental innovation.

The theoretical framework has implications for economic policymaking and for the analysis of the effects of globalisation. The rationale of economic policies must be defined in its specific institutional context. General guidelines and advice based on 'best practice' do not make sense. Confronted with similar problems, it is beneficial for LMEs to take advantage of its market-based coordination capacities, whereas CMEs will benefit from utilising its institutional capacities for non-market coordination. The adaptation of national systems in the era of globalisation is similarly guided by their specific institutional complementarities that generate disincentives to radical change. On the other hand, it is stressed that institutional reform in one sphere of the economy may also snowball into changes in other spheres as well. Globalisation threatens traditional practices in CMEs. Global financial markets, in particular, imply disruptions and pressures for adoption of practices characteristic of LMEs. However, although the long-term consequences are still uncertain, resistance to radical change and specific path-dependent adaptation patterns that retain the basic qualities of the CMEs are seen to be the dominant features.

There are other subsidiary elements in the theoretical framework. The role of culture, informal rules and history is explicitly mentioned. Formal institutions are supplemented and supported by informal institutions that contribute to the establishment of specific equilibria. Multiple equilibria are seen to exist, and what leads actors to a specific equilibrium is a set of shared understandings and common knowledge that leads actors to coordinate on one outcome, rather than another. This is seen as the entry point in the analysis of history and culture. It implies a role for discourse and ideology although this is hardly crucial in the framework compared to the core elements of the approach centred upon strategic interaction. In addition, the typological dichotomy is modified through the introduction of a Mediterranean type of capitalism and through a bifurcation of CMEs into industry-based coordination (Germany and other Northern European countries) and group-based coordination (Japan and South Korea). However such distinctions do not inform the discussion, in general, which is based on the two ideal types.

CRITIQUE AND ELABORATION

Hall and Soskice's book has been reviewed and criticised by quite a few since it was published in 2001. Others have tried to revise and/or supplement the analytical framework. To our knowledge, at least four review articles go beyond a mere summary and try to evaluate theoretical and empirical claims made by Hall and Soskice (Dore 2003; Edwards 2003 and Haggard 2003; Howell 2003). In addition a special issue of the *Journal of Comparative European Politics* contains three longer critical review articles (Blyth 2003; Goodin 2003 and Watson 2003) followed by a response by the authors. In *Capitalist Diversity and Change* (2005) Colin Crouch develops a detailed critique of the *Varieties of Capitalism* literature and lays the foundation for his alternative approach to comparative analysis and institutional change. Moreover a comprehensive overview and summary of the debate around comparative institutional analyses of capitalist diversity can be found in contributions by Jackson and Deeg (2006a, 2006b).

The three review articles published in *Comparative European Politics* question the validity of Hall and Soskice's theses, typology and empirical evidence. Mark Blyth (2003) argues that the evidence does not confirm the perceived differences between Germany and the USA, and hence questions the empirical basis for the typology. Michael Watson (2003) finds the reference to Ricardian comparative advantage inappropriate. In their response Hall and Soskice (2003) agree and explain that what they mean by 'comparative institutional advantages' is rather competitive advantage as it is coined in the management literature by Michael Porter (1998). Robert Goodin (2003, p. 207) makes an important observation: 'Only in 1979, under the ideological onslaught of Thatcher, did the UK become anything like a pure case of an LME'. This remark points to the relevance of ideas in public discourse for shaping policy outcomes. Hall and Soskice (2003, p.248) acknowledge that 'the coalitions that build specific institutions are multiply motivated'. Moreover, in their response, they seem to adhere to a conception of strategic behaviour which is distinctly different from the game-theoretic one: 'In short, although efficiency considerations of the sort our analysis identifies are relevant to institutional change, the latter is ultimately a political process driven by many factors and must be analysed as such' (ibid., p. 245). This political process is largely based on negotiation, or in other words, conflictual iterated interaction which is framed by institutional settings, but also shapes these institutional structures in return. However such a circular cumulative causation (Myrdal 1972) is in stark opposition to the behavioural logic of game theory as presented in Hall and Soskice (2001). This raises a fundamental question concerning the behavioural logic proposed by the authors.

In his review, Tony Edwards questions the focus on the national level. He adds that national differences may have been exaggerated as a consequence and stresses that a focus on the sectoral level could have qualified the picture. He has another very important point. The dynamic nature of national systems is not adequately theorised. 'While the central argument about institutional complementarities is convincing, I would have liked to hear more about how these complementarities were created, and how they persist and evolve' (Edwards 2003, p. 86). The existence of institutional complementarities is merely assumed, and 'there is relatively little material concerning cases where the "fit" between various institutions is uneasy' (ibid.).

Stephan Haggard makes the same point and sees a risk of functionalism in Hall and Soskice's approach: 'Institutions are seen through the lenses of their effects, and it is only a short distance to the genetic fallacy that institutions arose to solve the problems they do' (Haggard 2003, p. 252). Consequently it is ignored how the complementarities arose in the first place. He adds: 'A related problem is the equilibrium nature of the analysis and the question of the stickiness of institutional complexes. If institutions hang together in these very complex ways, where precisely is the source of the enormous change we have witnessed over the last decade' (ibid.). The theoretical framework stresses functionality and stickiness and has difficulties explaining rapid and radical change. This seems to point towards flaws in the micro-foundation of the approach.

In his review, Ronald Dore picks up on this weakness bluntly and straight away:

> The authors' avowed attempt to formulate their generalisations in the game-theoretic terms of 'strategic' interaction focuses attention on the self-interested rationality of choices at the expense of other motivations – loyalties, a sense of public responsibility, friendships. The 'concept of culture as a set of shared understandings' gets a page of brief acknowledgement in general terms, but no practical application in the analysis (Dore 2003, p. 359).

Overall, according to Dore 'economics tail-wags the political economy dog' (ibid., p. 359). He stresses that this is partly a matter of language but it is more than that. It implies 'economism' in the analysis such as, for instance, a stress on economic performance and an ignorance of 'other aspects of the quality of life – social cohesion and exclusion, crime, the strength of the family and friendship ties' (ibid., p. 360). Furthermore, quite in accordance with the aforementioned historical remark by Goodin, he also bemoans that 'ideology as an explanatory factor is ignored' (Dore 2003, p. 360).

In his thorough review article, Chris Howell substantiates his main critical points by confronting the theoretical framework of Hall and Soskice with two other recent contributions to comparative political economy (Coates 2005; Streeck and Yamamura 2003). Like other critics, Howell also picks upon the 'latent functionalism' of the approach by Hall and Soskice: 'capitalist economies, and the social relations that undergrid them, are fundamentally non-conflictual, such that the interests of different actors can be efficiently coordinated for long periods by institutions' (Howell 2003, p. 13). The *Varieties of Capitalism* approach is criticised for a tendency to underplay the importance of the *political* dimension of political economies. The framework offers 'an extremely thin notion of politics and state action, in which governments … act largely at the behest of employers' (ibid., p. 13). The latent functionalism in the image presented of a smoothly functioning, self-adjusting political economy makes it very difficult to 'explain, the moments of crisis and conflict which are a central part of comparative political economy' (Howell 2003, p. 17). According to the approach of Streeck and Yamamura, 'system coherence and integration has to be continuously defined, established and restored, and institutions emerge from experimentation, improvisation, co-evolution, elective affinities, and unintended consequences' (Howell 2003, p. 21). The historical process is 'replete with accumulating internal inconsistencies that make for a permanent need for reorganisation and reconstruction' (ibid.).

The absence of conflict and exercise of power in the *Varieties of Capitalism* approach means that not only politics is underplayed. In addition, labour is very much a minor actor and almost invisible. According to Howell, it is the virtue of the volume authored by Coates that it rearticulates the role of labour, power and conflict in comparative political economy. First, Coates offers a more thorough examination of LMEs which is much less developed than the analysis of CMEs in Hall and Soskice. Coates has most to say on the British case which is interesting because it is not obvious that it qualified as an LME prior to 1980. Since then, radical change has reconfigured the British political economy in a way which is unaccounted for in the *Varieties of Capitalism* framework. Coates explains this by class conflict and the purposeful strategic actions by employers and the Thatcherite state. Second, Coates emphasises the importance of the class context within which institutions operate, both in terms of capital–labour relationships and in terms of relationships between fractions of capital which is of particular relevance in the UK (finance versus industry). Third, in accordance with French Regulation Theory, he focuses on the temporal dimension of capitalist development. He identifies the periodic shifts in the underlying pattern and form of economic growth, and the manner in which these changes in the growth regimes themselves challenge the institutional configurations of a given political economy.

Colin Crouch warns that theoretical parsimony in a quest to win respect by economists can be overdone and lead to determinism, functionalism and a static and rigid analysis (Crouch 2005, p. 4). He questions the usefulness of neoclassical micro foundations to understand the behaviour of 'individual "warm-blooded" role-holders' and its appropriateness for institutional analysis (ibid., pp. 17–18). His scepticism includes game theory: 'Conventional economics and game theory make the single assumption of the maximization of gain as a goal, and take consistency in decision making for granted. This enables these approaches to make extraordinary progress at the level of theory-construction, but at the expense of becoming remote from reality' (ibid., pp. 19–20). Jackson and Deeg lament Hall and Soskice's insufficient micro foundation as well. They want to see the neoclassical model of behaviour replaced by a more pluralistic governance framework: 'In contrast to Hall and Soskice, who emphasize rational, strategic behavior within a set of fixed institutions, the governance framework pays more attention to social norms and "logics of appropriateness" in shaping actor behavior and institutional choices' (Jackson and Deeg 2006a, p. 24).

Other main critical points are directed toward first, the typology, second, the level of analysis and third the use of complementarity. Crouch criticises 'confusion between ideal types and cases' (ibid., p. 44). Instead of defining LME and CME theoretically, these categories stand for particular countries. In other words, the comparison between LMEs and CMEs is a comparison between USA/UK and Germany (Crouch 2005, p. 35). To overcome this dichotomy, further types may be added (ibid., p. 35). However this extension does not overcome the confusion between types and cases and it still hinders the analysis from being truly dynamic (ibid., p. 31). Jackson and Deeg also regard the analysis as 'relatively static' (2006a, p. 570) 'because it is apolitical and agentless – change comes only through exogenous pressures' (ibid., p. 572). The necessity of a dynamic analytical perspective is also one of five 'emerging challenges' Jackson and Deeg summarise at the end of their working paper (Johnson and Deeg 2006a, p. 38).

For Crouch the starting point for comparative institutional studies should be a much lower level of aggregation: 'Despite the claim to be firm-centred, the approach has been too concerned with the macro-level picture of whole economies, and the account of types has been too closely linked to the polemic between neoliberalism and social democracy' (Crouch 2005, p. 44). A more disaggregated analysis would show the normality of hybrid governance (ibid., p. 120). Crouch sees a combination of different types of governance in any institutional setting and therefore criticises Hall and Soskice's notion of the perfect fit of institutional arrangements in a particular country: 'Characteristics of economies have been bundled together as coherent wholes with inadequate attention being paid to the forces that produce the bundles' (ibid., p. 45). He points out that there are no perfectly integrated complementarities, no tendency to institutional congruence nor a strain towards institutional consistency (ibid., p. 79).

Jackson and Deeg add another critical point. They highlight that Hall and Soskice forget the 'Marxist insight' of class conflict: 'existing typologies are too focused on economic co-ordination rather than distributional outcomes, the politics of class compromise are often missing, and consequently the ... literature has failed to understand the dynamics of change in contemporary capitalism' (Jackson and Deeg 2006b, p. 571).

ALTERNATIVE THEORETICAL APPROACHES

One may ask whether such a typology is necessary at all to conduct cross–country comparisons in terms of performance, efficiency, equality or other areas of interest. In this section we will briefly relate to three contributions to the debate that do not think so.

As outlined above, in his review article Ronald Dore criticised the approach of Hall and Soskice for their focus on 'strategic behaviour' and lack of cultural specificity. In an earlier co-authored article he demonstrates that careful historical explanation can explain why Germany and Japan still differ from what he calls the 'Anglo-Saxon economies' (Dore et al. 1999, p. 117) and probably will do so in the future. Also the differences between the American and the British economic development in the 1990s are stressed as well as the distinct historical events that led to quite similar ideological outcomes in the US and UK (ibid., p. 114). In their attempt to describe particular patterns and variants of capitalism the authors focus on macroeconomic conditions, ideological influence (especially habits of thought among managers), union power and the particular legal system in the four countries under consideration.

In his introductory essay to *Capitalism in Evolution*, Geoff Hodgson (2001) does not refer to any typology of the varieties of capitalism. However he emphasises that deep seated habits and cultural values explain different economic developmental paths in different countries. Starting from a critique of Marx and inspired by institutional and evolutional economists Hodgson derives his 'impurity principle' which he defines as: 'The idea that every socio-economic system must rely on at least one structurally dissimilar subsystem to function. There must always be a coexistent plurality of modes of production, so that the social formation as a whole has the requisite structural variety to cope with change' (Hodgson 2001, p. 72). According to

Hodgson every system relies on its 'impurities' which are based on differences in historical experience, language and culture. From this principle he concludes:

> The particular subsystem, the nature of the combination, and the precise boundaries of the demarcation profoundly affect the nature of the specific variety of capitalist system. A corollary of the impurity principle is the contention that an immense variety of forms of any given socioeconomic system can exist. In particular, an infinite variety of forms of capitalism is possible (ibid., p. 74).

As a consequence of the impurity principle, the rich and diverse variety of capitalisms can not be pressed into a straightjacket of typology based on rational choice. A distinct shift in economic theory away from the standard approaches is necessary (that is an account of cumulative causation) to explain the diversity and its dynamics as well as the constraining and liberating force of institutions.

Franz-Xaver Kaufmann (2003) focuses on the welfare state in his comparative study of varieties of capitalism. His hypothesis is that a clear account of national idiosyncrasies is indispensable for an understanding of the development of welfare states, and that typologies do not help to account for this. He argues (aiming specifically at Gösta Esping-Andersen's typology of welfare regimes) that different countries tend to cluster in yet different groups depending on the aspects of welfare states chosen as criteria for the classification. He also claims that the kind of robustness suggested by statistical data is usually mistaken and problems of comparability tend to be ignored. In his opinion the historical method is better equipped to allow for the kind of flexibility which is necessary for cross–country comparisons. Kaufmann stresses that the efforts of the welfare state to solve problems of social integration and coherence are embedded in a normative public discourse which articulates problems and possible solutions in a particular way dependent on preceding wars, economic crisis, social upheavals and bargaining between unions and employers (Kaufmann 2003, pp. 31–33). Hence, he argues that the theoretical inclusion of distributional conflicts and the cultural-normative dimension is absolutely essential to explain national idiosyncrasies or what he calls the 'Gestalt' of a variety of capitalism compared to others (ibid., p. 51).

Dore et al., Hodgson and Kaufmann have in common that they all raise considerable doubts about the usefulness of typologies in cross–country comparative studies and stress the importance of cultural specificity and ideology. They all seem to view individual countries as specific 'cases' rather than representatives of a limited number of 'classes'. However, in the study of cases, ideal typical classes such as the typology of Hall and Soskice may be helpful. Crouch provides the arguments for such a methodological approach. He starts from a broader concept of the agent: 'human individuals are assumed to operate in a permanent dilemma between following the rules of the institution within which they operate and challenging, breaking, innovating against, those rules' (Crouch 2005 p. 19). His behavioural model is a Schumpeterian one of institutional entrepreneurs or historically and socially embedded path creators:

> Our agent, A, could find new paths only when there were some 'mongrel', even incongruent elements in her environment. We can therefore observe innovations of this kind only if our models of real-world institutions have allowed us to find elements of complexity and incoherence. This will not happen if a false interpretation of the law of parsimony requires us to simplify the cases we study so that they seem to be the embodiments of ideal types (ibid., p. 99).

This notion of 'mongrel' elements is very similar to Hodgson's impurity principle. Conflicting rationalities and interests, diversity of institutional forms or governance mechanisms and latent redundant capacities lead to degrees of freedom used by institutional entrepreneurs embedded and empowered by networks to bend path dependence by emulation and discovery of functional equivalents. Potential institutional change, according to Crouch, is constrained as well as enabled by path dependency. To analyse these processes clearly defined Weberian ideal types might be useful instruments, but: 'The fundamental point is: Empirical cases must be studied, not to determine to which (singular) of a number of theoretical types they should each be allocated, but to determine which (plural) of these types are to be found within them, in roughly what proportions, and with what change over time' (ibid., p. 26). He demonstrates how such an historically specific enquiry can be done at the example of what he calls 'The British Neoliberal Turn' (ibid., pp. 143–150).

Similarly, in Jackson and Deeg's reading, path dependency both limits deliberate institutional change, and at the same time enables it: 'Different institutional domains have their own unique logic (or *Eigengesetzlichkeit* following Max Weber) and thus evolve "historically" in the sense of being open to political contention and ideological reinterpretation' (Jackson and Deeg 2006a, p. 36). Hence, detailed case studies are needed to understand varieties of capitalism and institutional change.

A FRAMEWORK FOR CASE STUDIES

The two case studies on New Zealand and Denmark will refer to Hall and Soskice's dichotomy by means of an attempt to determine which of the two types are to be found within them, in roughly what proportions, and how this has changed over time. Generally the approach implies that we should expect to find hybrids rather than cases that confirm to ideal types. Such hybrids may constitute specific and heterogenous complementarities (Crouch 2005, pp. 50–60), rather than the ideal type institutional complementarities identified in Hall and Soskice.

Furthermore, the case studies take into account some of the critique presented in the previous section. Prior to the cases studies we will sum up this criticism supplemented by an inclusion of the variable of smallness. We will not refer to the criticism based on empirical evidence and neither will we include the more fundamental critique that questions the whole approach as such, but rather focus on the more constructive theoretical critique. We basically assume that variety of political economies is persistent, that there is no such thing as 'convergence towards best practice'. We believe that it is more fruitful to consider 'cases' rather than 'classes'. However, although historical specificities and path dependency make every national case unique we do not believe that it is a futile exercise to construct typologies such as the duality of LMEs versus CMEs. However we are not convinced that this is the most fruitful typology. In any case, 'classes' should be understood as ideal types that may help us to understand the specific combination of features in each unique 'case' rather than categories in which each case are supposed to fit more or less in its totality.

One of the most serious points of criticism relates to the crucial idea of institutional complementarities, which is seen as a cause for (latent) functionalism. A consequence of this is the failure to focus on founding moments and lost alternatives and other aspects of the process of the establishment of complementarities. Another consequence is the ignorance of ambiguities, 'uneasy fit', inconsistencies and tensions, and the need for continuous reconstruction of institutional complementarities. This requires a more open and historical approach but it is hardly incompatible with the *Varieties of Capitalism* approach as such. We will identify a few such uneasy fits and tensions in the two case studies.

A related critique focuses on the non-conflictual character of the approach. Hall and Soskice see coordination problems at the level of firms but these are not regarded as fundamentally conflictual. This is remarkable considering the background of the authors in the tradition of historical institutionalism. Within institutional theory the dimension of institutional genesis and change can be seen as one of the two crucial explanatory dimensions, the other being the relationship between individuals and institutions (DiMaggio 1998; Nielsen 2001). Historical institutionalism has always been characterised by a clear emphasis on the fundamental conflictual character of institutional genesis and change and the role of power and group conflict, but now Hall and Soskice rather seem to subscribe to the views of rational choice institutionalism and social constructivist institutionalism. Both these alternative approaches stress in different ways that institutionalisation and institutional change reflects efforts to solve coordination problems among individual actors rather than effects of conflicts (Nielsen 2001). In the case studies we will take account of this critique by means of a reinstatement of the role of the state as well as the role of labour.

A third important point of criticism is centred on the perceived stickiness and resistance to change and the consequent failure to account for rapid and radical change. This is related to the latent functionalism and the absence of a proper political dimension of the approach. It is crucial to introduce the role of ideas and ideologies and hegemonic struggles as part of such a political dimension. In this context, it would strongly improve the explanatory strength of the approach if it would introduce sensitivity to the temporal dimension of growth patterns in capitalist economies such as inherent in French Regulation Theory. The proposed amendments would certainly make the *Varieties of Capitalism* approach more complex but none of them seem fundamentally inconsistent with the overall theoretical framework. It is remarkable that Hall, in an earlier contribution, actually presents a well developed explanation of the conditions for radical versus incremental institutional change by means of the approach of social learning. He used the event of Thatcherism as an example of radical change (Hall 1998).

A fourth major point is the critique of the approach for representing 'economism' and for the limited role attached to culture, ideology and ideas. Hall and Soskice focus on the rationality of strategic interaction. However, other forms of rationality (communicative – Habermas 1995; as well as procedural – Hargreaves Heap 1989 and Simon 1997) should have equal weight as strategic considerations. Otherwise important aspects of dynamic change and adjustment will be overlooked or misinterpreted. From the vantage point of public choice theory (a close sibling to Hall and Soskice's approach in terms of emphasis on strategic interaction) it is not quite clear why governments should be prone to take a broader macro perspective or national point of view (Hall and Soskice 2001, p. 51). What induces or ensures that governments and other actors (firms, unions, associations and so on) will adopt the general public interest? What are the factors which facilitate deliberation, cooperation and commitment (ibid., 2001, pp. 32–33)? How can we explain 'trustworthiness and common knowledge' (ibid., p. 63)? Such phenomena cannot be explained merely through actions guided by strategic rationality but rather through other forms of rationality. The 'negotiated economy' model provides a different notion of 'common understanding' and the underlying institutional processes to support it (Nielsen and Pedersen 1991; Nielsen and Kesting 2003; Kesting 2005, 2007).

A fifth critical point relates to the stylised distinction between LMEs and CMEs. The exclusive reference to the US and Germany as extreme cases of LMEs and CMEs is not helpful. It makes all other national varieties intermediate cases characterised in terms of their variation from the two ideal type polar cases. One way of alleviating this problem is to expand on the number of ideal types. Hall and Soskice briefly mention the possibility of identifying a Mediterranean type without specifying its ingredient parts and its complementarities. Anyway, it may only be seen as a hybrid within the context of the theoretical framework and probably an unstable one as well. Other authors have expanded the typology in other ways. Kitchelt et al (2002) subdivides CMEs into sectoral versus national coordination, that is Central versus Northern Europe. Schmidt (2002) adds State Capitalism to LMEs and CMEs. Amable (2003) operates with five types. He adds the Mediterranean and Asian models of coordination to the LME and the sectoral and national variants of CME. An extended typology for Europe identifies 'four basic models of capitalism: Nordic, Center, Southern, and Anglo-Saxon' (Jackson and Deeg 2006a, p. 29). There is also a typology for Asia: 'Japanese community, Korean patrimonialism, and familial networks in Taiwan' (ibid., p. 29).

Our suggestion is to explore whether the inclusion of an analysis of small countries may contribute to the development of the typology. Does smallness represent distinct institutional traits that make it necessary to amend the typology, or does it question the foundation of the typology? Smallness is identified with specific features by Katzenstein (1985). Small countries tend to adapt more rapidly and flexibly to world market changes, which is made possible by a set of institutions that involve all major interest groups in the political decision making and compensate those who lose as an effect of the processes of adaptation (see the discussion of Denmark in Campbell et al. 2006). In a similar vein, it may be argued that small countries are capable of more rapid and even radical change because of their domestic institutional set-up. It may also be that small countries because of their spatial proximity and social cohesion are capable of combining elements of LME and CME in ways that are impossible in larger countries. Does smallness allow for other types or higher degrees of social capital? Do smaller countries achieve higher degrees of social embeddedness of markets into regions and communities?

In Hall and Soskice (2003), New Zealand and Denmark are mentioned as representatives of LMEs and CMEs, respectively. Hall and Gingerich (2004) uses a set of indicators to assess the overall balance between market and strategic coordination in labour relations and corporate governance which positions Denmark and New Zealand firmly in the camps of CMEs and LMEs respectively (Hall and Gingerich 2004, p. 16). However do New Zealand and Denmark really fit into the taxonomy of LME and CME? What are the institutional support systems for firms and industries in New Zealand and Denmark? Are they competitive and collaborative, respectively? To follow the logic of the *Varieties of Capitalism* framework they can be seen as the US and Germany writ small. Or maybe, the institutional characteristics of these two countries represent slightly modified versions of the ideal type cases. In the case studies below we present evidence that seems to indicate far more complex relationships. In the case of New Zealand, there is a focus on the simultaneous co-emergence of the neo-liberal revolution of economic and industrial policies and the new Resource Management Act that represents a completely different logic. This constitutes an 'uneasy fit' with the dichotomous typology proposed by Hall and Soskice. Also, in the case of Denmark, evidence showing the existence of complex unique complementarities is presented. In addition, the evidence also documents the implications of social embeddedness and social capital and the fact that the role of domestic compensation is still crucial.

CASE: NEW ZEALAND

The incredibly fast and radical change of New Zealand from one of the most regulated economies in the developed western world to an extremely deregulated market economy after 1984 followed by the construction and implementation of the Resource Management Act (RMA) in 1991 can serve as a good example to illustrate our arguments concerning smallness, uneasy fits, heterogeneous institutional complementarities, the importance of ideas and common understanding and the important role of the state and labour.

Before Roger Douglas became Minister of Finance in the Labour government led by David Lange in 1984, New Zealand was nothing if not the opposite of an LME in Hall and Soskice's sense. The preceding National Party government (1975–84) was ruled by their charismatic and autocratic leader Robert Muldoon who believed in the merits of a strong central state and did not seem to have much faith into the workings of the free market. The slogan for economic policy he created was 'Think Big', meaning state–funded infrastructure and industrial projects. Quotas and high tariffs were in place to protect the local industries. Inflation was high and unemployment hidden in social programmes and state–owned enterprises. Farming was heavily subsidised, for instance 'one was not able to buy margarine, that economically subversive substance, without a doctor's prescription until the mid-1970s' (Belich 2001, p. 414). This was meant to protect dairy farming from competition. Michael King describes the economic policy of Muldoon's National Government in the following way:

> At different points in its term it imposed a wage and price freeze, controlled rents, director's fees and dividends, and tried to force down interest rates. It invested heavily and ultimately unsuccessfully in a programme to make synthetic petrol, ammonia urea and methanol out of natural gas – the so-called "Think Big" strategy designed to make New Zealand self-reliant in energy and soak up unemployment (King 2003, pp. 485–6).

The failing of the National government's economic policy, which resulted in downward sliding living standards, led to a radical ideological turn in the political sphere: 'There is an element of "what would Muldoon do? – we do the opposite" apparent in the adoption of neoclassical ideas. Muldoon had, in some policy elites' eyes at least, discredited government intervention in the economy (Goldfinch 2000, p. 56). The tremendous frustration and dissatisfaction with the Muldoon type of economic policy led to a landslide victory of Labour in 1984.

Goodin's remark about the role of ideology in Thatcherism which was necessary to turn the UK into an LME (Goodin 2003, p. 207) is equally true for New Zealand. A minority of ministers in the new government were heavily influenced by radical liberal ideology (Easton 1997, p. 223; see also Goldfinch 2000, pp. 36–7). The newly elected Minister of Finance Roger Douglas, 'the son of a trade unionist, was from a traditional Labour family' (Massey 1995, p. 65). Nonetheless, the experience of the National government's failed interventionist policies turned him into a staunchly convinced free market advocate (Douglas 1993, p. 10). The mid 1980s were dominated by the ascendancy of Thatcherism and Reaganomics. In Britain, the union movement was in strong decline after the defeat of the miners' strike, the Soviet Union was in decline, and international organisations like OECD, IMF and World Bank were relentlessly propagating an international standard of free market policies. The New Zealand variant of neoliberalism is now known as 'Rogernomics', a term created in an analogy to 'Reaganomics'. The ideological support for the new Minister of Finance came from the Treasury which basically worked as a neo-liberal think tank to prepare the project of radical change (Goldfinch 2000, p. 40; Kelsey 1995, pp. 49 and 67; Roper 2005, pp. 157 and 163). 'From 1984 to 1990 the Treasury was able to use its dominant position to exercise an extraordinary degree of influence over the policy-making of the ... Government' (Roper 2005, p. 169). Further support came from the Reserve Bank and the New Zealand Business Roundtable, a liberal and free market oriented lobbying group. Within these circles the policy alternative to Muldoon's 'Think Big' and state control was adapted from a reservoir of internationally popular ideas.[1]

About two dozen likeminded and befriended people oscillating in overlapping careers between these key institutions (Cabinet, Treasury,

Reserve Bank and Business) constituted a powerful elite which was able to push for and implement very fast institutional change (Goldfinch 2000, pp. 65 and 84; Kelsey 1995, p. 49; Roper 2005, pp. 160–61). Such closeness and cohesion was supported by the smallness of New Zealand. The credibility and legitimacy of the 'technocrats' in Treasury and Reserve Bank (Kelsey 1995, p. 53) was further strengthened by their success in handling a major foreign exchange crisis in the early days of the Labour government (Roper 2005, p. 169).

The comprehensive deregulation and the free market policies that were installed by Labour– and National– led governments during the next 16 years can be seen as efforts at putting an almost ideal LME into place. In March 1985 the Minister of Finance announced the floating of the New Zealand exchange rate (Easton 1997, p. 231). The Central Bank became independent. A change in employment law weakened the bargaining power of unions considerably.[2] Quotas as well as farm subsidies were basically abolished and tariffs reduced step by step (Friede 1997, p. 9). State owned enterprises were, if not privatised, run more like business enterprises.

Of course these changes were met with opposition especially from trade unions and their allies in the Labour Party, but it remained weak and fragmented for several reasons explained by Kelsey (1995, p. 35): 'the capture of (neoliberal ideology by) a Labour Party historically committed to social democracy proved a major political coup and helped neutralize opposition from the left'. 'The trade union movement, in particular, refused to take on "its own" Labour government, fearful of a fate similar to the British unions under Thatcher if they lost' (ibid., p. 36). 'Many of the feminists, peace activists and environmentalists who chose to work within the Labour Party concentrated on their sectoral concerns' (ibid.). Overall Kelsey points toward a sedative political climate which led to stifled protest and opposition:

> Most … were paralysed by the pace and content of change, confused by the role of the Labour government, and trapped in nostalgia for a centralised welfare state which was disappearing before their eyes. While they felt uneasy about what was taking place, people generally remained isolated, insecure, defensive, unorganized and politically inert (ibid., p. 297).

Because of the ideological vacuum left by the frustration with the former political era of state intervention there was a lack of alternatives to the neo-liberal project. Moreover these new political ideas could be implemented with such an astounding speed because of the short distance between the centre and lower administrative bodies in New Zealand as a small country and with its simple parliamentary structure: 'The single-house, first-past-the-post, two-party system meant the winning party had absolute power to rule.

By maintaining a strategic ratio of ministers to MPs, the Cabinet was able to dominate decision-making in the caucus, while a rigid system of party whips ensured that all its MPs followed the Executive's line' (Kelsey 1995, p. 42). As emphasised and criticised by Kelsey and others, Roger Douglas used this lack of checks and balances quite successfully to override democratic processes of deliberation characteristic of what we call 'negotiated economy'. Easton has called this the 'blitzkrieg' approach: 'In each case the lightning strike involved a policy goal radically different from the existing configuration, to be attained in a short period, following a surprise announcement and a very rapid implementation' (Easton 1994, p. 215). 'Critics and opponents were always on the defensive and left debating last week's reforms. The major decisions would already have been taken; any consultation was limited to detail' (in Kelsey 1995, p. 33).

To sum up, the surprising speed and radical character of the New Zealand *revolution* (Russell 1996) after 1984 can be explained at least in part by the dominance of a particular set of ideas which was forcefully put into practice by a determined power elite whose manoeuvrings were facilitated by conditions grounded in the smallness of the country such as the proximity of the ruling network and a political system weak in such checks and balances that are typical of larger and especially federal countries. New Zealand was not an LME right from the start, but turned into one in a deliberately conducted, nevertheless, path–dependent process.

However, astonishingly, in these high times of installing a free market regime a pioneering piece of legislation was created as well, the Resource Management Act (RMA). We interpret this as an introduction of novel CME features and at least as a step towards a proper negotiated economy: here the environmentalist fraction within the Labour Party which concentrated on their concerns while neglecting economic policy can be interpreted as a source of heterogeneous complementarities. Julie Frieder, an American guest scholar who was invited to New Zealand to review this law, writes enthusiastically:

> In 1991, the New Zealand Parliament confidently added to its catalogue of 'firsts' – first country to give women the right to vote, first country to ban nuclear weapons – when it became the first country to sanction sustainability. The Resource Management Act of 1991 … is a public policy masterpiece designed for efficacy, efficiency, equity and transparency of process. It provides for the establishment of national policy direction, and standardized planning, permitting and enforcement, but extends to local and regional agencies the flexibility and autonomy to identify the most suitable and least costly implementation methods (Frieder 1997, p. 5).

Hence, besides the free market creed a quite different system of ideas was installed. How did this change come about? This rapid introduction of ecological 'sustainability' in public sentiment and policy could only happen in a small country. A window of opportunity opened up because environmentalists and the business community were equally dissatisfied with Muldoon's authoritarian 'Think Big' state–centralised approach. The plan of the central government of hydroelectric development at the Manapouri lake was seen as a symbol of the Muldoon approach and led to a strong environmental movement in New Zealand: The 'Save Manapouri Campaign … started a national debate on environmental issues, involving national and local body politicians, scientists, professional planners and members of the public' (King 2003, p. 441). 'There is little doubt that "the perceived indifference, if not open hostility" of the National government towards environmental interests was exploited by the Labour Party in the run up to the 1984 election' (Wheen 2002, p. 269).[3] The then new ideas of sustainability formulated in the Brundtland report thus found entry into a new piece of legislation, the RMA. Thus, the Manapouri Campaign is an event which initiated processes of argumentation and negotiation which led to a significant change in the pool of publicly expressed ideas.

On the other hand, 'The private sector was also satisfied that requirements for cost benefit analyses … would serve least-cost policy options and that property rights and consumer choice would give individuals, rather than central government, the key to resource management decisions' (Frieder 1997, p. 5). Hence RMA is a political compromise between these two interest groups and belief systems:

> Agenda status for both local government reform and resource management reform was achieved in part because of the consistency of these reforms with the broader reform thrust of the Labour Government, in part because the logic of the broader reforms suggested that they should also be entrenched in local government (not only New Right efficiency reforms but also accountability, procedural, and checks and balances reforms), and in part because of commitments that Labour had made to reform the structure of environmental decision making (Buehrs and Bartlett 1993, p. 116).

The RMA forces investors (for example real estate developers or mining companies) to attain resource consent for any economic projects at regional councils. This allows for interventions by the public (including environmentalist groups) during the process of approval and since economic development has to take place according to the Brundtland definition of sustainability it initiates negotiations between groups representing investment interests and others defending the diversity of species and other environmental issues. Investment projects in New Zealand are not based on economic calculation and market processes alone, but embedded in negotiation and bargaining processes which include a much larger value base than cost–benefit considerations.

Currently neither the environmentalists nor the business community are particularly happy with the bottom up, holistic and 'fair process'–oriented RMA which is based on a broad and open vision of sustainability. Environmentalists would like to see stricter rules. The executive director of the New Zealand Business Roundtable on the other hand criticises that the RMA limits the property rights of owners otherwise guarantied by common law (Kerr 2002). This indicates that in negotiations and bargaining processes business and environmentalist claims frequently clash. However most observers seem to agree with the following statement by Michael King: 'Given that the Act was always going to be a referee among competing interests, however, it was inevitable that few parties would be entirely satisfied by its operation. On balance, it does subject the country's use of finite resources to more rigorous, fair and transparent monitoring than was possible previously' (King 2003, p. 446).

The negotiations around resource consent set off an ongoing debate about environmental issues in relation to economic investment. At the moment it seems to be a way of balancing interests and different sets of ideas about the future, that is a procedure to ensure fair conflict resolution. However it can also be interpreted as an increment to a negotiated economy in which a more consensus–oriented way of negotiations about visions of the future might be implemented.

In a nutshell, the example of the RMA teaches us two lessons in regard to the *Varieties of Capitalism* approach: firstly, elements which can lead to a negotiated economy (which can be interpreted as an advanced state of a CME) can be found in a country which otherwise (in the economic sphere) would clearly be seen as an almost pure LME, and thus we need a different micro foundation from strategic interaction based on rational choice to integrate the influence of different sets of ideas in our explanation of particular political economic institutional arrangements; secondly, in small countries institutional change can happen quite fast and develop peculiar traits which might not fit perfectly with the ideal type institutional settings of CMEs and LMEs.

CASE: DENMARK

The Danish case has been analysed in an impressive recent volume (Campbell et al. 2006) which not only thoroughly describes its historical foundation and its current institutional fabrics but also links the Danish experience with both the *Varieties of Capitalism* and the *Small States* literature. The volume outlines the image of a peculiar hybrid of characteristics from both CMEs and LMEs which challenges the *Varieties of Capitalism* literature and supplements and elaborates Katzenstein's classical contribution to the literature on small states. In a follow up article, two of the editors of the book have summarised the conclusions of the book in relation to the Varieties of Capitalism literature (Campbell and Pedersen 2007). Contrary to the logic of this approach Denmark is seen to have developed a successful hybrid form by (a) increasing the exposure of actors to market forces and (b) decentralising collective learning and decision making. Such hybridization represents institutional complementarities but these are based on institutional heterogeneity rather than homogeneity. Case studies of Danish labour markets, vocational training and industrial policy illustrate the points. The authors conclude that the *Varieties of Capitalism* theory is logically flawed.

The hybrid characteristics of the Danish case are rooted in historical events and compromises but more recent developments such as globalization and neo-liberalism have contributed to further hybridisation (Nielsen and Kesting 2003; Campbell and Pedersen 2001). Generally, Denmark has adapted to the challenges of globalization and the advance of neo-liberal ideology by introducing new or strengthening old features that are normally associated with LMEs in ways that are compatible with the overall logic of the model.

One of the founders of the *Varieties of Capitalism* literature comments on the Danish experience in a postscript in the book edited by Campbell et al. (Hall 2006). Hall does not question the description of the actual characteristics of the model and its dynamics but he interprets it differently. He finds the Danish experience perfectly compatible with the *Varieties of Capitalism* framework. He points to the underlying stability of the institutions of 'a negotiated economy' that underpins the continuous mobilisation of consensus among the social partners and constitutes a genuine defining trait of coordinated market economies. He concludes that 'the Danish experience reminds us that markets have an important role to play in coordinated economies as well, and need not undermine strategic coordination, provided that they are configured so as to be complementary to it' (Hall 2006, p. 451).

Recently, the so-called 'flexicurity' associated with the Danish labour market and welfare state has been seen as a 'model' to follow in the context of both OECD, EU and ILO (OECD 2004, chapter 2; Wilthagen and Tros 2004; Bredgaard et al. 2005; Madsen 2006). The specific combination of features from CMEs and LMEs in relation to Danish flexicurity is the most obvious case for divergence from the ideal typical varieties of capitalism.

One of the Danish peculiarities is the low level of job security. Employment can be terminated at low cost and at short notice. This is considered socially acceptable because of the generous unemployment benefits and the strong efforts to retrain redundant workers. An influential model of the Danish employment system is the so-called 'golden triangle' (Madsen 2006, pp. 330–31) consisting of (a) a flexible labour market with a high level of worker flow in and out of employment and unemployment, (b) a generous system of economic unemployment support, and (c) active labour market policies aimed at upgrading the skills of the unemployed who are unable to return directly from unemployment to a new job.

The 'golden triangle' is a post-hoc rationalisation of emergent properties rather than a result of grand design. Each of the elements of the triangle has deep historical roots (Madsen 2006). The employers' right to freely hire and fire workers was accepted by the trade unions as part of the so-called September Compromise between the social partners in 1899. The generous unemployment support system originates from a large–scale reform of the unemployment benefit system in 1969. The present system of active labour market policy dates back to programmes introduced in 1979. All three elements have been basically maintained and elaborated since their initiation although the active labour market programmes were thoroughly reformed in the 1990s.

The specific Danish variant of flexicurity with generous unemployment benefits is in accordance with the practice of flexible adaptation to market changes combined with domestic compensation as stressed by Katzenstein. The 'golden triangle' is a reflection of an industrial structure that requires a high level of numerical flexibility of firms and represents a sort of implicit social contract between employees and employers. Furthermore retraining programmes and lax hire and fire rules imply a unique combination of functional and numerical flexibility which contributes strongly to the competitiveness of parts of the Danish industry. It can be seen as a specific incidence of institutional complementarities between the industrial structure, social and labour market policies. As such it accords with an important general element of the *Variety of Capitalisms* framework. On the other hand, the market relations in the sphere of job security diverge quite radically from the characteristics of the ideal type CME.

The Danish case also clearly diverges from the ideal type CME in another respect. LMEs are normally associated with a higher degree of exposure of labour to market forces than CMEs. Social policies in CMEs are typically more often based on citizenship rights than in LMEs. Denmark has introduced workfare policies with some similarities to those pioneered by the neo-liberal governments of Thatcher and Reagan. It is interesting that it was a social democratic government that in 1993 substituted the pre-existing system of generous passive support with an activation programme. Control with active job-seeking has traditionally been relatively tough in Denmark as a counterpart to the generous unemployment benefits. However, control was strengthened, the level of compensation was generally maintained but radically reduced for young benefit seekers and, most importantly, the duration of benefits was shortened radically. Furthermore the unemployed were guaranteed either education or subsidised employment for most of the period of support, individual action plans were introduced, and activation programmes were created also for recipients of social assistance. The program can be seen as a particular Danish version of workfare policies with an emphasis on empowerment through training (Torfing 1999).

While cuts in entitlements and compensation levels rarely happened, substantial reforms of the organisation of welfare state institutions have been initiated. These changes involved decentralisation of operational authority and responsibility for outcomes by putting it in the hands of line agencies while centralising control over the volume of spending. Under the name of 'New Public Management' market–like pressures were imposed on administrators and personnel of state agencies in order to foster competition and hence greater efficiency. In addition consumers became more involved in the production of these services as they were offered greater freedom in the choice of services and inclusion in the management of service institutions. Denmark was among the early movers in respect of implementation of new public management (Schwartz 1994). In Denmark, the social democrats passively supported the public sector modernisation programmes, when they were introduced by the previous conservative-led government, and further enhanced and deepened the efforts when they took over in 1993.

During spring 2007 major deals concerning new large funds for life–long learning of public employees were made after negotiations between the government and trade unions as strategic means to raise the quality of public services in an era with future prospects of both funding and labour market shortages. These measures complement deals made since the early 2000s between employers and unions that introduce substantial funds for life–long programmes among private employees. The trade unions were heavily involved in the reforms of the active labour market policies and the workfare policies in the 1990s. They have consistently supported policies of moderate wage increases exchanged by soft welfare measures as well as measures that increase productivity and competitiveness, most recently large funds for life–long learning.

The Danish experience shows that radical and relatively rapid change is possible in a CME context. Normally LMEs are associated with capacities for radical change but in the Danish case this has happened though bargaining and consensual policies have been maintained. Wage bargaining was decentralised in Denmark as in other developed countries. However the development did not, as in many other countries, move in the direction of wage setting ending up at the company level, but has the character of a 'centralized decentralization' (Due et al. 1995). Since the 1980s the influence of interest groups has declined in most developed countries compared to the neo-corporatist era of the 1960s and 1970s. In Denmark the interest groups continue to play a central role in the political system, but the collaboration between organised interests and the political system became more informal. It also became more open. The priority given to large business and labour market organisations was curtailed, and an increasing number of actors became involved. The transformation of the role of interest groups is linked to general changes in the process of political decision making. The preparatory phase always used to be crucial: the important work was carried out in committees and commissions where most often the interest organisations were represented and strongly influential, whilst Parliament played a subordinate and largely confirmatory role.

Macroeconomic policy is an area in which the formal influence of interest groups actually declined. However interest groups still have considerable influence in the discursive processes of agenda setting and formulation of frameworks for the actual decisions. The economists in the secretariats of the large interest organisations together with the Ministry of Finance, independent 'think-tanks' such as the Economic Council and other experts are influential participants in the on-going process of developing a 'socio-economic frame of meaning', that is a consensus around elaborate joint perceptions of the problems, challenges and opportunities of the Danish economy, that define the room for manoeuvre in actual economic policy making. In effect these expert circles helped to 'translate' and adjust neo-liberal ideas to the specific demands and problems of the Danish economy (Kjaer and Pedersen 2001).

Trade openness and free capital movements increase international competition and impose huge pressures for industrial restructuring of the OECD countries. The challenge of continuous structural upgrading creates even more pressure for small high-wage countries. In the case of Denmark this is particularly imminent because of the specialisation pattern of Danish industry with its strength in rather traditional low- and medium-tech branches of production. However Denmark has succeeded in maintaining and even improving its relative position among the developed countries (as measured by GDP per capita) in spite of this apparent handicap. The explanation is a high degree of change and flexibility in firms' use of resources, including rapid diffusion of new technologies in those low–tech and medium–tech industrial sectors where Denmark maintains its competitive advantage. The production equipment and manufacturing methods in the production of foodstuffs, furniture and clothing are highly advanced, often combined with high expertise in design and marketing (Lundvall 2002; Maskell 1998). These experienced-based knowledge assets in traditional industries have little to do with R&D and more with 'a close social interaction across the boundaries of organizations, departments and management levels. This interaction is supported by a system of education and a labor market with its own national idiosyncrasies' (Lundvall 2002, p. 74). One may add that wide–ranging structural reforms have been implemented in labour markets, product markets, taxation and education policies, and so on. The reforms have aimed at and apparently succeeded in enhancing flexibility and capabilities. In this context it is also important to stress that the Danish society is characterised by strong social cohesion. Danish firms have the advantages of a relatively high stock of social capital, that is a multitude of voluntary associations, cross-cutting social networks, and a high degree of mutual trust, which not only reduces costs of inter–firm transactions but also makes easier adaptation, learning and cooperation between business firms, state and civil society in local contexts as well as at a national level. The major Danish competitive asset is characterised as 'localized learning' based on 'shared trust' (Maskell et al. 1999). The recent initiatives to enhance life time learning further strengthen these capabilities. This particular solution to coordination problems at the level of the firm and its stakeholders can hardly be explained by mere strategic interaction.

CONCLUSION

The two case studies provide evidence that may add to the understanding of the complexity and alternative possibilities in institutional configurations. The Danish case has features of CMEs that are more ideal type than the German case. On the other hand, it combines such features with characteristics that constitute core features in the ideal type LME. It represent hybrid forms that are unaccounted for in the *Varieties of Capitalism* framework and in this way it resembles the New Zealand combination of full-blown neoliberalism and the embryo of a negotiated economy in the form of the Resource Management Act. Furthermore the New Zealand experience shows how radical change towards an LME was possible as a result of a specific political conjuncture, clever political engineering and a powerful stint of ideology. The Danish evidence shows that rapid and comprehensive changes are possible in spite of institutional features that are closely associated with CME and traditionally seen as impediments for such changes. Crucial explanatory factors are institutional complementaries across the boundaries of the LME and CME ideal types, social capital, the role of ideas, and maintenance of strong influence of interest groups. In both cases, smallness clearly contributes to the capacities for relatively smooth, rapid and even radical change. Another important common feature is the important role of ideas and common understandings in both LMEs and CMEs.

The inclusion of smallness as a variable certainly questions the validity of the dichotomous distinction between LMEs and CMEs. In many respects the two countries fit uneasily into these ideal type models. Whether this indicates that smallness should be accounted for by amendments to the *Varieties of Capitalism* framework through an emphasis on distinct features resulting from smallness as such in the spirit of Katzenstein (1985) is a future research area. In this context it is crucial to clearly identify the dependent variable, that is the effect of smallness. The specific effect of smallness is hardly similar institutional set-ups in small countries but rather similar political processes (Pontusson 2005)

NOTES

1. This interpretation resembles Crouch's analysis of what he calls 'The British Neoliberal Turn' where a similar role is played by the UK financial sector in London, the Treasury, neoliberal academic economists and 'think tanks' as well as some politicians in the Conservative Party (2005, pp. 143–150).
2. Union membership was compulsory in New Zealand until 1983 (Roper 2005, p. 105).
3. Another important event is the bombing and sinking of the Greenpeace organisation's flagship vessel Rainbow Warrior in Auckland Harbour by the French secret service (the DGSE) in July 1985 (King 2003, p. 443).

REFERENCES

Albert M. (1993), *Capitalism against Capitalism*, London: Whurr.

Amable B. (2003), *The Diversity of Modern Capitalism*, Oxford: Oxford University Press.

Belich J. (2001), *Paradise Reforged – A History of the New Zealanders*, Auckland: Allan Lane The Penguin Press.

Berger S. and Dore R. (eds) (1996), *National Diversity and Global Capitalism*, Ithaca: Cornell University Press.

Blyth M. (2003), 'Same as it Never Was: Temporality and Typology in the Varieties of Capitalism', *Comparative European Politics*, 1 (1), 215–225.

Boyer R. and Drache D. (eds) (1996), *States Against Markets*, London: Routledge.

Bredgaard T., Larsen F. And Madsen P.K. (2005), 'The flexible Danish labour market – a review', Carma Research Papers 2005:1, Centre for Labour Market Studies, Aalborg University.

Buehrs T. and Bartlett R.V. (1993), *Environmental Policy in New Zealand – The Politics of Clean and Green?*, Auckland and Oxford: Oxford University Press.

Campbell J.L., Hall P.A. and Pedersen O.K. (eds) (2006), *National Identity and the Varieties of Capitalism – The Danish Experience*, Montreal and Kingston: McGill-Queen's University Press.

Campbell J.L. and Pedersen O.K. (eds) (2001), *The Rise of Neoliberalism and Institutional Analysis*, Princeton and Oxford: Princeton University Press.

Campbell J.L. and Pedersen O.K. (2007), 'Varieties of Capitalism and Hybrid Success: Denmark in the Global Economy', *Comparative Political Studies*, 40 (3), 307–332.

Coates D. (ed.) (2005), *Varieties of Capitalism, Varieties of Approaches*, New York: Palgrave Macmillan.

Crouch C. (2005), *Capitalist Diversity and Change*, Oxford: Oxford University Press.

Crouch C. and Streeck W. (eds) (1997), *Political Economy of Modern Capitalism. Mapping Convergence and Diversity*, London: Sage.

DiMaggio P.J. (1998), 'The New Institutionalisms: Avenues of Collaboration', *Journal of Institutional and Theoretical Economics*, 154 (4), 696–705.

Dore R. (2003), 'Varieties of Capitalism (book review)', *British Journal of Industrial Relations*, 41 (2), 359–361.

Dore R., Lazonick W. and O'Sullivan M. (1999), 'Varieties of Capitalism in the Twentieth Century', *Oxford Review of Economic Policy*, 15 (4), 102–120.

Douglas R. (1993), *Unfinished Business*, Auckland: Random House.

Due J., Madsen J.S., Jensen C.S. and Kjerulf L. (1995), 'Adjusting the Danish Model: Towards Centralized Decentralization', in Colin Crouch and Franz Traxler (eds), *Organized Industrial Relations in Europe. What Future?*, Aldershot: Avebury.

Easton B. (1994), 'How did the Health Reforms Blitzkrieg fail?', *Political Science*, 46 (2).

Easton B. (1997), *In Stormy Seas – The Post-War New Zealand Economy*, Dunedin: University of Otago Press.

Edwards T. (2003), 'Varieties of Capitalism (book review)', *Industrial Relations Journal*, 34 (2), 185–7.

Esping–Andersen, Gösta (ed.) (1996), *Welfare States in Transition – National Adaptation in Global Economies*, London: Sage.

Frieder J. (1997), *Approaching Sustainability: Integrated Environmental Management and New Zealand's Resource Management Act*, report for Ian Axford (New Zealand) Fellowships in Public Policy, Wellington.

Goldfinch S. (2000), *Remaking New Zealand and Australian Economic Policy*, Wellington: Victoria University Press.

Goodin R.E. (2003), 'Choose Your Capitalism?', *Comparative European Politics*, 1 (1), 203–13.

Habermas J. (1995[1982]), *Theorie des Kommunikativen Handelns*, 2 Vols, Frankfurt a.M.: Suhrkamp.

Haggard S. (2003), 'Varieties of Capitalism (book review)', *Business History Review*, 77 (2), 352–4.

Hall P.A. (1998), 'Policy Paradigms, Social Learning, and the State', *Comparative Politics*, 25 (3), 275–296.

Hall P.A. (2006), 'Danish Capitalism in Comparative Perspective', in John L. Campbell, Peter A. Hall and Ove K. Pedersen (eds), *National Identity and the Varieties of Capitalism – The Danish Experience*, Montreal and Kingston: McGill-Queen's University Press, pp. 441–452.

Hall P.A. and Gingerich D.W. (2004), 'Varieties of Capitalism and the Institutional Complementarities in the Macroeconomy. An Empirical Analysis', *MPIfG*

Discussion Paper 04/5, Max-Planck-Institut für Gesellschaftsforschung, Cologne.

Hall P.A. and Soskice D. (2001), 'An Introduction to Varieties of Capitalism', in Peter A. Hall and David Soskice (eds), *Varieties of Capitalism – The Institutional Foundations of Comparative Advantage*, Oxford: Oxford University Press, pp. 1–68.

Hall P.A. and Soskice D. (2003), 'Varieties of Capitalism and Institutional Change: A Response to Three Critics', *Comparative European Politics*, 1 (1), 241–250.

Hargreaves Heap S. (1989), *Rationality in Economics*, Oxford and New York: Basil Blackwell.

Hodgson G.M. (2001), 'The Evolution of Capitalism from the Perspective of Institutional and Evolutionary Economics' in Geoffrey M. Hodgson, Makoto Itoh, and Nobuharu Yokokawa (eds), *Capitalism in Evolution: Global Contentions – East and West*, Cheltenham UK and Northampton, MA, USA: Edward Elgar, pp. 63–82.

Howell C. (2003), 'Varieties of Capitalism: And Then There was One?', *Comparative Politics*, 36 (1), 103–124.

Jackson G. and Deeg R. (2006a), 'How Many Varieties of Capitalism? Comparing the Comparative Institutional Analyses of Capitalist Diversity', *MPIfG (Max Planck Institute for the Study of Societies) Discussion Paper 06/2.*

Jackson G. and Deeg R. (2006b), 'Comparing Capitalism: Recent Debates (book review)', *British Journal of Industrial Relations*, 44 (3), 569–75.

Katzenstein P. (1985), *Small States in World Markets: Industrial Policy in Europe*, New York: Cornell University Press.

Kaufmann F.X. (2003), *Varianten des Wohlfahrtsstaats – Der deutsche Sozialstaat im internationalen Vergleich*, Frankfurt a.M.: Suhrkamp.

Kelsey J. (1995), *The New Zealand Experiment – A World Model for Structural Adjustment?* Auckland: Auckland University Press.

Kerr R. (2002), *The Resource Management Act: Fundamentally Sound or Fundamentally Flawed?*, speech for the Massey University Planning Programme, in Palmerston North 19 April 2002, retrieved from: www.nzbr.org.nz/documents/speeches/speeches-2002.

Kesting S. (2005), 'Countervailing, Conditioned and Contingent – the Power Theory of John Kenneth Galbraith', *Journal of Post-Keynesian Economics*, 28 (1), 3–24.

Kesting S. (2007), 'Mental Models as Language-Transmitted Means of Power', in Klaus Nielsen and Carsten A. Koch (eds), *Institutionalism in Economics and Sociology – Variety, Dialogue and Future Challenges*, Cheltenham, UK and Northampton, MA, USA: Edward Elgar.

King M. (2003), *The Penguin History of New Zealand*, Auckland: Penguin Books.

Kitchelt H., Lange P., Marks G. and Stephens J.D. (eds) (1999), *Continuity and Change in Contemporary Capitalism*, Cambridge: Cambridge University Press.

Kjaer P. and Pedersen O.K. (2001), 'Translating Liberalization – Neoliberalism in the Danish Negotiated Economy', in John L. Campbell and Ove K. Pedersen (eds), *The Rise of Neoliberalism and Institutional Analysis*, Princeton and Oxford: Princeton University Press, pp. 219–48.

Lundvall B.A. (2002), *Innovation, Growth and Social Cohesion*, Cheltenham, UK and Northampton; MA, USA: Edward Elgar.

Madsen P.K. (2006), 'How Can It Possibly Fly? The Paradox of Dynamic Labour Markets in a Scandinavian Welfare State', in John L. Campbell, Peter A. Hall and Ove K. Pedersen (eds) (2006), *National Identity and the Varieties of Capitalism – The Danish Experience*, Montreal and Kingston: McGill-Queen's University Press,

321–55.
Maskell P. (1998), 'Learning in the Village Economy of Denmark – the Role of Institutions and Policy in Sustaining Competitiveness', in H. Braczyk, P. Cooke and M. Heidenreich (eds), *Regional Innovation Systems – The Role of Governance in a Globalized World*, London: UCL Press, pp. 190–213.
Maskell P. et al. (eds) (1999), *Competitiveness, Localised Learning and Regional Development. Specialisation and Prosperity in Small Open Economies*, Routledge: London.
Massey P. (1995), *New Zealand – Market Lilberalization in a Developed Economy*, Houndsmills, Basingstoke and London: St Martin's Press.
Myrdal G. (1972[1944]), *An American Dilemma: The Negro Problem and Modern Democracy*, New York: Pantheon Books.
Nielsen K. (2001), 'Institutionalist Approaches in the Social Sciences: Typology, Dialogue, and Future Challenges', *Journal of Economic Issues*, 35 (2), 505–16.
Nielsen K. and Kesting S. (2003), 'Small is Resilient – the Impact of Globalization on Denmark', *Review of Social Economy*, 71 (3), 365–87.
Nielsen K. and Pedersen O.K. (1991), 'From the Mixed Economy to the Negotiated Economy: The Scandinavian Countries', in R.M. Coughlin (ed.), *Morality, Rationality, and Efficiency – New Perspectives on Socio-Economics*, Armonk, US and London: M.E. Sharpe.
OECD (2004): *Employment Outlook*, Paris: OECD.
Pontusson J. (2005), *equality and Prosperity: Social Europe vs. Liberal America*, Ithaca, NY: Cornell University Press.
Porter M.E. (1998), *The Competitive Advantage of Nations*, Basingstoke, Hampshire and New York: Palgrave.
Roper B.S. (2005), *Prosperity for All? Economic, Social and Political Change in New Zealand since 1935*, Auckland and Southbank: Thomson Dunmore Press.
Russell M. (1996), *Revolution – New Zealand From Fortress to Free Market*, Auckland: Television New Zealand and Images.
Schmidt V. (2002), *The Futures of European Capitalism*, Oxford: Oxford University Press.
Schwartz H. (1994), 'Small States in Big Trouble. State Reorganization in Australia, Denmark, New Zealand and Sweden in the 1980s', *World Politics*, 46 (July), 527–55.
Simon H.A. (1997), 'Rationality in Decision Making', in H.A. Simon (ed.), *An Empirically Based Microeconomics*, Cambridge UK: Cambridge University Press, pp. 3-31.
Streeck W. and Yamamura K. (eds) (2001), *The Origins of Nonliberal Capitalism: Germany and Japan in Comparison*, Ithaca: Cornell University Press.
Torfing J. (1999), 'Workfare with Welfare', *Journal of European Social Policy*, 9 (1), 1–31.
Watson M. (2003), 'Ricardian Political Economy and the "Varieties of Capitalism" Approach: Specialization, Trade and Comparative Institutional Advantage', *Comparative European Politics*, 1 (1), 227–40.
Wheen N. (2002), 'A History of New Zealand Environmental Law', in Eric Pawson and Tom Brooking (eds), *Environmental Histories of New Zealand*, Melbourne: Oxford University Press.
Wilthagen T. and Tros F. (2004), 'The concepts of "flexicurity": A new approach to regulating employment and labour markets', *TRANSFER – European Review of Labour and Research*, 10 (2), 166–87.

2. State Formation and the Construction and Maintenance of Institutions for Economic Growth in the West and the East, 1415–1846

Patrick O'Brien

INTRODUCTION: STATE FORMATION WITH SMITHIAN AND SCHUMPETERIAN GROWTH

Let us begin with a tautology. Efficient states govern successful economies that provide high standards of living for their citizens. Over the centuries per capita incomes have increased at differential rates around the world. Thus an efficient state is the one that over time somehow provided for relatively higher levels of social welfare. Among Anglo-American economists that outcome is now widely represented as emanating from a process of 'Smithian growth' – a label that includes the extension and integration of markets for commodities, land, labour and capital, as well as the formation of regimes for the recovery, storage, discovery and diffusion of useful and reliable knowledge for purposes of production (Hoselitz, 1960).

In recent decades Adam Smith's name has, alas, been misappropriated to support a 'Washington consensus' in favour of minimalist intervention by governments. But the founding father of modern economics who placed security before opulence explicitly forbade no actions by states (particularly in the geopolitical sphere) that might be in a nation's interest and his writings provide clear intellectual justifications for the provision of public goods. (Winch, 1996) Nevertheless, Smithian growth has now acquired a meaning that is congruent with antipathies embodied in economics – particularly new institutional economics and the spill-over of its vocabularies into early modern European history. For example, many economists and their acolytes in history and other social sciences represent most forms of 'interference' by states with the operations of competitive markets and private enterprise as futile, perverse and motivated by rent–seeking behaviour (Weede, 1996).

Furthermore the 'Smithian' assumptions that historically successful states promoted long-run growth in some regions of Europe (and Asia) basically by 'encouraging' the allocation of resources into activities and by motivating their utilization in ways that brought about a congruence between social and private returns can be contrasted with an alternative view that states ruling successful economies did much more than simply create incentives for positive change by redefining and protecting property rights, reducing transactions, search and negotiation costs for private production and exchange. This alternative tradition now labelled as 'Schumpeterian' can be traced back to the Renaissance (Jomo and Reinert, 2005). It remains alive and well in economics and economic history and perceives and conceives of an altogether wider and more positive role for states.

In contrast to the Smithian approaches (which are basically concerned with barter, markets and exchange) the Schumpeterian tradition is production-centred and emphasizes the historical role played by governments in encouraging, protecting and investing in activities that in outcome enjoyed increasing returns over the long run. Willy-nilly, intentionally (or historically as a by-product of political and strategic preoccupations) the policies implemented and capital formed by some states promoted the development of sectors, industries, organizations, technologies and institutions which embodied economies of scale, scope, potential for learning, investment and structural change (Reinert, 1999). In a Schumpeterian framework (as elaborated by Braudel for European economic history) rents, monopolies, defence and aggression, luxury consumption and other ostensibly 'wasteful' geopolitical expenditures by early modern states are not dismissed as politically malign impediments and obstacles for the long-run development (however slow) of national economies in the West, or for the Ming-Qing, Tokugawa, Ottoman and Mughal agrarian empires of the East (Braudel, 1981–84).

Adam Smith certainly realized that for several centuries before the Industrial Revolution, the primary and urgent concerns of states, in the West and the East, were not with the specification and protection of property rights, the reduction of transaction costs, the extension of markets, the terms of exchange and the promotion of competition, but rather with their own formation in contexts of intensifying geopolitical violence and threats of invasion across indefensible frontiers, as well as rivalries for control over resources with aristocratic magnates, urban oligarchies, ecclesiastical prelates, warlords, nomads and other serious contenders for political authority within their vulnerable borders. Power prevailed over profit by a long way in the priorities of all pre-modern states (Skinner and Wilson, 1976). Their main objectives included: dynastic survival, territorial security and aggrandizement, the monopolization of internal coercion and the integration of quasi autonomous territories and regional, ethnic and religious populations into national or imperial polities, made subject to laws, promulgated, adjudicated and enforced by a sovereign source of authority (Lachmann, 2000).

EUROPEAN TRAJECTORIES FROM MEDIEVAL TO WEBERIAN STATES

'Weberian state' is a handy label for a state that has become secure from external takeover and is politically stable enough to enjoy 'sufficient' degrees of sovereignty, information, administrative capacity and the revenue required to formulate strategies and sustain conditions for the facilitation of Smithian and/or the promotion of Schumpeterian growth. When, where, how and why cities, regions, estates, countries and empires around the world obtained and retained the kind of autonomous centralized and effective government required to support modern economic growth is a core question for global economic historians to pursue. To do that they will need, however, to acquire some comprehension of the long and complex processes of state formation that occurred in Europe, China, India and other parts of the world (Mann, 1986).

In the West the beginnings of the process can be traced back to the powers and functions exercised by feudal rulers who emerged in the Middle Ages from the turmoil of dynastic rivalries among territorial warrior magnates for the status of *primus inter pares* (Ertman, 1997). Their role as 'monarchs' allowed them to deploy their own considerable resources, and to convene and coordinate military forces under the control of other powerful feudal lords for: the 'collective' defence of confederated polities (which often included estates, fiefdoms, bishoprics and cities); for 'collaborative' attacks on rival confederations and for 'cooperation' to maintain internal order and to preserve some kind of stability in the distribution and control over property and wealth, particularly land and natural resources (Bonney, 1991).

Over centuries of violent and hazardous transition and evolving from a multiplicity of feudal confederations, into federations and on to states with more or less effective and efficient monopolies over the means (armies, navies and revenues) for coercion, Europe's sovereigns attempted to centralize and to realize the economies of scale, scope and specialization embodied in more effectively organized, increasingly capital-intensive armies and navies, equipped with modern technologies for defence and aggression. Geopolitical imperatives driven by dynastic rivalry as well as advances in the technologies, organization and fiscal costs associated with and delivery of violence, prompted rulers everywhere to attempt to move on from acting as coordinators of military and naval power available within their frontiers, towards positions of virtual command over the means of coercion required for the defence of vulnerable territories, national wealth and royal or rather 'domestic' fiscal bases (Poggi, 1990).

Their 'trajectory' towards 'centralization' (proceeding falteringly along diverse routes at different speeds across the continents within political arenas of embryo nations loosely governed by Weberian states in the making) is a history marked by varying degrees of stronger and weaker opposition from estates, aristocracies, urban oligarchies, churches and other networks of power. Constrained by historically embedded centrifugal forces, rulers of Europe's feudal polities constructed and reconstructed several types of state that first became viable and stable, but only gradually autonomous enough to govern effectively within the geopolitical spaces and political contexts over which they prematurely and pretentiously claimed to be sovereign (Tilly, 1990).

European historians have latterly reconfigured their continent's process of state formation as a record of inter–related coercion, cooperation and co-option which took centuries to complete and which was marked by accident, contingency relapses and political discontinuities of every kind. Acting within the imperatives of a violent, unstable and competitive geopolitical order, centralizing monarchies, oligarchies and power elites (funded by resources appropriated from accessible fiscal bases) 'struggled' to construct states that could protect and govern emergent but disintegrated national economies. They simultaneously coerced and co-opted rival claimants to local powers (ancient kingdoms, estates, territorial magnates, ecclesiastical authorities, cities, towns and potentially rebellious artisans and peasants) into compliance with their missions to fund and construct sovereign states. (Dyson, 1980) Co-option, which is now recognized to have been as significant as coercion in the formation of Europe's ancien regimes, involved sovereigns and their advisers in complex political settlements with aristocracies and other seigneurs over: the separation of powers; rights to assess, collect and profit from royal revenues; patronage to appoint to senior positions in the armies, navies, churches, judiciaries and bureaucracies of realms and republics. Protracted 'negotiations' and compromises between rulers and insubordinate elites occurred in the formation and management of all departments and organizations of monarchical or oligarchial states (Reinhard, 1996).

Historians of state formation and political economy have long recognized that the scope, difficulties and costs of maintaining administrations and organizations to supply public goods required to provide external security, political stability and internal order, let alone for the coordination of economic activities, varied with geographies and with degrees of cultural difference among nominally subject populations, which also changed gradually through time (Epstein, 2002). Rulers of compact contiguous territories surrounded by water and containing populations of similar ethnic and religious identities, pervaded by cultures of patriotism and deference to hereditary authorities did not confront either the same logistical problems or the resistance and enforcement costs as rulers constrained of dispersed territories with long frontiers that contained *multi*-lingual, *multi*-ethnic and *multi*-religious populations. Compare, for example, the problems faced and sovereignties enjoyed by England's Hanoverian and Austria's Habsburg monarchies in the early modern period (Teichova and Matis, 2003).

Everywhere in Europe the formation of stronger, more centralized and stable states involved divisions of power and the sharing of resources with established stakeholders in national wealth and with territorial authorities – regardless of whether the settlements over terms for coordination, collaboration and cooperation were reached and maintained formally after due process with 'unrepresentative' assemblies of notables. Alternatively they invariably and implicitly shared power: firstly in the ways that ostensibly autocratic decisions were made and secondly carried into effect by 'private' organizations 'under contract' to ruling houses and oligarchies or implemented by hierarchical administrations of their own making and, in theory, under their command and management (Hall, 1985).

Historical trajectories along which Europe's competing polities evolved into Weberian states are histories of contrasts which political historians have traditionally analysed in teleological terms as precocious or protracted transitions to freedom and democracy. Nevertheless, the preoccupations of philosophers, political scientists and historians since the Enlightenment with the constitutional forms of Eurasian states reveal that they were rarely correlated either to the priorities accorded by those forming and running states to the development of economies or to the kinds and qualities of organizations and institutions set up to promote sustained Smithian or Schumpeterian growth (Weiss and Hobson, 1995). Correlations between the forms of states (absolute, despotic, monarchical, oligarchical, parliamentary and democratic) and the functions that they performed more or less effectively to promote economic growth were not at all stable or unambiguous before the 19th century (Persson and Tabellini, 2003). Constitutions for liberty or autocracy were not strictly correlated with conditions for economic growth (Epstein, 2002).

NEW INSTITUTIONAL ECONOMICS AND POLITICAL HISTORY

Although economic historians are as concerned with freedoms as other historians, until causal relations between constitutional forms and economic activities become clearer, they will remain less involved than political historians with evolutions towards democracy, civil rights and parliamentary forms of government (Macfarlane, 2000). In recent decades they have become more interested in those forms of new institutional economics which have drawn attention to connexions between particular organizations, laws, rules, customs and culturally conditioned behaviour for the promotion of long– term economic development (Menard and Shirley, 2005). Meanwhile modern economics has, at last, expanded its remit to include matters that Cunningham recommended to Marshal and now sustains an enlightening programme of classifying, theorizing (but only occasionally measuring) how a range of institutional variables conditioned both the flow and the productivity of the classical inputs of land, labour, capital, technology and other proximate determinants of national economic growth, elaborated within the rigorous but parsimonious taxonomies of production functions (North, 1990).

Perhaps economic historians, engaged with traditions of enquiry going back to the German historical school, and who retained links with history, had less need than their colleagues in economics to be reminded that production and exchange across early modern Eurasia were embedded in less than enabling frameworks of law, institutions and cultures (Hodgson, 2001). Although the insights derived from this still relatively new and evolving branch of economics are certainly helpful and illuminating to consult, there is one foundational premise where theory seems seriously ill-informed and under-specified. Ships adrift on uncharted waters certainly deserve credit for every mile travelled in the right direction, but the new institutional economics has hardly left harbour when it comes to analysing and explaining the behaviour of states (Field, 1981).

That represents a serious *lacunae* because states created and sustained the legal frameworks and institutions within which productive and counter-productive activities occurred. States defined and enforced property rights. States solved or failed to solve both the legal and the infra-structural problems involved in extending and coordinating markets. States reordered, or neglected to reorder, ideologies, religions and cultures of behaviour that reduced shirking, cheating, free-riding and encouraged thrift, work and innovation. Above all, states supplied economies (bounded by vulnerable frontiers and engaged in 'foreign' trade) with those overwhelmingly important 'public goods', external security and internal order without which investment, innovation, production, exchange and overseas trade could only have remained at much lower levels (Chang, forthcoming 2007).

Of course, during peaceable interludes of time, a great deal of subsistence (and 'embodied') production, as well as local and regional (but rarely international) trade continued without reference to states on the basis of custom and traditional patterns of behaviour, based upon widely accepted norms derived from religious or other cosmologies of belief. But the conclusions derivable from European history are that without states and the laws, institutions and protection that they provided, potential gains from trade, specialization and innovation remained unrealized (Platteau, 2000).

That is why history from below is not enough and unless economic historians become (like neo–classical economists) willing to 'endogeonize' the actions and policies of states and support predictions and retrodictions that the constitutions of states and frameworks of rules and institutions (for the operation of economic activity that they supported) altered as and when it became 'sufficiently profitable' for 'rulers', 'bureaucracies', 'innovators' or 'revolutionaries' to bring about positive change, they conclude that new institutional economics lacks anything approximating to a general theory of state formation or state behaviour. Without those foundations any general theory purporting to explain the construction, functioning or absence of institutions is simply aspirational (Smelser and Swedberg, 2006).

Alas history has not been helpful to social scientists struggling to construct new theories, even though the preoccupations of historians have always been with the evolution of states, empires, laws, rules, religions, ideologies and cultures conditioning personal and group behaviour in the economic and other spheres of social activity. History's libraries are dominated by volumes of research into these matters for particular places at particular times. Most historians do not believe, however, that the formation and policies of early modern states took place in arenas that can be simulated to market places. They do not find attempts to model the actions, inactions or failures of early modern rulers and their servants with reference to 'trade-offs', 'rent seeking' or 'revenue maximizing' behaviour, particularly illuminating (Ekelund and Tollison, 1997). There is too much violence, path dependence, vested interest, custom, inertia and bargaining recorded for national and local histories of political evolution and no overriding and persistent aim or even a set of rational objectives that rulers attempted to maximize for economic theory to be of serious help with the interrelated problems of state formation, the formulation and the implementation of central policy (Blockmans, 1997).

Rational choice political theory might become (like perfect competition) a point for reference or departure (Helpman, 2004). Insights into the operations of states are, however, more likely to flow from theories formulated to model the evolution of competitive advantages embodied in large–scale, hierarchically organized firms, producing goods and services for sale to consumers (Prendergast, 1999). These theories could be extended to expose conditions for efficiency among complex organizations with less clear–cut objectives than private firms but charged to deliver public goods, such as external security, health, education and protection against crime as effectively as possible under given constraints (Dixit, 2002). Unfortunately too much effort has, in recent years, been ideologically concerned simply to expose bureaucratic failures, superficially represented as: corruption, rent seeking, inertia, rigidities and other obvious attributes of organizations, designed and run by states for multiple purposes, but which were historically and for explicable reasons loosely connected to requirements for economic growth (Ekelund and Tollison, 1981).

THE ORGANIZATIONAL CAPACITIES AND EFFICIENCIES OF PRE-MODERN EUROPEAN STATES

For centuries organizational defects continued to be an omnipresent feature of all states and to almost predetermine the performance of their armies, navies and bureaucracies (Tilly, 1975). The political constraints on developing departments and institutions nominally under the control of rulers and their advisers attempting to secure legitimacy and compliance by trying to deliver public goods at lower fiscal and political costs were then formidable and continue now to be very difficult to achieve. Historians, in touch with primary sources and aware of the constraints surrounding rulers, their political advisers and the pre-modern technologies available for administration, recognize that the modes and scale of public and quasi-public institutions in place for the recruitment of personnel, levels of corruption, degrees of rigidity and rent seeking simply exemplify the multiple priorities and restraints operating upon Europe's ancien regimes of every conceivable constitutional form (Blickle, 1997). On the one hand rulers made 'unavoidable' political bargains, deals and comprises required to secure stability, but their interest on the other was to maintain and increase power by supplying external security, victories in war, and internal order on terms that did not threaten their own status, powers, survival and claims to rule (Downing, 1992).

During the long transition to degrees of sovereignty which provided scope for functional levels of efficiency, the administrative and organizational technologies available before the 19th century to every conceivable kind of political regime (imperial, parliamentary, republican and absolutist alike) remained limited and extremely difficult to extend and deepen (Elias, 1982). That may seem less obvious at the courts and capitals of emperors and kings and the chambers of oligarchies where many rulers with pretensions to absolutism benefited from the advice and support from talented 'servants', often recruited from the church and the law, or in China through a meritocratic examination system – admired by Voltaire, Leibniz and other enlightened intellectuals of the day (Brook and Blue, 1999). These loyal servants of sovereigns are superficially represented by neo-liberal economists as corruptible rent seekers, pursuing interests, antithetical to economic progress, or as paternalistic mandarins more concerned with stability and social welfare than growth with 'creative destruction'. Nevertheless, their albeit sometimes sycophantic devotion to hereditary rulers and opposition to rival centres of power implies that they pursued missions to centralize and to rationalize the formulation of rules; to universalize, monitor and enforce their execution, and to build up procedures for adjudication (Poggi, 1990).

For centuries serious, and persistent, problems for the formation and efficiency of states arose in varying degrees across the entire range of administrations responsible for the provision of public goods even in those key hierarchical departments of government: armies and navies where aristocratic officers often pursued strategies and agendas of their own to the cost and detriment of rulers and national economies (Genet and le Mené, 1987). Early modern states had no choice but to resort to markets and franchising to execute policies, however formulated. Private firms networked in tandem with politically appointed hierarchies to deliver public goods and even to assess and to collect taxes. The very sinews of power had to be delegated to private administrations of tax farmers (Bonney, 1995).

European political history has exposed two inescapable features concerning the formation of Weberian states. First even in the West the process took centuries to achieve and secondly, some polities such as England and Holland constructed and managed the bureaucracies, departments and complex organizations required to raise revenues, solve problems, preserve stability and deliver arrays of public goods, including external security, that promoted economic growth sooner and more effectively than others (e.g. Spain, Poland, Austria and other states) (Bonney, 1999). Prerequisites for Smithian growth may also have been established in Tang-Song China centuries before Europe and in parts of Europe before the Russian Empire and long before Africa where the slow formation of sovereign states now appears as a key factor behind the poor economic performance exhibited by most of that continent's national economies since independence (Herbst, 2000).

Meanwhile neither historians nor social scientists have much to offer by way of theory that explains either the chronology or exposes mechanisms and connexions between state formation, political behaviour and the construction of efficient institutions for long-term economic growth. Historians and some historical sociologists tend to handle the foundational problem of state formation by elaborating upon the geographical, geopolitical and cultural specifities that favoured the emergence of prototype Weberian states in some polities before others. Unsurprisingly they resort to historical narratives that lead explanations towards profound conjunctures in the political evolution of states when fundamental discontinuities occurred in response to crises of internal stability (the English and French Revolutions, the American Civil War), the break up of the Spanish empire or to exogeneous shocks from victory or defeat in geopolitical conflicts (e.g. the Franco-Prussian and Great Wars) (Mooers, 1991). These 'conjunctures' can be plausibly represented as exercising profound effects on the pace and shape of state formation and by extension upon the construction of institutions further down the line (Hall and Schroeder, 2006). Alas if significant and persistent variations in economic institutions are to some degree explicable as the outcome of past geopolitical settlements, civil wars and internal revolutions, then prospects for the formation of any parsimonious and general theory for institutional change continues to look entirely problematical. There may well be nothing out there but history (Zmera, 2001).

STATES AND STATE FORMATION IN THE WEST AND THE EAST, 1415–1846

Meanwhile global economic historians who have recently re-engaged with illuminating exercises in comparative history across continents have drawn attention to clear and potentially significant contrasts between the divergent political (and by implication, economic) trajectories taken over these centuries by the economies of Western Europe on the one hand and China, India and the Ottoman empire on the other (Bayly, 2004). For centuries before the First Industrial Revolution most economic activity (agricultural, industrial and commercial) to the east of Eurasia took place within frameworks of laws, rules, cultural conventions and institutions established and sustained by imperial systems of governance – over the Ottoman Dominions in West Asia and the Balkans, the Mughal Empire in India and the Ming-Qing Empire in China. Of course, large areas of economic activity in Western Europe also fell within sovereignties claimed by the Habsburg empires of Spain and Austria and Russian's Romanov empire – expanding to the east and south of Eurasia (Lieven, 2000). Nevertheless, and simply for purposes of pursuing any potential illumination derivable from exercises in macro comparative history, we should at least consider the Weberian hypothesis (as repeated and reformulated in a hegemonic tradition of occidental writing on oriental political economy) which posits that Western firms and economic agents derived relative advantages from operating within Europe's competitive state system – compared to their counterparts constrained by the regulatory frameworks and institutions maintained by oriental empires and despotisms to the east (Landes, 1998). Although everyone recognizes that the precise significance of rather clear contrasts in state systems across Eurasia compared with variations in natural endowments and technologies will remain open for discussion and unmeasurable (Pomeranz, 2000). For present purposes the major elements of the argument that Europe's competitive state system could well have been more functional for long–term economic growth will be elaborated in implicit and rather general terms with reference to geopolitical rivalry among the states of Portugal, Spain, the Netherlands, France, Britain, Prussia, Scandinavia and others on the one hand, compared to the relative political stability maintained within three major empires (Ming-Qing China, the Ottoman Dominions and Mughal India) on the other.

MERCANTILISM IN THE WEST, 1415–1805

The international economic order which prevailed during an era labelled as mercantilism refers essentially to the centuries between the conquest of Ceuta by the Portuguese in 1415 to the achievement of hegemony at sea by the British navy at Trafalgar in 1805. These centuries were marked by dynastic conflict and imperial rivalry and intense competition erupting frequently into warfare among European powers in order to exploit the gains to be made from trade overseas and in particular from transcontinental colonization and commerce within a proto-global economy of intensified connexions between Europe, Africa, Asia and above all the Americas (Black, 1998).

By no means all of the frequent lapses into warfare, which invariably included predation upon the foreign investments and trade of rival European polities, could be ascribed to economic causes. Nevertheless, the persistence of dynastic religious, colonial and commercial warfare has been represented as ultimately benign for the formation of powerful states and the construction of functional institutions in the West (Glete, 2002).

Cold warfare continued, moreover, even during interludes of peace when international trade was conducted within the constrictions of a mercantilist economic order in which Europe's sovereign governments attempted to regulate flows of commodities, labour, capital and useful knowledge across their own frontiers and the borders of their territories overseas in terms of a strategically conceived national interest. They pursued common (and mutually irreconcilable) policies in order to exploit colonies in the interest of the metropolis, to favour domestic over rival economies and to widen and deepen the fiscal bases upon which the internal power and geopolitical status of all states rested (Coleman, 1969). Mercantilist 'beggar thy neighbour' policies were designed to centralize the monopoly of coercive powers within polities, to maintain external security against foreign rivals and to project power overland and overseas to acquire more taxable territory, assets and populations (Magnusson, 1998).

Given that Western mercantilism remained preoccupied for centuries with policies for the formation of powerful centralized sovereign states (and not, except contingently, with economic development and social welfare) the focus upon trade in strategic commodities and upon exports compared to imports seems in retrospect to have turned out neither as irrational nor as misconceived as modern liberals continue to suggest (Tracy, 1991).

Fiscal opportunities, especially accessible fiscal bases in maritime cities and towns, expanded as colonization and commerce overseas increased. Favourable balances of trade provided national economies with surpluses of gold and silver bullion (the era's internationally accepted media of exchange) which became available to states for (a) the mobilization of armies and navies; (b) the import of weapons, warships and other strategic goods; (c) the expansion of metropolitan money supplies and as reserves extension of financial intermediation; and (d) the import of raw materials and manufactures upon which programmes of import substitution could be promoted (Blitz, 1967).

As liberal economists observed, for decades before and for centuries after Adam Smith's famous synthesis of 1776, dynastic conflicts, imperial rivalries, religious intolerance – reinforced support for a mercantilist economic order, riven by barriers to trade and factor mobility, severely restrained prospects for higher levels of economic welfare for the populations of Western Europe (Hutcheison, 1988). There can be no doubt that a liberal international economic order of the kind Smith advocated, that became possible when Britain achieved command of the oceans in 1805, and which came gradually on stream over the 19th century, could have operated as a superior geo-political and economic order for material progress long before 1846 (Gomes, 1987). Nevertheless, historians will remind economists that the order that actually prevailed for several centuries from 1415 to 1805 was one of mercantilism intensifying in the wake of European expansion overseas and the break-up of Christendom after the Reformation (Tracy, 1991). It is simply anachronistic rhetoric to deplore the fact that European states operated in terms of its logic and tenets and failed to take the advice of Adam Smith and a long line of enlightened intellectuals to somehow establish a geo-politically superior and economically more efficient order much before the mid-19th century (Mokyr, 2006). Meanwhile a more interesting meta question for global economic historians to address is: did these centuries of intense and violent competition within and among European states for sovereignty, internal stability, external security and geo-political power carry any benign and unintended consequences for the long-run growth of Western economies? Were comparable advantages not available to economies evolving within more stable, less violent and competitive orders maintained by rulers of empires in East, South and West Asia?

In the West geopolitical warfare and mercantilist rivalry surely increased the powers of centralizing elites (Weiss and Hobson, 1995). As Charles Tilly's epithet put it: states made war and war made states (Tilly, 1990). Threats to external security clarified the need for external security, and thereby raised social levels of compliance with demands for a widening and deepening of national fiscal bases upon which state policies for defence and aggression with development ultimately depended (Winch and O'Brien, 2002). Furthermore, the support accorded by European rulers with foresight to merchants and investors engaged in expansion and colonization overseas contributed to the growth of maritime cities as *pôles de croissance*, and augmented the political influence of nouveau riche merchants in the councils of monarchical and aristocratic states. In turn they commercialized, monetized and agglomerated economic activity in the hinterlands of their cities (Tracy, 1991).

Furthermore, Western enterprise in expansion overseas connected the Atlantic, Indian and Pacific oceans and brought the coastal economic regions of Europe, the Americas, Africa and the already well-connected maritime regions of East Africa, South and East Asia into regular and slowly rising levels of commercial relations with each other (Thompson, 2000). Such connections (a form of early or proto-globalization) matured into an embryo world economy which offered expanded opportunities to reap profits and other gains from trade and plunder which accrued (many would argue accrued disproportionately) to Europeans prepared to take risks and back their drives for wealth with superior naval power (Chaudhuri, 1990). Expanded trade which combined opportunities for taxation with mercantile profits became one (possibly the major) source of funds for net incremental investment in infrastructures, networks and the manufacturing sectors of Europe's famous port cities (Pohl, 1990), while the cultivable lands (emptied of indigenous peoples) and the abundant resources of the Americas attracted Europe's surplus population. Migration maintained higher wages and helped to sustain the search for labour-saving technologies, new forms of energy and good order required for transitions to urban industrial market economies in the West (Canny, 1994).

Europe's competitive state system also facilitated what Albert Hirschman famously referred to as 'exit and voice' (Hirschman, 1978). His phrases recognized that in a state and a geopolitical system marked by mercantilism the demands of merchants would be listened to and to some degree acted upon by monarchs, oligarchs and their coteries of noble advisers more attentively than would be the case in empires ruled by hereditary monarchies, landed aristocrats, ecclesiastical prelates and mandarins with disdain for the avarice associated with commerce and profits of middlemen (Arrighi, 1994). More significantly, the European polities with their permeable frontiers allowed agents with liquid savings, knowledge and skills to migrate into countries and cities where their skills and investible funds would be welcomed. To escape religious persecution and political oppression they could conceivably, and indeed did, move to sites where their human and liquid capital realized higher private, social and fiscal returns (Braudel, 1985).

All of these contingent, unintended, but possibly benign, consequences that flowed from geo-political rivalry and violence among states in the West should not, however, be conflated with familiar theoretical arguments in favour of competitive commodity and factor markets. Obtained at enormous human and economic cost, rivalry and violence that flowed from the failure of Western states to construct a more liberal and peaceable geopolitical order prevailed until centuries of mercantilism had elapsed. Warfare crowded out an even greater potential for higher rates of growth for early modern Europe (Jones, 2003). Adam Smith wrote decades before his time, but the *Wealth of Nations* should be lauded for exposing and undermining the intellectual basis and sub-foundations for an international economic order, based upon the rationalities and principles of mercantilism (Winch, 1996).

ASIAN EMPIRES AND THEIR FISCAL AND FINANCIAL SYSTEMS

For purposes of comparison narratives of global history now offer 'stylised' analyses of the imperial governance surrounding, constraining and helping the efforts of economic agents (farmers, industrialists, merchants, skilled workers and investors) operating in the agrarian empires of China, India and the Ottoman Dominions during the centuries that witnessed intensified rivalry and mercantilism among states in the west of Eurasia (Blaut, 2000). There is a venerable Eurocentric tradition of denigrating imperial states of the East for acting persistently in autocratic, arbitrary and predatory ways in their treatment of the peoples, societies and economies under their rule (Macfarlane, 2000). Latterly that tradition has been virtually degraded by a generation of historical writing on all three 'oriental despotisms', which has been concerned (a) to correct the conflation of constitutional forms with the content and substance of economic governance; (b) to bring into the balance sheet some of the relatively benign and economically efficient features of imperial rule; and (c) to represent salient contrasts between the West and the East as emanating from the entirely limited fiscal resources and inefficient monetary systems available to oriental dynastic regimes to fund sustained, centralized penetrative rule over and provide public goods and services for the economies of their vast and diverse empires (O'Brien et al., 2009).

Agreed: interludes of violent disorder and confiscation of mobile forms of wealth certainly marked the early years of conquest of new territories, assets and populations by empires in the East as well as states in the West (Abernathy, 2000). Nevertheless, where and whenever Eastern empires and western states moved on from pacification, plunder and the extraction of tribute to secure regular and stable flows of tax revenues into metropolitan centres of power, they all confronted the same unavoidable task of constructing fiscal systems to fund the public goods (principally internal order and external security) that they supplied for all their subjects, and domestic or imperial economies in order to achieve regularized flows of taxation (Doyle, 1986).

For several plausible reasons the fiscal systems maintained over these centuries by all three oriental empires look weaker and less responsive to the demands of their central, ostensibly powerful and autocratic governments than political and administrative arrangements set up by the monarchies, aristocracies and oligarchies in charge of most states in Western Europe.

Furthermore, historians are beginning to solidify this unorthodox view of the Orient into a validated contrast by using evidence from fiscal accounts of the day to quantify the amounts of tax revenue (calibrated into comparable grams of the silver grain equivalents or hours of labour time) which were made available on a regularized basis to the central governments of several European polities and to rulers and bureaucracies of the Ottoman, Mughal and Qing empires (O'Brien et al., 2009). Needless to say, the archival research required for these exercises is incomplete and arduous – not least because data for Western Europe has to be collected on a country-by-country basis (Bonney, 1999). Ambiguity surrounds both the accuracy and conceptual comparability of most figures currently published in secondary sources, mainly because internal order, external security adjudication and other public goods required to sustain and support states and the maintenance of institutions required for growth and structural change in the early modern world were provided and funded in very diverse ways across Eurasia (Ardant, 1971–72).

Before the mid-19th century, the classic Weberian model of a centralized state providing services funded by universally applied taxes assessed and collected in standardized monies of account, from well-defined national (or imperial) fiscal bases, could be exemplified (and even then not entirely) by a single case – Great Britain (O'Brien, 2006). In varying degrees all other states on the mainland of Europe and across Asia left the supply of public goods to subsidiary authorities, who mobilized the resources (troops and labour) required for warfare, defence, good order and construction directly. These local authorities levied taxes and fees for the performance of services and provision of public goods upon a provincial, regional or even a village basis, nominally in the names of their imperial and national rulers. Between 1415 and 1805 'confederated', 'devolved' and 'localized' systems of governance remained as key features of all states in formation over centuries of transition to centralized Weberian states that not only claimed, but actually exercised sovereignty, over taxation and government expenditures (Hall and Schroeder, 2006). During that protracted transition states proceeded along a diversity of path-dependent trajectories at different speeds across Eurasia. Nevertheless, and in so far as historians can track and measure it in terms of an acceptable set of potentially quantifiable indices for the centralization of power, evidence is beginning to stack up that European states (particularly Britain, the Netherlands and France) possessed far greater fiscal and financial capacity to fund any of the strategies and policies their ruling elites decided to pursue than the so-called oriental despotisms of west, south and east Asia (Bayly, 2004).

At present the statistical evidence used to support this premature generalization is still under construction and is of contestible provenance and reliability, but it includes sets of provisional data, calibrated to measure and to compare the following list of indicators that can plausibly represent degrees of centralized and eventually sovereign power (Hoffman and Norberg, 1994):

1. Amounts of tax revenue made available to central governments (sovereign rulers) per (a) square mile of territory, (b) per head of population, (c) per unit of national or imperial product – or better still a denominator that includes the potentially taxable incomes or outputs derived from the agricultures, industries or commerce of national and imperial economies (Levi, 1988).
2. Perceptions (information) of the scale and scope of the sovereigns' fiscal base assessable for taxation as conceived and estimated by his advisers.
3. Amounts of wealth, incomes and outputs legally assessed for taxation compared to the sums collected, which in effect measures a sovereign's views of taxable capacities and actual compliance with his demands for revenues.
4. Shares of total tax revenues assessed, collected and delivered by franchised private agencies, compared to professional, properly funded fiscal bureaucracies.

5. Taxes collected on behalf of sovereign authorities actually delivered to central governments which quantifies the administrative costs and the political powers of sovereigns to collect and to spend revenues on purposes and in ways under their direct control. Most of this critical gap between sums collected and amounts received as disposable income by metropolitan treasuries consists of the 'negotiated' (hypothecated) expenditures sovereigns had reluctantly agreed to make in particular localities or on pre-negotiated objectives, which in effect weakened their discretion over the allocation of revenues. Costs of collection include rents, fees, bribes, misappropriations of funds by franchised agents or officials responsible for the assessment and collection of taxes – all of which could add up to a really significant share of taxes nominally and legally due to the central state (O'Brien, 2002).
6. Proportions of taxes paid in monies on account or in kind which indicates the extent to which the fiscal process had been effectively monetized.
7. Scales of sovereign debt which can be measured in relation to total annual tax revenues or as the share of tax revenues devoted to servicing such debt. High ratios denote the confidence of creditors in the political will, power and fiscal capacities of states to meet contractual obligations to their creditors, and especially to foreign creditors, while the rates of interest paid by rulers for loans is another and related indicator of their standing as creditors (Caselli, 2008).
8. Size and quality of bureaucracies employed by sovereigns to implement their decisions.

These eight indicators represent tests currently applied by economic historians to ascertain the relative capacities and powers of states to fund and deliver such major public goods as external security, internal order, the protection of property rights, the adjudication of contracts, standardized weights, measures and means of payment etc. required for the functioning of economies and economic growth under pre-modern conditions (Bonney, 1995).

Needless to say, none of these potentially measurable indicators of state formation are securely in place, but any review of secondary sources now in print leaves the impression that (with all their imperfections) the states of Western Europe look better placed to assist entrepreneurs, merchants, commercial farmers, manufacturers, transporters and other businessmen to carry forward processes of Schumpeterian or Smithian growth, based upon securing increased gains from trade and specialization than their less well served and protected counterparts operating within the Mughal, Ottoman and Ming-Qing empires, who, prima-facie, seem to have been less adequately provided with the good order, legal frameworks, monetary systems and social overhead capital to support extending and expanding internal or external trade on a European scale. In short, imperial rulers lacked sufficient power or foresight and above all fiscal and financial resources to either interfere (positively along Schumpeterian lines) or to provide much by way of an infrastructure of communications, and institutions for the formation and coordination of markets, across the vast territories and diversified populations and disconnected regions over which they claimed sovereignty.

In theory these large and, for centuries, expanding imperial political units might well have offered better prospects for the realization of gains from trade and specialization than the smaller-scale competitive states of the West. However, in time all three imperial systems reached their politically viable frontiers (Struve, 2004). For the Mughal and Ottoman Empires contraction if not decline had set in before 1700 (Bayly, 2004). Although Qing emperors continued to extend their frontiers for another century it is doubtful that the territories annexed by the Manchu dynasty for geopolitical reasons in central Asia added anything much to the overall volume of intra-imperial Chinese trade and almost certainly not enough to cover the extra costs of conquest and local administration (Perdue, 2005).

Only the rulers of China invested and maintained anything approximating to an infrastructure of transportation and communications to link regional economies of an empire together (Crossley et al., 2006). None of these oriental states established and maintained fiscal monetary legal and other institutions for standardization designed to reduce transaction costs and to push their heterogeneous empires in the direction of integrated single markets (Adshead, 1995 and Pamuk, 1987). In general, the stance of rulers and their bureaucracies towards merchants, bankers and other agents who fostered and profited from intra-imperial trade varied over time from neutrality and indifference to bouts of repressive hostility and regulation (Deng, 1993 and 1997). Merchants who ventured beyond imperial frontiers overland or sailed their ships for commerce overseas received virtually no support or naval protection from these states. The Mughal and Ottoman regimes preferred to leave foreign trade, to a large extent, in the hands of Westerners and ethnic minorities (Richards 1995 and Quataert 2000), while the Chinese rulers remained suspicious (and rightly so, given the European record of predation in Asia) of prospects for significant benefits from intensified commercial and other connections with the West over the centuries from the Portuguese conquest of Ceuta (1415) through the takeover of India to the Opium War of 1839–1842 (Deng, 1993).

CONCLUSION

Temptations to stress contrasts in exercises devoted to the construction of binary comparisons between amorphous macro entities labelled 'the East' and 'the West' are not easy to resist, particularly by those still inclined to foreground the deviant case of Britain as a paradigm for Europe as a whole (Wong, 1997). Nevertheless, on investigation it does seem that for this era at least Europe's competitive state system embodied unforeseen advantages that turned out to be more functional for a process of Smithian growth as the path to modernity than the states nominally in charge of the imperial economic systems of Asia.

This outcome probably had a lot less to do with the Eurocentric over-emphasized and endlessly repeated perceptions of differences in the constitutional forms assumed by states across Eurasia or with the exaggerated military (not naval) superiority of the West and rather more with the relative levels of support that various states accorded to institutions and agencies for the extension, coordination and eventual integration of markets (Modelski and Thompson, 1998).

Liberal political economists who have publicized an otherwise laudably negative view of the violence and mercantilism associated with the geopolitics and state formation in the West, right down to the era of free trade, have conspicuously failed to take notice of more positive features of the system for the formation of Weberian states and the construction of institutions conducive to higher rates of Smithian growth leading to increasing returns from trade, associated with urban agglomeration, networking and eventually technological innovation.

It is arguably the case that the otherwise malign geopolitics of the period certainly contributed (some historians argue contributed massively) to the formation of a finite number of viable centralized states with the coercive powers, bureaucracies and above all monetized fiscal and financial resources required to pursue some kind of governance on behalf of the smaller territories, more cohesive societies and better integrated economies over which they claimed sovereignty. Within Europe, it is not coincidental that the most commercialized economies of these centuries (Northern Italy, Flanders, Portugal, Spain, Holland and England) enjoyed the services and public goods (internal order, external security and protection for trade, shipping and colonization overseas) provided by reasonably and relatively well-funded states. That outcome derived from loans as well as taxes, depended partly on coercion but also upon collaboration and levels of compliance secured from bodies of more or less culturally homogeneous and patriotic taxpayers, who recognized their stakes in the power and efficiency of 'their' royal and aristocratic masters (Braudel, 1985).

To the East, what (Eurocentric?) economic historians interested in the political cum institutional basis for modern economic growth now see are no longer the hydraulic societies, Asiatic modes of production or predatory oriental despotisms of yesteryear (Weiss and Hobson, 1995). When they survey an emerging body of statistical evidence, calibrated to expose the resources (taxes, loans, salaried bureaucrats, properly paid and equipped armies and navies) available to the rulers of the Ming-Qing, Mughal and other empires, the inferences drawn from the data and resources available to their emperors, divided by the square kilometres of territory and large diverse populations over which they claimed to rule, they are prepared to suggest that these over-extended landed Eurasian empires were somehow held together by under-funded and weak states (Lieven, 2000).

Before Britain's takeover of their empire, Mughal rulers continued, however, to provide relatively superior levels of external security, but had witnessed deceleration in their rates of territorial expansion. In an age of primitive systems of transportation and communication they lacked the resources and penetrative powers to connect and integrate the scattered ethnically heterogeneous and culturally diverse populations spread across vast territories into a better integrated imperial market for commodities, land, labour and capital (Wade, 2004). To maintain stability they fell back upon exemplary but episodic displays of despotism, paternalistic ideologies and religious ideologies. All three empires basically refrained from constructing the kind of fiscal base and mobilizing the resources required to govern, protect and develop empires of that scale and diversity (Leonard and Watts, 1992, and Pamuk, 1987). Their courts and capitals impressed Western visitors, but of effective and sustained economic governance there seems to have been some centuries of salient contracts between the Occident and the Orient.

REFERENCES

Abernathy D. (2000), *The Dynamics of Global Dominance. European Overseas Empires 1415–1980*, New Haven.
Adshead S. (1995), *China and World History*, Basingstoke.
Ardant G. (1971–72), *Histoire de l'impot*, 2 vols, Paris.
Arrighi G. (1994), *The Long Twentieth Century. Money, Power and the Origins of our Times*, London.
Blaut J. (2000), *Eight Eurocentric Historians*, New York.
Bayly Ch. (2004), *The Birth of the Modern World 1780–1914*, Oxford.
Black J. (1998), *War in the Early Modern World*, New Haven.
Blickel P. (ed.) (1997), *Resistance, Representation and Community*, Oxford.
Blitz R. (1967), 'Mercantilist Policies and the Pattern of World Trade 1500-1750', *Journal of Economic History*, 27 (2), 39–55.

Blockmans W. (1997), *A History of Power in Europe: People, Markets, States*, Oxford.

Bonney R. (1991), *The European Dynastic State*, Oxford.

Bonney R. (ed.) (1995), *Economic Systems and State Finance*, Oxford.

Bonney R. (1999), *The Rise of the Fiscal State in Europe*, Oxford.

Brook T. and Blue G. (1999), *China and Historical Capitalism*, Cambridge.

Braudel F. (1981–84), *Civilization and Capitalism*, 3 vols, London.

Canny N. (ed.) (1994), *Europeans on the Move. Studies on European Migration 1500-1800*, Oxford.

Caselli F. (ed.) (2008), *Government Debts and Financial Markets in Europe* (from Chatto and Pickering).

Chang H.J. (ed.) (2007), *Institutions for Economic Development. Theory, History and Contemporary Experience*, Tokyo, University Press.

Chaudhuri K. (1990), *Asia Before Europe. Economy and Civilization of the Indian Ocean from the Rise of Islam to 1750*, Cambridge.

Coleman D. (ed.) (1969), *Revisions in Mercantilism*, London.

Crossley P. et al. (eds) (2006), *Empire at the Margins: Culture, Ethnicity and Frontier in Early Modern China*, Berkeley.

Deng G. (1993), *Development Versus Stagnation. Technological Continuity and Agricultural Progress in Pre-modern China*, Westport.

Deng G. (1997), *Chinese Maritime Activities and Socio-economic Developments c. 2100BC–1900AD*, Westport.

Deng G. (1999), *The Premodern Chinese Economy. Economy, Structural Equilibrium and Capitalist Sterility*, London.

Dixit A. (2002), 'Incentives and Organizations in the Public Sector', *Journal of Human Resources*, 37 (4), 697–727.

Downing B. (1992), *The Military Revolution and Political Change. The Origins of Democracy and Autocracy in Early Modern Europe*, Princeton.

Doyle M. (1986), *Empires*, Ithaca.

Dunstan H. (1996), *Conflicting Counsels to Confuse the Age. A Documentary Study of Political Economy in Qing China, 1644–1840*, Ann Arbor.

Dyson K. (1980), *The State Tradition in Western Europe. A Study of an Idea and an Institution*, Oxford.

Ekelund R. and Tollison R. (1981), *Mercantilism as a Rent Seeking Society*, College Station Texas.

Ekelund R. and Tollison R. (1997), *Politicized Economies: Monarchy, Monopoly and Mercantilism*, College Station Texas.

Elias N. (1982), 'The Civilizing Process', Vol. 2, *State Formation and Civilization*, Oxford.

Epstein S. (2002), *Freedom and Growth. Markets and Sates in Premodern Europe*, London.

Ertman Th. (1997), *Birth of the Leviathan. Building States and Regimes in Early Modern Europe*, Cambridge.

Field A. (1981), 'The Problem with Neoclassical Institutional Economics', *Explorations in Economic History*, 18, 174–98.

Genet J.P. and Le Mené M. (1987), *Genèse de l'Etat moderne*, Paris.

Glete J. (2002), *War and the State in Early Modern Europe*, London.

Gomes L. (1987), *Foreign Trade and the National Economy*, Basingstoke.

Hall J. (1985), *Powers and Liberties*, Oxford.

Hall J. and Schroeder R. (2006), *An Anatomy of Power. The Social Theory of Michael*

Mann, Cambridge.
Helpman E. (2004), *The Mystery of Economic Growth*, Oxford.
Herbst J. (2000), *States and Power in Africa*, Princeton.
Hirschman A. (1978), 'Exit, Voice and the State', *World Politics*, 31 (1), 90–107.
Hodgson G. (2000), *How Economics Forgot History*, London.
Hoffman P. and Norberg K. (1994), *Fiscal Crises, Liberty and Representative Government*, Stanford.
Hoselitz B. (ed.) (1960), *Theories of Economic Growth*, New York.
Hutchison T. (1988), *Before Adam Smith*, Oxford.
Jomo K.S. and Reinert E. (eds.) (2005), *The Origin of Development Economics*, London.
Jones E. (2003), *The European Miracle*, Cambridge.
Lachmann R. (2000), *Capitalists in Spite of Themselves. Elite Conflict and Economic Transitions in Early Modern Europe*, New York.
Landes D. (1998), *The Wealth and Poverty of Nations*, New York.
Leonard J. and Watts J. (eds) (1992), *To Achieve Security and Wealth. The Qing Imperial State and the Economy, 1644–1911*, Ithaca.
Levi M. (1988), *Of Rule and Revenue*, Berkeley.
Lieven D. (2000), *Empire. The Russian Empire and its Rivals*, London.
Macfarlane A. (2000), *The Riddle of the Modern World of Liberty, Wealth and Equality*, Basingstoke.
Magnusson L. (ed.) (2002), *Mercantilist Economics*, London.
Mann M. (1986), 'The Sources of Social Power', Vol. 1, *A History from the Beginning to 1760AD*, Cambridge.
Menard C. and Shirley M. (eds) (2005), *Handbook for New Institutional Economics*, Norwell.
Modelski G. and Thompson W. (1998), *Seapower in Global Politics, 1494–1993*, London.
Mokyr J. (2006), 'Mercantilism, the Enlightenment and the Industrial Revolution', in Findlay R. et al. (eds), *Eli Heckscher, International Trade and Economic History*, Cambridge, MA.
Mooers C. (1991), *The Making of Bourgeois Europe*, London.
North D. (1990), *Institutions, Institutional Change and Economic Performance*, Cambridge.
O'Brien P. (2002), 'Fiscal Exceptionalism. Great Britain and its European Rivals from Civil War to Triumph at Waterloo', in Winch and O'Brien.
O'Brien P. (2006), 'Contentions of the Purse between England and its European Rivals from Henry V to George IV: A Conversation with Michael Mann', *Journal of Historical Sociology*.
O'Brien P. et al. (eds) (forthcoming 2009), *Fiscal States in Europe and Asia*, Cambridge.
Pamuk S. (1987), *The Ottoman Empire and European Capitalism, 1820–1913*, Cambridge.
Perdue P. (2005), *China Marches West. The Qing Conquest of Central Eurasia*, Cambridge, MA.
Persson T. and Tabellini G. (2003), *The Economic Effects of Constitutions*, Cambridge.
Plateau J.-P. (2000), *Institutions, Social Norms and Economic Development*, Paris.
Poggi G. (1990), *The State: Its Nature, Development and Prospects*, Cambridge.
Pohl H. (ed.) (1990), *The European Discovery of the World and its Economic Effects*

on Pre-Industrial Society 1500–1800, Stuttgart.

Pomeranz K. (2000), *The Great Divergence. China, Europe and the Making of the Modern World Economy*, Princeton.

Prendergast C. (1999), 'The Provision of Incentives in Firms', *Journal of Economic Literature*, 37, 7–63.

Quataert D. (2000), *The Ottoman Empire 1700–1922*, Cambridge.

Reinert E. (1999), 'The Role of the State in Economic Growth', *Journal of Economic Studies*, 26 (415), 268–326.

Reinhard W. (ed.) (1996), *Power, Elites and State Building*, Oxford.

Richards J. (1995), *The Mughal Empire*, Cambridge.

Skinner A. and Wilson T. (eds) (1976), *The Market and the State; Essays in Honour of Adam Smith*, Oxford.

Smelser N. and Swedberg R. (eds) (2006), *Handbook of Economic Sociology*, Princeton.

Struve L. (ed.) (2004), *The Qing Formation in World Historical Time*, London.

Teichova A. and Matis H. (eds) (2003), *Nation, State and the Economy in History*, Cambridge.

Tilly Ch. (1975), *The Formation of National States in Western Europe*, Princeton.

Tilly Ch. (1990), *Coercion, Capital and European States 990–1990*, Oxford.

Thompson W. (2000), *The Emergence of Global Political Economy*, London.

Tracy J. (ed.) (1991a), *The Rise of Merchant Empires. Long Distance Trade in the Early Modern World 1350–1750*, Cambridge.

Tracy J. (ed.) (1991b), *The Political Economy of Merchant Empires. State Power and World Trade 1350–1750*, Cambridge.

Vries P. (2003), *Via Peking and Back to Manchester: Britain, the Industrial Revolution and China*, Leiden.

Wade R. (2004), *Governing the Market. Economic Theory and The Role of Government in East Asian Industrialization*, Princeton.

Weede E. (1996), *Economic Development, Social Order and World Politics*, London.

Weiss L. and Hobson J. (1995), *States and Economic Development*, Cambridge.

Winch D. and O'Brien P. (2002), *The Political Economy of British Historical Experience*, Oxford.

Winch D. (1996), *Riches and Poverty. An Intellectual History of Political Economy in Britain 1750–1834*, Cambridge.

Wong R.B. (1997), *China Transformed and the Limits of European Experience*, Ithaca.

Zmera H. (2001), *Monarchy, Aristocracy and the State in Europe, 1300–1800*, London.

3. Contemporary Capitalisms and Internationalisation: From One Diversity to Another

Charlie Dannreuther and Pascal Petit

INTRODUCTION

Regulation Theory (RT) developed an analysis of capitalist development centred mainly around the growth of nation states. This characterisation was especially clear as a description of industrial growth in the three decades following WWII that redefined and strengthened the role of the nation state in the international system. Fordism was an efficient techno-organisation of mass production that tied wage gains to the expansion of mass consumption through a series of nationally defined social and political institutions. Part of RT's characterisation of Fordism was the assumption that sources of crises in accumulation were endogenous and derived from the contradictory nature of relations under capitalism and that these tensions were managed through institutional compromises at the national level. Fordist capitalism was typically presented as supporting broadly similar national level institutional forms that governed the wage relationship, forms of competition, the use of money, the role of the state and the organisation of international relations. Reflecting nationally contingent economies, these national level compromises supported patterns of accumulation and economic growth that have been described as Keynesian.

This Regulation Theory perspective led to a distinction between modes of social regulation (MSRs), corresponding to institutional characteristics and contexts, and regimes of accumulation (RAs), that corresponded to macroeconomic Keynesianism.[1] Under Fordism, the institutionalised nexus between wage and labour (in for example tripartite decision-making processes) played a central role in the overall development of Fordism because, under Fordist production principles, the stabilisation of the labour force was central to the smooth accumulation of capital under mass production and consumption. It therefore influenced how the other forms (such as finance and the state) evolved and impacted on accumulation processes (such as credit management and social policy). If these modes of social regulation conditioned the accumulation regimes they did not determine them. National compromises were also influenced by the international environment, for example. The Bretton Woods system therefore afforded stability in the international economy by guaranteeing most-favoured-nation access to overseas markets for the disposal of surplus production (the GATT), the dollar-based foreign exchange system provided international financial stability (IMF), and a lender of last resort provided access to credit (IBRD and World Bank).

Although until recently the domestic/international relation was seen as secondary to the wage–labour nexus in RT, it was integrally related to the other four structural forms (such as the State, money, the forms of competition or the wage–labour nexus). With the demise of Fordism this has become increasingly apparent as the exposure to international competition has been a central experience in all the once nationally organised modes of social regulation associated with Fordism. The wage/labour relation has been shattered through the changing international division of labour and the associated access of even small companies to cheap labour across the world. Finance has radically altered in scope and scale after the removal of credit controls and the deregulation of financial markets in the 1980s and states now often seek to enable markets, through privatisation and normalisation, rather than intervene to direct them. The corollary of these processes has been that new forms of competition have entered each of the main modes of social regulation.

Many have explained these changes broad societal changes through the term 'globalisation'. While there are sufficient problems with globalisation as a concept in itself (Rosenberg 1999, 2006), for RT it is an unsatisfactory explanation as it prioritises exogenous sources of change – such as technological, increased international competition, greater influence of hedge funds – in explaining shifts in accumulation. RT seeks to explain change in the first place through endogenous sources and this forces us to question the role of globalisation as determining social change. After the crisis of Fordism, the internationalisation of the developed economies has strongly contributed to new forms of competition. But this competition has not led to convergence among these economies as institutions are resistant to change even when policies attempt to direct change along a similar path. There has been since the early 1980s the dismantling of much of the social and political institutional infrastructure that underpinned Fordism as the turn to liberal markets led to greater internationalisation, deregulated finance and labour markets and the reform of social protection. Still by the mid 1990s the diversity of capitalism remained a major characteristic of modern economies that overshadowed any sustained trend of convergence.

The Regulation Theory analysed in depth in the mid 90s this diversity of market economies. Studies on national systems of innovation had stressed how idiosyncratic systems of innovation remained, although they were at the core of emerging knowledge-based economies (Nelson, Lundvall). Regulation Theory underlined that this diversity is not only supported by systems of innovation, but also by the whole structures of institutions grounding growth regimes. This led to the identification of various types of capitalism (Amable, Barré and Boyer 1997; Amable and Petit 2002; Amable 2003). The persistence of diversity does imply that convergence of institutional structures is not taking place but it does not imply that no change in the structure of this diversity is occurring. The various paths to internationalisation have successfully reshaped the relative positions of national economies. Some have evolved in ways common to all models, others are more country specific and transform the clustering of countries. The redeployment of manufacturing activities, for example, may feature as a common change in most developed countries as they are faced with competition from low wage cost countries. Conversely the reorganisation of service activities may lead to more idiosyncratic changes, as they respond to universal trends for regulatory reform. The reason is tied to the more embedded nature of services markets which have for long been considered as sheltered activities and which are now more exposed to international competition and its influences.

In this chapter we shall see that another explanation for the changes associated with the change in regime is the movement from a wage/labour relation, organised around the modern corporate form of large firms, to a consumer/producer relation, where the form of the small and medium-sized enterprise (SME), modern and traditional plays a new role. This chapter will investigate the diversity of responses to the challenges of internationalisation. As well as examining the issue of convergence we will also try to assess the extent to which there has been a reordering of the country clusters through this process of internationalisation.

The first section will recall the various types of capitalism identified in previous RT works on the basis of their institutional characteristics in the mid 1990s. The second section will try to underline the main traits of the national institutional contexts after the first wave of deregulation that occurred at the turn of the 1980s and 1990s following the crisis of Fordism in the mid 1970s. These differences in terms of regulatory pressures will be investigated in the three following sections:

– the regulation of labour market activity by the state, (section 3),
– the monitoring of private national transactions (section 4) and
– in the ruling of transnational transactions (section 5).

From these observations, the sixth section will draw conclusions on the future of the diversity of capitalisms.

DIVERSITIES OF CAPITALISM

The institutional diversity of developed economies is due to the contingent ways in which institutions develop. There is a systemic dimension to these dynamics. The complementarity between pairs of institutions as developed in Aoki (1994) and in RT does not consider institutions in isolation but as part of a whole. The existence and function of an institution in one sector is therefore often enhanced by the institutional arrangements in another.[2] The plasticity that comes from these complentarities means that as changes occur in a country's structural forms, as they adjust to forces impacting all countries, country specificities are not erased.

We now have to reconcile the idea of a growth regime, prevalent for a given historical period across many countries, with the lasting institutional diversity that describes their specific contexts. We may then be able to account for the relative performances of countries by examining institutional differences by specific domains of activity. Thus labour markets can be more or less regulated; wage bargaining can be more or less centralised; and the financial systems more or less reliant upon the banks, or on the freedom that they give to the financial markets. Education is organised quite differently from one country to the next, with more or less close ties to industry and universities are more or less independent. Finally competition between private companies may be more or less intense according to the regulation of markets.

One way of examining economic performance is to add up the types of institutions that prevail in the most efficient domain. But collecting 'best practices' is not feasible as institutional change is evolutionary and so contingent. 'Re-engineering' institutions cannot guarantee anticipated outcomes but will lead to a hybrid that corresponds to expectations both more and less than intended. Change occurs over long periods of time, and so under quite different structural conditions, so there only a very limited amount of learning will be planned. During the 1990s, for example, the transition of post-communist countries to market economies was a cruel example of the unintended consequences of organisational reform, despite the best efforts of many experts. Monitoring change is also hard as it may be hidden by the slow pace and unpredictable nature of reform.

We thus have to consider the diversity of institutions and examine the extent to which they have adapted to the structural conditions of the time and evolved into new types of capitalism. The typologies of capitalism derived here are from empirical investigation and are therefore not likely to endure indefinitely. A new type can appear, another may disappear and national economies may shift from one category to another so that what is happening in the present period of transition from the old Fordist regime (with its variety) to a new post-Fordist regime (with its own variety) may describe very different forms of capitalism. Another way to put it is that in this chapter we try to investigate the main features of a post Fordist regime by looking at the varieties that it produces. Numerous studies have focused on the different kinds of capitalism and the specificity of national models. Some studies have emphasised national specificities, considering that each country constitutes its own category, while others base their understanding of diversity on two polar extremes (i.e., the United States and Germany in Hall and Soskice (2002)) and classify countries according to their differences, or similarities, to these extreme cases.

For the purpose of this chapter we shall retain the five forms of capitalism distinguished in Amable and Petit (2002) on the basis of a data analysis of the structural forms of 21 OECD countries[3] in the mid 1990s. These models have performed consistently over the 1990s as shown in various OECD studies on productivity, convergence and institutional settings. The empirical analyses explored subsystems relating to 1) scientific and technological fields, 2) economic structure, 3) educational system, 4) labour market. These are all fields used extensively in investigations on innovation system. To these were added 5) the form of internationalisation (foreign trade and direct investment) and 6) the financial domain.

Five main clusters were identified that seemed to occur in a majority of the above six fields:

1. A group comprising those countries that best embody the *market-based* model – including the United States, Great Britain, Canada, Australia.
2. A group comprising those countries that embody the *social-democratic* model, including basically the Scandinavian countries (Finland, Sweden, Denmark[4]).
3. A *mesocorporatist* group where large firms play a key role in organising welfare structures, with Korea and Japan.
4. A *European continental* group, where the State was playing a central role, made up of France, Germany, the Netherlands, Belgium and Ireland[5].
5. A *Mediterranean* variant of the European continental, comprising Spain, Italy, Greece and Portugal.

This typology stresses the heterogeneity of European capitalism. The distinction of a Mediterranean model, for example, acknowledges the typology developed by Esping Andersen (1990). This highlights the role of family support in social security provision in addition to other factors that distinguish this Mediterranean sub group, such as low R&D expenditures. There are of course weaknesses in this model. First a comparative analysis of national institutional contexts in the mid 90s does not tell us how institutions have evolved during the last decade, during a period when internationalisation has increased in many ways from cross-border investments to international flows of information and knowledge. Second, beyond the rough clustering of capitalist countries featured above, a non-negligible variety does remain within clusters. For instance a joined analysis of wage formation and working conditions leads to the clustering described above while separate analyses of wage formation and working conditions do not (Davoine and Erhel 2006). This intra cluster diversity may imply significant breaks and reshuffles as countries are met with specific challenges associated with different engagement with internationalisation. It is important to acknowledge this weakness in the model if we are to appreciate the impact of the main institutional changes that have taken placed since the emergence of post-Fordist growth regimes.

DEGREES OF BUSINESS REGULATION AFTER THE FIRST WAVE OF LIBERALISATION IN THE FIVE TYPES OF CAPITALIST COUNTRIES

We can begin to confront the overall clustering of capitalisms mentioned above (and built on current structural indicators in each field) with a general assessment on market regulations done in an expert survey by the OECD in 1998. In this survey experts were asked to rank between 0 and 6 the degree of regulation bearing at the end of the 1990s on various type of activities, distinguishing external activities, standard internal market activities and activities under more or less close public monitoring. Table 3.1 shows the situation at the end of the 90s. States have removed controls once used to control international business transactions such as in trade and investment. As all the states had made a commitment to do this with their membership of the GATT it is perhaps of little surprise to see that it is precisely in the realm of external activities that the level of regulation is rather generally low. Membership of regional trading blocs have also precipitated the acceleration of the removal of such barriers, notably in the EU's Single Market Programme, frequently seen as a benchmark for neo liberal capitalism (Albert 1992; Rhodes 1997).

Table 3.1: Degrees of Business Regulation (indicators ranging from 0, fully liberalised, to 6, fully regulated)

Type of Capitalism	Inter-national[1]	State Regulatory Control		State Discretionary Control		Overall Regulatory Environment[6]
		Domestic[2]	Enterprise[3]	Public Sector[4]	State Control[5]	
Market-based						
Australia						
Canada	0.4	1.2	1.1	0.8	1.8	0.9
USA	2.2	1.0	0.8	1.2	1.4	1.5
GB	0.9	1.1	1.3	0.8	0.9	1.0
	0.4	0.5	0.5	0.	1.2	0.5
Nordic						
Sweden	0.8	1.7	1.8	2.3	0.6	1.4
Finland	0.6	2.3	1.9	3.3	1.9	1.7
Denmark	0.5	1.9	1.3	2.3	2.7	1.4
Mesocorporatist						
Japan						
Korea	1.0	1.8	2.3	0.7	2.1	1.5
	1.7	2.7	3.1	2.5	2.2	2.4
European Continental						
Germany	0.5	2.7	2.1	1.2	2.5	1.4
France	1.0	2.7	2.7	2.3	3.0	2.1
Belgium	0.6	2.7	2.6	2.0	3.8	1.9
Ireland	0.4	1.1	1.2	1.3	0.5	0.8
Netherlands	0.5	1.8	1.4	2.6	1.9	1.4
Mediterranean						
Spain						
Portugal	0.7	2.2	1.8	2.0	3.4	1.6
Italy	1.1	2.1	1.5	2.7	3.0	1.7
Greece	0.5	3.3	2.7	4.4	3.3	2.3
	1.3	2.7	1.7	3.4	4.5	2.2

Notes: Column 1: degree of regulation of international business transactions, barriers to trade and investment; Column 2: degree of regulation of domestic business transactions; Column 3: degree of small business regulations, barriers to entrepreneurship; Column 4: size of the public sector; Column 5: degree of control of economic activities by the State; Column 6: general degree of regulation of economic activities.
Source: indicators taken from Nicoletti, Scarpetta and Boylaud (2000), constructed using experts' scores from 0 (extremely liberal) to 6 (extremely strict regulation) for the various fields. The indicator in Column 2 is the average of the indicators in columns 3, 4 and 5. In other words national characteristics have been maintained even when external regulations are enforced allowing national characteristics to inform key political choices about the regulation of economic behaviour. National capitalisms can still be described according to the institutional make up of the economy. This reflects both the practices and routines of actors in the economy as well as providing clear categories for the classification of markets.

It is worth noting that the groupings identified above do not break according to trading bloc membership but rather retain national characteristics. This is in part because the nation states have negotiated the terms of economic integration in ways that reflect and preserve the interests of key players in economic policy. While coalitions between states inevitably emerge during negotiations, the intergovernmental character of regional trade arrangements guarantees the rights of governments to veto clauses not in their national interest. In the EU, where genuine supranational powers are far more developed than any other regional bloc, member states have dominated in the main treaty negotiations over pillar one (Moravcsik 1993). But even the Single Market Programme was only possible through the use of directives (which allow member states to decide how to achieve shared goals) and legal principles such as mutual recognition (which allow companies to trade on the basis of their national regulatory requirements) (Burley and Mattli 1993). National capitalisms were thus preserved.

Figure 3.1 supports the main results showed in Table 3.1 on the levels of 'regulation' in various developed economies at the end of the 90s. Specifically it confirms that:

a) barriers to trade are now low across the board of countries,[6]
b) significant diversity remains in administrative and economic regulation,
c) little correlation exists between the levels of economic regulations (the degree of regulation of sectoral activities) and the levels of administrative regulation (the role of the state in the economy).

Figure 3.1:

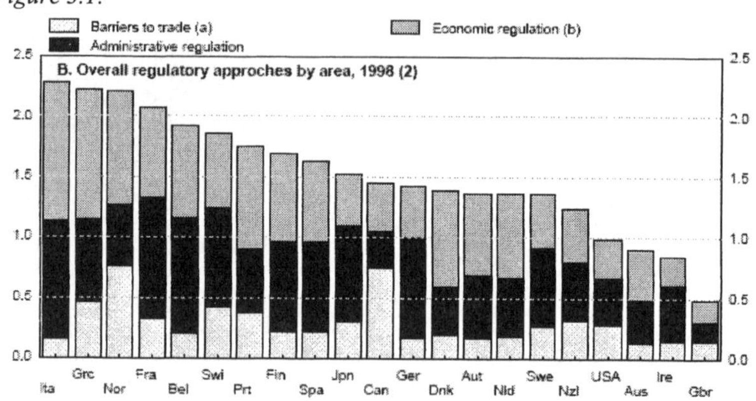

Notes: Using indicators from Nicoletti et al. (2001), as done in Table 3.1, 'barriers to trade' includes trade and FDI restrictions, 'economic regulation' includes barriers to competition and state control.
Source: Serres (2003) p. 46.

These results show that the transformation experienced across many countries was not just because the states began at with different degrees of business regulation. Data on regulatory stances in non-manufacturing industries over a long period (between 1978 and 1998) shows that deregulation changes occurred nearly everywhere (see Figure 3.2).[7] Furthermore changes have been more important in countries that already had relatively low degrees of market regulations: market-based economies ranked first, followed by Nordic economies, then European continental system and finally the Mediterranean group.

Market economies, in other words those that employ a preponderance of market mechanisms for social coordination, tend to have become more market orientated with time (see Figure 3.2). Conversely those with the most regulated economies initially have travelled less far towards the market model, despite the various pressures to conform. A lot of countries remained in a rather intermediary situation between convergence and divergence from the market-based model.

Travelling towards the market model in the experts' eyes seems to imply some kind of convergence process. But markets are themselves social constructions and the changes associated with internationalisation appear to have entrenched existing social relations. This places the focus back on endogenous nature of change in varieties of capitalism and how it plays out between complementary institutions. Institutions in a given country are not randomly associated but are linked within a pattern of interrelationships. This complementarity between national institutions (Amable 2000) implies complex dynamics of changes.

Figure 3.2:

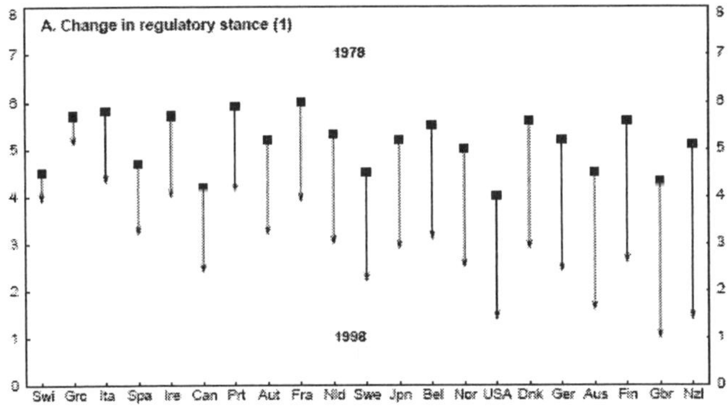

Notes: Using indicators from Nicoletti et al.(2001), as done in Table 3.1, 'change in regulatory stance' combines indicators of degree of regulation in seven non-manufacturing industries (gas, electricity, post, telecommunication, passenger air transport railways and road freight).
Source: Serres (2003) p. 46.

Institutional changes under internationalisation are thus simultaneously carrying the diffusion of market mechanisms and allowing national diversities to reproduce themselves by entrenching national social traits. We shall illustrate this process of dual transformation by assessing some of their underlying features in this second section. To illustrate the kind of changes that a changed regulatory role of the state can effect, we shall examine the flexibilisation of the labour market in the third section. In the fourth section we shall demonstrate that changes in the economic regulation of product markets have affected change in the key service activities. Finally the fifth section will examine how specific changes associated with the liberalisation of external activities has led to a new role played by SMEs. These three case studies should help us to assess the convergence and/or divergence among diverse kinds of capitalism and to investigate what kind of growth regime these transformations may lead to in the next decade. Specifically it will help us to account for some of the renewed features of diversity at work under the structural changes experienced by all the economies under view.

THE REGULATORY ROLE OF THE STATE

In many political debates the main issue about liberalisation has focused on labour market regulations. The OECD job study of the mid 80s made a general call for more flexibility in labour markets as a precondition for full employment and most national policies, whatever the type of country capitalism concerned, complied. But if we look more closely we can see that the reforms undertaken in the name of liberalisation were borne more by some categories of job than others and not by all kinds of jobs. Table 3.2 shows that labour market regulations are quite distinct from one cluster to another. Not surprisingly degrees of labour market regulations can be clearly discriminated between country clusters: low levels of regulation are to be found in market based economies, continental and Mediterranean maintain tighter regulatory frameworks in their labour markets, while Nordic countries are in between.

Table 3.2 shows that by the end of the 1990s differences in labour market regulations were still marked in both regular jobs and temporary jobs. This may partly explain why some policy recommendations continue to demand further labour market deregulation to promote higher flexibility of labour markets. This is despite many years of promoting this policy of flexibility.

Table 3.2: Degrees of Labour Market Regulation

Type of Capitalism	Degree of Protection of Temporary Jobs	Degree of Protection of Regular Employment
Market-based		
Australia	1.2	0.9
Canada	0.3	0.9
USA	0.3	0.1
GB	0.3	0.7
Nordic		
Sweden	1.8	3.0
Finland	1.9	2.3
Denmark	1.2	1.7
Mesocorporatist		
Japan	2.3	3.0
Korea	2.3	-
European Continental		
Germany	2.5	3.0
France	3.7	2.5
Belgium	2.6	1.6
Ireland	0.3	1.7
Netherlands	1.5	3.2
Mediterranean		
Spain	3.7	2.8
Portugal	3.2	4.3
Italy	3.6	3.0
Greece	4.5	2.6

Source: the indicator of labour market regulation EPL(Employment Protection Legislation) is drawn from OECD, *Employment Outlook* 1999. The higher the indicator, the more restrictive is the relevant labour market policy.

Still there are today numerous contentions that the stated objectives of greater flexibility have been achieved and that the flexibilisation of labour markets should not come first on the policy agenda. Even the OECD, which widely advocated stepping up labour market flexibility as its preferred remedy for restoring full employment and growth in the 1980s, has devoted much less emphasis on the need to bolster labour market flexibility in its recent Job Strategy (2006). There is now a good deal of empirical evidence doubting the claim that a more flexible labour market systematically contributes to boosting competitiveness. A recent ILO study even finds that there is a positive correlation between average length of service and the growth in hourly productivity. This suggests that, all other things being equal, the claims for flexible labour markets are not guaranteed (Auer et al. 2005).

Figure 3.3a: Regular Employment: Changes in EPL between the late 80s and the late 90s

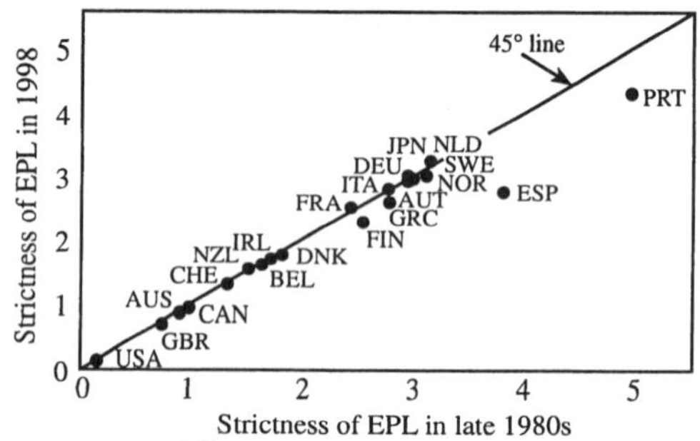

Figure 3.3b: Temporary Employment: Changes in EPL between the late 80s and the late 90s

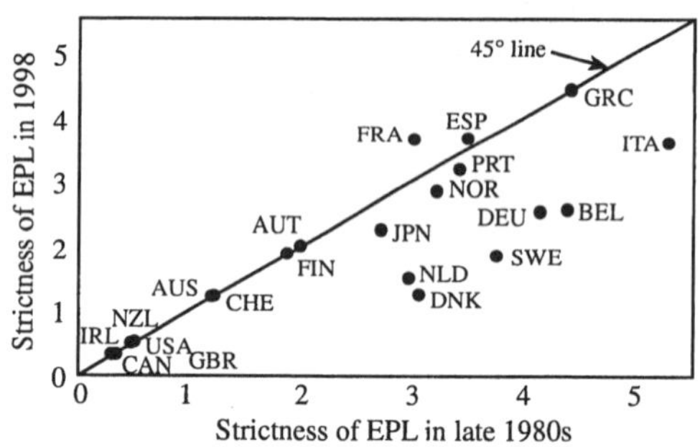

Note: The indicator of strictness follows from expert advice, ranking countries' performances from 6 for the strictest to 0 for the most flexible.
Source: Serres (2003); EPL indicator, see OECD (1999) Employment Outlook.

Countries have achieved flexibility by developing a more dual labour market, and in doing so strongly distinguishing between regular and temporary employment. Temporary employment has expanded in most labour markets, accounting much more than labour market liberalisation for the achievements in terms of flexibility. Figure 3.3a shows this stability in strictness of EPL (Employment Policy Legislation) indicators for regular jobs. Beyond the expansion of temporary employment jobs, most of the changes towards deregulation have also concerned these jobs (see Figure 3.3b). But these changes in temporary employment regulation have been diverse among countries. They seem to have been especially marked in Nordic countries, leaving them at the core of the flexicurity model (see Boyer 2006). In Denmark, for example, increased mobility, especially in temporary jobs, has been supported by some certainty to be reemployed elsewhere, after some paid training if needed.

These regulatory variations, obligation and changes all have a common theme. The main change that has characterised the shift from Fordism to post Fordism has been the reorientation of the regime of accumulation from around the core relation of the wage/labour relation, epitomised in national collectivist bargains, to the relations between producers, consumers and markets, that characterise the new forms of competition. In these forms of competition service activities as well as all types of SMEs are playing key structural roles.

Evidence for this change is clear in the shifts in the modes of social regulation described in the paragraphs above notably in relation to the type of capitalism and the evolution of the sector in the domestic economy. While corporate sectors may experience convergence due to obligatory compliance with regulatory standards, auditing practices and the demands of financial markets, small firms and service activities have frequently been either exempted from such obligations or allowed to retain special regulatory exemptions. In that respect they have been the main loci of entrenched social relations that helped to perpetuate and renew the diversity of national capitalisms.

For this reason SME policy is often the point at which the distinction between universal corporate form and the contingent cultural economy is defined. SME definitions have much to tell us about the resilience of the diversity of capitalisms. For example, in the 'market based' model of capitalism (e.g. UK, USA) there are very few regulatory requirements to comply with in advance of trading. But in the 'European continental model' there are very many, including registering with a Chamber and complying with often old legal obligations prior to trading. Social democratic company law obliges companies to cooperate with their workforce and contribute significant taxes to the sustenance of the welfare state, while in the Mediterranean variant, post-WWII national economic development has been far more dependent on small firms than in the European continental models.

Flexible work and management practices are all associated with the growth of self employed people and their deployment in companies as part time workers. Most importantly the change in reduction of regulatory burdens on business has been consistently associated with the greater political significance of the SME sector across the industrialised world and is a view promoted through the mechanism of supranational and international governance such as the EU, the OECD and the IMF as well as across nation states. In short many of the characteristics associated with these diverse economies and the contemporary reforms that they have experienced, including the greater exposure of the hidden service economy, are associated with the economic and political re-emergence of the small firm.

The *Global Entrepreneurship Monitor* (GEM) surveys indicate a relationship between levels of education and entrepreneurship. In low income economies, people with low education tend to become self employed. In high income economies, people with high levels of education tend to become self employment (Minniti 2005). While there has been much debate on whether entrepreneurship can be taught, a more educated workforce may see self employment as an opportunity rather than as a necessity. The rise in post material consumption placed a premium on the small batch production techniques that favoured SMEs, and the growth in the service sector and especially in value adding services such as marketing and advertising have all contributed to greater opportunities for SMEs.

Flexible labour markets are seen as Anglo American models and as in opposition to the more regulated European continental models. This is normally seen to be the consequence of better trade union organisation and better protection for workers through centrally managed state legislation and social compact in the continental models. However there are a number of problems with this assumption. First the EU's economy is predominantly a small firm economy and as such compliance with labour market, or any other form of regulation, is very hard to monitor let alone ensure. This is in comparison to the Anglo American economies which are based on large relatively corporate bodies with a relatively higher level of work force organisation within larger establishments.

Second the idea of a flexible labour market was initially introduced as a critique of new forms of work organisation in the UK by John Atkinson of the Institute for Manpower Studies. It was a critique of a growing practice amongst employers of separating workers according to a core workforce to 'conduct the organisations' key, firm specific activities, surrounded by a cluster of peripheral groups' (Atkinson 1984, p. 3).

These peripheral groups would provide the numerical flexibility that the employers wanted during the recession of the early 1980s. The core group would preserve their job security by being functionally flexible according to the needs of management. This practice represented a 'significant break with the conventional, unitary and hierarchical internal labour markets with dominate[d] manpower management both in theory and practices' (Atkinson

1984, p. 3).

While the practice of subcontracting was not a new one in the UK or any other European economy, this notion of flexibility introduced a way of managing the labour force through a significantly increased number of self employed. At one level the peripheral workers allowed companies to introduce non-unionised labour to perform 'non core' tasks, such as cleaning, or employ new entrants to the labour force at lower rates of pay and poorer conditions than those enjoyed by core workers. The large increases in part-time female employment in the UK from this period reflects their greater role that women played in small firms, non-manual labour and sectors with low trade union membership and limited collective bargaining (Bruegle and Perrons 1998, p. 107). This pattern fits well with the service sectors.

To conclude major structural changes – the diffusion of SMEs in the economy and the rise in female employment – seem to have accompanied the transformations of labour markets giving them more flexibility, rather than changes in regulatory stance. This is underlined by the observation that both changes have acted to sustain nationally specific segmentations, thereby reproducing the new bases for the diversity of nations despite the pressures of internationalisation for convergence.

PRODUCT MARKET REGULATIONS

In the above we stressed that SMEs were central to the working of flexible labour markets and in the reproduction of national specificities, especially in service activities. But clearly services are also areas where large network services operate too. In large network services idiosyncratic organisations appear regularly across all countries and are not restricted just to non-market based ones. Looking at Table 3.3, which compares the strictness of regulations in seven non-manufacturing industries, one can see that in every country some large network service activities remain subjected to strict regulations, even in countries which are generally considered as market based. This underlines how services have developed in ways very specific to countries and that despite the general trend for deregulation (shown in this case in Figure 3.2) some of it remains.

Table 3.3 shows us, however, that some countries have achieved more extensive deregulation of these sectors than others. In the group of market-based countries the levels of regulation are on average quite low. Conversely in continental Europe and even in Mediterranean countries, levels of service regulation remain high across nearly all of the services under review (again despite the general move towards deregulation observed in Figure 3.2). A similar observation could be drawn with the regulation of professions (such as medical, financial services and legal). In the UK, for example, reducing regulation, red tape or regulatory impacts has been at the top of all UK political agendas since the mid 1980s. A similar situation exists in the other market based economies of the USA and Australia.

This shows that the diversity of capitalisms is in part perpetuated by lasting product market regulations in areas of economic activity which are traditionally prone to public tutelage. In other words more or less 'flexible' labour markets is not the only way in which we can differentiate between varieties of capitalisms.

Beyond the general lesson that can be drawn concerning variable levels of product market regulations, the fact that some industries remain more regulated than others is telling of the contingency of relationships that underscore capitalism. The Canadian market-based economy for example has a highly regulated electricity market according in table three, which is due to political tensions between the various provinces:

> Rather than developing a national grid system, or even substantial regional grids, to take advantage of efficiencies and low-cost producing abilities of some provinces, the bickering between provinces prevented the development of a mechanism that could have regulated the transmission of electricity across provincial boundaries. (Griffin Cohen 2002, p. 21)

Similar contingencies in national political system, or political opportunity structures, explain the difference in use of nuclear power between France and Germany (Kitschelt 1986). Similar divergence among large network service industries is evident among EU countries despite the commitment taken by Member States to adopt a common road map for deregulation in most of these activities. The breadth of political sensitivity of electorates to the deregulation of their services was highlighted in the Service – or Bolkestein – Directive that threatened to deregulate services of a general interest across the EU.

EU Member States also vary considerably in the ways that they consult and evaluate regulatory burdens. While the EU has promoted administrative simplification for many years, there are significant variations in how states undertake the process that reflect national political traditions (Radaelli 2004). The remaining differences in product market regulations are therefore not marginal but indicators of major differences in the political communities and what binds them together.

Table 3.3: Levels of Regulation in Some Networked Service (1998)

Type of Capitalism	Retail Trade	Truck Transport	Mobile Phone	Fix Phone	Air pass. Transport	Electricity	Rail
Market-based							
Australia							
Canada	0	0	2	2	2	0	0
USA	2	2	-	2	4	6	2
GB	0	0	2	2	0	4	0
	4	0	2	2	2	0	2
Nordic							
Sweden	2	2	2	2	2	0	2
Finland	4	2	2	2	2	0	6
Denmark	4	-	2	2	2	4	6
Mesocorporatist							
Japan							
Korea	6	4	-	-	4	4	-
	2	0	2	2	4	-	6
European Continental							
Germany	2	4	2	2	2	2	0
France	6	-	-	-	4	6	6
Belgium	4	4	2	2	2	4	6
Ireland	2	-	2	2	2	4	6
Netherlands	2	4	2	2	0	4	0
Mediterranean							
Spain							
Portugal	4	4	6	2	2	4	6
Italy	4	2	2	6	6	4	-
Greece	4	6	6	2	2	6	6
	6	6	2	6	6	6	-

Source: Indicators of regulatory strictness are taken from Nicoletti (2001).

ON TRANSNATIONAL TRANSACTIONS

The previous sections have described two sources of difference in the regulation of modern capitalist economies. These exist within a general pattern of economic growth where forging new forms of competition has been the main driving process of the economic governance of nations. In this section we consider how international transactions, where the trend for deregulation has been more comprehensive, have changed in the late 1990s (see Figure 3.4). There has been a broad liberalisation of transnational transactions in terms of trade and in foreign direct investment during this period. Our emphasis is that this process, combined with the extended technical capability to service large networks at a global level, has significantly enlarge the reach of SMEs at international level. This structural change has changed both the form of international transactions and also the international division of labour among developed economies. Specifically it has demonstrated the greater and relatively new significance of SMEs in international transactions.

Changes in International Trade Patterns

Changes in trade patterns indicate shifts in the international division of labour as national market regulations (including labour rights and capital mobility restrictions) are removed to ease the export of production to economies where the labour costs are lower. Both these changes have been the consequence of the relaxing of national level controls described in the previous sections. With the breakdown in national trade barriers (Table 3.1), there has been far greater opportunity for SMEs to compete beyond their national boundaries as market harmonisation exposes new market niches abroad. In other words as the position of large firms as national champions was no longer protected by national market regulations, subsidies or preferential purchasing agreements, SMEs have been able to exploit their size advantages either by directly entering new markets or, more easily, through alliances across national boundaries. SMEs enjoy various advantages that they are able to exploit in the process of transnational transactions.

First as large firms have become less flexible in response to less predictable post-Fordist markets, small firms were better able to compete. The 'new Competition' outlined by Best and many others has demonstrated the relative competitiveness of small firms in fluctuating markets (Best 1990). The WTOs regime on the transfer of intellectual property rights (TRIPs) has protected SMEs in high value sectors enabling them to establish strategic alliances with far larger firms, as in the pharmaceutical sector (Figure 3.5).

Second as financial markets and consultants have redefined large firms in the pursuit of 'share holder value', cost centres that are not deemed sufficiently profitable have been sold off and the function contracted out (Williams 2000). This has followed the long standing practice of large firms contracting out functions to small firms. Functions too costly to be done in the firm due to tax or labour law obligations would be contracted out. Or large firms might capitalise on other local market competitive advantages of an SME to gain access to a specialist capability provided by a smaller service company. In telecoms, for example, mergers and alliances with local SMEs has been a popular way for larger telecoms companies to expand into new markets (Figure 3.6).

Figure 3.4: Cross-Border Alliances Involving SMEs, 1988–2000

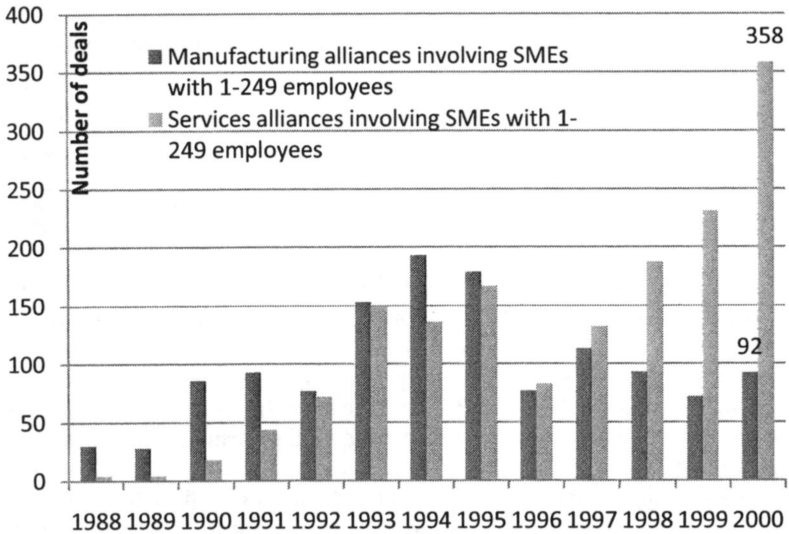

Source: OECD, based on Thomson Financial. Reproduced from page 13 of Kentaro Sakai Industry Issues Global Restructuring: implications for small firms STI Working paper 2002/4 OECD.

Figure 3.5: Pharmaceuticals: Cross-Border Alliances by Firm Size, 1990–2000

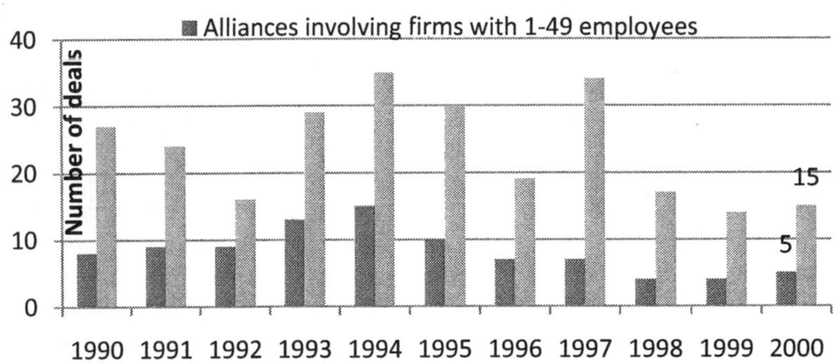

Source: OECD, based on Thomson Financial Reproduced from page 24 of Sakai 2002, op cit.

Figure 3.6: Telecommunications: Cross-Border Alliances by Firm Size, 1990–2000

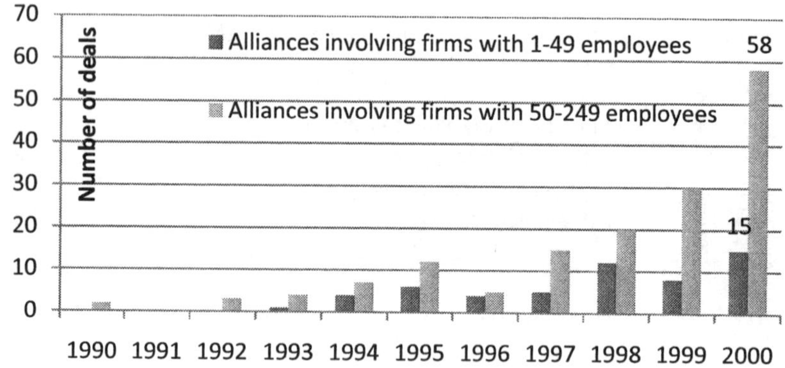

Source: OECD, based on Thomson Financial. Reproduced from page 26 of Sakai 2002, op cit.

Third, high-tech small firms have also come to use alliances to access capital for research. As Figure 3.7 shows, even in the USA where risk capital is in relatively high supply in comparison to European markets, partnering provides more funds for SME biotech research than private and venture capital funding combined, even after a steady increase in the latter. This may be because the time frame in this sector is very long for venture capitalists while the risk remains high. It could also be due to the predatory practices of larger pharmaceutical corporations.

Figure 3.7: Pharmaceuticals: US Biotech Industry's Fundraising, 1996–2000

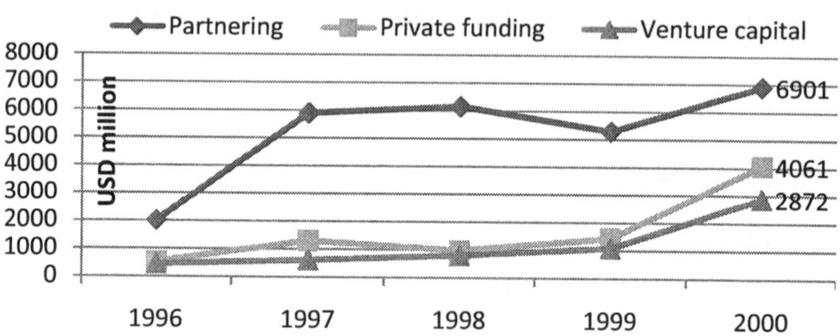

Note: Partnering figures are based on disclosed transactions' value.

Source: Burrill & Company (1998, 2000a), and PricewaterhouseCoopers (1998c). Reproduced from page 25 of Sakai (2002), op cit.

ICTs and the Coordinating Economy

But in addition to these structural changes that have allowed SMEs to engage equally in larger markets, small firms have been well suited to provide services to businesses. With more small firms operating in the economy, the institutional costs of economic coordination are no longer carried internally in larger corporations. Rather the market has been guided through various coordinating mechanisms such as ISOs, new regulatory frameworks and auditing functions that have been implemented by small firms in business services. These include lawyers, accountants and management consultants, regulated themselves as professions and so able to offer bespoke interpretations to the relevant parties. The growth in B2B (business to business) services has been a key element to the use of the internet and to the idea of a knowledge economy. The EU has promoted it enthusiastically through its 'info economy' policies which have been targeted at the SME sector.

Figure 3.8: Growth of e-Business Use By Sector 1994–2004

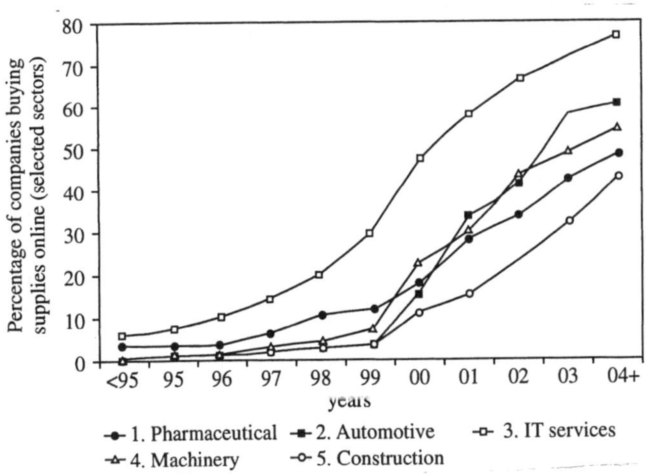

Source: Reproduced from 'B2B Group Meeting Latest developments in the field of B2B e-markets' Brussels, 10 May 2006' downloaded 01/10/2008 from http://ec.europa.eu/enterprise/ict/policy/doc/b2b_2006_05_10_dev.pdf

SMEs are now broadly recognised as integral to the fabric of international transactions. More importantly for this chapter their participation in international economic exchange heightens another important dimension of diversity under contemporary capitalism – the political economy of the small firm. SMEs are now at the core of policy interventions at all levels, and since the EU's Lisbon process and the OECD's Bologna Charter have been actively promoted by international organisations.

CONCLUSION

There has been a shift from one diversity to another as capitalism evolved from the national Fordism of the mid Twentieth Century into the service economy regulated more by post national institutions. The policy trend for regulatory reform often introduced as a policy response to greater internationalisation has contributed to the transformation of the modes of national economic regulation. In this chapter we have focused on how developed economies during the 1990s varied in their responses according to three key areas:

1. how dualism in labour markets was maintained through non regular forms of employment;
2. how large network services, with a long tradition of public tutelage, operated especially in relation to the external effects of the services they provide;
3. how SMEs were able to extend their reach at international level and act as efficient intermediaries in the most competitive domains.

Certainly the clusters identified at the beginning of the chapter will change, especially in the more heterogeneous group, such as the European continental cluster. The Mediterranean group may also merge with this group despite the 'old' vs 'new' Europe distinctions that have been mooted in recent years. The Nordic countries have a rather specific and successful profile with an effective flexibility on the labour market close to the one of market-based economies but combined with a high redistributive mechanism ensuring a security at least equal to the one provided in continental Europe.[8]

Despite these changes contingent variables remain central. The replication of Nordic models is not likely to be possible as the relative small size of the Nordic states and the trust built up in social capital inherited from a century of modern development make their experiences very specific. The governance of service sectors is also an area of variation which has persisted despite the greater international exposure of all services. SMEs have become important again despite decades of economic centralisation under Fordism. The resilience of these two sectors to change, especially in the EU, indicates that there may be other dimensions of comparison beyond the labour, state and corporate sector dimensions that RT has promoted in the past. How important, for example, have social compromises between small firms and welfare states been in the sustenance of capitalist relations? What role did these compromises with the middle classes play in facilitating the transition from Fordism to post-Fordism and to what degree have they enabled the reproduction of other dimensions of social regulation?

This chapter has shown that the RT framework, developed to explain the relationship between national mass production and consumption regimes, can help us to understand the processes of accumulation under global regulation and fuelled by niche production and high value consumption. Its ability to provide historical as well as geographical comparison also allows us to raise other important questions. Was globalisation really a force that could not be challenged or a change made possible through the dismantling of institutions once sustained through national level commitments? If the break up of these compromises was replaced by new forms of social regulation, how new are they and in what ways are the costs of these regulatory mechanisms to be distributed? While the diversity of capitalism over space and time may be an enduring feature of its form, there is much to learn from exploring how the way that it has changed reveals the underlying relations that sustain it.

NOTES

1. For an overview of mature works of the regulation school as it stood in the late 90s see Aglietta (1998) , Petit (1999), Jessop (2001), Boyer and Saillard (2002).
2. To give standard examples of complementarity, if certain conditions are met, negotiations between social partners in a given labour market can create the sort of stable compromises that could help the workforce to receive a high level of training. In addition, physical investment is facilitated by the existence of close relationships between banks and firms. In this scenario, the existence of durable relationships, and of proximity between banks and firms, enhances the implementation of long-term investment projects, and *in return* this facilitates the establishment of stable compromises in the labour market. Conversely, a flexible labour market, one that facilitates employee mobility, is seen here as complementing a financial system that facilitates the reversibility of commitments and the liquidation of investments. This means that the range of potential complementarities can be extended to cover such areas as innovation, professional training systems, etc.
3. The 21 countries were: the United States, Japan, the United Kingdom, Canada, Australia, Italy, Spain, Portugal, Greece, France, Belgium, Denmark, Norway, Sweden, Finland, Germany, Austria, Switzerland, the Netherlands, Ireland and Korea. This draws on the theoretical analysis and international comparisons of Amable et al. 1997) which highlighted four main types of 'capitalism': market-based (United States, Great Britain, Australia and Canada); a social-democratic type (Scandinavian countries); a mesocorporatist (Japan); and a 'European continental' type (France, Germany, Italy and the Netherlands).
4. With the exception of Norway which, due to its natural resources is linked up with Canada and Australia in many sub-system data analyses.
5. Ireland is an outlier in this group as a small economy.
6. If only for Norway and Canada where it is linked to the importance of natural ressources in their trade.
7. In this case the relative exception may be of Greece and Switzerland.

8. Moreover some small countries have also been quite successful at the turn of the century, such as Ireland and Finland for specific reasons much linked with the part they took in the whole system of international relations.

REFERENCES

Amable, B. (2000), 'Institutional complementarity and diversity of social systems of innovation and production', *Review of International Political Economy*, 7 (4), 645–87.

Amable, B. (2003), *The Diversity of Modern Capitalism*, Oxford: Oxford University Press.

Amable, B. and P. Petit (2002), 'La diversité des systèmes d'innovation et de production dans les années 90', in *Innovation et Croissance*, collective volume edited by P. Touffût, Paris: Albin Michel (English version: CEPREMAP Working Document No. 2001-15).

Aoki, M. (1994), 'The contingent governance of teams: analysis of institutional complementarity', *International Economic Review*, 35 (3), 657–76.

Auer, P., J. Berg and I. Coulibaly (2005), 'Une main d'oeuvre stable est-elle bonne pour la productivité?', *Revue Internationale du travail*, No. 3, 2005.

Best, M. (1990), *The New Competition – Institutions Of Industrial Restructuring*, Cambridge: Polity.

Boyer R. (2006), 'La flexisécurité danoise: quels enseignements pour la France?' Paris: Ed. ENS rue d'Ulm.

Bruegel, I. and D. Perrons (1998), 'Deregulation and women's employment: the diverse experiences of women in Britain', *Feminist Economics*, 4 (1), 103–25.

Burley, A.-M. and W. Mattli (1993), 'Europe before the court: a political theory of legal integration', *International Organization*, 47 (1), 41–76.

Coriat, B., P. Petit and G. Schmeder (eds.) (2006), *The Hardship of Nations: Exploring the Paths of Modern Capitalism*, Cheltenham, UK and Northampton MA, USA: Edward Elgar.

Davoine, L. and C. Erhel (2006), 'Monitoring Employment Quality in Europe: European Employment Strategy Indicators and Beyond', Working Document, CEE, No. 66, July, Paris.

Esping Andersen, G. (1990), *The Three Worlds of Welfare Capitalism*, Cambridge: Polity Press.

Griffin Cohen, M. (2002), 'From Public Good to Private Exploitation: Electricity Deregulation, Privatization and Continental Integration', *Canadian Centre for Policy Alternatives – Nova Scotia.*

Hall, P. and D. Soskice (2001), *Varieties of Capitalism: The Institutional Foundations of Comparative Advantage*, Oxford: Oxford University Press, 1–70.

Hoeckman, B. and A. Winters (2006), 'Trade and employment: stylised facts and research findings', WPS3676, World Bank.

Kitschelt H. (1986), 'Political opportunity structures and political protest: anti-nuclear movements in four democracies', *British Journal of Political Science*, 16 (1), 57–85.

Marglin, S.A. and J.B. Schor (eds) (1990), *The Golden Age of Capitalism*, Oxford: Clarendon Press.

Minniti, M. (2005), 'Characteristics of the Entrepreneur', *Global Entrepreneurship Monitor Presentation*, Babson College London, January 20 2005.
Moravcsik, A. (1993), 'Preferences and power in the European Community –a liberal intergovernmentalist approach.', *Journal of Common Market Studies*, 31 (4), 473–524.
Nicoletti, G. (2001), 'Regulation in Services: OECD Patterns and Economic Implications', *Economics Department, Working Paper* No 28, June, Paris: OECD.
Nicoletti G., S. Scarpetta and O. Boylaud (2000), 'Summary Indicators of Product Market Regulation with an Extension to Employment Protection Legislation', *Economics Department, Working Paper* No. 226, April, Paris.
Noord Van den, P., N. Girouard and C. André (2006), 'Social Safety Nets and Structural Adjustment', *Economics Department, Working Paper* No. 517, Paris: OECD.
North, D. (1990), *Institutions, Institutional Change and Economic Performance*, Cambridge: Cambridge University Press.
Reich R. (1992), *The Work of Nations*, Random House, New York.
Sakai, K. (2002), 'Global industrial restructuring: implications for small firms', *STI Working Paper* 2002/4.
Serres de A. (2003), 'Structural policies and growth: a non technical overview', *Economics Department, Working Paper* No. 355, OECD , Paris.
Thelen K. (2004), *How Institutions Evolve: the Political Economy of Skills in Germany, Britain, the United States and Japan*, New York: Cambridge University Press.
Williams, K (2000), 'From shareholder value to present-day capitalism', *Economy and Society*, 29 (1), 1–12.
World Bank (2005a), *Investment Climate, World Development Report 2005*, Washington DC.
World Bank (2005b), *Doing Business*, Washington DC.

4. Towards an Historically Relevant Economics of the Firm

Michael Dietrich and Jackie Krafft

INTRODUCTION

The basic sub-text or conjecture of this chapter is that an adequate economics of the firm should be historically relevant. The terms 'adequate' and 'relevant' imply, in the current context, that theoretical frameworks allow explanation of historical developments rather than a rationalisation of these developments. Two possible implications follow from this conjecture. First, given the complexity of historical reality a single theoretical approach to the firm may be inadequate as a general framework to understand actual events. It follows, therefore, that a historically relevant economics of the firm may imply theoretical pluralism. The possible nature of this pluralism is explored in this chapter. Secondly, and following on from the first point, if the importance of theoretical pluralism is accepted, different frameworks or approaches to the firm may be relevant in different historical circumstances. Among other things, pluralism might therefore imply a requirement for empirically driven theory. In our context empirically driven suggests that historical reality is an important motivator for the economics of the firm rather than being something that is interpreted as an end product.

To develop an economics of the firm consistent with these principles, it would seem to be necessary to echo the approach of Coase. He emphasised (1937, p. 386) that we require 'a definition of a firm … which is … realistic in that it corresponds to what is meant by the firm in the real world'. In reality the firm is obviously a technical unit i.e. it is a unit that transforms factor inputs into outputs. Following Machlup (1967), this involves how production and cost functions interact with demand on the market. But equally the firm is an institutional unit involving questions of basic definition, identity, internal structure and external boundaries (Hodgson, 2002). It follows that the firm in the 'real world', to echo Coase once again, is both technical and institutional.

If this basic duality in the nature of the firm is accepted a fundamental analytical requirement is that technical and institutional theoretical aspects to the firm are not built on inconsistent principles. This consistency is required not only for theoretical-logical reasons, but also so that we can switch between technical and institutional views on the firms without creating conceptual problems. An inability to switch between definitions would introduce particular problems in the current context. It would undermine an ability to undertake an historical investigation of, for instance, how the boundaries of the firm have changed in the context of the interaction between cost structures and market pressures.

But recognising this duality in the nature of the firm introduces a central complexity at the heart of this chapter. There is no single view of the firm as an institutional unit with the implication that there is no single mapping between institutional and technical definitions. To simplify matters it is suggested here that the firm as an institutional unit exists in two guises: the firm as an economiser and the firm as a strategiser (for want of a better term), or equivalently the firm as a follower and the firm as a leader. In terms of the institutional firm as an economiser or follower, the core theoretical focus is on efficient motivation, as exemplified in the transaction cost work of Williamson. The institutional firm as a strategiser or leader emphasises the long-run focus of the firm, as exemplified by the neo-Austrian work of Langlois. Recognising the potential relevance of both these views suggests an inevitable complexity in the conceptualisation of the firm.

The rest of the discussion is organised as follows. In the next section the nature of this integrated view of the firm is developed. Following this, possible historical implications for the perspective on the firm suggested here are developed. This leads into a more explicit historical analysis based on the work of Chandler. In brief it is argued that different interpretations of Chandler's work can be viewed as specific examples of the conceptual framework developed in this chapter.

AN INTEGRATED PERSPECTIVE ON THE FIRM

This section of the discussion will develop in more detail the possible characteristics of the firm as both a technical and institutional entity as summarised above. To reiterate the earlier summary: the economics of the firm can be understood in two distinct contexts: technical and institutional. The technical context involves the production of goods and services in particular market settings. Two alternative institutional views on the firm appear to exist in economics: the firm as an efficient motivator and the firm as a long-run strategic unit in which emphasis is placed on generating strategic focus. Using Nooteboom (2004) we can understand that these two firm types are not merely theoretical devices but they also carry empirical content because of different cognitive requirements. Homogeneity of cognition within a firm is a necessary characteristic of efficient production. Variety and novelty of cognition is relevant when innovation is strategically crucial. But this necessary variety implies that generating focus is a key organisational/managerial task with attendant costs.

The particular traditions that might be placed under these two headings of efficient motivator and long-run focus will be explored shortly. Before doing this we emphasise the point made above that the insights gained from these two institutional approaches are driven by the conceptual linkages created between institutional and technical factors. In schematic terms the two institutional approaches can be summarised as follows:

Figure 4.1:

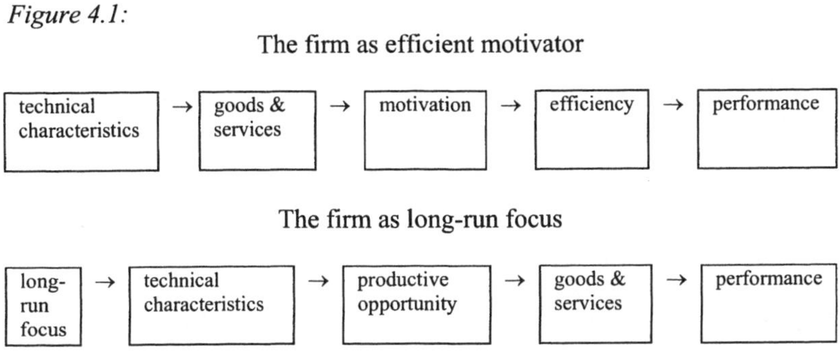

A number of particular approaches can be highlighted as examples of these firm types. Perhaps the most obvious example of the firm as efficient motivator is Williamson's (1975, 1985) transaction cost economics. Here, basic technical characteristics, and in particular asset specificity, along with bounded rationality and opportunism, produce motivation problems. The problems are managed using the most efficient, i.e. transaction cost minimising, institutions. This approach is explicitly ex-post in its logic, i.e. the firm as an institution emerges following motivation problems. But the same abstract reasoning is evident with the ex-ante logic of agency theory in which optimal contracts are developed to manage motivation issues given information asymmetries (for example Hart's (1995) financial theory of the firm). Finally, the property rights approach of Alchian and Demsetz (1972) illustrates the same abstract logic in which team production produces motivation problems and a requirement for hierarchical management. Presenting the 'efficient motivator' approaches in this way reveals that they all have a common methodological root grounded in a comparative static logic. The firm as an institution emerges in response to exogenous technical characteristics. This is transparent in, for example, new institutional approaches to accounting (see Dietrich 2001).

The following approaches can be highlighted under the general heading of the 'firm as long-run focus'. Perhaps the most interesting of these long-run approaches (at least in the opinion of the authors of this chapter) is the neo-Austrian approach of Langlois and Robertson (1995). Here a distinction is drawn between long-run and short-run transaction costs. Short-run transaction costs are those that exist in traditional (Williamsonian) theory. Long-run transaction costs are incurred with the management of strategic reorientation. The approach is neo-Austrian because ignorance and tacit knowledge produce profit opportunities for particular firms. But the exploitation of these opportunities is not costless, as appears to be the case in traditional Austrian economics (for example Hayek, 1945), but rather involve investment in managerial and complementary assets. These long-run transaction costs would not exist in a world in which long-run, firm-specific, profit opportunities did not exist.

Consistent with the neo-Austrian approach is the competence approach to the firm (for example, Foss and Loasby, 1998). This builds on the earlier work of Penrose (1959), Richardson (1972) and Nelson and Winter (1982). The idea of managed long-run focus is explicit in the work of Penrose; the term 'productive opportunity' in the flow diagram just presented is taken from her work. In the work of Richardson and the evolutionary approach of Nelson and Winter long-run focus still exists but is more emergent (to use Mintzberg's (1990) term) rather than explicitly planned. But whether firm-specific opportunities are emergent or planned is somewhat irrelevant for the abstract logic that firm performance is not explained as a comparative static response to exogenous technical characteristics. Instead, the technical characteristics of the firm (involving cost and market structures) are endogenous to the long-run focus of firms.

Presenting the institutional approach to the firm in the manner suggested here, i.e. as essentially two general schools of thought, reveals that the linkages are to some extent partial or incomplete. To develop an integrated economics of the firm a more fully connected set of linkages can be recognised. In schematic terms this fully connected model can be presented as shown in Figure 4.2.

Link (1) defines conventional new institutional economics, as considered above. Link (2) defines neo-Austrian and related approaches to the firm, as also just considered. These first two approaches constitute what might be considered the recognised literature on the economics of the firm. For this reason they are perhaps less interesting than the 'alternative' frameworks defined by links (3)–(6).

Figure 4.2:

An inter-connected model of the firm

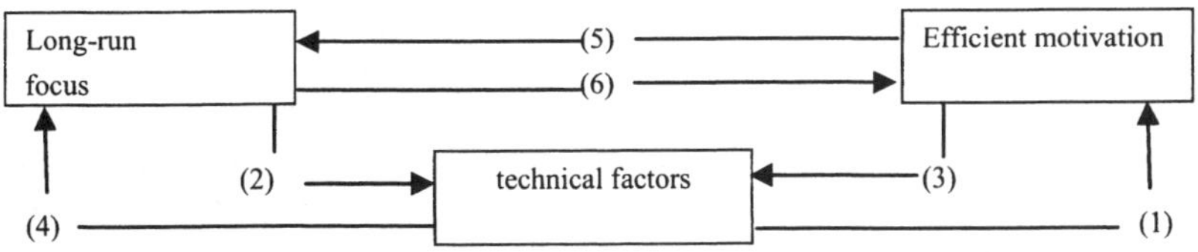

The nature of link (3) can be explained in the following way. The causation operates from efficient motivation to the technical characteristics of the firm, i.e. the reverse of traditional new institutional economics. For example, economising on transaction costs implies contracting or organisational productivity gains. Such gains must be based on a more effective management of search, negotiation and/or policing matters, i.e. more effective control of factors of production. At the technical level such improvement will become apparent as improved labour and/or capital productivity. Using a standard production function analysis of the firm, an increase in factor productivities will increase production–based scale economies (or reduce diseconomies) and hence influence firm size and market structure. An alternative way of conceptualising this link is to follow Morroni (1992) and suggest that organisational indivisibilities, arising from the management of transaction costs, produce economies of scale. Either way of conceptualising link (3) suggests the same conclusion: the management of efficient motivation can impact on the technical characteristics of the firm.

The characteristics of link (4) can be explained in one of two ways. First using a standard structure–conduct–performance approach, it can be suggested that different market structures can impact on firm objectives and hence performance. In the neo-Austrian writing cited above this possible impact of market structure is marginalised. Monopoly power is characteristically viewed as a return to entrepreneurship, a common feature of non-equilibrium Austrian analysis. A second possible explanation is suggested by Langlois and Robertson (1995). When firms are making investment decisions, i.e. decisions involving long-run focus, the variable costs of existing ventures will be compared with the total costs of new ventures. With significant sunk costs this can produce what might be called technological path dependence, i.e. a bias towards existing ventures and technologies. This path dependence will generate inertia in the long-run focus of firms. Of course these two possible explanations of link (4) are connected. Technological path dependence is likely to be greater with a degree of monopoly power for existing firms.

Link (5), from efficient motivation to long-run focus, can be considered the organisational analogue of link (4). Given the sunk costs of setting up and managing contracting and motivation systems a bias towards the use of existing organisational methods and processes will be introduced. If strategic re-orientation involves fundamental organisational change such re-orientation can be rationally blocked, i.e. long-run strategies and focus will be constrained and channelled in particular directions. Mintzberg (1990) suggests that organisational rigidities, in our context path dependence, might exist because strategies are filtered through existing learning processes. Similarly, Nooteboom (2004) suggests that recognising the centrality of individual and collective cognition implies the existence of path dependencies. Alternatively the same result might follow from recognising that particular firm strategies reflect the orientation and interests of particular professional groups inside the firm (Dietrich, 1997). Strategic coordination is then required around the objectives of a particular professional grouping, if coordination failures are to be avoided. Firm strategic change can be understood as a change in coordination equilibrium; or, in management speak, organisational turnaround, a notoriously difficult process.

The nature of link (6) can be summarised under the shorthand of strategising or economising. Or as indicated above, the same idea can be captured under the distinction between firms acting as leaders or followers. For firms as institutional entities, leadership is not simply based on exploiting costless subjective knowledge, as traditional Austrian theory suggests. Instead if firms act as market leaders, investment in organisational assets is required to be able to develop new strategies or to manage the flexibilities required to effectively exploit market opportunities. Such assets are not necessary for follower firms (Langlois, 1986). In turn the required capabilities for effective innovation and flexibility will impact on organisational motivation systems. In short, organisational motivation need not be simply an efficient response to exogenous technical characteristics but in addition can depend on long-run objectives. One way of conceptualising these impacts is to distinguish between long-run and short-run economising. With short-run economising firms respond to cost and revenue potential. For long-run economising cost and revenue potential are endogenous to firm strategies, with higher costs being required for the management of faster or more fundamental change. In terms of the above diagram, link (5) is based on the dominance of short-run economising whereas link (6) has long-run economising being dominant.

THE FIRM AND ITS HISTORICAL CONTEXT

The model suggested above indicates the potential complexity involved when analysing the firm in its concrete historical detail. In addition to identifying links (1)–(6) the complexities involved can be increased by combining the links, as is done by theorists who suggest that competence and transaction cost approaches are complements rather than substitutes (for example, Foss, 1993; Langlois and Robertson, 1995). Arguably a full development of the complexities here would introduce significant conceptual diminishing returns, particularly given the objectives of the current discussion. In terms of economic investigation into the firm, and in particular economic investigation based on historical analysis, two strategies would appear to exist to manage the complexities involved. First, emphasis might be placed on identifying the key linkages in particular circumstances. But an implication here is that linkages relevant in different historical epochs need not be the same. Such a research strategy is empirically driven. The second approach is theoretically driven: a particular conceptual framework can be adopted, but non-core frameworks (linkages) can be recognised and introduced as constraints. But, once again, the nature of the constraints is likely to be contingent on historical circumstances.[1]

To simplify analysis of the complexities indicated by earlier discussion we argue that the two ways of thinking of the institutional nature of the firm in an historical context (i.e. as an economiser, follower, efficient motivator versus strategiser, leader, long-run focus) are in fact the natural outcome of different interpretations that can be provided from the pioneering work of Alfred Chandler. In linking history with the economics of the firm, the author has received two essential interpretations: one by Williamson, which is centred on information coordination; and one by Lazonick and also Langlois, centred on productive coordination.

Today, this separation still holds since, in the recent literature, there are two different ways under which connections between history and the economics of the firm are conducted (Krafft, 2004). The first way is to use data collected by business historians to answer key questions that structure the economics of the firm. Here, a selection of economic models on the firm are used, with the objective being to provide a consistent interpretation of empirical data over the long run. The second way proceeds the other way around, since it involves the questioning of economic results on the firm by referring to puzzles and questions emerging from business history archives. Here, long-run historical data is generally used as a way to increase the variety of economic models able to understand these questions and puzzles, rather than to select them a priori.

The existence of these two ways suggests the importance of theoretical pluralism. In line with this reasoning, it is also possible to show that the first way essentially concerns major neo-institutionalist theories of the firm, namely transaction costs approaches, agency theories and property rights analyses. Alternatively, the second way often necessitates elaborating new theoretical perspectives, especially by fostering approaches focusing on innovation and competences (Krafft, 2005). These theories of the firm provide complementary advances, and one is never superior to the other in absolute terms.

In addition, however, we also have to acknowledge that the empirical question which is addressed in this chapter (i.e. historical reality) necessarily drives us to select one set of theories and reject another set of (time inferior) theories. In addition, the elaboration of an historically relevant economics of the firm is largely an interdisciplinary exercise, that is dependent on two conditions. First, taking history seriously into account should permit one to observe at the same time general results or regularities in the economics of the firm that are not determined contextually, but also critical differences and anomalies that, throughout history, make certain firms unique. Second, the confirmation of general conclusions obtained in the economics of the firm should not obscure or leave apart important results extracted from history. In the further development of the chapter, we will see that this latter problem was present for a long time, though it tends to be less predominant in more recent contributions (see below recent evidence on the case General Motors/Fisher Body).

THE HISTORICAL RELEVANCE OF THE EFFICIENT MOTIVATOR VISION OF THE FIRM

One of the preliminary connections between history and economics of the firm started with the interpretation of Alfred Chandler by Oliver Williamson. The main object of Chandler in his book *The Visible Hand* published in 1977 is to understand major characteristics of the industrial revolution that started at the end of the 19th century in the USA and subsequently shaped the modern industrial system. Chandler focuses on the reasons why the US economy is so largely dominated by large companies for a major part of the 20th century. Starting from monographs of significant companies, the projected outcome is to draw major characteristics of long-term viable companies over large panels of population. Chandler then generates two essential characteristics. The first characteristic is that companies which are engaged in massively capital-intensive activities were generally confronted by a major problem of coordination. This problem was to articulate mass production with mass distribution. The second characteristic is that the problem of coordination of capital-intensive activities could generally not be resolved automatically, relying on market forces alone. Within these capital–intensive industries, vertical integration (backward or forward) could permit firms to avoid bottlenecks on the supply side and to generate new demand opportunities by the coordination of different yet complementary productive units. The argument is that managerial coordination superseded market coordination in industries characterised by high economies of speed, i.e. in which production is sufficiently high and rapid to decrease unit costs. Investment in organisational capacity to manage vertically-related units emerged as a key to competitive success. As a matter of fact, companies which did not invest in organizational capacity exited, while companies which invested became the leaders of the industry.

Oliver Williamson, in Chapter 5 of his book *The Economic Institutions of Capitalism* published in 1985, uses different cases of vertical integration examined by Chandler as empirical evidence for his own theory based on transaction costs. Williamson argues that firms involve the minimisation of transaction costs in specific situations, as discussed earlier. In this theoretical framework, the proposition is that the higher (respectively the lower) the transaction costs, the higher the chances to allocate resources within a firm (respectively within a market). In this framework, vertical integration represents a 'paradigmatic problem' (Williamson, 1985, p. 150) for the theory of the firm based on transaction costs. Williamson acknowledges that the empirical verifications of his own theory on the basis of the monographs done by Chandler are to some extent preliminary and rudimentary. However, the major outcome is that, in most cases, business history on vertical integration supports the theoretical proposition based on transaction cost, and discards alternative theoretical proposition. In conclusion he stresses that a predictive theory of vertical integration should essentially refer to asset specificity and opportunism.

Three comments result from this connection between history and the economics of the firm. The first comment is that Williamson derives from this connection the dominant explanation of why the US economy was characterised in the early 20th century by large, vertically integrated companies. Vertical integration appears as the optimal governance structure (minimising transaction costs) since opportunism linked up with asset specificity is eliminated. The second comment is that Williamson argues from this connection that transaction costs theory of the firm is superior to any other theories of the firm developed so far. Former theories of the firm can essentially identify technical determinants explaining basic mechanisms of integration (mundane integration), but sophisticated forms of vertical integration (exotic integration) are explained by a transaction cost approach to the firm. The reason is that in addition to production costs integrated within traditional theories of the firm, Williamson focuses on the minimisation of the sum between production and transaction costs. The third comment concerns economies of speed. This notion leads to erroneous conclusions for Williamson, since it leads to justifying vertical integration in industries in which there is no asset specificity. This notion introduced by Chandler does not differ from technical complementarity argument advanced in traditional analysis of the theory of the firm. As such, transaction cost theory is not able to capture the large diversity of integration forms.

THE HISTORICAL RELEVANCE OF THE LONG-RUN VISION OF THE FIRM

In his book *Business Organization and the Myth of the Economy* published in 1991, Lazonick criticizes the interpretation provided by Williamson of the work of Chandler. For Lazonick, the Williamson–Chandler relationship is not a pure connection between theory (based on transaction costs) and facts (based on business history). Rather, this relation should be considered as the confrontation between two distinct theories on the specific issue of vertical integration. In this perspective, it appears that Williamson essentially proposes a theory of adaptive firms, i.e. a theory in which the behaviour of firms is constrained by the structure of the environment. On the other hand, Chandler suggests advances in the field of innovative firms on the basis of a theory in which the behaviour of firms shape the structure of the environment.[2] The relevance and importance of this distinction is clear from earlier discussion.

The argument is the following. First, the economies of speed characterised by Chandler cannot be assimilated into pure technical problems as described in Williamson's book. Second, the emergence of vertical integration analysed by Chandler cannot be assimilated to the reaction against opportunistic behaviours which is so central to Williamson. The four essential cases examined by Chandler (Duke, Kodak, Swift and Singer) were concerned with the emergence of technological innovations, but the essential thing in each of these cases was that new forms of organisation were to be elaborated in order to coordinate mass production with mass consumption. Vertical integration dominated because it was one of the possible solutions to this specific problem of coordination of productive activities. In fact, well before the technological innovations came out on the market, networks of production and distributions were in development. The implementation of a capital-intensive programme was generally required for the company to maintain a regular flow of input for the effective utilisation of productive capacity, as well as a sufficient flow of output structuring the establishment of a market which formerly was nonexistent. When these conditions were not observed, the weight of sunk costs generally highly questioned the viability of the innovative firm.

For Lazonick (1991, pp. 198–9), the essential problem lies in the transformation of high fixed costs into low unit costs. Chandler (1992) confirms that economies of speed generally implied strengthening of productive capacity as well as the intensity of utilisation of this capacity. In addition, these increased fixed and sunk costs required a counterbalancing low unit costs in final production. The engagement of a triple investment, i.e. the elaboration of distribution networks, the elaboration of networks in commercialisation and marketing, and the definition of a specific organisation dedicated to coordinate the different phases of the process of production, was crucial to the coordination of mass production and mass market. This triple investment was the source of durable competitive advantages. In labour–intensive industries, however, such triple investment was not observed, essentially because in that case investments were neither fixed nor irreversible. With this interpretation, the explanation of the dominance of vertical integration goes largely beyond the problem of opportunism linked with asset specificity.[3] Instead, emphasis is placed on the firm as a strategic leader. The management of cost structure involves shifting the organisational focus of the firm.

In 1992, Chandler provides a contribution in which he clarifies his position on the economics of the firm within history. To him, the firm is necessarily at the centre stage and its essential functions, i.e. first production and second, exchange, require an in-depth investigation. Neoclassical visions of the firm, but also agency and even transaction costs theories, are of no help solving this problem (Chandler, 1992, pp. 85–6).[4] Within neoclassical approaches the firm is exclusively considered as a technical unit dedicated to maximize a specific function, on the basis of a closed set of information. This clearly does not correspond to the concrete production problems that a firm has to face throughout business history. For reasons set out above, the firm in the 'real world' requires a coupling of technical and institutional factors. Within agency theory and transaction costs theory, the basic unit of analysis is not the firm but rather the transaction or any contractual arrangement. In fact, the empirical phenomenon he has collected and analysed are much more in coherence with an analysis in terms of evolution of competences. More specifically, Chandler advances that the alternative theory of the firm which is more in accordance with his work on business history is certainly the analysis in terms of dynamic competences, the origins of which are in Marshall, Schumpeter, Penrose and the more recent developments in Teece, Dosi, Lazonick and Nelson (ibid., p. 86). As a matter of fact, Chandler criticises thus some of the utilisation of his own work, and especially the interpretation by Williamson which was however considered as one of the key mode of connection between history and the economics of the firm. Another important teaching is that the emerging collaboration between business history and the theory of dynamic competences. Using the framework set out earlier, this suggests that the relevant coupling between institutional and technical factors is link (2) not link (1).

RECENT EVIDENCE ON THE CASE GENERAL MOTORS/FISHER BODY

GM/FB has certainly been one of the most extensively discussed historical case in the literature on vertical integration and the boundaries of the firm. For a long time, and for most of the commentators (Klein, Crawford and Alchian, 1978; Joskow, 1988; Shelanski and Klein, 1995; Crocker and Masten, 1996), this case was essentially considered as an example of hold up in the presence of asset specificity. In 1926 General Motors was led to acquire its supplier of automobile bodies, Fisher Body, because Fisher Body held up General Motors. It is generally claimed that Fisher Body did this by locating its body plants far away from the General Motors assembly plants and by adapting inefficient methods of production, thus increasing both the cost of producing bodies and the profits of Fisher Body under its cost-plus contract. This factual evidence justified the historical relevance of the institutional interpretation of the economics of the firm, based on the minimization of transaction costs (Tirole, 1988; Carlton and Perloff, 1994; Williamson, 1985; Ricketts, 1994).

In a recent issue of the *Journal of Law and Economics* (2000), however, new historically-based evidence is provided by key contributors in the domain of the economics of the firm (Klein; Coase; Freeland; Casadesus-Masanell and Spulber) that tend to suggest that the dominant explanation based on problems of coordination of information and transaction costs is not necessarily the correct one, and even that such an explanation has tended to neglect and obscure other major determinants of vertical integration.

Within these new developments, the dominant hypothesis H0 according to which 'holdup is the main rationale for vertical integration' is only confirmed by Klein, who reaffirms his initial idea with Crawford and Alchian that the facts of the GM/FB case are fully consistent with the hold up description. To him,

> the evidence unambiguously demonstrates that while the contract initially worked well, this contract broke down in 1925 when GM's demand for Fisher bodies increased dramatically. Fisher then refused to make the necessary capital

> investments required to produce bodies efficiently for GM, in particular refusing to build an important body plant close to GM production facility in Flint, Michigan. These contractual difficulties were the primary reason GM decide in 1926 to vertically integrate with Fisher Body (Klein, 2000, p. 106).

In reaffirming the dominant argument, Klein clearly supports a unilateral relationship between technical factors and efficient motivation that identifies the conventional new institutional economics (termed link (1) in this chapter). Basic technical characteristic, and especially asset specificity, along with bounded rationality and opportunism, produce motivation problems that can only be managed using the most efficient institution (here, vertical integration which guarantees transaction costs minimisation).

Coase, alternatively, supports the idea that H0 is rejected by historical facts. To him, asset specificity is only a potential rationale for vertical integration, not sufficiently high enough in the present case to justify vertical integration. Three reasons motivate the argument. First, 'What General Motors acquired in 1926 was the 40 percent of the shares of Fisher Body that it did not already own' (Coase, 2000, p. 15). Second, 'Fisher Body did not locate its plants far away from the General Motors assembly plants' (ibid.). Thirdly, 'it is also most implausible, for many reasons, that the Fisher brothers would have used inefficient methods of production' (ibid.). Consequently, there is no evidence that a holdup occurred. H0 is thus rejected, and an alternative hypothesis is suggested, H1 'Asset specificity (with or without hold up) is normally handled satisfactorily with long term contracts without requiring vertical integration'. In this case, technical factors appear thus as the point of departure of the reflection, but do not necessarily produce efficient motivation problems. Link (1) is not the ultimate interpretation, since technical factors can also generate long run aspects (Link (4)), such as the complete acquisition of a company which was already partially owned, or the location of plants which was part of a broader strategy implemented by the acquired company. In turn, these different long-run elements may have impacted on the methods of production of this latter company which could have been be viewed as inefficient from outside, and especially from the acquirer point of view (Link (2)).

Freeland also rejects H0, and suggests that hold up never occurred. He advances a different interpretation of the case based on the role of human assets in determining the boundaries of the firm. To him, vertical integration was 'caused primarily by the desire to acquire and retain the specialised knowledge and services of the Fisher brothers' (Freeland, 2000, p. 35). Further he also shows that if hold up occurred it is after integration, since because of their specialised knowledge, competences and skills the Fisher brothers could significantly shape the strategies of the integrated company.

Thus, we can define H2, supported by Freeland, according to which 'Access to specialised human capabilities favours vertical integration which may, in turn, produce holdup situations'. There again, using the earlier framework, link (1) is not the selected interpretation. Rather, the implementation of a long-run strategy in terms of how to recruit and retain human capital have had an impact on technical factors (link (6)), and may also have degenerated into inefficient motivation outcomes if not adequately treated (link (6)).

Finally, Casadesus-Masanell and Spulber also reject H0, for the following reasons. First, the stress that 'the historical record indicates close collaboration and trust between the companies, which contradicts supposed contract failures. The extensive participation of the Fisher brothers in GM management beginning in 1921 also indicates an absence of alleged opportunism by Fisher' (Casadesus-Masanell and Spulber, 2000, p. 68). Second, 'the initial acquisition in 1919 also accompanied by substantial investment by GM in Fisher and a voting trust arrangement in which executives from the two companies had equal control over Fisher's board of directors, which contradict the need for property rights to exercise control' (ibid.). Thirdly, 'Fisher Body did not price opportunistically under its manufacturing contract. Many Fisher Body plants already were located next to GM plants before 1926' (ibid., p. 69). In addition, 'the supposed transaction-specific investment in metal presses and dies is inconsistent with Fisher's manufacturing technology, which was wood based and labor intensive and therefore flexible and not transaction specific' (ibid.). This leads authors to suggest an alternative hypothesis, more closely oriented towards the coordination of production in an innovative context. As a matter of fact, 'the closed auto bodies made by Fisher represented quality and comfort and were a source of competitive advantage for GM in its competition with Ford. Vertically integrating into auto body manufacturing allowed GM better to coordinate the management of inventories, production and purchasing given the transportation, communications, and data-processing costs existing at that time' (ibid.). Thus H3 can thus be termed as 'the coordination of production in an innovative context stimulates vertical integration'. What is supported here is thus that technical factors, such as plant location and pricing issues, were embedded into a long-run strategy of the acquired company (links (2) and (4)). Also, close collaboration and voting trust arrangements between the acquired and acquiring firms were shaped by, and also shaped themselves by, the long-run focus (links (5) and (6)).

FROM CONFIRMATION TO CONFRONTATION: HOW HISTORY CAN GENERATE NEW PERSPECTIVES ON THE ECONOMICS OF THE FIRM

New evidence on the case GM/FB is especially interesting to us in this chapter since it shows the progression in the connection between history and the economics of the firm. Though empirically driven research sustained for a long time the predominance of vertical integration by transaction costs economics, and to some extent confirmed the only body of analysis to be tested, it seems that things have now changed. As summarised in Table 4.1, and on the basis of a new series of observations on historical archives, H0 is confirmed by some authors but rejected by other authors.

Table 4.1: New Evidence on the General Motor/Fisher Body Case – Synthesis

Empirical implications of models	H0: holdup in presence of asset specificity explains vertical integration => NIE is confirmed => predominance of link (1)
Empirical observations	4 series of observations on historical archives: 1) Klein, 2) Coase, 3) Freeland, 4) Casadesus-Masanell and Spulber
Acceptance/Reject of hypotheses	1) H0 is confirmed 2) H0 is rejected 3) H0 is rejected 4) H0 is rejected
New formulations	1) no new formulation => NIE is confirmed => predominance of link (1) 2) H1: Asset specificity (with or without hold up) is normally handled satisfactorily with long-term contracts without requiring vertical integration => Refinements into transaction costs economics => Investigations into links (2) and (4) 3) H2: Access to specialised human capabilities favours vertical integration which may, in turn, produce holdup situations.

=> Investigations into specialised competences and human capital
=> Investigations into links (2) and (6)
4) H3 can thus be termed as 'the coordination of production in an innovative context stimulates vertical integration'
=> Investigations into innovation and the coordination of production
=> Investigations into links (2) and (4)
=> Investigations into links (5) and (6).

When H0 is rejected, then new propositions for a theoretical background on the economics of the firm are provided. Moreover, these new propositions tend to move progressively from a vision of the firm as an economiser or follower to the firm as a strategiser or leader. These new propositions stimulate the investigation of a wider spectrum of links to interpret historical facts (links (1) to (6)), which was however not implemented in earlier developments. For instance, in the interpretations of the work of Chandler, either link (1) or link (4) (i.e. the Williamson version or the Lazonick version) could exclusively be analysed. This recognition of a wider theoretical spectrum leads to the economics of the firm having a greater historical relevance.

CONCLUSION

The aim of the chapter was to draw the lines of an historically relevant economics of the firm, i.e. based on theoretical pluralism and empirical content. The first step was to closely insert this project within the current development of the economics of the firm which is essentially based on a dual vision of the firm, i.e. technical and institutional. Our contribution was to go beyond this traditional duality and provide an integrated perspective on the firm since, within history, technical and institutional aspects are largely intertwined. In this integrated perspective, we explicitly relate technical and institutional aspects of the firm and rediscover how the different theories of the firm can be incorporated and classified. Apart from the two dominant, and largely opposed, frameworks that relate, on the one hand, technical factors and efficient motivation institutional factors (link (1), such as new institutional economics, agency theory and property approaches) and, on the other hand, long-run institutional factors and technical factors (link (4), such as Austrian, Post-Marshallian and evolutionary analyses), another set of four different interpretations can also be derived (links (2), (3), (5) and (6)). Moreover we show that these different interpretations are crucial to the development of an historically relevant economics of the firm. In fact, at a more applied level, when we analyse how business history and economics of the firm have interacted in the past, we come to the conclusion that the initial attempts supported essentially either one or the other dominant interpretations. Evidence was given in this chapter of the two opposite interpretations of the work of Chandler, first by Williamson in terms of efficient motivation, and second by Lazonick in terms of long-run focus. However, in more recent combinations between economics of the firm and business history, such as the re-examination of the case General Motors/Fisher Body, though the earlier distinction still holds, a more complex set of interpretational linkages can be derived, mixing technical factors, efficient motivation institutional factors, and long-run institutional factors. We consider these recent interdisciplinary developments as a significant progress in the insertion of the economics of the firm within history. Only robust confrontation between economic frameworks and historical archive can prevent important elements being neglected, and thus guarantee progress towards an historically relevant economics of the firm.

NOTES

1. This potentially historical specificity of economic theory is consistent with the arguments developed by Hodgson (2001).
2. See also Lazonick (2002, 2003).
3. Again, according to Lazonick (1991, pp. 242–3), 'In referring to Chandler's material on Swift, Williamson demonstrated his unwillingness (or inability) to comprehend the Chandlerian emphasis on high throughput and economies of speed. Paraphrasing Chandler on the reasons for Swift's ultimate success, Williamson argued that 'despite the opposition from the railroads and butchers, Swift's 'high quality and low prices' combined with 'careful scheduling' prevailed'. Compare this statement with the quote from Chandler that I have just reproduced and emphasised. For Williamson, it was not worth mentioning the other factors 'high volume and the speed ... of product flow' – that Chandler included in the same phrase as 'careful scheduling' (the factor that Williamson did quote) as ways in which Swift attained the 'high quality at low prices' that enabled him to win the market'.
4. See also Chandler et al. (1997, 1998, 2000).

REFERENCES

Alchian A. and Demsetz H. (1972), 'Production, information costs, and economic organization', *American Economic Review*, 62, 777–95.

Carlton D. and Perloff J. (1994), *Modern Industrial Organization*, New York: Harper Collins College Publishers.

Casadesus-Masanell R. and Spulber D. (2000), 'The fable of Fisher Body', *Journal of*

Law and Economics, 43 (1), 67–104.
Chandler A. (1977), *The Visible Hand*, Cambridge: Harvard University Press.
Chandler A. (1992), 'Organizational capabilities and the economic history of the industrial enterprise', *Journal of Economic Perspectives*, 6 (3), 79–100.
Coase R. (1937), 'The nature of the firm', *Economica*, 4, 386-405.
Coase R. (2000), 'The acquisition of Fisher Body by General Motors', *Journal of Law and Economics*, 43 (1), 15–31.
Crocker K. and Masten S. (1996), 'Regulation and administered contracts revisited: lessons from transaction-costs economics for public utility regulation', *Journal of Regulatory Economics*, 9, 5–36.
Dietrich M. (1997), 'Strategic Lock-in as a Human Issue: The Role of Professional Orientation', in L. Magnusson and J. Ottoson, *Evolutionary Economics and Path Dependence*, Cheltenham, UK and Lyme, USA: Edward Elgar.
Dietrich M. (2001), 'Accounting for the economics of the firm', *Management Accounting Research*, 12.
Dosi G. (1988), 'Sources, procedures and microeconomic effects of innovation', *Journal of Economic Literature*, 26, 1120–71.
Foss N. (1993), 'Theories of the firm: contractual and competence perspectives', *Journal of Evolutionary Economics*, 3, 126–44.
Foss N. and Loasby B. (eds) (1998), *Economic Organization, Capabilities and Co-ordination: essays in honour of GB Richardson*, London: Routledge.
Freeland R. (2000), 'Creating hold up through vertical integration: Fisher Body revisited', *Journal of Law and Economics*, 43 (1), 33-66.
Hart O. (1995), *Firms, Contracts and Financial Structure*, Oxford: Oxford University Press.
Hayek F. (1945), 'The Use of Knowledge in Society', *American Economic Review*, 35, 519–30.
Hodgson G. (2001), *How Economics Forgot History: the problem of historical specificity in social science*, London, Routledge.
Hodgson G. (2002), 'The legal nature of the firm and the myth of the firm–market hybrid', *International Journal of the Economics of Business*, 9, 37–60.
Joskow P. (1988), 'Asset specificity and the structure of vertical relationships: empirical evidence', *Journal of Law, Economics and Organization*, 4, 337–55.
Klein B. (2000), 'Fisher–General Motors and the nature of the firm', *Journal of Law and Economics*, 43 (1), 105–141.
Klein B., Crawford R. and Alchian B. (1978), 'Vertical integration, appropriable rents and the competitive contracting problem', *Journal of Law and Economics*, 31, 265–97.
Krafft J. (2004), 'Entry, exit and knowledge: evidence from a cluster in the info-communications industry', *Research Policy*, 33 (10), 1687–706.
Krafft J. (2005), 'Business History and the Organization of Industry', in M. Dietrich (ed.), *The Firm: analysis, evolution and history*, London: Routledge.
Langlois R. (1986), 'The New Institutional Economics: an introductory essay', in R.N. Langlois (ed.), *Economics as a Process*, Cambridge: Cambridge University Press.
Langlois R. and Robertson P. (1995), *Firms, Markets and Economic Change: a dynamic theory of business institutions*, London: Routledge.
Lazonick W. (1991), *Business Organization and the Myth of the Economy*, Cambridge: Cambridge University Press.
Machlup F. (1967), 'Theories of the firm: marginalist, managerial, behavioural',

American Economic Review, 57, 1–33.

March J. and Simon H. (1958), *Organizations*, London: John Wiley and Sons.

Mintzberg H. (1990), 'Strategy Formation Schools of Thought', in J.W. Fredrickson (ed.), *Perspectives on Strategic Management*, New York: Harper & Row.

Morroni M. (1992), *Production Process and Technical Change*, Cambridge, Cambridge University Press.

Nelson R. and Winter S. (1982), *An Evolutionary Theory of Economic Change*, Boston, Harvard University Press.

Nooteboom B. (2004), 'Governance and competence: how can they be combined?', *Cambridge Journal of Economics*, 28.

Penrose E. (1959), *The Theory of the Growth of the Firm*, Oxford, Basil Blackwell.

Richardson G. (1972), 'The organization of industry', Economic Journal, 82.

Ricketts (1994), *The Economics of Business Enterprise: an introduction to economic organization and the theory of the firm*, New York: Harvester Wheatsheaf.

Shelanski H. and Klein B. (1995), 'Empirical research in transaction costs economics: a review and assessement', *Journal of Law, Economics and Organization*, 11, 335–61.

Tirole J. (1988), *Theory of Industrial Organization*, Cambridge: MIT Press.

Williamson O. (1975), *Markets and Hierarchies*, New York, Free Press.

Williamson O. (1985), *The Economic Institutions of Capitalism: firms, markets and relational contracting*, New York: Free Press.

5. The Export of Varieties of Capitalism: The Cases of Wal-Mart and IKEA

Sue Konzelmann, Frank Wilkinson, Charles Craypo and Rabih Aridi

INTRODUCTION

The liberalization of trade and capital movements has resulted in increasing global interdependence and integration. Customers and investors are demanding that firms be responsive to changes in technologies and market requirements and that they deliver high quality products and services at low prices. Companies are being urged to prioritise shareholder interests, continuously improve short-term financial results and be publicly accountable. But despite these pressures, a growing body of literature suggests that national systems are evolving in ways that maintain significant variety within capitalism. One strand of the research distinguishes shareholder from stakeholder varieties, with much of the debate centring around issues of convergence towards and divergence from the dominant 'Anglo-American' shareholder model (Hutton, 1995; Hansmann and Kraakman 2001; Dore 2000). Another differentiates systems on the basis of their institutional characteristics.[1] Hall and Soskice (2001), for example, distinguish 'liberal market economies' from 'coordinated market economies', the former being characterized by hierarchies and competitive market relationships and the latter by networks, other forms of collaboration and 'relational contracting'. Jacoby (2005) differentiates capitalist systems according to the role and relative importance of production requirements and markets, locating systems along a continuum ranging from organization- or institution-oriented systems to market-oriented systems; and while he finds that most systems are moving towards the market pole of the continuum, they are maintaining key components and competitive capabilities of their traditional systems.

Neither the co-existence and endurance of national systems within the global system, nor the processes by which they extend and reproduce themselves at home and abroad, has been sufficiently examined and explained. Most studies are descriptive and as such fail to take into account the 'black box' of production, the dynamics of production within and among national systems and the dynamic interaction through which they determine market requirements and outcomes. This chapter uses the productive systems method to examine the ways in which institutional structures and priorities shape 'varieties of capitalism' through production and market relations. It considers the nature of these relations and their interaction within the domestic economy and the ways that firms and national systems interact globally. It examines the processes by which trading standards are transported via supply chain relationships, which eventually become embedded in products and recognized by purchasers at each stage of the supply chain through to the end consumer. The cases of Wal-Mart and IKEA show how national systems expand globally, how they affect various business environments differently, and how they ultimately impact supply chain inter-relationships and organizational performance.

The following section describes productive systems and explains the interactions among them and the determinants of competitive market outcomes. Section three extends the framework to distinguish varieties of capitalism based on the extent and nature of this interaction. Section four examines the cases of Wal-Mart and IKEA. Section five concludes.

PRODUCTIVE SYSTEM RELATIONSHIPS AND COMPETITIVE OUTCOMES

Productive systems theory[2] provides a dynamic non-equilibrium framework for understanding how firms and national systems evolve and how they reproduce and expand globally, backward through supply chains and forward through distribution networks. It views the productive system of an individual firm as one embedded in a wider industry system, which itself is part of broader national and global systems. While the level of analysis determines the boundaries of a particular system, the system itself is a coherent entity within which wider boundaries are constantly being re-drawn. Relationships among firms in an industry relate to those within the nation's productive system just as those among nations relate to the global system. The quality and consistency of relationships determine the competitiveness and relative performance of productive systems at all levels of analysis.

Productive system relationships have technical and social dimensions at all levels of analysis. Technical relations link various agents and factors of production as they exchange relevant information through progressive stages of production. Objective and impersonal in nature, these relationships are shaped by the type of product or service involved and the way it is produced. Their effectiveness is determined by the level of cooperation within the system and the degree to which individuals fully perform their productive functions: the higher the level the greater the efficiency. Social relations are the subjective and personal relationships among human productive agents. They form the social function within productive systems and thus are critical to the effectiveness of technical relations. Because there are inevitable but legitimate differences in the interests and objectives of individuals and groups within the system, particularly with respect to distribution, social relations also work to resolve conflict so that productive agents are willing to participate cooperatively. Social relations are thus central to the system's dynamic ability to achieve operating efficiency.

The hallmark of high quality productive system relations is that individuals and organizations work together and provide open-ended commitments to cooperate. However, because the returns from cooperation are uncertain and long-term, they depend on a mutual trust that commitments will be honoured. In systems where there is little institutional support for such levels of confidence, effective performance depends on the ability of individuals and groups themselves to create and enforce appropriate standards of behaviour.

Mutuality and power asymmetries structure the internal social and political framework of productive systems and the environment in which they operate. This is particularly the case regarding the role, interaction and evolution of the broader institutions that represent the collective interests of managers, shareholders, customers, suppliers and society. Trade unions, employers' and trade associations, the state, international organizations and other agencies represent these interests, but negotiated outcomes among them reflect relative power differences among constituents. Trade unions and employers' associations, for example, have many shared objectives but their internal organization reflects a balance of power between sectional interests.

State activities also are shaped by the coincidence of mutual dependence and power differences. Public education, health, law and order and regulated labour relations further the common interest by enhancing production and curbing destructive sectional interests. They can also serve particular interests: for example, in the case of capital, by curbing worker organization, providing services that individual capitalists cannot and abetting the corrosive effect of competitive price cutting on labour and other productive resources; or, in the case of labour, by lifting the burden of market disadvantage through poverty, disease and ignorance. These forces guide state intervention in the matters reflecting class and sectional divisions.

At the international level, nation states conclude treaties and establish international institutions – such as the IMF, World Bank, World Trade Organisation and European Union – to regulate trade, international payments and capital flows in order to avoid the potential damage from unilateral attempts to control global mobility through trade and monetary cooperation. Their form and behaviour, however, reflect the relative power of nation states, trading blocs and economic regions and of particular interest groups within states.

The quality of productive system relationships determines how organizational outcomes should be measured. In Anglo-American systems, for example, successful performance is measured in terms of short–term net profits, which in most cases is limited to shareholder returns. Markets are prioritized and production effectiveness assessed in terms of the value of company shares. Scandinavian productive systems, by contrast, measure performance in terms of long-term production efficiency, balanced by stakeholder returns. The production process is prioritized and productive effectiveness is realized in the market.

NATIONAL PRODUCTIVE SYSTEMS AND VARIETIES OF CAPITALISM

Varieties of capitalism stem from differences in institutional frameworks, in social relations of production and in the quality of system relations, which is to say, the forces that shape production and market requirements and resolve conflicts of interest in diverse systems. Recent literature distinguishes between production-oriented and market-oriented capitalism (Jacoby 2005). Production-oriented systems focus on production cooperation aimed at market competitiveness. They try to reconcile the interests of the firm and its shareholders with those of the employees, suppliers and other stakeholders in order to best meet customer needs. By contrast, market-oriented systems are grounded in neo-liberal beliefs regarding the superiority of markets to optimize productive efficiency and distributional justice. Collective cooperation is inherently anti-competitive and hence economically damaging. This ideal is institutionalized in economic, legal and business ideology and practice. As such, it centralizes corporate decision-making in top management but requires it to give priority to shareholder rather than stakeholder interests. Markets thus drive productive system relationships with consequent weak institutional mediation to reconcile competing interests.

Production-oriented systems ideally combine leading edge HRM practices and close relations with suppliers and customers (Appelbaum and Batt 1994; Best 1990). Work organization is participatory and non-hierarchical and inter-firm links are intimate and co-operative rather than hands-off and antagonistic. The more effective mobilization of worker commitment, skills and knowledge that results raises thus efficiency, improves quality, and generates faster product process and organizational innovation. It creates competitive environments that foster organizations designed to fully exploit the co-operative nature of production. In market-oriented systems, by contrast, introducing limited degrees of worker involvement and other 'high performance work system' practices into existing managerial structures and forms of corporate governance achieves only temporary competitive advantages because it does not change 'the fundamental nature of the production system or threaten the basic organisation or power structure of the firms' (Appelbaum and Batt 1994, p. 22). Most studies find that although new workplace techniques generate substantive productivity and quality gains, even the promising ones prove difficult to sustain over time (Baker, 1999; Huselid, 1995; Ichniowski et al., 1996; Konzelmann 2003; Pfeffer, 1996, 1998).

The degree to which a national productive system is market or production (institution or organization) oriented importantly influences industry structure and firm behaviour and the way by which varieties of capitalism reproduce and extend themselves globally. Because dominant firms compete in the home country and in the host markets of suppliers and consumers abroad, alternative systems come into conflict with one another in both constructive and destructive ways. The following section examines two successful global retailers in the mass consumer market, Wal-Mart and IKEA. They originated and evolved in quite different capitalist traditions and therefore behaved differently when the national system expanded globally.

THE CASES: WAL-MART AND IKEA – ORGANIZATIONAL STRUCTURE AND CUSTOMER RELATIONS

Wal-Mart

Sam Walton founded Wal-Mart in 1962 as a single store in semi-rural Arkansas. Today it is the largest retailer in America and the world, with more than a hundred million shoppers a week passing through its doors in the US alone. In 2005, global sales totalled $285 billion, employees 1.7 million and stores nearly 5,300. More than 350,000 employees and two of every three stores were outside the US.

Wal-Mart operates four types of stores: the standard Discount unit, a medium-sized outlet that carries a wide range of general merchandise at prices typically below those of competing department and variety stores; the Supercenter, a 'big box' outlet that offers 24-hour, seven-day sales of tens of thousands of food and merchandise items and ranges in size from 100,000 to more than 300,000 thousand square feet; the Sam's Club, a membership discount outlet that stocks and sells selected items in bulk quantities; and the Neighborhood Market, Wal-Mart's scaled-down version of the urban residential convenience shop, designed for 'grab and go' rather than 'one stop' shopping. Particular formats typify operations in particular countries. Whereas regular discount stores dominate in the UK, Canada, Mexico and Brazil, Supercenters are the exclusive format in Germany, South Korea and Argentina and the smaller Neighborhood stores prevail only in Puerto Rico. Wal-Mart's original and still most frequent outlet outside the US is the Discount store, but the company's top performer and fastest growing format is the Supercenter; and at home and abroad, Wal-Mart is steadily converting existing discount stores into Supercenters.

Between 2000 and 2006, the number of foreign Wal-Mart stores grew by 150 per cent, considerably faster than its domestic growth rate, although from a much smaller base; and by 2006, Wal-Mart had wholly-owned subsidiaries in 15 countries. Although Wal-Mart's origins and headquarters are in a high-income country, it thrives in low-income economies. Matching store locations and growth rates with per capita income levels, Wal-Mart stores are concentrated in localities where populations are poor – and the appeal of low prices powerful – and where the lack of regulatory protection makes productive systems vulnerable.

In the United States, Wal-Mart rose to prominence in the non-union, largely unregulated American South and then expanded across the continent, aided by deindustrialization and the accompanying decline of unions and high wages and the systematic deregulation of domestic product, labour and financial markets. Wal-Mart is the largest retailer in both Canada and Mexico, where expansion was both logical and easy, given their proximity to Wal-Mart's US supply and distribution systems.

Expansion in China is currently Wal-Mart's primary overseas objective. By 2005 it had 43 stores in China with plans to build several more, including its first Supercenter in Shanghai. Yet Wal-Mart is not the only global retailer with aspirations in a country of more than a billion people. Both French Carrefour and German Metro are well ahead of Wal-Mart in China. Shanghai, the country's major commercial centre, boasts nearly 100 domestic and foreign owned big box stores. Carrefour currently ranks first among foreign chains in China and fifth largest overall on the basis of annual sales while Wal-Mart is placed nineteenth but says it will double its stores by 2007.

Apart from supply chain advantages in Europe and Asia, Wal-Mart is less successful in those regions, notably in Germany – the only country in which it operates fewer stores today than when it entered the market – and in Japan, where it has never made money but recently acquired sole ownership of a major chain in need of modernization, despite the fact that Japanese consumers have not yet taken to one-stop, discount shopping. In the UK, Wal-Mart's experience competing with Tesco has not been encouraging. Asda, its subsidiary in the UK, accounts for nearly half the company's foreign sales and earnings but recently has not been as profitable as Wal-Mart would like.

Asda's difficulties can be attributed to its inability to apply Wal-Mart's usual expansion formula in land-scarce, commercially regulated England. Although it has sufficient financing, Asda finds itself hemmed in by zoning ordnances and stiffening community resistance. Moreover, whereas Wal-Mart's no-frills, rock bottom prices approach had come to dominate mainstream retailing in the UK, shoppers took price cuts for granted and also wanted wide aisles, appealing shelf selections and informed clerks as well. The difference between Asda and others in this regard is that it is less inclined to sacrifice cost-price-cutting priorities in order to win over enough customers to maintain its earlier momentum. Wal-Mart's future in the UK is not in jeopardy but is less than certain (Rigby 2004).

Entrenched German chains have demonstrated their ability and willingness to match Wal-Mart's price cuts; and they have shown themselves far better at understanding and observing shopper preferences there. German state regulation has also worked for and against Wal-Mart. On the positive side, the government acceded to pressure from volume retailers and urban residents to keep stores open longer on evenings and weekends (Konzelmann 1999, p. 14). Yet no sooner had it done this than the Cartel Office ordered Wal-Mart (along with Aldi and Lidl) to stop selling staple products such as milk, butter and flour at less than wholesale cost as part of their price wars; and it threatened serious fines against any company found in violation (Andrews 2000; Associated Press 2000). This experience may explain why Wal-Mart has not ventured into any other Nordic country despite similarly prosperous shoppers. Wal-Mart also stays out of France, presumably because its rules and customs protect small retailers and Wal-Mart does not want to go up against Carrefour, the second largest global retailer and the model for Sam Walton's initial big box stores.

In sum, Wal-Mart's strategy with respect to market entry and expansion is to locate stores where its business philosophy and practices are most likely to succeed. This entails going into countries either steeped in free market ideology or offering low-wage labour, low-income shoppers, ineffective unions and few social protections: places where government is committed to unregulated industry or deregulation, where workers are bereft of unions and social protections and where communities are without alternative job and revenue sources.

IKEA

Like Wal-Mart, IKEA began as a single store, in Almhult Sweden in 1958, and has grown to become the world's largest home furnishings retailer. The name IKEA is an acronym for the initials of its founder, Ingvar Kampard, the farm where he was brought up, Elmtaryd, and his South Sweden village, Agunnaryd. Kampard's first store stocked goods from food to magazines. But in the late 1940s he noticed that the price of furniture had risen much faster than that of other household items, not because of shortages of labour or raw materials but largely due to tight industry control by manufacturers and retailers that prevented most Swedes from purchasing quality furniture. Here Kampard recognized a business opportunity that also would benefit society. So he modelled the IKEA concept on offering a wide range of well-designed, functional home furnishing products at prices most households could afford. This approach dictates the way IKEA develops and purchases products and then distributes and sells them around the world.

To ensure that IKEA continues to grow and retain its original philosophy beyond his direct involvement with the company, Kampard registered the company as a foundation. IKEA thus is owned by the Stichting INGKA Foundation – a charitable foundation incorporated in the Netherlands – and as such is immune from potential disruptions by self-interested family members or shareholders. The Kampard family owns IKEA Systems BV, which controls the IKEA concept and trade-name. In 2004, IKEA reported sales revenues of 13.6 billion Euros ($16.8 billion) up from 4.4 billion in 1994 (IKEA Annual Report 2005). At the end of 2005 it had 233 stores in 34 countries, most of them belonging to the Foundation and the remainder owned and run by franchisees licensed by Inter IKEA Systems. IKEA employs around 84,000 people in 44 countries. In 2004, nearly a half billion customers visited IKEA stores, more than triple the number ten years earlier.

Since 1951 the IKEA catalogue has spear-headed marketing, with more than 145 million copies in 25 different languages published annually. IKEA gets bigger geographically by starting with a single store and then expanding in carefully coordinated phases managed by a central group responsible for store location and layout, training, logistics and marketing. The team also ensures that IKEA subsidiaries maintain financial control. But once operations are streamlined and fully functional, local teams take over from the expansion group. IKEA began offshore operations in Norway in 1963; and after success in Scandinavian countries, it moved into Western Europe a decade later and into Asia and North America within a few years after that. IKEA has stores not only where Wal-Mart has been successful but also where it chooses not to go or has little success. IKEA owes its success to low price plus quality (as opposed to Wal-Mart's historic focus on price alone) which appeals to customers everywhere it operates. Since the early 1980s, 81 per cent of IKEA's annual turnover has been in Europe. It currently has 18 stores in France; and Germany accounts for 20 per cent of IKEA's sales, a figure which is growing, as Germany serves as a launching pad for IKEA's expansion into Eastern Europe. Sales in the UK, its second largest market, have grown steadily but development restrictions on out-of-town areas prevent IKEA from locating large warehouses and stores in those locations. As a result, IKEA now intends to open smaller stores in town centres across the country, ten by 2007.

In 2006 IKEA opened its fourth store and what is for it a massive outlet (42,000 square metres) in Beijing, its largest store behind the flagship store in Stockholm. Such a key market is China that IKEA plans to open two new stores there annually through 1010. Low per capita income presents a unique challenge however. In addition to having low, but reportedly rising disposable incomes, Chinese households have one of the highest saving rates in the world; and Chinese entrepreneurs habitually sell knock-off goods at a fraction of their regular prices. Not surprisingly, shops located near IKEA stores offer low-priced imitations of IKEA products. After slow sales initially in China, in 2001 IKEA slashed its prices by 44 per cent and as a result increased sales 500 per cent over the next few years. The deep price cutting was possible because most of the items sold there are made in China, compared to 23 per cent on average in IKEA stores worldwide. Moreover, IKEA is considered a trendy western brand of high quality and service rather than a discount home furnishings retailer. Its products accommodate customer needs and fancies alike: woks and chopsticks on the one hand, and placemats to commemorate the year of the rooster, some 250,000 plastic sets of which sold out in three weeks. IKEA claims to be on track to achieve profitability in China but declines to say when.

IKEA indeed adapts to local culture in general. The United States has been a particular challenge in this regard because of the size and diversity of customer tastes. From its earliest experiences there IKEA learned that its dining room tables were too small for Thanksgiving turkey dinner; its bed sizes, sold in centimetres rather than in the 'Queen', 'Full' and 'Twin', were unfamiliar to Americans; its Scandinavian-style bookshelves were too small to hold American television sets; and its European-style bath towels were too small and thin by American standards. Americans were buying IKEA vases to use as drinking glasses because IKEA glasses were too small. As a result, IKEA re-designed products to better suit American tastes; and because

Americans like to drink water as they shop, IKEA introduced fountains in its US stores. In other areas, IKEA has been culturally bold and progressive. It was, for example, the first company to use gay couples in its American television commercials because while it knew the risks of doing so it also felt the value of social diversity.

IKEA is creative in anticipating and responding to customer needs, so shopping at IKEA is a unique and comfortable experience, resulting in powerful customer loyalty. In some UK stores, IKEA employees (using radio communication) direct shoppers to car park spots to help ease driving frustration. Most IKEA stores have playrooms, or 'Smaland', where parents leave children while shopping; but they are so popular that some parents have been found to use them as free day-care centres while they run errands elsewhere. Elsewhere in Europe, IKEA stores feature dining clubs designed to help retired persons socialize and save money on meals. 'From Munich in the South to Kiel in the North, IKEA is increasingly turning into a welfare centre for pensioners, young moms, low-earners and the unemployed.'

Despite its attentiveness in customer relations, IKEA faces some of the same systemwide problems that other discounters face. The rush of customers at store openings and everyday traffic congestion are two. More than 22 people were injured by crushing crowds at a store opening in Edmonton, England, forcing IKEA to close its doors after only 45 minutes. Observers were surprised at IKEA's failure to prepare for the obvious danger in view of the fact that six months earlier at least three people were killed at an opening in Saudi Arabia. Another problem is ongoing traffic snarls in and around store parking lots, prompting community activists to resist big box retailing, whether Wal-Mart or IKEA (Dicker 2005, pp. 191–3).

Relationships With Suppliers

Wal-Mart

To the extent that Wal-Mart's success anywhere in the world depends ultimately on its ability to duplicate the American experience of increasing market share through 'everyday low prices', it must cut operating costs to the bone, incessantly and ruthlessly. As a practical matter, cost cutting entails making good use of economies of large-scale operations and deftly applying modern information technology. Wal-Mart does these well and as a result has long been an industry leader in both areas. But because other large retailers do the same, that alone is not enough.

Wal-Mart's relentless cost cutting begins with its suppliers. Walton's operating premise was that every wholesale price is always negotiable and open to competitive bidding. Big and small vendors alike are forced to compete, largely under Wal-Mart's unilateral and inflexible terms

(Blumenthal 1991; Tosh 1993). More recently, with an estimated 65,000 large and small suppliers worldwide, Wal-Mart has been placing greater emphasis on working closely with suppliers to ensure reliable, marketable goods that are made to order, specified product design and quality and delivered in a smooth, timely fashion. But it still demands low prices, reportedly annual reductions of 2–6 per cent.

Despite such concessions from domestic suppliers, Wal-Mart is increasingly reliant on global suppliers. Dependence on Chinese manufacturing, for example, is reflected in its sophisticated logistics centre in Shenzhen, from which the company annually tracks, packs and directs tens of billions of dollars worth of consumer goods to US outlets. But the dynamic drive to undercut the competition by importing from China and other low-wage productive systems is, among other things, contributing to America's steadily mounting trade imbalances and overall debt. In 2005, the US deficit with China rose by one-fourth to more than $200 billion. This accounted for more than a quarter of the nation's total deficit that year, twice that with the OPEC countries; and it makes Wal-Mart a leading cause and disproportionate beneficiary of the staggering increase in the import share of total retail sales in America. In 1965, three years after Sam Walton opened his first discount store in the US, the import share of the largest eight categories of consumer purchases in the US was 10 per cent or less; 20 years later, the shares ranged between 10 and 70 per cent and by 1995 between 40 and 70 per cent in all but one category, which was itself nearly 30 per cent (Petrovic and Hamilton 2006, p. 120). Thus while Chinese imports may be good for Wal-Mart's supply chain and for consumers' pocketbooks, they bode ill for the future of the US dollar at home and abroad, for those who will inherit huge foreign debts and for America's increasingly debilitated productive system.

Wal-Mart stores sell similar or same items worldwide, which minimizes wholesale cost by maximizing purchases from a common supply chain. What is good for the discount retailer, however, is not always good for host country productive systems. Domestic producers not part of Wal-Mart's supply chain will produce less and less of what the country's stores sell and its households consume. Such exclusion also damages national trade balances. Wal-Mart's rapidly expanding share of the Mexican market reduced the ratio of domestically supplied retail sales from 80 per cent in 1997 to 45 per cent by 2002, making Wal-Mart the leading contributor to that country's trade deficit. In response, Wal-Mart's largest Mexican competitors created their own centralized supply chain by combining wholesale purchases, which further depressed domestic supply prices and lowered supplier margins (Durand 2005). Wal-Mart's shift from African to Brazilian coffee exports all but excluded Uganda from the trade and was instrumental in bringing in Vietnam (Anholt 2005, pp. 28–30). Elsewhere, when Wal-Mart acquired Asda in 1999 it promptly cut the number of domestic produce suppliers from 250 to 20 'to simplify its supply chain, streamline costs and ultimately provide better value for the consumer', according to a leading British trade journal. This was despite Asda's stated policy of using local suppliers.

The transfer of market power from producers to retailers thus has an often adverse impact on productive agents. Volume buyers force traditional suppliers to maintain competitive product quality and design while steadily lowering the prices paid them. Vendors have to shift product lines in compliance with chain marketing objectives. After Wal-Mart and other discounters made it clear they preferred in-buying the leading one or few brands in each product category (instead of a wider variety of items), for example, Kraft, the largest food processor in the US, had no choice but to reduce its portfolio of branded products by 20 per cent, which forced the closure of 20 plants and elimination of 8,000 jobs (*Business Week* 2006).

Such squeezing also forces many manufacturers that can do so to outsource operations offshore. Instead of a single or even major producer, the retail buyer either assumes direct control over production or contracts responsibility to a principal supplier. This fragments previously integrated production systems by outsourcing various stages of production to different contractors in different countries and operating environments. The more cost-efficient and contractually reliable outbid the others, while the less proficient find themselves in performance difficulty. In response, they seek primarily structural solutions, such as mergers (acquisitions) with (by) other, more adaptive producers or larger ones that are better able, financially, to survive in the changed environment (Lynn 2005; Petrovic and Hamilton 2006). But not every current or potential vendor is willing to accept Wal-Mart's conditions. Simplicity, for example, a manufacturer of high-end lawn mowers, acquired the company that produced low-end mowers for Wal-Mart. When Wal-Mart offered to make Simplicity its major supplier, the owner refused, preferring to maintain the quality (and reputation) of Simplicity mowers. 'Once you get hooked on [Wal-Mart's] volume, it's like getting hooked on cocaine. You've created a monster for yourself', he explained (Fishman 2006, p. 117).

IKEA

Low price and cost also are important objectives for IKEA, but not at the expense of product quality or social and environmental responsibility. Like Wal-Mart and other global retailers, IKEA makes extensive use of economies of scale in production and distribution. It also invests in innovative production methods and smart design to keep costs low but without sacrificing product quality; and it became a global organization in order to provide infrastructure, service and support to its various business units and suppliers and help them identify and implement state of the art technology. IKEA's approach to delivering high quality products at low prices begins at the development stage. Before the product is even designed, an affordable price is set and innovative ways devised to produce and distribute it accordingly. To do so, IKEA assists particular long-term suppliers to ensure efficiency and quality at each step of the subsequent production process. Most IKEA production occurs in low-cost countries: only 8 percent in Sweden but 20 per cent in China and 12–13 per cent in Germany, Italy and Poland each, the remainder in various locations globally (AFX Europe, July 2005).

Once a supply relationship is established, IKEA requires compliance with national laws and regulations as well as with international conventions protecting the environment, working conditions and child labour. In 1998, it established the IKEA Way on Purchasing Home Furnishing Products (IWAY) to guarantee high legal, employment, social and environmental standards and responsibilities within IKEA and among its suppliers and other business partners.[3] IWAY requires that suppliers not use forced, bonded or child labour or wood from either intact natural forests or high conservation value forests. Suppliers must provide a healthy and safe working environment, pay legal minimum wages or local industry standards, and pay overtime. If housing is provided, suppliers must ensure reasonable privacy, quietness and personal hygiene; and they must not engage in improper employee discipline or prevent employee association or trade union activity. Suppliers must submit an action plan detailing how they intend to meet other IWAY standards. In return, they are assured that they can expect IKEA to be reliable, to adapt products to suppliers' production methods and otherwise contribute to efficient production. IKEA also pledges to care for the environment, to support material and energy-saving techniques, to clarify desired working conditions, to respect cultural differences, and to provide clear and mutually agreed commercial terms.

To ensure vendor compliance, both IKEA and its contracted auditors monitor and inspect regular vendors. In cases of non-compliance, they require – within a month – a written corrective plan, names of responsible persons and a timeline for completion; and auditors later return for follow-up inspections. IKEA's demanding code of conduct and its tough enforcement has had an impact. Non-compliance led to 49 terminations in 2004 alone and a much larger IKEA today works with 1,500 suppliers compared with approximately 2,700 in the late 1990s. China has been particularly challenging. Producers often claim to be observing standards but it is widely believed that Chinese customers and retailers favour low prices regardless of social costs. A Chinese local NGO director remarked, 'of course, on paper, the policies are the same. But in reality, they are different. Wal-Mart is a classic example. Lots of written commitments and policies, but the reality of the "dig dan" (order placement) process reveals the true nature of the retail business here: to get the cheapest price, with little consideration for the supplier's environmental or social responsibility.' Failure to comply with IKEA's code resulted in significant reductions in the number of its Chinese suppliers.

IKEA works with suppliers to help them meet not only price and quality expectations but also IWAY requirements. Shaw Wood in Nova Scotia, Canada, is a case in point. In 1998 it became IKEA's first North American furniture plant. From the start, it was treated as a partner and given extensive technical and creative support. Representatives visited IKEA Swedwood factories in Europe. During start-up IKEA provided Shaw Wood with critical technical and engineering assistance, including the selection of production equipment based on performance-based specifications capable of delivering the required levels of quality and productivity. President Robert Shaw himself confirms that IKEA has little tolerance for suppliers failing to live up to its production and policy standards. 'IKEA's quality people are in our factory constantly,' and, according to him, everywhere else their furniture is made. IKEA auditors recently judged Shaw Wood a level three producer in its four-level quality programme, a goal Shaw Wood is actively pursuing. Meanwhile it is in compliance with IKEA's forestry practices programme: 'We have a long paper trail between all of our lumber mills and harvesters to show IKEA that our lumber did not come from any old-growth forests or national parks, and that it was harvested in the right way.' And also its social standards and employment conditions: '[T]hey inspect all of their supplier plants around the world in these areas and apply the toughest laws set by any one nation as their standard. They do this to level the playing field among competing suppliers. It's a bit of a pain to meet all of these things but it sets us up to be more competitive and a better supplier down the road' (Christianson 2001, p. 63).

IKEA's partnering with suppliers not only benefits long-term performance but also has a positive impact on the community. In 1999, for example, IKEA lent Nicholas Boros the money to purchase a state-owned factory in Romania. Then, he says, they taught him the business, including how to bring the run-down facility into compliance with IKEA standards. He also has to see that his suppliers know and follow IKEA's code of conduct, including paying fair wages and on time. Borsos credits IKEA's code requirements and compliance assistance with an improved community situation and a fivefold increase in factory sales.

IKEA has 27 strategically positioned distribution centres in 16 countries. These highly automated structures make sure the route from supplier to customer is as direct, cost-effective and environmentally friendly as possible.

Maximum space utilization achieved by the industry's first robotic storage and retrieval system produces considerable operating savings. Another IKEA trademark is to sell furniture in flat packs retrieved and assembled by customers, a cost-saving practice also pioneered by IKEA. Not only is IKEA highly innovative when it comes to minimizing costs in product design, manufacturing and distribution, but where possible it uses under-valued and under-utilized resources. Once, at an open food market in China, Kampard was mesmerized by rows and rows of plucked chickens and asked what was done with all the feathers. They were simply discarded, he was told. Out of that experience IKEA has made and sold millions of feather duvets at prices much below those using duck or goose feathers. Similar stories abound: sofas made partly with shopping cart wire; tables made with excess materials from shirt, ski, window and door factories; even picture frames made from scrap rubber from a Volvo factory.

Employment Standards

Wal-Mart

The labour extraction process presents another opportunity for Wal-Mart to cut operating costs. The company has developed exploitive labour recruiting and supervising strategies that generate a steady supply of low-wage workers having few employment alternatives and therefore willing to accept the terms and conditions offered. Managers reportedly agree to work long hours for modest base salaries in the expectation of receiving large performance bonuses and then retiring before the associated stresses take their toll. Hourly workers agree to work for low wages, poor benefits and exacting supervisory demands out of diverse combinations of fear of losing their job, personal pride in a job well done and misplaced loyalty to a company that promotes a few from the ranks but otherwise seldom reciprocates (Cleeland et al. 2003; Tower 2002). But retailing is a low-wage industry in general and Wal-Mart's rates tend to be equal or only slightly below those of competitors.

Its real advantage has been an ability to work employees 'off the clock', that is, without pay. Store managers, under threat of disciplinary sanctions, must cut to the bone the number of paid labour hours in specified time periods. To meet such quotas, they have persuaded or forced employees to work through scheduled lunch and break times or when necessary, they have simply locked the doors at closing time and not let the employees out until the store is ready for business the next morning. As a result, several dozen employee class action lawsuits have been filed, most still pending in the courts. Wal-Mart so far has paid employees millions of dollars in back wages as a result of voluntary settlements and jury findings of guilt in cases alleging wage and hours violations, including settlements in three states and jury convictions in three others, the latter resulting in fines, including $172 million in California. State governments have also fined the company for multiple and repeated violation of child safety ordinances, wage and hour regulations, anti-discrimination mandates and illegal immigrant laws. But the modestly punished yet recidivist nature of these offences suggests that Wal-Mart, along with many other American employers, consider them a cost of doing business (O'Brien 2002; Schafer and Helderman 2001).

Unions might have made a difference here but to date not one American Wal-Mart store recognizes and bargains with a union despite ongoing efforts for more than two decades by the United Food and Commercial Workers (UFCW). It has won only one of about 20 recognition elections, that involving a small unit of meat cutters at a Texas Supercenter. Wal-Mart attempted to overturn the results but was denied, whereupon it discontinued meat cutting in all of its stores and substituted pre-wrapped products instead, voiding the Texas certification and precluding similar outcomes elsewhere. Several years later, the provincial labour board in Quebec, Canada, certified UFCW Canada as bargaining agent for all hourly workers at a Wal-Mart store there. Again Wal-Mart appealed and lost. This time it closed the store outright, claiming 'poor operating performance' but the board rejected this and ordered it to bargain (Barbaro 2005).

A report on US labour standards by the Geneva-based International Confederation of Free Trade Unions (2004) revealed that between 2000 and 2003, Wal-Mart was involved in more than 100 unfair labour practices, primarily involving union organizing attempts. Since 1995, the National Labor Relations Board (NLRB) had filed some 60 complaints ranging from illegal firing of union sympathizers to unlawful surveillance, intimidation and threats. While many of these complaints were dismissed at the first step, numerous others resulted in formal hearings and findings of guilt. The typical Board penalty in such cases, however, is an order requiring Wal-Mart 'to post notices in various stores that it will no longer threaten employees who engage in "concerted activity", deny their right to organize, require employees to report their contacts with unions, or discipline or fire workers who engage in concerted activity.'

Wal-Mart Germany experienced recurring worker actions including brief walkouts relating mainly to its failure to observe prevailing industry pay and employment standards. Wal-Mart reportedly had difficulty recruiting and retaining qualified employees as a result. There was also the matter of different cultural expectations, as when Bentonville tried to introduce an 'employee ethics code' patterned after its US model. Along with their monthly pay checks, German employees were told that the new, mandatory code of behaviour prohibited them from accepting gifts from or entering into romantic relationships with employees in positions of influence and that they were expected to inform on fellow workers they might observe breaking company rules. Failure to do so could result in termination. When imposing the code, however, Wal-Mart's German managers added that it had not originated with them but rather from their Arkansas superiors and when the union vowed to resist in court, they declined to comment (Deutsche Welle 2005). A German employee rights expert rightly pointed out that American workers tolerate such strictures more than European, and Wal-Mart's code therefore might not travel well. Within weeks a German tribunal, in response to union complaints, declared the rule changes illegal and dismissed this trans-Atlantic directive (Morning News Beat 2005).

Wal-Mart's UK subsidiary, Asda, has also experienced strained labour relations under Wal-Mart ownership. GMB union members at Asda distribution centres repeatedly voted to strike depots at two sites and on at least two occasions did so. In one dispute, Asda offered workers 10 per cent pay rises but on the condition they give up future bargaining rights. When workers rejected the offer overwhelmingly, Asda offered a 7.75 per cent increase over two years, half of what the union was demanding, but informed half the depot's 600 workers they might be laid-off as a result. At another site, the company announced plans to increase by one-fourth the number of warehouse items the workforce was expected to lift during the regular 8-hour shift, on the grounds that Tesco employees lifted that much. When workers protested the speed-up, management suspended a GMB shop steward. A third dispute arose after Asda said it was eliminating some 14,000 store manager and headquarters jobs in response to market losses to Tesco and Sainsbury. GMB claimed it was because large numbers of Asda junior managers were becoming union members and it was obligated to resist the reductions on their behalf and in support of its claim that labour relations and standards in retailing had deteriorated since Wal-Mart's arrival (Donaldson 2005; Goldsmith 2005; GMB 2005).

Relations in China have been more complicated. Although poor working conditions in Third World countries in general are documented, the evidence regarding China is contradictory. Reporting on a recently opened Wal-Mart in Guiyang, a *Fortune* writer noted that workers were dressed in red smocks, organized into distinctive cells and singing motivational songs – all too reminiscent of the Cultural Revolution. They exuded seemingly staged joy and commitment for the benefit of onlookers but numerous interviews with them away from the store convinced him they were indeed 'swept up in enthusiasm for the store and the culture and the collective'. When he challenged them to admit that the pay was inadequate and the work 'hateful' and 'depressing', they insisted the opposite: 'No, I love it, it's much better, it pays more than any job I could get at the other store', said one, referring to prior employment at state-owned locations. 'Wal-Mart oddly has really dialed into the psyche of these workers', he concluded. But when a Chinese-American film maker interviewed Wal-Mart workers in Beijing, she got mixed responses. 'The floor people work long hours, 10 hour days, 6 days a week, with a half-hour break', she wrote. 'But they said they have it the easiest, that the loaders and the people who actually make the products are worse off.' A young woman from a small fishing village transformed by government edict into a manufacturing centre of 10 million people said that had she stayed there she would be working 12 hours a day, 7 days a week, and earning \$3 a day instead of the \$4 she made in Beijing, although this was doubtless a commentary on big-city wages in general rather than Wal-Mart generosity in particular. It is not that Wal-Mart jobs are so good, the alternatives are so bad and in the land of bad jobs the half-bad job is king.

Surprisingly, in view of the ubiquity of official unions in China, Wal-Mart's workers there remained non-union longer than one might think. Wal-Mart says it is because they did not want to belong. So when the All China Federation of Trade Unions publicly pressured Wal-Mart to recognize and bargain with its 20,000 employees in 2004, Bentonville explained that it should be up to the workers themselves. 'Should associates request formation of a union, Wal-Mart China would respect their wishes and honour its obligation under China's Trade Union Law', according to a company spokesperson (Associated Press 2004b). This is precisely what happened in late 2006 when the ACFTU announced it had overcome attempts by Wal-Mart management to suppress unionization efforts in its stores and established itself in several locations. Wal-Mart soon entered into negotiations and eventually agreed to recognize the union throughout the country. 'I fully anticipate working collaboratively with ... union organizations at all levels to create a model working relationship', said the president of Wal-Mart's Asian operations, words no other union movement has ever received from a Wal-Mart excutive (Kahn 2006).

IKEA

IKEA, by contrast, does not get the most out of employees by capitalizing on their labour market disadvantages but instead by developing their skills and commitment to the organization and in the process encouraging them to fully participate in the productive system. According to an IKEA executive, successful employees

> are people who accept our values and are willing to act on our ideas. They tend to be straightforward rather than flashy, and not too status-conscious. They must be hardworking and comfortable dealing with everyone from the customer to the owner to the cashier. But perhaps the most important quality for an IKEA is 'odmjukhet', a Swedish word that implies humility, modesty and respect for one's fellow man. It may be hard to translate, but we know it when we see it. It's

> reflected in things like personal simplicity and self-criticism. (Barlett and Nanda 1996, p. 5)

IKEA believes this employee culture is central to its philosophy and success and therefore conducts appropriate training and mentoring programmes throughout the organization. It also tries to export the culture to suppliers and to maintain diversity within the workplace. In Germany, for example, IKEA aims to increase the share of women in senior-level positions from 30 per cent now to 50 per cent or more within three years, and in the UK to hire more workers 55 years or older.

To meet its employment commitments, IKEA pays good wages and provides benefits including full health care to employees working at least 20 hours a week. New parents are eligible for parental leave of seven paid weeks for mothers and one week for fathers and adoptive parents. Other benefits include quiet rooms (for meditation or prayer), on-site childcare facilities in many stores, entertaining rooms (where employees can receive family and friends) and lactation rooms (for nursing mothers). Employees also get subscriptions to wellness magazines, rewards for losing weight or stopping smoking and full college course fees.

When IKEA saw that some employees did not take full advantage of these efforts, it created a programme called 'life balance and diversity'. Among other things, it introduced flexible work weeks and hours, job sharing and telecommuting. Employees can coordinate work schedules with those of spouses, particularly where they have small children and one or the other must be home at all times. The programme also provides video-conferencing to help employees avoid excessive business travel at the cost of family time. By all accounts, these measures are highly motivating. By 2004, it is estimated, 65 per cent of IKEA's full-time employees and 10 per cent of part-timers had taken advantage of this flexibility. Despite the substantial cost of these policies the benefits are said to far outweigh the costs. Executives insist that they make all employees feel their contributions are valued and have contributed directly to a dramatic decline in employee turnover: from 76 per cent annually in 2001 to 56 per cent the following year and 35 per cent in 2003, nearly half the industry rate of 60 per cent. This in turn lowers recruiting and training costs, an important gain considering that analysts calculate the cost of replacing a worker at 1 to 1.5 times regular salary.

By all appearances, IKEA maintains comparable employment standards everywhere it operates. American employees, for example, have the same benefits and growth opportunities as those in IKEA's German stores. Yet difficulties and challenges do arise from different social, economic and political norms and standards. When American and Scandinavian employee attitudes are surveyed, differences are apparent. 'Because of low job security,

American employees are always looking for guidance despite their higher education and need to achieve. The IKEA way requires openness and a willingness to take responsibility. We want people to stand up and disagree with authority if they have confidence in their beliefs. Despite intensive training programs it has been hard making the IKEA way their way of life here in the United States' (Barlett and Nanda 1996, p. 10). Because most large US retail stores experience high employee turnover rates, IKEA employs many who previously worked at other retail outlets, including Wal-Mart, and bring with them undesirable remnants such as insecurity and low self-esteem. Such negative attitudes seriously challenge the employee culture IKEA is seeking to develop in the US. Nevertheless, in January 2005, *Fortune* magazine named IKEA one of the country's top 100 employers. This is especially noteworthy considering the overall reputation of the US retail industry for low wages, poor benefits and harsh working conditions.

Social Responsibility

Wal-Mart

At home, Wal-Mart faces a barrage of criticism from labour, environmental and equal opportunity organizations, forcing it to devote unprecedented time and money in control damage. Discount retailing gives shoppers bargain prices, ample parking spaces and controlled indoor climates; it also promises communities thousands of jobs and increased tax revenues. But chains like Wal-Mart make calculated use of communities when it comes to achieving economies of scale from huge distribution centres and an excess number of big box stores. Community well-being suffers from consequent traffic jams, increased welfare costs and, eventually, closed or abandoned buildings of the wrong size and location. Moreover, existing class and race tensions stemming from industrial decline of one sort or another often intensify.

As Wal-Mart's promise of low prices becomes increasingly tarnished by low wages, small business bankruptcies and costly local tax subsidies and abatements, community groups debate whether to host such stores. White-collar suburbs increasingly resist them while blue-collar, deindustrialized communities tend to welcome them. The outcome depends on relative political power. Discount chains, low-income shoppers, tax-starved local governments and low-wage or unemployed workers are pitted against local retailers, labour unions, environmentalists and women's, minority and religious groups. In Chicago, for example, Wal-Mart wanted to build a regular discount store in a low-income, racial and ethnical minority neighbourhood on the West Side and another in a similar South Side location. Besieged by both camps, Chicago Aldermen approved the company's West Side bid and rejected the other. The West side had waged an aggressive campaign, calling attention to the 80 per cent youth unemployment level in the ward. 'We need those jobs. Something beats nothing', an Alderman argued, 'and we look for low prices'. An anti-Wal-Mart Alderman painted a broader picture. 'Wal-Mart does not just affect these two wards. It affects the whole of Chicago. There will be a race to the bottom in wages, benefits, full-time versus part-time employment', he warned (Associated Press 2004b; Mihalopoulos 2004; Grant and Daniel 2004).

Concern over the rise of discount retailing initially focused on harm to existing stores and shops (Stone 1997; Artz and McConnan 2001; Hicks and Wilburn 2001), but has shifted to taxpayer subsidies. A Congressional staff report estimated that each Wal-Mart employee costs $2,103 a year in public health care, food stamps, housing and energy assistance to low-wage households (Miller 2004). A Los Angeles County survey put the cost of Wal-Mart coming into the region at $2.8 billion due to long-term declines in jobs and earnings. Another found that Wal-Mart received at least a billion dollars in state and local government subsidies related to store and warehouse location and construction (Good Jobs First 2005).

Criticism of Wal-Mart extends to actions affecting workers and environments in developing nations. Long-time corporate watchdog National Labor Committee interviewed women workers in Chinese factories making things for American discount chains. Conditions at three plants turning out handbags for Wal-Mart were 'among the worst' of the 21 investigated. Sewers worked six 10-hour shifts a week, earned between 18 and 23 cents an hour – or $2.30 a day at most – and received no benefits. Still, they took home little more than half that amount per week after food and lodging deductions. Warehouse workers earned as little as 13 cents an hour. At the time Chinese labour law mandated 8-hour days and 40-hour workweeks and voluntary overtime at premium pay. Subsistence wages were about 87 cents an hour. Wal-Mart insisted it inspected the factories for violations, but workers insisted plant managers knew in advance and had time to correct violations and tell employees what to tell visitors (National Labor Committee 1998, pp. 20–4, 29, 45). Wal-Mart refuses to supply names and locations of offshore supply factories, but pledges to hold vendors to labour and environmental standards. 'You'll see Wal-Mart taking a stronger stand over the next several months', CEO H. Lee Scott said in 2005. 'If somebody wakes up and finds out that children that are down the river from that factory where you save 3 cents a foot in the cost of garden hose are developing cancers at a significant rate so that the American public can save 3 cents a foot, those things won't be tolerated and they shouldn't be tolerated' (Kabel 2005). But when Massachusetts school children gathered at a local store to ask Wal-Mart to stop using Third World sweatshops, management called the police and had them and their parents removed (Siek 2005).

IKEA

IKEA has an established track record of good corporate social responsibility, beyond that of most companies. In the area of children's rights, it has little tolerance for child labour and works hard to prevent the practice among suppliers. In 1994 the company was identified as a buyer of carpets made in Pakistan under child-bondage conditions, contrary to law. It served as a wake-up call for IKEA owners, managers and customers. The company quickly ended such sourcing and has since worked to eliminate it elsewhere, including a joint programme with UNICEF affecting 500 villages in the heavily populated 'carpet belt' of India and aimed at eliminating child labour by addressing its root causes: debt, poverty, illiteracy, disability and poor health. The object was to help families escape the vice-like grip of loan sharks who often also owned the carpet factories (Luce 2004). Around 75,000 children have started school and nearly 300,000 infants and expectant mothers inoculated against serious diseases who otherwise would not have been. (Unicef Press Center, March 2004). On the environment, IKEA works with Chinese authorities to preserve state-owned forests under the Forest Stewardship Council (FSC), a German-based NGO that provides forest standards, trademarks and accreditation; and in Germany, IKEA cooperates with Opel in a fuel cell vehicle test programme.

Despite such successes, progress in Asia is moving at a much slower pace and critics say IKEA must do better, especially in South East Asia. IKEA nevertheless insists that most of its suppliers are in compliance with a majority of the IWAY criteria and that non-compliance cases take time to remedy because they require fundamental, difficult cultural, social and political change.

CONCLUSION

Since the end of World War Two, the industrial structure of the global retail sector has profoundly changed. Under the earlier system, a few dominant firms in each of the basic supplier industries produced and sold retail product lines to department stores, variety chains, independent specialty shops and supermarkets, more or less on terms set by the supplier; and retailers gladly offered consumers fashionable, brand-name products, manufactured by well-known companies whose relative size and scope gave them the bargaining leverage to present the retailers with 'take-it-or-leave-it' wholesale prices. But with the rise of the giant discount retailers like Wal-Mart and IKEA, the system shifted to one where suppliers were forced to play by the retailers' rules.

It is in this context that Wal-Mart and IKEA compete, with a comparable degree of power and influence in their relations with suppliers. However, the two companies exercise this power in very different ways, with vastly different outcomes both in terms of the impact of the corporate productive system on its social and economic environment (domestic and global) and in terms of the long-term performance of the company, those within its supply chain and the communities in which its suppliers and retail stores are located. Whereas Wal-Mart uses its market power to squeeze suppliers and other stakeholders in order to minimize cost and price, with adverse effects on the socio-economic conditions in localities in which they trade, IKEA's power is used in a constructive way. IKEA works with suppliers in order to help them deliver low prices without compromising product quality or social and environmental standards; it provides good terms and conditions of employment and behaves responsibly with respect to the communities in which it does business. In so doing, IKEA exports the high quality of customer/supplier, employee and societal relationships expected of Swedish companies to its suppliers in developing countries and its retail outlet employees and customers, to the mutual benefit of these stakeholder groups, host localities and IKEA itself. The cases of Wal-Mart and IKEA thus demonstrate the process by which national varieties of capitalism enforce themselves on companies originating within their borders, which in turn transport dominant features of the national variety of capitalism globally, backward through the supply chain and forward to employees and customers at home and abroad.

Essentially, Wal-Mart's ability to contain costs, hold down prices and turn a profit derives from its capacity to make others pay a significant portion of the cost of doing business: suppliers through rock bottom wholesale prices and loss of control over the production process, workers through low wages and benefits, communities through direct and indirect operating subsidies and the national welfare through disruption and decimation of its productive system. By contrast, IKEA's ability to cut costs without sacrificing quality or high social and environmental standards offers an alternative way forward and one that poses a significant threat to the long-term performance viability of companies like Wal-Mart, which depend on a consumer orientation for low price at any quality. In the long term, companies like IKEA are likely to have the advantage because when given the choice, customers will inevitably prefer better quality for given prices.

As the cases of Wal-Mart and IKEA demonstrate, markets will operate as destructively or constructively as they are permitted by the national productive system in which they are located; and companies originating and/or operating within them will behave accordingly. Wal-Mart, for example, is a product of American neo-liberal ideology embodied in American capitalism, which idealizes free and unrestricted markets; views large size and market dominance as the reward for successful competition; and considers managerial prerogative as the efficient way of coordinating relationships within large firms. Because cooperation and collective organization are assumed to be inherently anti-competitive and hence economically damaging, fierce opposition to unions is justified; and lax laws with respect to labour and corporate standards permit exploitation of weaker stakeholders at a relatively low cost to the company. The strong preferences of American consumers for low price, their high tolerance for exploitation and social and environmental irresponsibility and their increasing dependence on cheap goods and services as more and more households find themselves among the 'working poor', lends support to the proliferation of deep discount retailers like Wal-Mart, contributing to their success in the US market.

Not surprisingly, Wal-Mart avoids locations where its business philosophy and practice is unwelcome, illegal and likely to be unsuccessful. The less regulated the national economy and the lower the standard of living among shoppers and workers, the better Wal-Mart fares. The company has had its greatest successes in English-speaking nations steeped in free market ideology and, alternatively, in low-wage developing countries with weak unions and social protections. Accordingly, Wal-Mart's most recently targeted markets are in Eastern and Central Europe. By contrast, Wal-Mart avoids economies like Sweden, which are characterized by high family incomes, narrow earnings differentials and comprehensive social programmes.

IKEA is a product of the Swedish variety of capitalism, with its strong tradition, ideology and societal value for social democracy, distributional equity and corporate and personal social responsibility. Access to the Swedish market requires a high standard of quality, social and environmental responsibility, which in turn underpins the country's high social and labour standards. Evidence of the social imposition of high national standards of corporate behaviour and social responsibility on Swedish companies can be found in such things as IKEA's immediate and pro-active response when the exploitation of child labour was discovered in its Pakistani supply chain. IKEA's constructive response demonstrates the embeddedness of these high standards in the company's corporate culture and the ability to transfer them globally to the mutual benefit of all of the system's stakeholder groups. By contrast, in the case of Wal-Mart, recent pressure in reaction to the company's widely publicized bad behaviour is generating a public relations counter-response rather than a reflective change in corporate behaviour. In the case of Wal-Mart, the boundaries of minimal accepted standards are being tested in the US, and driven even further downward, to the disadvantage of all but the short-term interests of the dominant stakeholders in the system.

IKEA's success and that of its suppliers and other stakeholders demonstrate the contribution to long-term performance effectiveness that high quality cooperative productive system relationships can make. But the ability to maintain these relationships is based on a supportive institutional framework and the ability to secure a high level of mutual and reciprocal trust that commitments made will be honoured. In the IKEA case, high quality productive system relationships are enforced at the corporate, national and societal levels. IWAY, for example, contractually requires of suppliers a high standard of social, economic and environmental responsibility, good terms and conditions of work and recognition of independent representatives of weaker stakeholders, such as trade unions. IKEA's system of corporate governance in the form of the IKEA Foundation ensures that commitments made by the company to its various stakeholders (such as employees, suppliers and local communities) are not undermined by the requirements of a dominant stakeholder group. The Swedish national system provides both institutional support for IKEA's strategic approach from a social, legal and economic perspective and imposes high standards of corporate behaviour and responsibility on IKEA and, by extension, the companies with which it does business.

As is evident in the cases, corporate concentration in retailing has directly affected the trade fortunes of developing countries, whose major export sectors are vulnerable to the supply chain relations of global buyers. Wal-Mart's approach demonstrates the process by which discount prices based on low living standards reverberate through the entire retail system to the detriment of domestic manufacturing; and given the global nature of production systems, the vicious circle moves from one national system to another. By contrast, IKEA's approach shows that it is possible to deliver low price and good quality while at the same time adhering to high standards of social, economic and environmental responsibility at home and abroad. Whereas the Wal-Mart case illustrates the potential costs of a market-based, 'low road' approach to global sourcing, the IKEA case demonstrates the potential benefits of an organization-oriented, 'high road' strategy to long-term system performance for the corporate, national and global productive system of which it forms a part.

NOTES

1. See, for example, Berger and Dore (1996); Hall and Soskice (2001); Hollingsworth and Boyer (1997); Quack, Morgan and Whitley (1999); Whitley and Kristensen (2001).
2. For further elaboration, see Birecree, Konzelmann and Wilkinson (1997); Wilkinson (1983); and Wilkinson (2002).
3. IWAY was fully implemented by September 2000.

REFERENCES

AFX Europe (2005), 'IKEA Launches New Catalogue with Average Two Percent Price Cut Around World', *Financial Times*, July 29: electronic edition.

Anholt, S. (2005), *Brand New Justice: How Branding Places and Products Can Help the Developing World* (rev. ed.), London: Elsevier.

Andrews, E. (2000), 'Germany Says Wal-Mart Must Raise Prices', *New York Times*, September 9.

Appelbaum E. and Batt R. (1994), *The New American Workplace: Transforming Work Systems in the United States*, New York: ILR Press.

Artz, G.M. and McConnan, J.C. (2001), 'The Impact of Wal-Mart on Host Towns and Surrounding Communities in Maine', paper presented at the *NAREA Meeting, Bar Harbor*, Maine, June 10–12.

Associated Press (2000), 'Germany to Retailers: Raise Prices', *Washington Post Online*, September 8.

Associated Press (2004a), 'Wal-Mart Gains Chicago Toehold', *Chicago Tribune*, May 27.

Associated Press (2004b), 'Wal-Mart concedes China can make unions', *New York Times*, November 23.

Baker, T. (1999), *Doing Well By Doing Good: The Bottom Line on Workplace Practices*, Washington, DC, Economic Policy Institute.

Barbaro, M. (2005), 'Wal-Mart Chief Defends Closing Unionized Store', *Washington Post*, February 11: E1.

Barlett, C. and Nanda, A. (1996), *Harvard Business School Case Study: Ingvar Kamprad and IKEA*.

Berger, S. and Dore, R. (1996), *National Diversity and Global Capitalism*, Ithaca: Cornell University Press.

Best, M. (1990), *The New Competition: Institutions of Industrial Restructuring*, London: Harvard University Press.

Birecree, A., Konzelmann, S. and Wilkinson, F (1997), 'Productive Systems, Competitive Pressure, Strategic Choices and Work Organisation: An introduction', *International Contributions to Labour Studies*, 7 (1): 3–17.

Blumenthal, Karen (1991), 'Wal-Mart Set to Eliminate Reps, Brokers', *The Wall Street Journal*, December 2.

Business Week (2006), *Cuts at Kraft*, February 13, p. 30.

Christianson, R. (2001), 'IKEA Supplier Gets Lean: Shaw Wood Implements Big and Small Improvements to Curb Production Costs and Become More Globally Competitive', *Wood & Wood Products*, December 1.

Cleeland, N., Iritani, E. and Marshall, T. (2003), 'Scouring the Globe to Give Shoppers an $8.63 Polo Shirt', *Los Angeles Times*, November 24: A-1+. [#2: LA Times W-M series].

Deutsche Welle (2005), *Wal-Mart ethics code angers Germans* (English edition), March 15.

Dicker, John (2005), *The United States of Wal-Mart*, New York: Tarcher, Penguin.

Donaldson, H. (2005), 'Wal-Mart and Unions in the UK', *International Union Rights*, 12 (2), 8–9.

Dore, R. (2000), *Stock Market Capitalism, Welfare Capitalism: Japan versus the Anglo-Saxons*, Oxford: Oxford University Press.

Durand, C. (2005) 'Externalities from FDI in the Mexican self-service retailing sector', unpublished paper, March.

Fishman, Charles (2006), *The Wal-Mart Effect: How the World's Most Powerful Company Really Works–And How It's Transforming the American Economy*, New York: Penguin.

GMB (2005), 'Protest Meeting Tomorrow in Support of Suspended ASDA Shop Steward', *gmb.org.uk*, June 27. http://www.gmb.org.uk/Templates/PressItems.asp?NodeID=91936.

Goldsmith, J. (2005), 'Asda Workers Strike', *Retail Weekly Online*, July 27.

Good Jobs First (2005), *Disclosures of Employers Whose Workers and Their Dependents Are Using State Health Insurance Programs*, March 7.

Grant, J. and Daniel, C. (2004), 'Chicago Keeps Wal-Mart Waiting for Zoning Decision', *Financial Times*, May 6, 2.

Greenland, R. (2004), 'Sam Walton's visit to Cannon Mills', E-mail message from Greenland, a former Cannon Mills official, to Charles Craypo, January 5.

Hall, P. and Soskice, D. (eds) (2001), *Varieties of Capitalism: The Institutional Foundations of Comparative Advantage*, Oxford: Oxford University Press.

Hansmann and Kraakman (2001), 'The End of History for Corporate Law', *The Georgetown Law Journal*, 89, 439–68.

Hicks, M.J., and Wilburn, K.L. (2001), 'The Regional Impact of Wal-Mart Entrance: A Panel Study of the Retail Trade Sector in West Virginia', *The Review of Regional Studies*, 31 (3), 305–13.

Hollingsworth, R. and Boyer, R. (1997), *Contemporary Capitalism: The Embeddedness of Institutions*, Cambridge: Cambridge University Press.

Huselid, M. (1995), 'The Impact of Human Resource Management Practices on Turnover, Productivity, and Corporate Financial Performance', *Academy of Management Journal*, 38 (3), 635–72.

Hutton, W. (1995), *The State We're In*, London: Jonathan Cape.

Ichniowski, C., Kochan, T., Levine, D., Olson, C., and Straus, G. (1996), 'What Works at Work: Overview and Assessment', *Industrial Relations*, 35 (3), 299–333.

International Confederation of Free Trade Unions (2004), 'Internationally Recognized Core Labour Standards in the United States', *Report for the WTO General Council Review of the Trade Policies of the United States*, Geneva, January 14–16.

Jacoby, S. (2005), *The Embedded Corporation: Corporate Governance and Employment Relations in Japan and the United States*, Princeton: Princeton University Press.

Kabel, Marcus (2005) 'Wal-Mart nudges foreign suppliers', *Washington Post*, October 21: D2.

Konzelmann, S. (1999), 'Comparative Trends in Retail Labor Standards in Germany and the UK' (unpublished paper), August 13.

Konzelmann, S. (2003), 'Markets, Corporate Governance and Creative Work Systems: The Case of Ferodyn', *The Journal of Interdisciplinary Research*, 14 (2), 139–58.

Luce, E. (2004), 'IKEA's Grown Up Plan to Tackle Child Labour', *Financial Times*, September 14: Electronic Version.

Lynn, Barry C. (2005), *End of the Line: The Rise and Coming Fall of the Global Corporation*, Doubleday: New York.

Mihalopoulos, D. (2004) 'Wal-Mart Gets Half a Loaf', *Chicago Tribune*, May 27.

Miller, George (2004), 'Everyday Low Wages: The Hidden Price We All Pay for Wal-Mart', *Report of the Democratic Staff of the Committee on Education and the Workforce*, U.S. House of Representatives, February 16.

Morning News Beat (2005), *The MNB Wal-Mart Watch*, June 20. ttp://www.morningnewsbeat.com/archives/2005/06/20.html.

Morning News Beat (2006), *Saying 'no' to Wal-Mart*, January 19.

National Labor Committee (1998), *Made in China: Behind the Label*, New York, March.

National Labor Committee (2001), *'Made in the U.S.A.'? Nightmare at the Daewoosa Factory in American Samoa*, New York, March.

O'Brien, R. (2002), *Crippled Justice: The History of Modern Disability in the Workplace*, Chicago: University of Chicago Press.

Petrovic, Misha, and Gary G. Hamilton (2006), 'Making global markets', *Nelson Lichtenstein, Wal-Mart: The Face of Twenty-First Century Capitalism*, New York: New Press.

Pfeffer, J. (1996), 'When It Comes to "Best Practices" Why Do Smart Organizations Occasionally Do Dumb Things?', *Organizational Dynamics*, 25 (1), 33–34.

Pfeffer, J. (1998), 'Seven Practices of Successful Organizations', *California Management Review*, 40 (2), 96–124.

Quack, S., Morgan, G. and Whitley, R. (eds) (1999), *National Capitalisms, Global Competition and Economic Performance*, Amsterdam: John Benjamins Publishing Company.

Rigby, E. (2005), 'Tesco Aims To Go Global After £2bn Profit', *Financial Times*, April 13, 15.

Rohwedder, Cecilie and Ann Zimmerman (2006), 'Wal-Mart gets smaller in the U.K.', *Wall Street Journal*, February 21, B2. F.

Schafer, S. and R.S. Helderman (2001), 'For Wal-Mart, Discomfort Over Disabled', *Washington Post*, August 2, E14.

Seik, Stephanie (2005), 'Children protest outside Wal-Mart', *Boston Globe*, December 12.

Stone, K. (1997), 'Impact of the Wal-Mart Phenomenon on Rural Communities,' *Proceedings: Increasing Understanding of Public Problems and Policies*, Chicago: Farm Foundation.

Tosh, Mark (1993), 'Wal-Mart Defends Direct Dealing', *Supermarket News*, March 15.

Tower, W. (2002) 'Sam's Dream', *Washington Post Magazine*, October 6, 6–22.

UNICEF (2004), *Through UNICEF, IKEA Supports Children's Right to Play*, UNICEF Press Center, March 12.

Whitley, R. and Kristensen, P.H. (2001), *The Multinational Firm: Organising Across Institutional and National Divides*, Oxford: Oxford University Press.

Wilkinson, F. (1983), 'Productive systems', *Cambridge Journal of Economics*, 7, 413–29.

Wilkinson, F. (1998), 'Co-operation, the Organisation of Work and Competitiveness', *ESRC Centre for Business Research*, Working Papers No. 85.

6. Modern Economic Predation: War, Corporate Fraud and the Cruel Chimera of Labour Market Reform

James K. Galbraith

INTRODUCTION

My topic is 'Modern Economic Predation' and I choose it to evoke a memory of Simon Kuznets and his 1966 classic *Modern Economic Growth*. Just as growth defined the age of which Kuznets wrote, so predation defines ours. For Kuznets, growth was a phenomenon whose origin needed explanation because its persistence was to be expected. For us predation holds a similar place in the hierarchy of significant but inadequately comprehended ideas.

In 1899 Thorstein Veblen published the first and still the definitive theory of economic predation, *The Theory of the Leisure Class*. The metaphor is of course evolutionary and Veblen's treatment is a high point in evolutionary political economy. Veblen writes that predation is a phase in the evolution of culture, 'attained only when the predatory attitude has become the habitual and accredited spiritual attitude when the fight has become the dominant note in the current theory of life'. Moreover, 'the transition from peace to predation depends on the growth of technical knowledge and the use of tools'.

Eventually, 'emulation under the circumstances of a predatory life [leads to] ... a form of marriage resting on coercion, and on the other hand the custom of ownership'. (Veblen here shows his pioneering feminist streak.) The two institutions are not distinguishable, 'initially, but soon ownership becomes the prevalent way to display predatory prowess accumulated property more and more replaces trophies of predatory exploit as the conventional exponent of prepotence and success'.

I establish the pedigree of predation in order to propose updated applications in three topical fields: war, corporate governance and the campaign for what is called labor market reform. Each offers, in its way, a fine example of the predatory principle's interpretive power.

WAR CHALLENGES…

War challenges the modern economist's sensibility, perhaps because of its apparently profound irrationality and the evident absence of occasion to apply the standard tools of market theory. Our profession has an intimate link to modern warfare, as this year's Nobel Prize to Thomas Schelling acknowledges. The link illuminates the early careers of such luminaries as Kuznets, Rostow, and Kindleberger, not to mention the work of Galbraith, Kaldor, Schumacher, Baran and others on the United States Strategic Bombing Survey in 1945. But the profession is populated – to our credit – mainly by pacifists. Economists going back to Adam Smith understand the costs of war; but we do not do as good a job with the causes. These we tend to leave to historians and political scientists; at the risk of gross generalization one might say the former focus on blunders and miscalculations while the latter develop models of confrontation between rational nation-states. There are exceptions, and the work of Mary Kaldor (1999) is notable for her flat insight that 'warfare is a predatory social condition'. But they are rare.

The predatory principle teaches us to focus on the relative position of the predatory agent within the society initiating conflict. In the case of the present-day United States, one may usefully call attention to, say, the Office of the Vice President, Mr Cheney, author of the modern doctrine of preventive war.

What does Mr Cheney really think? Clearly the United States did not invade Iraq in authentic pursuit of weapons of mass destruction. Indeed, the WMD issue nicely illuminates the modern predatory view of law, much taught in American business schools, which regards the law not as rules designed to guide behavior but as lines laid down to define the limits of unpunished conduct. Mr Cheney and his colleagues seized on the WMD issue as a rationalization for a war they knew would otherwise be legally condemned. This insight, however, does not by itself give us the reasons why they wished to commit the crime in the first place.

Does Mr Cheney really hold the Philip II theory of imperial conquest – the idea that the silver of Mexico and the gold of Peru would make the fortune of Spain? Have 500 years of economics, beginning with the mercantilist understanding that trade trumps war, passed Mr Cheney by? It's possible. But theories of ignorance and irrationality explain too much; they should be held in reserve, for use only when other possibilities have been ruled out.

On the other hand, when we focus not on oil, but on graft, not imperial control but commercial contracts, not on the price of oil but on the value of the stocks of arms companies – as analyzed in the important recent work of Luc Mampaey and Claude Serfati (2004) – things become quite clear. Why did the Vice President's energy task force take the time, back in 2001, to examine lists of oil-field contractors in Saddam Hussein's Iraq? Curious minds wish to know. Proof comes later, of course – first you need the hypothesis and the research program. The predatory principle provides these. And a great many phenomena, including the lack of accounting for reconstruction funds in Iraq, are at least consistent with the principle in ways that other explanations for the conduct of the war, apart from incompetence, are not.

Is predation the only force behind modern American military strategy? Of course not. But it is a neglected force, and one which can be detected, one might add, in the historical record of the entire period of Cold War militarism from which Mr Cheney emerges, going back to the pressure for preventive nuclear war against the Soviet Union that came, relentlessly, from General Curtis LeMay in the 1950s and 1960s (see Galbraith and Purcell, 1994). There is no reason to regard Mr Cheney as anything other than the faithful product of his formation.

PREDATORY PRINCIPLE IN CORPORATE GOVERNANCE

The predatory principle in corporate governance has been explored by Akerlof and Romer (1993) in their paper on 'Looting', and it now reaches the status of a full-fledged theory in the work of William K. Black (2005) on control fraud. Black was the whistle-blower in the Savings and Loan and Keating Five scandals and is now our premier economic criminologist. The theory of control fraud addresses the situation where the leader of an organization is a criminal actor; it leads to concrete implications that strongly challenge the fashionable neoclassical doctrines of law and economics.

For example, in the Savings and Loan episode, it was widely argued that top accounting firms would protect their own reputations by ferreting out fraud. Black showed that in every case major corporate fraud was protected by clean audits from top accounting firms. The worst fraud, Lincoln Savings and Loan, headed by Charles Keating, sought and received a recommendation from Mr Reputation himself, Alan Greenspan.

Further, the doctrine of moral hazard shifts the blame for financial collapse to the incentives implicit in deposit insurance and predicts that all rational players will expose themselves to excessive risk. But Black showed that the large frauds were all committed in institutions previously taken over for that purpose by criminal networks. Institutions not taken over were largely unaffected.

Finally, standard theory held that the disaster deepened as banks in trouble 'gambled for resurrection' – redoubling their risk in order to have a chance of recovery. But Black showed that the survival rate of high flying S&Ls was zero percent. This can only mean that the destruction of the underlying enterprise was a deliberate act – a fact richly corroborated by the underwriting behavior of the control frauds. This finding has important implications for evaluating the conduct of those who brought us Enron, Tyco, WorldCom, and perhaps also the bankruptcy of the major airlines such as Delta and the impending collapse of the major automotive firms. Perhaps it may have implications, at some point in our lifetimes, for the survival of the largest global corporations.

The principles of predation displayed in corporate governance easily extend themselves to national governments organized along corporate lines. The model of the corporation described by John Kenneth Galbraith (1967) in *The New Industrial State* provides a template for governance in the Corporate Republic, as I have earlier described it:

- There is the essentially clientelist character of decisionmaking, unable to deliberate in an extended, goal-seeking way, because of internal structures of deference. Thus we have the capture of strategic direction, in national security, finance, regulation and other areas, by cliques (resembling JKG's Technostructure) that can lay claim to expertise not available to outsiders, thus manufacturing bogus expertise at will, and claiming the privilege of dispensing it without fear of substantial contradiction.
- We have had, until recently, the rubber-stamping board of directors, to which we refer in the United States by the honorific name of 'Congress'.
- We have shareholders, nominal owners and participants in occasional elections, which the management arranges never to lose.
- We have the Chief Executive Officer as a specialist in public relations, the front man who spends his time on the golf course (or, more precisely, on the ranch) in order to show that he can, to advertise that things are under control. Or, more precisely, to conceal the fact that they are not.
- And we have the larger public relations apparatus of the corporate propaganda machine, featuring an inability to tell a truthful story that is consistent from one day to the next. Yet like the press releases of large corporations the apparatus nevertheless expects and receives deferential treatment from the press, while challengers and critics are treated as the financial papers handle trade unionists and tort lawyers.

LABOR MARKET REFORM

I call attention to this last feature because it brings me to my final topic, a predatory campaign in which economists are prominently featured, namely to legitimate a program of labor market reform, so-called.

The characteristics of the campaign for labor market reform are a steadfast reasoning from first principles, refusal to confront the logical critiques of those principles going back to Keynes's *General Theory*, studied indifference to the evidence, and a dogmatic recommitment to the same program in the face of failure to reach designated goals. All failure is invariably attributed to insufficient zeal.

Thus we have the proposal in 2005 by Hans Werner Sinn, President of the Ifo Institute, who criticized the German reform program as too weak and called for radical surgery, specifically reduction of average wages in Germany by 10 to 15 percent and those of less-skilled workers by one-third – implying a major rise in the inequality of the wage structure. This we have to concede is a robust proposal and a worthy basis for debate.

So let us ask: What is the evidence in favor? Where are the cases of countries that returned to full employment by cutting wages and increasing inequality?

It is often claimed that the United States comprises such a case but it does not. As I have shown on repeated occasions, wage inequality in the broad working population of America declined as we moved toward full employment in the late 1990s. Using the precise sense of Mr Sinn, labor market flexibility in the US declined as unemployment fell. It did not rise, and no part of the decline of unemployment can be attributed to increasing inequalities of pay.

Equally, there is no evidence within Europe that countries with more internal labor market inequality have better employment records. Quite the reverse, as anyone can see and everyone knows. Denmark has less unemployment than Kosovo, or Greece, or Spain.

Theory of course exists to interpret what evidence shows. The Rehn–Meidner (Meidner and Rehn, 1951) model taught how a deliberate program of solidarity and wage compression could speed the evolution of industrial competitiveness, and when combined with active labor market policy yield full employment. The Harris–Todaro (1970) model of wage differentials and migration explained how high inequality in structures of pay would generate equilibrium job search and structural unemployment.

In our 2004 paper on inequality, unemployment and the policy of Europe, Enrique Garcilazo and I rely on these theories to help explain the demonstrable fact that equality of pay is associated with less, not more, unemployment. And to this we add evidence of strategic wage-setting in the controlled labor markets of Austria and late-1990s Ireland, evidently designed to reduce unemployment in those countries by setting wages in the traded-goods sectors at a slight discount to Germany and the UK, thus importing employment from the larger neighbor. This is an effective tool available only to small countries with fully inflexible labor markets.

CONCLUSION

In addition, we show precisely how all regions of Europe saw a common pattern of rising unemployment following the adoption of the Maastricht Treaty – evidence which by itself debunks the notion that reform of national labor market institutions can effectively reduce the unemployment rate in, say, Germany or France. Plainly a European phenomenon requires a European solution.

What then are we to make of the persistence of labor market reform as a slogan for politicians and a research program for economists? The evidence, I fear, does not support the hypothesis that this is an honest and open scientific discussion in which all rigorous arguments meet on an equal footing, especially in what are called the mainstream journals, in which economists find they have to publish in order to secure professional advancement. We are left with two alternative views, incompetence and predation. As an economist, once again, I'm trained to treat the irrationality postulate as a last resort, particularly when observed errors are not random but always biased in a single direction.

That leaves me with the predatory principle – that labor market reform dominates the political agenda simply because it serves the interests of the influences behind the political class. Why, for example, do we see the emphasis on the right to fire? Is it really plausible that this is a program offered in the larger interests of society, to relieve employers of an irrational fear of adding employees in order to earn profits that are otherwise plainly in view? Or is it more likely that easing job protections in slow times would lead to more firings, downsizing, and intimidation of trade unionists and other troublemakers? I ask this as a scientific question – which of the two hypotheses, do you think, is really easier to believe?

In 'The Means to Prosperity' Keynes (1991) wrote, 'I call attention to the nature of the problem, because it points to the nature of the remedy'. Predators exist. They are a normal feature of any ecosystem, as are scavengers, parasites and ordinary pests. The point is not to eliminate them. That can't be done, and if it could, new predators would spring up as they always do to occupy the niche. The point is rather to understand the phenomenon, from a scientific point of view. And it is to deploy that understanding in the quest for an acceptable measure of control.

We have, of course, established tools for the purpose. In the labor market, there is what my father long ago christened the countervailing power of the trade unions. Among economists, there is or ought to be the enduring intellectual authority of Keynesian economics and the moral authority of scholarly standards. In the sphere of corporate governance, there is the power of law and regulation, given adequate resources for investigation and prosecution, again buttressed by clear understanding of theory of the case. And in the case of those who would wage predatory war – well, for some levels of predation there can be no tolerance in a free and civilized world.

REFERENCES

Akerlof, George and Paul Romer (1993), 'Looting: The Economic Underworld of Bankruptcy for Profit' *Brookings Papers on Economic Activity*.

Black, William K. (2005), *The Best Way to Rob a Bank is to Own One*, Austin: University of Texas Press.

Harris, J.R. and M.P. Todaro (1970), 'Migration, Unemployment and Development: A Two-Sector Analysis', *The American Economic Review*, 60 (1), 126–42.

Galbraith, James K. and Enrique Garcilazo (2004), 'Unemployment, Inequality and the Policy of Europe, 1984–2000', *Banca Nazionale del Lavoro Quarterly Review*, LVII (228), 3–28 March.

Galbraith, James K. and Heather Purcell (1994), 'Did the United States Military Plan a Nuclear First Strike for 1963?' *The American Prospect*, 19, 88–96.

Galbraith, John Kenneth (1967), *The New Industrial State*, Boston: Houghton-Mifflin.

Kaldor, Mary (1999), *New and Old Wars: Organized Violence in the Global Era*, Stanford: Stanford University Press.

Keynes, John Maynard (1936), *The General Theory of Employment Interest and Money*, London: MacMillan.

— The Means to Prosperity (1991), *Essays in Persuasion*, New York: W.W. Norton.

Kuznets, Simon (1966), *Modern Economic Growth: Rate, Structure and Spread*, New Haven: Yale University Press.

Mampaey, Luc and Claude Serfati (2004), 'Du capitalisme managérial au capitalisme actionnarial: quels changements pour les industries d'armement?', Paper presented at *The Forum International John Kenneth Galbraith*, Paris, September.

Meidner, R. and G. Rehn (1951), *Fackföreningrsrörelsen Och Den Fulla Sysselsättningen*, LO.Stockholm.

Sinn, Hans-Werner (2005), 'How to Combat German Unemployment', *IFO Viewpoint 61*, at http://www.cesifo-group.de, Accessed March 16, 2006.

Veblen, Thorstein (1948), 'Theory of the Leisure Class', in Max Eastman, ed., *The Portable Veblen*, New York: Viking, pp. 71–4.

7. A New Global Military–Terrorism–Hegemony Social Structure of Accumulation for Long-Wave Upswing?

Phillip Anthony O'Hara

INTRODUCTION

The question addressed in this chapter is the degree to which the new configuration of terrorists and pre-emptive strikes in the global political economy over the past decade or so is affecting long-term socioeconomic performance. We believe that global military–terrorist activities have an impact on performance through the building or otherwise of potential social structures of accumulation (SSAs). The key factors to consider are the impact of the current military–terrorism structure on levels of stability and conflict resolution. If stability and the resolution of conflict are at a high level this is likely to stimulate economic activity through higher levels of consumption, investment, trade, tourism, GDP, utility and welfare. But if the current forces are creating higher levels of instability and conflict in the global political economy then this is inhibiting the development of institutions to promote economic activity.

The study starts with a section on the major planks of the current global military–terrorism system. Afterwards we analyse the nature and degree of stability and conflict resolution in the military system. The final major section outlines some critical transmission mechanisms linking instability and conflict with declining performance. A conclusion follows.

MAJOR PLANKS OF THE GLOBAL MILITARY–TERRORISM SYSTEM

The current global military–terrorism system is evolving in multiple directions that are difficult to delineate precisely. But some fairly obvious trends and patterns are emerging that are becoming fairly durable and dynamic. The first plank situates the US as a powerful imperial force, though with much less absolute power than in the 1950s and 1960s. Militarily it has 'soft' hegemonic military dominance since while it is more powerful relatively than in the 1980s, its economic strength has been diminishing, which places limits on its military strength (Wallerstein 2002; Gulick 2004). More significantly, though, we are concerned here with strategy, in particular the recently amplified policy of the US 'going it alone' (with some allies) in military and related affairs. This can be neatly schematized by calling the first plank the unipolar and first strike tendencies of the US imperial system.[1]

With the imperial trend the US dominates militarily and seeks to prevent other powers from threatening its pre-eminence. With the recent heightened focus on unilateralism, the US has created a military alliance with its 'coalition of the willing', including the UK, Australia, Japan, Pakistan, Saudi Arabia and Israel. The doctrine of pre-emptive strike has been introduced by the US, to replace the old doctrine of deterrence which is argued not to be valid in an environment of global terrorism and rogue states. The US often seeks to go into battle and undertake international relations on its own terms, eschewing, for instance, many critical international protocols, courts, agreements, conventions and so forth (see below) while unilaterally attacking 'terrorists' and 'rogue states' in association with its coalition partners. It also undermines multilateral institutions by forcing its power on them, such as happened in several UN forums and the Chemical Weapons Convention.[2]

Foreign policy in the second Bush Administration has been very ideologically coherent with the rise to pre-eminence of the neo-conservatives and assertive nationalists. These hawks such as Richard Cheney, Donald Rumsfeld, Condoleezza Rice, Paul Wolfowitz, Robert Zoellick, Stephen Hadley, Elliott Abrams and John Negroponte believe in taking an assertive position to prevent attacks on the US through first strikes and invasions to destroy rogue states and terrorists. Realists, such as Colin Powell, are now out of favour since they adhere to 'old-fashioned' notions of balance of power, international stability and predictable alliances (Kern, 2005). It remains to be seen how the new administration in Washington affects the processes associated with this tendency.

The second plank is the multilateralism trend. While the US is taking a unilateral direction, it does also at times cooperate beyond the coalition of the willing through the UN, NATO and nations in the Middle East and South and North America. But for the US, multilateral or bilateral relations are really just an extension of its unilateral tendency, since it wants to choose whatever strategy it thinks is relevant to its 'national interest'. The dominant states of Europe, especially France and Germany, prefer a consistently multilateral approach to international relations, since it correlates with the rule of law, compromise and agreements to solve complex problems. Such multilateral forces include the UN, NATO, the Kyoto Protocol, the Anti-Ballistic Missile Agreement, an expanded European Union and the Chemical Weapons Convention. This trend seeks to solve conflicts via institutionalized accords between the major parties, in the belief that this reduces instability and conflict. When it suits the US it too contributes to multilateral agreements, but it reserves the right to act unilaterally where it thinks this is in the 'national interest'.

The third plank of the system is the emergence of a relatively new form of terrorism. The old style terrorism of the IRA, the Red Brigade and FARC was the classic variety of small–scale attacks and abductions in order to gain media attention and influence government. They tended to eschew major attacks for fear of alienating the general population. They were content to enhance the cause of independence and attacks on the establishment thorough regular incursions that kept their concerns in the public eye. The new form of terrorism associated with radical Islamic groups has a new agenda of attacking US hegemony in the Middle East, Western influence in regional areas and corrupt, pro-Western and/or relatively secular governments. They have announced a war that seeks major civilian casualties against the US and its coalition of the willing. Moreover, they seek to escalate the conflict in order to entice the US to overreact and try to reinforce their power base in the Middle East and elsewhere. In this fashion they champion the fundamentalist Islamic cause.

The new form of terrorism has four main characteristics: (a) a marked expansion in the number of casualties per attack, (b) a majority of non-state terrorists being religious-Muslim in origin, (c) a growing global network of resources, and (d) a concern to destroy US hegemony in the Middle East. Many authors have questioned the newness of this trend, but these four tendencies do seem to prevail.[3] The world is currently experiencing a war between the US and its allies and a global network of non-state terrorists that are effectively attacking the foundations of US dominance in the region. The war is likely to play out over several decades and to dominate the lives of most nations in Europe, the US, the Middle East, northern Africa and parts of south-east Asia and Oceania.

The fourth plank is a series of so-called 'rogue states' that also appear to be 'challenging' US power. Nations such as Iraq, Afghanistan, Iran, North

Korea, Cuba, Lebanon, Syria and the Sudan have variously been included, over recent years, in this category of states that have been trying to enhance their power through an independent foreign policy, acquisition of nuclear weapons and/or support for various forms of 'terrorism' around the globe. Indeed, it was the activities of such states that 'justified' the US (with UN support) invading Afghanistan to root out the Taliban in the search for Al Qaeda terrorists, and also for the foray into Iraq due to *supposed* weapons of mass destruction and support for terrorists by Saddam Hussein. This is a critical part of the recent US policy of engaging in pre-emptive first strikes where thought necessary. Gone are the old principles of the US respecting the sovereignty of established governments. They seek to be more proactive in encouraging changes to regimes that are obviously anti-American.

The fifth plank of the military–terrorism system is the 'oil regime' and the 'corporate state'. Corporations are a critical part of the system through the production of armaments, military hardware, trained specialists, financiers and strategists. The state also trains military personnel, establishes a military bureaucracy and associated intelligence and defence organizations. The US President is the chief of the armed forces, while Congress provides financial support and nationalistic fervour legitimizes the practices. Oil, however, is more important than some analysts have been led to believe. The Middle East would be seen like much of sub-Saharan Africa without oil, and no government seeking global power would bother to invade nations without such rich resources. Known reserves of oil are likely to decline by 50 per cent between now and 2050, while the Middle East share is expected to increase from 20 per cent to 45 per cent over the same period (Clark, 2003).

The sixth plank is the dominance of a neoliberalism policy framework. Starting with the Reagan and Thatcher revolutions, most nations of the world have reformed their governance structures to adhere to the free market ideology. Special reference has been given in national and international policy settings to moderating budget deficits, reducing the size of government, and protecting property rights. Fundamental to this view is the notion that the role of government is to provide a set of laws and institutions to protect the rights to private property, democracy and association. This is an important rationale for the recent unilateral push in the White House, since military and so-called 'defence' activities are core parts of the 'rule of law' and the 'protection of private property'. The idea is that, once these public goods are in place, the entrepreneurial spirit can emerge free of the fetters of regulations so as to enhance innovation and productivity. The supply side of the economy is thus seen to be critical to long-term economic performance; demand in the form of investment and consumption will naturally flow once the basic structures are in place.[4] The importance of neoliberalism is outlined in the core national security strategy developed by the White House (Bush,

2002, ch. VI).

The seventh plank of the global military–terrorism system is increasing dominance of the 'American way of life' through most nations and regions. American culture, economy and polity are being adopted through the four corners of the globe. However, this does not necessarily translate into absolute American hegemony or even the uniformity of culture. But it does provide a pattern to the processes affecting the global system. It may lead to the creation of alternative sources of power, and to the emergence of new cultural forms. Critical to this is a parliamentary system of checks and balances, regular elections, and a sophisticated corporate media/news apparatus. The neoconservatives seek to stimulate and if necessary force on rouge states a world in the image of the US, with free markets, parliamentary democracy and an open society. As the revised US national security strategy says, it is critical to 'expand the circle of development by opening societies and building the infrastructure of democracy' (Bush, 2002, p. 21).

CONTRADICTIONS OF THE GLOBAL MILITARY–TERRORISM SYSTEM

Emanating from these seven planks of the global military system are several contradictions, amplifying factors and enabling processes. Contradictions of the global military system are those tendencies that simultaneously promote positive and negative elements, and which are potentially destabilizing to the system. Through time the negative elements will tend to prevail unless major changes are made to promote stability, conflict resolution and performance. Contradictions are those paradoxes, ironies and oppositions that lead to endogenous instabilities and conflicts if not suitably checked by institutional constraints, accords and agreements. Every institutional apparatus has imbedded contradictions, but they will only become manifest when the vested interests take control in their narrow self-interest; when instrumental efficiency is not a critical part of the dynamic of the system; where financial and military activities dominate over productive relations and processes; and when instability and conflict arise from unstable power and authority structures (O'Hara 2005). The core contradiction, other contradictory processes, amplifying factors and relationships of interdependency are illustrated in Figure 7.1.

Terrorism and the wars associated with it are complex phenomena, and therefore it is necessary to situate it in a combined social, political and economic environment. Figure 7.1 illustrates the interdependency between nine factors. Usually there is the core contradiction and a number of secondary contradictions. The core contradiction lies in the relationship between the creation of a power vacuum from the global military imbalance of the demise of the Soviet system, and the tendency of the US to impose forms of relative hegemonic dominance in the Middle East. The other contradiction important in this context is that between the generation of global neoliberalism and the associated tendency towards uneven development. Also critical are certain amplifying factors that produce a divergence between the direct costs of terrorism and war (deaths, injuries, destruction of property, etc.) and the much wider generation of fear and intimidation among the population (which affects utility, satisfaction, quality of life, apparent security, the social and business climate and so forth). It is necessary to see all these factors in dynamic linkage and realistic practice.

Figure 7.1: Contradictions, Amplifications and Circuit Affecting Instability and Conflict

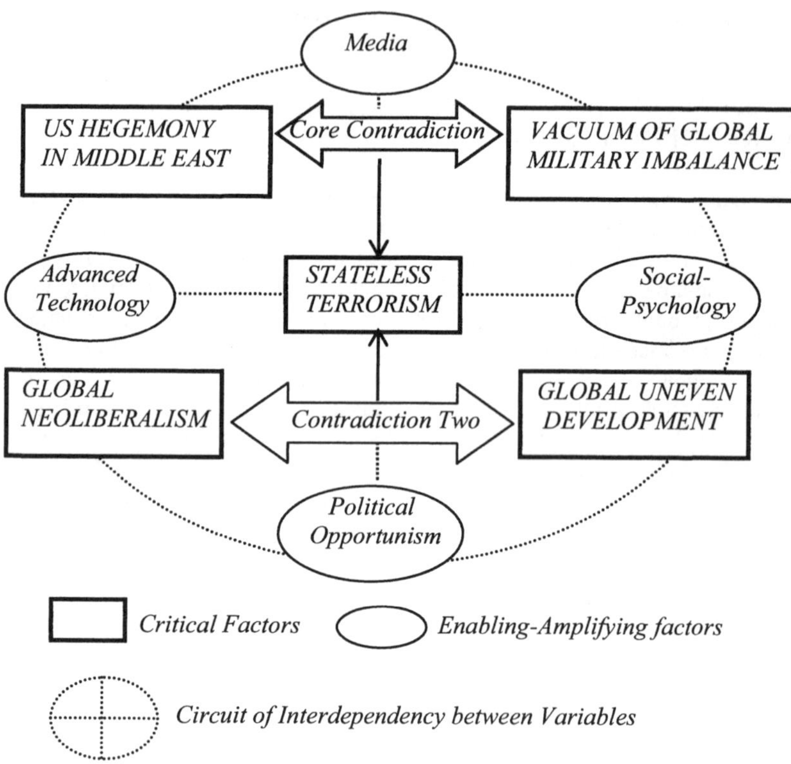

The Core Contradiction vis-à-vis the 'military–terrorism SSA' relates to the interface between the military vacuum posed by the demise of the USSR and the rise of US relative hegemony in the Middle East. The current global military system is in metamorphosis from the old cold war system to a new one the nature of which is somewhat indeterminate. Cold war stability rested on the superpowers knowing that both sides had the ability to destroy their enemies through 'mutually assured destruction'. It was unlikely that one of the superpowers could strike first without the prospect of retaliation. Various agreements and consultations were reached among the major powers for controls on armaments, nuclear weapons and long-range missiles which prevented an escalation into full-scale war, even (eventually) during the Cuban missile crisis of 1962. While during the 1950s, 1960s and early 1970s absolute US hegemony ruled much of the world, on the military side a perceived 'relative balance' existed that prevented major war.

With the demise of the Soviet Union around 1990, such an institutional balance was upset, and a military power vacuum was generated into which various groups and nations quickly moved. Indeed, the very process of destroying the power of the USSR in Afghanistan created the potential for radical Islamic groups to move into this vacuum, since they were supported heavily by the US and its allies. Afghanistan was a theatre within which Al Qaeda developed critical skills, networks and knowledge through which their power could multiply. Saddam Hussein also was supported by the US and its allies, and Iraq's foray into Kuwait (which led to the first Gulf War) was a result of a desire to expand its power in the post-Soviet vacuum. The terrorist activities of Al Qaeda and associates through the 1990s and 2000s gradually grew, culminating in the 'event that changed the world': 9/11. This could never have happened without the demise of the Soviet Union which created instability in the global military system. As Bob Riggs (2003, p. 4) says:

> When bin Laden changed the face of contemporary warfare by launching well-planned attacks on symbolic civilian targets, he wrote a new chapter in modern military history. … Bin Laden … show[ed] that the strategic and effective use of violence against symbolic civilian targets makes it possible for small, well-organised and ruthless terror groups to destabilise the most seemingly all-powerful of governments, and even the stability of the world order.

This transition process to a new military–terrorism configuration is enhancing instability as the US deepens its imperial role and neoconservative bent while radical Islamic elements seek to be included in the emerging power system. Out of the power vacuum created from the demise of the USSR Islamic radicals are seeking to be taken seriously as military and cultural elements of a new world system. The battle between the imperial and neoconservative forces and the Islamic elements are currently being played out in numerous theatres in Iraq, Afghanistan, Pakistan, Saudi Arabia, Palestine/Israel and numerous other areas of the world. The US alliance is sharing an unstable power system with Islamic radicals, and the battle is likely to continue until some degree of sharing of power is undertaken in global and regional decision-making. Until then battles will be fought, resistance against the US and its allies will continue, and military-security instability will continue.

The instability created by the power vacuum will play out over many years to come until a dynamic relative balance of power is (possibly) generated. In the meantime, military conflicts will continue, and likely become worse before they moderate. What we are currently seeing is a historic shift towards the re-emergence of Islamic power in global politics, while absolute US economic power declines, European potential rises and China and its archipelago emerges as a dominant player. US relative hegemony in the Middle East, in particular, is currently in question through conventional and terrorist battles in Iraq, Israel/Palestine, Europe, Northern Africa and elsewhere. The problems of so-called terrorism and the war on terrorism are thus likely to get worse until Islamic interests are able to impinge on the world system. The recent terrorist suicide attacks in New York, Bali, Morocco, Spain, London, Iraq and elsewhere are likely to be the mere start of a long campaign of re-establishing Islamic interests.

The current multilateral–unilateral system is generating instability from both sides. On the multilateral side, for instance, the United Nations has been in crisis mode for a number of years, as the US seeks to challenge its legitimacy; it was inadequate in the face of the Kosova crisis of the late 1990s; and was reluctant to strongly support the invasion of Iraq in the face of lack of evidence of weapons of mass destruction and Iraqi support for major terrorists. The multilateral foundation of the UN is constantly being threatened by the US as it moves in a unilateral direction, along with members of the 'coalition of the willing'. This lack of UN unity is increasing instability in international relations. Multilateral ineffectiveness is stimulating US unilateralism, while unilateralism is contributing to the ineffectiveness of multilateralism. This crisis of collective security is leading to greater conflict and war in the global system. As one analyst says:

> A world in which the paramount international security institution is unable to solve or even effectively address the most dramatic and dangerous threats to security is a world on the verge of regressing to a system of self-help. Neither bashing multilateralism nor singing its praises will resolve anything. Rather policymakers must acknowledge that multilateralism entails benefits as well as problems, and that it is necessary to develop the political will and determination to subject multilateralism to thorough review and, if the need arises, radical reforms. Only then can we bring about the kind of international order that both sides of the Atlantic as well as the greater international system so desire. (Krause, 2004, p. 57).

On the other hand, the unilateral trend of the US and the dominance of the neo-conservative-cum-nationalist wings of the Republican Party have enhanced instability. They have led an invasion of a country that was previously stable, to one that is now a theatre and global stimulus for growing networks of Islamic militants. The US invaded Iraq with insufficient ground troops, inadequate border control, lack of appreciation of the problems of governance, and inadequate recognition of the potential for heightened instability. Bin Laden and the Al Qaeda network undertook 9/11 to provoke US retaliation in the hope of creating a theatre where radical Islamic networks could flourish. This is exactly what the Iraqi war did – increase instability, promote effective resistance to the US and its allies, and increase conflict not only regionally but throughout much of the world.

The Hawks in Washington argue that increasing short-term instability will in the intermediate to long run reduce conflict. They say that having pre-emptive strikes on terrorists and rogue states may create some degree of regional instability – such as in the Middle East and the Korean Peninsula – but that this is the short-term price of long-term stability and resolution of conflict. However, this ignores critical counter-arguments such as the following problems suggested by Ikenberry (2002). While the US creates a core principle of the first strike, this may engender other states to put it into practice. Pakistan, Russia, China, North Korea and so on may decide that they need no firm evidence of attacks to strike first and destroy the enemy. It may also encourage states to accelerate their programmes of weapons of mass destruction to deter the US. First-strikes and invasions before evidence is available will likely increase the number of wars, and increase the resources necessary for state-building and peace-keeping for perhaps decades into the future. These wars and state-building programmes increase the degree of uncertainty regarding the future course of invaded states. It is likely to increase the number of invaded and changed regimes, but the future course of events may evolve in an unanticipated fashion, creating imperial overreach where the US requires long-term resources from others but has already alienated potential coalition partners.

The unilateral trend requires multilateral cooperation in intelligence, logistics, legality and socioeconomic policy. But potential partners are less likely to cooperate after being passed over in favour of more compliant junior partners such as Australia. Acting imperially in security and military matters is unlikely to generate cooperation in other areas such as trade liberalization, financial stability and organized crime. The US imperial trend may accelerate the demise of US power by creating an international backlash against the US. Numerous other states may rebel against the imperial US order. US military dominance and war-mongering may incite rebellion by other states, even those previously sympathetic to US power.

What is the link between this heightened global instability and conflict? For the first time in recent centuries a major attack has been unleashed on the mainland of the relatively most powerful nation in the world. This is an unprecedented attack on US power: the most significant challenge to a dominant nation since the demise of British power in the late 1800s. Radical Islamic militants are developing global networks against a major power, which is manifesting in a series of mostly suicide attacks against the US and its 'coalition of the willing'. The terrorist statistics compiled by the US Department of State and others are useful because they enable us to assess the degree of military action against the US, since their definition of terrorism ignores US-backed (or generated) terrorist activities.

Using these statistics we generate an 'Index of Anti-US Terrorism' (IAUST) for the period 1990–2006, divided into two periods: 1990–97 and 1998–2006. For each major attack against US interests an impact figure of between 0 and 10 points is given, depending on the severity of the attack. A summation of the Index is shown in Table 7.1. Using this IAUST Index we found that non-state terrorist attacks in the past nine years (1998–2006; Table 7.1b) have been much more proactive against the US "alliance" than in the seven years before then (1990–97; Table 7.1a). There was thus an increase in conflict associated with this expansion of instability in the wake of the power vacuum creating radical Islamic terrorism and unilateralism.

Table 7.1a: Index of Anti-US Terrorism (IAUST), 1990–97: Six Most Critical Non-State Terrorist Attacks Against the 'US Alliance'

Date	Place(s)	Target(s)	Civilians Killed
Feb/Mch 1991	Istanbul & Anarp, Turkey	Contract Workers US Defence Dept	2 US Citizens
March 1992	Bogota, Columbia	US Diners Club	1 US Citizen
Feb 1993	New York City	World Trade Centre	6
Oct 1994	Luxor, Egypt	Tourists	1 UK Citizen
Nov 1995	Rijadh, Saudi Arabia		7 (5 US Citizens)
Feb 1997	New York City	Empire State Building	1 Danish Citizen
			∑ = 18 Killed

Date	Technology Used	Strategic Impact	∑ IAUST Impact Score
Feb/Mch 1991	Revolver	Minimal	1
March 1992	Revolver	Minimal	1
Feb 1993	Bomb Materials	Significant	6
Oct 1994	Bomb Materials	Slight	2

Nov 1995	Bomb Materials	Moderate Significant	3
Feb 1997	Revolver	Moderate	3
			∑ = 16/60 = 27%

Table 7.1b: Index of Anti-US Terrorism (IAUST), 1998–2006: Seven Most Critical Non-State Terrorist Attacks Against 'US Alliance' and Its 'Protectorates'

Date	Place(s)	Target(s)	Civilians Killed
August 1998	Kenya, Tanzania	US Embassies	301
September 2001	New York Washington	Icons of US Power	3,000
October 2002	Bali, Indonesia	Nightclub (Western Tourists)	180
May 2003	Casablanca, Morocco	5 Western Tourist Sites	30
March 2004	Madrid, Spain	5 Trains (Commuter)	191
July 2005	London, England	5 Trains & 1 Bus	65
2003–2006	Various Places, Iraq	Mosques, Markets, Streets, etc.	141,542
			∑ = 145,309 Violent Deaths

Date	Technology Used	Strategic Impact	∑ IAUST Impact Score
August 1998	Bombs	Moderate	3
September 2001	Aeroplanes, Large Buildings	'Changed Course of History'	10
October 2002	Bombs, Buildings	Australia Vulnerable – Member of COW	4
May 2003	Bombs, Buildings	Moroccans Turn from Islam	2
March 2004	Bombs, Trains	COW Govt Defeated in Election	6
July 2005	Bombs, Trains, Bus	Internal Attack on COW England	7
2003–2006	Gunfire, Bombs, Suicide Missions	Enhancing Al Qaeda Networks	10
			∑ = 42/70 = 60%

Source: Adapted from NCC (2005); US Department of State (1992–2004); Fratianni and Kang (2004); Burnham et al. (2007); Kalpakian (2005).

These figures show that before the radical Islamists became organized there were far fewer challenges to US power, in the Middle East in particular. The six most critical attacks against US strategic interests during 1990–97 – in Turkey (1991), Columbia (1992), New York City (1993), Egypt (1994), Saudi Arabia (1995) and New York City (1997) – were collectively fairly minor incursions into the US power base, although the New York City ones were symbolically important as an attack on the mainland with seven civilians killed. The strategic, economic and social impacts of the attacks were minor, with an overall 'impact score' of 16/60 or 27 per cent. During the early–mid 1990s many of the so-called international terrorist attacks (as defined by the State Department) were by secular groups, such as FARC in Columbia which was protecting agricultural communities against terrorist actions by US-supported military and paramilitary forces.[5] Small-scale terrorist actions for diplomatic and/or media attention seem to have been the norm among FARC and related groups.

It took the radical Islamic groups a decade or so to institute sufficient networks against US power to pose a formidable threat after the demise of the US–USSR relative military balance of power. Once they organized themselves and learnt the techniques of large-scale suicide missions, by the late 1990s successes were forthcoming. They had bases such as in Afghanistan and Pakistan with which to organize campaigns, and during the early 2000s the majority of international terrorist groups were religious (mainly radical Islamic) in nature, as shown by Table 7.2 (see Schmidt, 2004).[6]

Table 7.2: Terrorist Groups Primarily Religious/Non-Religious in Focus, 1968–2002

	1968	1980	1992	1995	2002
Number Religious*	0	2	11	25	38
Number Non-Religious*	11	62	37	33	36
Percent Religious*	0	3	23	43	51
Percent Non-Religious*	100	97	77	57	49
Percent Fatalities by Religious Terrorists**	n.a.	n.a.	n.a.	58%	n.a.

Source: Adapted from Hoffman* (1997, pp. 48, 52); US State Department** (2003, pp. 99, 125).

'Religious' terrorist groups as a percent of all terrorist groups (defined by the US State Department) rose from 0 (1969) to 3 (1980) to 23 (1992) to 43 (1995) to 51 (2002); becoming the majority by 2002, while their contribution to total terrorist fatalities had already well exceeded 50 per cent by 1995.

This was, by-and-large, a new form of terrorism more intent on major attacks against US hegemony in the Middle East and elsewhere in the world. The late 1990s and 2000s thus saw an escalation in significant attacks, with the suicide bombings of US Embassies in Kenya and Tanzania (1998) leading the charge with 301 civilian deaths and 5,077 injured. This was followed by the most significant attack on the US homeland ever, the 9/11 suicide plane crashes in New York City and Washington DC (2001), killing around 3000 civilians.

The 9/11 attacks stimulated a whole series of network plans throughout the Middle East, Asia, Europe and North Africa as radical Islamists gained confidence in their cause. Hence the suicide bombs set off in Bali (2002), which killed 180 civilians; similar attacks in Casablanca (2003, a haven for especially British tourists), killing 30; the 10 suicide train bombs in Madrid (2004), killing 191 and responsible for the defeat of the government in the elections; and the main suicide attacks on the train and bus networks in London (2005), killing about 65 civilians. Al Qaeda, along with its informal global networks, and the US and its allies have declared war on each other. The ongoing Afghan war after 9/11 ironically helped Al Qaeda by forcing them to become non-state combatants with no territory and increasing network power throughout the world. Having no state to protect and amorphous networks enhanced their cause, and make it difficult for the US to retaliate against them.

Wanting the US to retaliate and spread their imperial power through the Middle East even more forcefully helped Al Qaeda and their allies immensely. Iraq then became a major theatre for Islamic militants to engage in serious war against the US, gaining critical experience and honing the craft of suicide bombings and Guerrilla Warfare. The 2003 US invasion of Iraq was a serious mistake and illustrates the contradictory limits of neo-conservatism. According to the only scientific estimate of total Iraqi casualties during the Iraqi war (aggregate figures for the period March 2003 to June 2006) (Burnham et al. 2007; an update of Roberts et al. 2004), since the US invasion, an estimated 601,027 Iraqis were killed by violent methods. This was a social survey of Iraqi households, undertaken between 20 May and 10 July 2006, backed up in over 90 per cent of cases by a death certificate; with the results published in the *Lancet*. Of the 601,027 Iraqi deaths by violent means, 24 per cent were killed by 'Other' groups such as Al Qaeda and their allies in association with religious-ethnic reprisals (141,241 people); 31 per cent were killed by the 'Coalition of the Willing' (188,422 people); and 45 per cent were killed by 'Unknown' personnel (271,364 people; likely a combination of Al Qaeda-inspired groups, religious-ethnic reprisals and Coalition members). Thus, the number killed by Al Qaeda in association with other Islamic groups, 141,241, can be seen as a very likely underestimate of the amount of anti-US terrorism (including terrorism which questions the presence of the Coalition in Iraq) during the first 40 months of the Iraq War. The number of total Iraqis violently killed by all groups increased from 90,154 (2003–04) to 180,308 (2004–05) and 330,565 (2005–06), with the total killed by 'Other' groups, including Al Qaeda and other Islamists, increasing over the same period from 8,114 to 34,259 and 99,169 people. These Iraqi's killed, especially by Al Qaeda et al. can be seen as a major threat to the US invasion and their broader imperial pursuits; hence the impact, '10', is very likely broadly equal to the 9/11 attacks in terms of morale and geo-political significance.

Hence, 9/11 and the Iraq War were the most critical events promoting radical Islamic strategy against US power. Therefore, overall, the 'impact score' for the 1998–2006 attacks against the US is 42/70 or 60 per cent. This is a more than double the strategic importance of the attacks earlier, in the 1990s.

Greater conflict has thus emanated from instability associated with the failures of multilateral–unilateral security; the vacuum created by the scrapping of the US–USSR balance of power system; and (declining) 'US hegemony' in the Middle East. An amorphous World War now exists between the forces of US power (including its allies) and radical Islamic religious–military groups. At present this war has no balance of power institutions to moderate the conflict, and therefore is likely to escalate into the future. In doing so, it will likely lead to more loss of life, declining utility and diminished socioeconomic performance for many nations. The link between instability, conflict and declining performance is analysed in more detail in the next section.

INSTABILITY, CONFLICT AND PERFORMANCE

The major hypothesis of this study is that the emergence of a military–terrorism SSA depends upon positive levels of stability, conflict resolution and performance. The relationship between these factors is illustrated in Figure 7.2.

The central hypothesis isolates the importance of linkages between levels of stability in military–terrorism institutions, conflict resolution and socioeconomic performance. Instability within and between these institutions stimulates high levels of conflict and war, contributing to anomalous performance. In the previous section we showed how instability within and between the unilateral and multilateral relationship is promoting conflict, war and terrorism in the global system. This section presents evidence that such instability and conflict is inhibiting socioeconomic performance, and thus preventing the formation of a military–terrorism SSA to stimulate long wave upswing in the global political economy.

Figure 7.2: Formation of a Military–Terrorism SSA

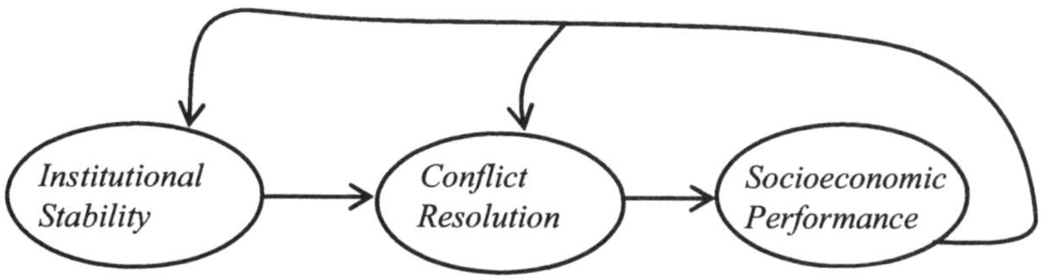

We now come to Contradiction 2 (see Figure 7.1, above) concerning the spread of global neoliberalism and the process of uneven growth and development. A major problem is the inability of US neoliberal policy hegemony in the Middle East to improve the performance of Arab nations. US influence in the area and the work of US-inspired IMF–World Bank institutions heavily influenced Arab nations to globalize and deregulate. Arab nations were told that if they opened their economies to international capital, privatized government enterprises and deregulated labour markets this would lead to improved performance. There are two problems here. The first is that many Middle Eastern nations did open up to markets, but such action did not materially improve their standard of living, as shown from the work of Peter Nunnemkamp (2004).

The evidence is fairly clear that, through time, living in an environment in which economic performance is sub-standard, political repression is strong and there are significant numbers of sympathetic educated people, provides a perfect breeding ground for radical Islamic networks. This has been the environment of most Arab nations in the Middle East (Testas 2004). Educated radicals are in high demand for their skills in areas such as information and communications technology and the ability to fit into a foreign environment. Also they are more likely to be interested in political activity and be committed to the cause. The political environment in most Arab nations is also conducive to terrorism as many national governments are affiliated with the US and provide few forums for radicals to be included in decision-making. Lastly, deteriorating performance provides an incentive for radical change to improve the conditions of Islamic people, even if Islam requires a balance of economic and social considerations. Internal tensions and conflict exacerbate these problems.

It is in this complex environment that radical Islamic networks have developed. US relative hegemony in the Middle East has stimulated a host of corrupt and repressive regimes, such as in Saudi Arabia, Turkey and Egypt; the promises of neoliberalism failed to materialize vis-à-vis socioeconomic performance; and therefore many educated (and other) people have flocked to the message of the Wahabism Brotherhood and their modern followers such as Al Qaeda, Al-Salafiya, Ansa Al Qaeda Brigades and Jemaah Islamiya (Katzman, 2005).

The 'New Terrorism' associated with radical Islamic networks is bent on greater fatalities in their war against relative US hegemony (along with its allies) in the Middle East and elsewhere. The Hawks in the Bush Administration are similarly bent on unilateral intervention in the region through violent regime change and wars. This has increased conflict in the Middle East and elsewhere. There have been attacks on civilians from both sides, whether as direct targets or the unconcerned effects of war. The costs of such terrorism and war are multiple, with transmission mechanisms negatively affecting performance in all directions. Some of the transmission mechanisms are illustrated in Table 7.3, below (see Frey et al., 2004a), although these examples are heterogeneous and do not concentrate purely on the 'new' terrorism.

These studies show that terrorism and the wars and conflicts caught up with it affect every major aspect of the economy. The most important components of private sector demand, consumption and investment, are significantly affected. Consumption expenditure can be affected through adversely impacting consumer confidence as people become fearful, reducing their geographical mobility and desire to visit certain shopping centres. Investment spending is usually impacted as a drop in business confidence increases uncertainty and expectations of profit decline. Critical aspects of the international economy, such as trade, FDI, tourism and airlines are impacted. Imports tend to decline as domestic demand suffers, while exports decline as the quality of products and innovation deteriorate. FDI falls off as domestic corporations perform below par and the overseas businesses are less inclined to operate in areas impacted by terrorism. Tourism and commercial airlines suffer as people go to places with more safety and protection, or develop alternative consumption patterns.

Contagion affects vast areas as nations not attacked yet linked to nations that are attacked are affected. This is an important amplifying affect associated with people's tendency to implicate whole areas that seem on the surface to be relatively homogenous. High levels of terrorism adversely affect GDP levels as consumption, investment, trade, FDI and tourism declines have negative impacts on the multiplier and accelerator. But broader measures of performance such as utility and life satisfaction seem to be more heavily impacted than the narrower variables. So affected by higher apparent levels of personal risk are people in the terrorism-affected areas that they are willing to pay very high prices for plane tickets, for instance, if terrorism would decline to zero. This is said to reflect their diminished levels of utility. And lastly, life satisfaction has been demonstrated to decline to create a 'peace premium' where the affected population are prepared to forgo very large levels of income for terrorism to decline to low levels when it has become part of everyday life.

Table 7.3: Impact of Terrorism on Socioeconomic Performance

Variable/ Author	Region	Period	Cost	Problem
Consumption (Eckstein and Tiddson, 2004)	Israel	1950–2003	C ↓ 5% per annum	Drop in Demand
Investment (Fielding, 2003)	Israel	1988-98	I_c↓ 28% I_m↓ 15%	Drop in Demand
International Trade (Nitsch and Schumacher, 2004)	Numerous	1968–79	Doubling Terrorism ↓ Bilateral Trade 4%	Lower Trade
FDI (Enders and Sandler, 1996)	Spain, Greece	1975–91 1976–91	12–14% ↓ FDI	Declining Investment
Tourism (Enders et al., 1992)	Europe	1974–88	$16.145b	Lower Growth
Tourism (Drakos and Kukan, 2003)	Meditterannean	1991–2000	89% of loss flows out of area	Contagion Spreads through Region
Airline Tickets (Ito and Lee, 2004)	USA, 9/11	2001–2003	10% ↓ in Yield	Corporate Bankruptcy
GDP per Capita (Eckstein and Tiddson, 2004)	Israel	1950–2003	'High' Terrorism ↓ GDP by 3.5% pa	Declining Performance
Terrorism Risk Factor (Viscusi and Zeckhauser, 2003)	Experimental Methods	2002	Willing to Pay 70% ↑ for Plane Tickets (for no terrorism)	Utility Loss
Life Satisfaction (Frey et al. 2004b)	Northern Ireland	2003	Willing to Forgo 41% of Income for 'Low' Terrorism level	Peace Income Premium

Overall, the aggregate costs of much higher than average levels of terrorism and war characteristic of the new form of terrorism are likely to be vast for those regions where radical Islamic networks and/or coalitions of the willing are active. This is true despite the fact that terrorism often has very limited direct affects. Much of the cost of terrorism is due to the fear and intimidation imposed on the civilian population, through social-psychological linkages to military force, technology, the media and opportunistic governments. As O'Hara (2004) and Mueller (2005) point out, relatively speaking very few people die of terrorist attacks compared with homicides, suicides, tuberculosis and heart attacks. Yet the social-psychological impact is often immense as systemic over-reaction by most parties amplify the costs many–fold.

CONCLUSION

This chapter has sought to analyse whether a new global military–terrorism social structure of accumulation (SSA) has emerged to contribute to long wave upswing in the early years of the new millennium. We found that the most important thing for the construction of an SSA is a series of institutions that promote global stability and conflict resolution, which contribute to socioeconomic performance. We delineated the main features of the current evolving military–strategic system. These included the imperial trend of US unilateralism, multilateralism, a new form of terrorism, a series of 'rouge states', the oil regime with the corporate-industrial state, neoliberalism and the increasing dominance of the US way of life. This structure of institutions was found to be promoting greater levels of instability and conflict, since the dual system of unilateralism–multilateralism is in disarray, new forms of terrorism linked to US unilateralism are heightening wars and disputes, the oil regime is contributing to conflict and corruption, while neoliberalism and the US way of life are creating a wave of insurgency against the 'infidels'. A major problem is the power vacuum since the demise of the Eastern Bloc and the emergence of even more conflicting groups such as the radical Islamic networks and the neo-conservatives in Washington.

Then we turned to the question of socioeconomic performance and found that the current structure of institutions is enhancing terrorism and war in the global system. Neoliberal reforms in the Arab world have failed to contribute to performance and hence stimulated the anger of Islamic radicals who abhor US institutions that fail to advance the cause of Muslims. Greater levels of terrorism associated with the new system is reducing private consumption and investment demand; adversely impacting FDI, tourism and trade; and reducing GDP growth, utility and life satisfaction. Greater levels of instability and conflict in the global system will likely continue reducing performance in critical areas. Therefore, it cannot be said that a new military–terrorism social structure of accumulation is emerging to enhance long wave upswing in the global political economy.

NOTES

1. While there are of course unilateral and multilateral trends in the current system, Frank Harvey is correct when he says that: 'there are no purely unilateral or multilateral strategies or policies; every major foreign policy initiative falls somewhere on a continuum (and often includes components of many strategies coexisting simultaneously). There are "principled" and "instrumental" forms of unilateralism, bilateralism and multilateralism, and these foreign policy options are often applied concurrently and strategically by all states at different points in time, occasionally within the same crisis' (Harvey 2003–04, p. 24).
2. Bob Rigg (2003) argues that the US underlined the Chemical Weapons Convention through demanding that the independently minded re-election of Director-General, Jose Bustani, be withdrawn; and ensuring that Iraq was prevented from joining the Convention. The US also encouraged Israel to expand its stock of weapons of mass destruction, despite the double standard that this perpetuated; and it is not bound by its earlier undertaking to refrain from using nuclear weapons against states that do not have them.
3. For instance, Isabelle Duyvesteyn (2004) critically analyses the notion of the 'new terrorism' and argues against it. Her critique is based on 'new terrorists' (a) 'acting transnationally', (b) 'being religious fanatics', (c) attacking as many people as possible, and (d) 'indiscriminately targeting victims'. She negates every one of these points, although not much is argued on the fourth point. The four parts of the 'new Terrorism' criteria used in this chapter, shown in the text of this chapter, are mostly different from her list. She ignores the tendencies, global networks (not simply 'transnational') and anti–'US Hegemony' aspects of the new terrorism. Many authors accept this change towards 'new Terrorism', including, for instance, one of the first to argue this (Hoffman, 1997) and, more recently, Kometer (2004), who says that 'The real difference is that for the militant Islamic movement, the strategy is a coherent one, where all four operational areas – motivation, organization, support, and operations – are congruent because they point to the same mechanism: global insurgency that gradually builds strength for a final takeover of the world. This is the nature of the war on which we are embarked' (p. 74). While I agree with this in large measure, I disagree with the 'final takeover of the world' remark as an exaggeration.
4. A related part of neoliberalism is the increasingly global economy, expanding the free movement of money capital, plus goods and services. National economies are becoming more global in the sense that they are increasing their dependency on the world market, capital is becoming more mobile, and corporations can move transnationally with few barriers to entry and exit. Through the WTO attempts are being made to limit tariffs on the movement of goods and services, minimize subsidies to exporters and domestic producers, and expand intellectual property rights. Through the workings of the IMF developing and emerging nations have been encouraged to reform state finances and open up capital markets to global competition. The World Bank has been encouraging underdeveloped nations to restructure their economies to promote markets to foster technological innovation and industrial development (see O'Hara, 2006).
5. FARC refers to the Revolutionary Armed Forces of Columbia, and has contributed a 'significant' (usually isolated) number of the so-called terrorist attacks listed in the US State Department statistics. FARC supported and often represented the rural peasants who prefer to have land ownership and collective structures of association rather than the government creating large land ownership structures with the dispossessed moving to the cities as wage labor. By the late 1990s, FARA controlled 60 per cent of the country, including the provision

of schools, decentralized judicial structures, and hospital services (Brittain, 2005, p. 23). Many peasants migrated to the FARC areas. There has been a history of US support for the central government, including recently with 'an attack on rural areas where local peasant farmers support ... FARC' (former US General James Hill), 'not against the guerrilla army itself' (Brittain, 2005, p. 28). In response, FARC has 'been moving away from small-scale operations and into large-scale, continuous, direct confrontations implemented through well-orchestrated, simultaneous attacks on state forces in many parts of the country' (Brittain, 2005, p. 31).

6. These statistics define religious as 'primarily religious', and therefore do not include terrorist groups that are primarily nationalist or fighting for independence for their homeland unless the religious element is the core aspect of the nationalism. The IRA, for instance, according to these figures, is primarily nationalist in orientation (rather than religious). If groups such as this were defined as religious then the statistics and argument would have to be re-analysed.

REFERENCES

Brittain, James J. (2005), 'The FARC-EP in Columbia: A Revolutionary Exception in an Age of Imperialist Expansion', Monthly Review: *An Independent Socialist Magazine*, 57, 20–33.

Burnham, Gilbert, Riyadh Lafta, Shannon Doocy and Les Roberts (2007), 'Mortality after the 2003 Invasion of Iraq: A Cross-Sectional Cluster Sample Survey', *Lancet*, 11 October 2006, www.theLancet.com (9 pages). (Accessed 15 May 2007)

Bush, George W. (2002), *The National Security Strategy of the United States of America*, Washington DC: White House.

Clark, William (2003), *Revisited – The Real Reasons for the Upcoming War with Iraq*, Mimeo, January.

Drakos, Konstantinos and Ali M. Kutan (2003), 'Regional Effects of Tourism on Tourism in Three Mediterranean Countries', *Journal of Conflict Resolution*, 47, 621–41.

Du Boff, Richard (2003), 'U.S. Hegemony: Continuing Decline, Enduring Danger', Monthly Review: *An Independent Socialist Magazine*, 55, 1–15.

Duyvesteyn, Isabelle (2004), 'How New is the New Terrorism?', *Studies in Conflict and Terrorism*, 27, 439–54.

Eckstein, Zvi and Daniel Tsiddon (2004), 'Macroeconomic Consequences of Terror: Theory and the Case of Israel', *Journal of Macroeconomics*, 51, 971–1002.

Enders, Walter and Todd Sandler (1996), 'Terrorism and Foreign Direct Investment in Spain and Greece', *Kyklos*, 49, 331–52.

Enders, Walter, Todd Sandler and Gerald F. Parise (1992), 'An Econometric Analysis of the Impact of Terrorism on Tourism', *Kyklos*, 45, 531–54.

Fielding, David (2003), 'Modelling Political Instability and Economic Performance: Israel Investment During the Infidada', *Economica*, 70, 159–86.

Fratianni, Michele and Heejoon Kang (2004), 'Borders and International Terrorism', *Working Paper*, Bloomington, Indiana: Graduate School of Business, Indiana University.

Frey, Bruno S., Simon Luechinger and Alois Stutzer (2004a), 'Calculating Tragedy: Assessing the Costs of Terrorism', *CESifo Working Paper*, 1341, Zurich: Institute for Empirical Research in Economics, University of Zurich.

Frey, Bruno S., Simon Luechinger and Alois Stutzer (2004b), 'Valuing Public Goods:

The Life Satisfaction Approach', *CESifo Working Paper*, 184, Zurich: Institute for Empirical Research in Economics, University of Zurich.

Gulick, John (2004), 'A Critical Appraisal of Peter Gowan's "Contemporary Intra-Core Relations and World Systems Theory": A Capitalist World-Empire or U.S.-East Asian Geo-Economic Integration?', *Journal of World-Systems Research*, 10, 502–15.

Harvey, Frank P. (2003–04), 'Addicted to Security: Globalized Terrorism and the Inevitability of American Unilateralism', *International Journal*, 22, 1–31.

Hoffman, Bruce (1997) 'Terrorism and WMD: Some Preliminary Hypotheses', *The Nonproliferation Review*, 5, 45–53.

Ikenberry, G. John (2002), 'America's Imperial Ambition', *Foreign Affairs*, 81, 44–60.

Ito, Harumi and Darin Lee (2004), 'Assessing the Impact of the September 11 Terrorist Attacks on U.S. Airline Demand', *Journal of Economics and Business*, 15, 22–44.

Kalpakian, Jack (2005), 'Building the Human Bomb: The Case of the 16 May 2003 Attacks in Casablanca', *Studies in Conflict and Terrorism*, 28, 113–27.

Katzman, Kenneth (2005), 'Al Qaeda: Profile and Threat Assessment', Washington DC: *Congressional Research Service*, Library of Congress.

Kern, Soeren (2005), 'Who is Running US Foreign Policy?', *USA-Transatlantic Dialogue*, 23, 1–9.

Kometer, Michael W. (2004), *The New Terrorism: The Nature of the War on Terrorism*, Maxwell Air Force Base, Alabama: Air University Press.

Krasner, Stephen D. (ed.) (1983), *International Regimes*, Cornell University Press: Ithaca & London.

Krause, Joachim (2004), 'Multilateralism: Behind the European Views', *The Washington Quarterly*, 27, 43–59.

Mueller, John (2006), 'Six Rather Unusual Propositions about Terrorism', *Terrorism and Political Violence*, 18, 15–32.

NCC (National Counterterrorism Centre) (2005), *A Chronology of Significant International Terrorism for 2004*, Washington DC: NCC.

Nitsch, Volker and Dieter Schumacher (2004), 'Terrorism and International Trade: An Empirical Investigation', *European Journal of Political Economy*, 20, 423–33.

Nunnenkamp, Peter (2004), 'Why Economic Growth has been Weak in Aran Countries: The Role of Exogenous Shocks, Economic Policy Failure and Institutional Deficiencies', *Kiel Discussion Paper*, 409. Kiel: Kiel Institute for World Economics.

O'Hara, Phillip Anthony (2004), 'The War on Terrorism, Political–Economic Contradictions and Policy Measures', in P.A. O'Hara (ed.), *Global Political Economy and the War on Terrorism: Performance, Institutions, Problems and Policies*, London and New York: Routledge.

O'Hara, Phillip Anthony (2005) 'The Contradictions of Neoliberal Globalization', *Journal of Interdisciplinary Economics*, 33(3), 231–59.

O'Hara, Phillip Anthony (2006), *Growth and Development in the Global Political Economy: Social Structure of Accumulation and Modes of Regulation*, London and New York: Routledge/Taylor & Francis.

Rigg, Bob. (2003) 'International Law or US Hegemony: From Chemical Weapons to Iraq', *Open Democracy*, 3, 1–6.

Roberts, Les; Riyadh Lafta, Richard Garfield, Jamal Khudhairi and Gilbert Burnham (2004), 'Mortality Before and After the 2003 Invasion of Iraq: Cluster Sample Survey', *Lancet*, 29 October 2004, 1–8.

Schmidt, Alex P. (2004) 'Frameworks for Conceptualising Terrorism', *Terrorism and Political Violence*, 16, 197–221.

Testas, Abdelaziz (2004), 'Determinants of Terrorism in the Muslim World: An Empirical Cross-Sectional Analysis', *Terrorism and Political Violence*, 16, 253–73.

US Department of State (1992–2004), *Patterns of Global Terrorism*, Washington DC: USDS. Numerous Years.

Viscusi, W. Kip and Richard J. Zeckhauser (2003), 'Sacrificing Civil Liberties to Reduce Terrorism Risks', *Journal of Risk and Uncertainty*, 26, 99–120.

Wallerstein, Immanuel (2002), 'The Eagle Has Crash Landed', *Foreign Policy* July/August, 60–68.

PART TWO

The (Welfare) State, The New Economy And New Institutional Deals

8. New Deals of New Social Entities. Evolution of Old Friends: Workers – Firms – Classes – States

Michael Scheibenreif and Hardy Hanappi

INTRODUCTION

Traditionally economics has considered its set of relevant social entities to be rather stable, even in the long–run. On the other hand scholars from different schools of thought placed a different emphasis on the importance of certain of these concepts: while classical economists evidently thought that individual human decisions are logically dependent on the social role in which the individual is embedded, economists propagating the marginalist revolution in the late 19th century preferred to turn the main direction of determination around. Class membership was considered to be co-determined by individual predisposition. A special case was Schumpeter's approach, emphasizing that entrepreneurs were thought to be a very special breed whose innate properties lay at the roots of the class of capitalists. Another, formally extremely appealing approach assumed representative individuals that exhibit features of all classes in a unified manner. Class relations thus were modelled to be resolved within the structure of each human individual, the relations between individuals therefore might be formulated without them and could be freewheeling, i.e. being solely dependent on preference–driven market forces. The roots of today's mainstream economics still can be traced back to this variant of the marginalist school.

Only with the dawn of the world economic crisis in the 1930s did the emphasis of economic theories shift back towards larger social entities. With Keynes's work a surrogate of the old working class – now called 'effective demand' – entered the scene again. And, to be sure not to miss important players in a world profoundly changed by the interference of the labour movement, Keynes also re-introduced the state, a regulating institution reflecting the prevailing results of class compromise – as well as the class of rentiers, a far cry from the old feudal class. With this new regulating organization, the state, temporarily stable relations between relevant social entities assumed the character of a deal, i.e. an agreement of conflicting parties that specifies the rules of behaviour of all players. If the dynamics of the political economy develop in a way that endangers the survival of the old players, then it needs a new deal.

This chapter puts forward the rather daring hypothesis that in the last decades the global political economy has been entering a stage that has started to dissolve the set of old relevant social entities. In particular such central concepts as 'worker', 'firm', 'class' and 'state' have to be redefined or substituted, or amended by more adequate concepts. In the body of the chapter a more detailed criticism of these concepts will be provided. Implicitly it is assumed that adequacy also means that concepts are apt to be understood as instruments to change social evolution; they have to be potential instruments for groups in society that want to take their fate in their own hands. For that reason it is also important to take a look at empirically observed dynamics in the global economy. Economic theory in the new millennium surely needs a sharp methodological turn from iconoclastic introspection towards empirically oriented and theoretically sound socio-economic and political investigation and design. What is provided in this chapter, are just some outlines hinting at necessary future research directions.

In the final part of the chapter it is discussed in which way the concept of a deal has to be transformed if the change of the set of players proposed above is taken seriously. In the old, Keynesian setting it was very clear that the arena where a deal was struck by a set of players was the nation state. With continental economic players, a changed physiognomy of production units and globally extremely diverse household and working structures (to name only a few difficulties), the environment for deals has changed dramatically. Again we try to contribute some innovative ideas to these problems, and conclude with a confession that this chapter hopefully contributes to the progress of the work of other researchers while it will certainly remain work in progress for a longer time period.

THE LANDSLIDE OF THE GLOBAL POLITICAL ECONOMY AFTER WORLD WAR II

After sixty years a look back at the dramatic changes that took place in this comparatively short span of time since World War II reveals that many of the traditional methods economists are trained to use when describing their subject of investigation are not adequate any more. While prospects for a revival of the type of capitalism experienced in the two centuries before seemed to be doomed immediately after the war, a new type of capitalist mode of production seized hold of the world economy – first disguised behind a veil of adaptive corrections, the so-called 'social market economy', forced by socialist and social-democratic policy interventions, later (in the early 1980s) followed by a clearly conservative policy stance. During these decades the most advanced economies not only experienced a continuous and unprecedented growth boom, they also became extremely interdependent.

As a consequence the nation state, the prime political unit of theoretical considerations of economists up to Keynes, changed its physiognomy. Internal intervention was increasingly bound to convene to international relations; today the major institutional players in political economy are now continental units. This change, already anticipated in Bretton Woods, had a deep impact on the abilities of nation states to use certain policy instruments; e.g. exchange rate regimes are arrangements between nations, where size, economic and military power evidently translates into bargaining power. In that sense any consideration of national economic policies immediately has to be considered in the light of the overall political setting. Macroeconomics has been even more likely to be understood as political economy dynamics in recent decades. There is no room any more for innocent questions like 'Why is one nation wealthier than another one?' (Adam Smith), or 'Can a nation state compensate for cyclical recessions of private business activity by using temporary public deficits?' (J.M. Keynes). To be operationally useful each such question must be embedded in a well-defined global political situation from the outset.

But it is not only the structure and the more interwoven character of political units that makes analysis more difficult. The second major change that occurred concerns production units, in vulgar economic theory often called firms. While the assumption of a model of a representative firm never really made sense – even a concise reading of Schumpeter reporting 19th century structures implies essential differences between firms – the divergence of types of production units has really exploded in the last sixty years.[1] Given the common basic characteristic that a capitalist production unit is bound to make profits to survive, there still are worlds in between the working modes – that is how this goal is achieved. Indeed large parts of profits today are made by transnational enterprises using deteriorating exchange rates of low-income countries. These profits clearly are politically enforced and mediated by international currency markets. On the other hand an increasing share of the small and medium-sized enterprises (SMEs) in Europe has to receive parts of their profits as payments from public institutions to be profitable at all.[2] Again this turn to a more politically-oriented profit source has diverted the economic activities of SMEs away from the traditional goals of revenue maximization and cost minimization, and considerable time nowadays is devoted to political lobbying. With this new type of diverse behaviour of production units new institutions representing agents with similar goals gained power: Formal organizations (unions, chambers of commerce and the like), but in particular also informal networks of associations that escaped any systematic recording of national or international agencies, are combining forces in changing coalitions that to a large part determine global economic policy.

To understand the working of the supply side of the economy in the new millennium thus involves a thorough analysis of institutional dynamics, at least on a continental basis. The ancient notion of entrepreneurship fails completely to enhance our knowledge about R&D developments, not to mention education, invention and knowledge dynamics in general. As a closer look at the classic contributions of evolutionary economists reveals, the concept of entrepreneurship was never meant to explain the emergence of knowledge at all.[3] Capitalism was characterized as the process of unintentional productivity gains (in the long–run socially beneficial for all) that occur due to the side-effects of capital allocation of profit-seeking capital owners. Capitalists as a political class among many other things implement political regimes and combine elements of existing technical and social knowledge to increase the profitability of their capital. They do not act as knowledge producers per se, they do not even provide social environments that enhance knowledge production, what they actually do is that they only embed new combinations of what they encounter as profitable ideas in certain given social environments. Nevertheless this task is not trivial and will have to be taken care of in the future – but it is not knowledge production.

Knowledge production proper has always been the activity of scientists financed primarily by political authorities using tax revenues.[4] Though this fact today is sometimes hidden by the titles given to this type of funding (e.g. money spent for 'national defence' in the USA) it is evident that major universities as well as the funds of the most important laboratories are mainly financed with public money. In that sense they also are responsible to the public, and not to the profitability criteria put forward by firm representatives that are so omnipresent in current debates. Societies thus via indirect and mostly little developed feedbacks could and should control the directions and diversity of their knowledge production. As a matter of fact a broader and more informed debate on education and knowledge production design has only started in the recent decade. The difficulties that are accompanying it are mainly due to the rapidly increasing amount of noise, i.e. inadequate information that often is hard to distinguish from valuable knowledge. Why noise and knowledge are exploding can be traced back to two interacting forces: maintenance of political power by ideological means and support of this objective by a boost of information and communication technologies (ICT).

The two central representative devices of the ICT revolution are computer networks and mobile phones (compare Figures 8.1 and 8.2, source: UNCTAD, 2004). They are currently responsible for a profound change of cognitive capabilities and communication habits of the human species; their impact can hardly be overestimated.

Figure 8.1: The Information Technology Revolution

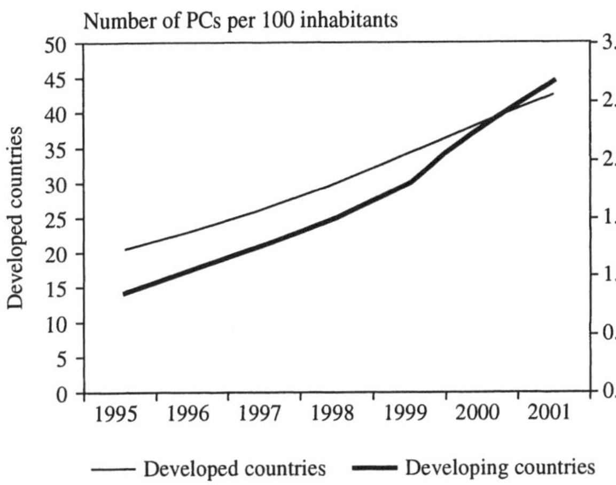

Figure 8.2: The Communication Technology Revolution

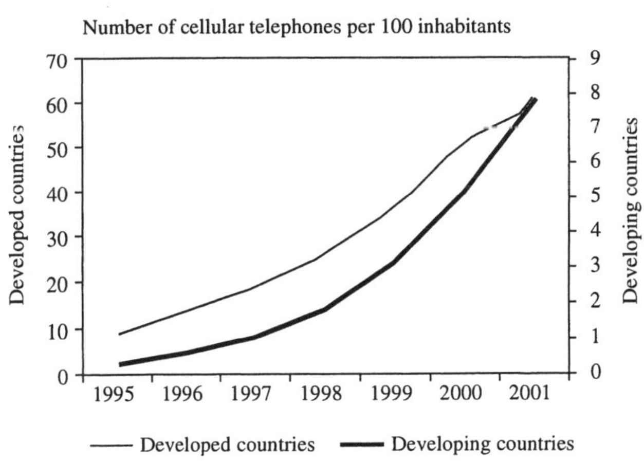

The overall mid-term impact on the global political economy is extremely hard to predict. What seems to be sure is that these devices in principle have the potential to enhance the design of a global democracy – though its implementation surely is a different story.

What currently can be observed rather resembles a quickly growing income difference between major groups of states of the world economy and somewhat slower increasing income differences within most states.[5] There is not much evidence that the deeply rooted properties of social and economic structures that are different between states started to converge after World War II (compare Figures 8.3 and 8.4, source UNCTAD, 2004). It rather seems to be the case that under the surface of a converging information sphere of the ruling elites in the big cities (e.g. finance and fashion), the current mode of globally integrated capitalism exploits and deepens local, often historically grown, inequalities.

Figure 8.3: Global Inequality in Output

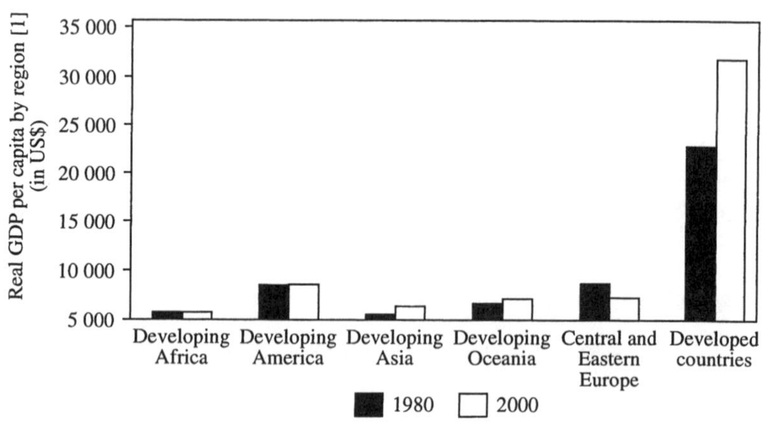

As a consequence the old perspective of the labour movement, namely that an internationally united working class will emerge – 'The worker does not have a home country', Karl Marx proclaimed – seems to be misleading. It is rather clear now that capital does not have a homeland and uses the homeward–bound cultural and economic specificities of workers to divide and conquer by means of ICT–supported ideological power.

Figure 8.4: Global Inequality in Productivity

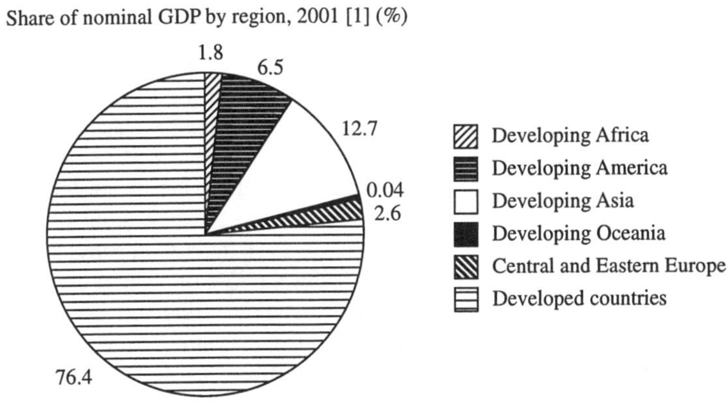

WORKERS – FIRMS – CLASSES – STATES

In the framework of classical political economy a worker was defined as a human individual in a capitalist economy that produced surplus value. This definition presupposed the existence of a capitalist, i.e. a blueprint of typical behaviour of an owner of means of production, as well as the validity of an adequate concept of social value. As sketched in the last chapter actual developments in the world economy in recent decades have blurred both notions. On the one hand labour productivity has soared and labour inputs thus can be provided by a decreasing number of workers.[6] In particular the related upsurge of profits enabled capital owners to entertain a whole scale of structured payments to split workers into different strata[7] – they are split within production units, between labour types, between regions and more recently between continents. To experience one's own position in society in terms of political economy, namely as a worker, a provider of surplus value, has become increasingly unlikely. In addition social value, for classical political economists 'labour value', is not a concept that can easily be grasped, not to mention quantification of a surplus. Workers today often feel exhausted due to the enormously increased labour intensity, but the permanent ideological influence of a subjectivist interpretation of individual use values lets any thought of being exploited dissolve in a feeling of personal failure.

As a consequence it probably will be the duty of professional knowledge producers, of scientists, to develop an adequate theory of social values. Such a theory evidently will be in sharp contrast to moral aspirations and religious attitudes which misuse the concept of social values today. Only with such a well elaborated concept at hand[8] can it be attempted to determine the position of the different strata of the global political economy today. And only with such a scientific evaluation at our disposal can the political implementation of improvements in a labour movement perspective be envisaged.

Production units will always be needed, though what will be produced will (and has always) changed rather dramatically. Looking at the long–run the nature of production units seems to return to its early roots in merchant capitalism: as in the early times (e.g. the East India Company) the fate of large companies is tightly interwoven with the fate of large political units – the political economy in the literal interpretation of the concept re-emerges. In between, in the age of industrial capitalism[9] prevailing from the 18th to the early 20th centuries, a somewhat different setting seemed to take on shape: all political agendas, including a monopoly on coercive and ideological power, are concentrated in the hands of the nation state. Within this nation state a regime free from all power relations, only regulated by market forces that work between independent individuals, prevails. So far the vision – the actual political world in which it had emerged–vanished in World War I and had to give way to ideologically oriented movements (e.g. Fascism, Stalinism) and large–scale production systems (e.g. Fordism and Stalinist production systems: Hanappi, 1994, pp.112–61). With World War II the first competitor for a new political economy model, Fascism, failed, and the overwhelming hegemonic power of the United States enabled its firms to become truly transnational models for global production units. Some European and Japanese firms, mainly due to their advantage of starting with brand new capital stocks after World War II, managed to produce some imitators. Already during that period it became evident that different strata of types of production units would build the production system of the future. When in the early 1990s the remaining competitor of the US model, the Soviet union, crashed as a political system, the surviving production units in its former hemisphere added a new variety to the strata of the global production system.

In the last ten years another variant of a Stalinist production system, the Chinese model, has flourished and now is producing the majority of goods traded in the world economy. To be very clear: this most successful contemporary model is based on a congruence of military, political and economic power – a political economy in the immediate sense of the word. Production units in China are not really exposed to internal market forces, but rather work as command systems, external relations of China are to a large extent politically centralized. Though business relations in the large centres, like Shanghai, are changing quickly it would be simply wrong to consider these production units to be in the same category as US firms or European firms. At the moment it is not clear at all which type of global division of labour related to the different strata of production unit types is emerging – and is feasible in the mid-term. Decision-makers in this process will be changing coalitions of military, political and economic elites, with power probably distributed in exactly this order.

As the discussion of workers and firms already vividly shows, an innocent and simple debate on classes and class relations is not possible. If there is no easily determined proletariat as a self-conscious class, then the simplistic notion of the dictatorship of such a class is pointless. The negation of the alienating features of industrial capitalism evidently can take place rather as a revival of ever larger, though nevertheless faster (thanks to ICT) political feedback loops. These feedbacks will come from a very complicated structured public, a global public that must not only be well nurtured but also well educated – something very far away from the current situation. If the concept of class is to evolve into such a new concept of a structured, public sovereign of last resort, then the major stumbling blocks towards this goal are religious movements. Whenever enlightenment and education fail, religious leaders step in to use ideological (increasingly ICT supported) power for exploitation. Together with the return of politics in economics comes the return of the battle for atheism, i.e. the agenda of the enlightenment. It is a necessary component for the further evolution of what was previously known as the class concept. Global coalitions of political feedback groups are not a strange idea; indeed international finance mechanisms – increasingly populated by public funds, e.g. pension funds – are already paving the way for more conscious and politically legitimated ways for such linkages.

In a certain sense this evolutionary task is the hardest of all since it runs completely counter to current trends. It therefore might emerge under the disguise of rather surprising forms, like international finance. It might also get some additional support from groups gaining their consciousness in political economics by being confronted with global environmental problems. In any case the difficulties of organizing, focusing and above all providing the theoretical basis for intelligent design will be enormous.

Finally it has to be kept in mind that nation states will change their role, but will not vanish. Their possible future importance will not stem from their agency in economic policy; they will rather be instruments, local devices and sensors, in this respect. What might be their major contribution could be their role as units of cultural identity. In providing diversity within the larger units of the political economy they could act as safeguards against monolithic aspirations of central framing authorities. By translating ideas to and from different cultural languages, seeing them in different contexts, the overall space for reactions to new challenges is extended. As shown with respect to the innovation activities of firms in a recent paper (Hanappi and Hanappi-Egger, 2004) there is an inverse relationship between the change of speed of the environment and the optimal diversity of behavioural responses. Too little internal diversity makes large units extremely vulnerable if environments change fast, on the other hand too much diversity in slowly changing environments is an unnecessary luxury. Nation states thus could serve as culture pools that breed potential social innovation for the larger political economy unit. If this suggestion turns out to be correct it is evident that Europe has a promising starting position.[10]

CONCLUDING REMARKS ON NEW DEALS

Who will be the parties that will have to strike a deal? And first of all, what does the concept of a deal imply?

The history of social evolution comes in time packages: for each time package a certain set of social relations, rule systems, law systems and corresponding executive powers seem to be frozen – at least when they are compared to the short periods of extraordinary fast dynamics and flux that divide the frozen states. A deal usually is an attempt to freeze relations, either immediately after a period of turmoil or even during this transition phase. It is meant to pave the way towards a new state of temporary stability.

To reach out for a *new* deal implies that the old deal does not work any more. In other words, the relative stability the old deal once provided is vanishing. As a matter of fact, new deals usually are not only characterized by new agreements to be formulated by the same old bargaining partners, they most often are also new because new players have entered the scene.

Roosevelt's famous New Deal was a proposal made after the Great Depression to implement a new mechanism between firms, the state and workers to prevent similar economic catastrophes in the future. What Roosevelt proposed for the domestic economy of the US was a new deal; and with a similar motivation what Keynes proposed in Bretton Woods as a fixed exchange rate system for international economic relations was a new deal proposed for nation states. Players in these deals were contemporary, but different. Interestingly enough most of the deals struck in this period were intact for an incredibly long period. Only the most recent developments – mainly initiated by the breakdown of the Soviet hemisphere and the follow-up of a Bush administration that aggressively has been changing most written and unwritten laws of international conduit – have made it evident that a new deal is waiting to be designed.

In the light of the discussion of the previous chapter it is clear that the new players that could strike such a deal have not yet been constituted. Of course, there are some old players, like the UNO or the OECD, who certainly will be important again. Other important bargaining partners, e.g. the international scientific community, have not found an organizational form, not to speak of a consistent mindset.

Others again, like China, are of utmost power and influence but lack any appreciative physiognomy in the views of their possible bargaining partners. China's future economic policy is perceived to be like an unguided missile: everybody hopes to benefit and at the same time is afraid of being destroyed.

Latin America is currently entering a period of industrial revolution. In a few respects this process is comparable to the corresponding classical period in Europe, but in most others this development should be characterized by a learning process, and should circumvent the well-known painful experiences the old world had to go through.

In this debate another extremely important bargaining partner comes into sight: international finance. Who's that? There is no global institution to manage world finance yet.[11]

Other potential bargaining partners at the moment only exist as latent forces too. Most pressing are the needs for a voice of those masses of the population that do not have any education or socioeconomic perspective at all, where some 30 thousands die every day from starvation.

This short and eclectic list should be sufficient to show how enormous the task envisaged by a new deal really is. Only to name the potential bargaining partners, to constitute them, is more difficult than dozens of human genome projects – it probably is more urgent too. But still a success would only be the starting point for designing and bargaining. Despite these difficulties, and as the old masters of new deals have shown so impressively, there is no room for despair; there is an incredibly large and growing community of scientists out there that – if it joins forces – might be able to act as a catalyst.

NOTES

1. There is a rich body of literature documenting and interpreting this process, starting with Chandler, (1977) and still flourishing today (e.g. Hollingsworth and Boyer, 1997; Whitley, 2000).
2. Subsidies for farmers are only one outstanding example, tax exemptions, cheap credit or low land rents are other forms of this wide variety of forms with which public bodies are aiming to help businesses to survive.
3. A good example is Schumpeter (compare Hanappi and Hanappi-Egger, 2004).
4. This even holds for the scholars financed by monarchs in the late middle ages. Today political authority has usually been passed over to the democratically elected governments of nation states.
5. An interesting study of parallels (between now and the late 19th century) of global income inequalities – both theoretically and empirically – is Aghion and Williamson (1998).

6. As Wood and Ridao-Cano (1996) show the emergence of the corresponding skill difference of workers might in turn speed up the divergence between developed and less developed parts of the global economy.
7. Already in the 1850s, while Marx was publishing his 'Das Kapital', the British ruling class was busy ameliorating the fate of the local working class. A conscious and decisive attempt to disperse resistance and to export exploitation – a very successful attempt indeed.
8. It still seems to be the methodology of augmented and enhanced, dynamic input–output frameworks, which is most promising as a starting point for this research project.
9. For a more precise definition of industrial capitalism compare Hanappi (1988).
10. There are indeed the first signs of a reversal of the brain drain from Europe to the USA that occurred during and immediately after World War II (compare e.g. Rifkin (2004). The preference formation of academics sometimes is a good indicator for prosperity.
11. To discuss the issues related to international finance would go beyond the scope of this chapter. Recent work in much the same direction of what is proposed here can be found in Aglietta and Rebérioux (2005).

REFERENCES

Aghion Ph. and Williamson J.G. (1999), *Growth, Inequality and Globalization*, Cambridge University Press, Cambridge (UK).

Aglietta M. and Rebérioux A. (2005), *Corporate Governance Adrift: A Critique of Shareholder Value*, Edward Elgar, Cheltenham, UK and Northampton, MA, USA.

Chandler A.D. (1977), *The Visible Hand*, Harvard University Press, Massachusetts.

Hanappi H. (1988), 'The Stages of Industrial Capitalism', in: *Proceedings of the International Workshop on Technological and Social Factors in Long Term Fluctuations*, Siena 1986, Springer, Heidelberg.

Hanappi H. and Hanappi-Egger E. (2004), 'New Combinations. Taking Schumpeter's concept seriously', *International Schumpeter Society*, bi-annual Conference 2004, Bocconi University (Milano, Italy), 2004.

Hodgson G.M. et al. (eds) (2001), *Capitalism in Evolution*, Edward Elgar, Cheltenham, UK and Northampton, MA, USA.

Hollingsworth R. and Boyer R. (1997), *Contemporary Capitalism: The Embeddedness of Institutions*, Cambridge University Press, Cambridge (UK).

Rifkin J. (2004), *The European Dream*, Penguin Books, New York.

UNCTAD (2004), *Development and Globalization: Facts and Figures*, United Nations.

Whitley R. (2000), *Divergent Capitalisms*, Oxford University Press, Oxford.

Wood A. and Ridao-Cano C. (1996), 'Skill, Trade and International Inequality', *IDS Working Paper 47*, University of Sussex, Sussex (UK).

9. The Death of the Family? Evolution of a New Deal Between Biological and Social Reproduction

Hardy Hanappi and Edeltraud Hanappi-Egger

INTRODUCTION

Since in many discourses on the development of the family biological, social and ideological lines of argument often appear to be intermingled, the first section of the chapter tries to disentangle these components and to arrive at a more appropriate description of the relations between these spheres. Evolutionary biology, in particular a fashionable part of it called socio-biology, reached out to explain the dynamics of human families in terms of descriptions of animal behaviour. Since the latter clearly is strongly linked to the conditions experienced by groups of animals – including the respective responses of the members of the group, eventually consisting of different biological species – there seems to be good reason to call this behaviour 'social'. Nevertheless it has to be clearly distinguished from the use of the term 'social' in the sciences concerned with human societies. For the humanities the special characteristic of the human species that distinguishes it from other mammals also implies that social behaviour cannot be naively derived from animal behaviour. In a further reaching argument it is also evident that the confusing misuse of concepts is not just a random error, it rather follows rules of ideological combat between opposing scientific – if not to say political – camps. The baseline positions of these camps are to be outlined to get a clearer picture of what really is at stake if the transformation of family structures is investigated.

The second section then concentrates on a description of the old (post - World War II) deal that was struck between macro-determinants of family structures and micro-opportunities and restrictions of individuals constituting the families. As will become clear from our argument, revolt from below as well as destruction from above was an unavoidable endogenous development starting in the mid-1960s and leading to the current state of dissolving and reshaping forms. The determinants of the revolt from below are diverse. They range from a crisis in the demand for education that cannot be adequately fulfilled within the families to the emancipation of women blowing up traditional gender roles. Destruction from above is mainly a consequence of the forces of advanced integrated capitalism, which penetrate families via the necessities transmitted by labour markets that in turn are accompanied by manipulative ideological role models. Of course, even the new form of advanced integrated capitalism will need a small social unit of about the size of a family. But what will it look like, and can it be reconciled with the aspirations coming from the revolts from below?

In the third section we take a look at the possibilities for a New Deal. Indeed, the enormously increased interdependence between social entities – economically, ideologically, even biologically (global catastrophes) – makes any such new arrangement an implicitly global design of a future political economy. Families, sometimes disguised in the more economically oriented concept of a household, are just one element in a rich setting of institutional structures encompassing economic and political activities. Institutional change, as a response to the evolution of political economy and initiator of further development of the latter, in many ways implies changes in family structures. Permanent or at least more fluent institutional change enforces and enables more fluent changes in family structures. Nevertheless there have to be lower limits for the inputs to the reproductive functions – economically, socially and culturally – that families are providing, and the institutional framework must ensure that these limits are respected. Indeed this is one of the foremost goals that institutional design – however evolutionary it might be – has to put on its agenda. A few spotlights on important issues are presented here.

FAMILY: A MULTI-LAYERED CONCEPT

From the point of view of a scientific discipline that is concerned with living systems in general, i.e. biology, the smallest unit of reproduction of a species is indeed an extremely fascinating object of investigation. Though it sometimes escapes the attention of scientists, it is nevertheless evident that the life-span of individual members of a species is finite – it is only a limited countermovement of organized behaviour against the second law of thermodynamics – while the transformation of individual life into new-born individual life enables the emergence of a considerably longer lasting existence of a living system labelled species. The locus of this transformation which (in somewhat philosophical terms) negates the finiteness of individual life is the family.

Darwin, the biologist, has to be credited for the revolutionary insight that species are not a given set – as the dominant ideological institution of his time, the church, proclaimed – but are themselves subject to evolution. At any moment the variety of existing species is in a state of transition, and Darwin's most celebrated idea of a mechanism of evolution therefore is just an immediate consequence of his aforementioned hypothesis: If you do not believe[1] in the existence of a given set of living systems that Noah saved on his ark, then you are obliged to describe the dynamics that explain the currently observed species. Inheritance and variation, mutation and finally selection are the sub-processes that can be distinguished in these dynamics – and they presuppose an interaction between individuals of a species. The space of this smallest unit of (re-)production of a species is delimited by the group of interacting individual members; it is the biological ancestor of the family (abbreviated as BAF).

In the animal kingdom Darwinian evolution – the mechanism itself, not only its material – comes in many varieties. In many respects the central concepts necessary to describe it are copy-making[2] and random variation. At the nodes where individual life is transformed into new individual life, i.e. in the BAF, these two concepts play a crucial role too as a brief look at the model of the genetic algorithm immediately reveals. Note that for matters of consistency the Darwinian mechanism must itself have been evolutionary selected.

Interaction within one BAF is linked to other BAFs as well as to other outside circumstances, the environment. Indeed, as the investigation of species shows, copying and producing variety not only needs organization within each BAFs but also organization of the local group of BAFs, inter-BAF organization. This two-fold organization, within BAFs and in between BAFs, constitutes a species. The growth of a species thus simply is the growth of the number of BAFs it organizes. As the environment as well as the inter-BAF relations change with growing and resource–competing species, variety becomes more important.[3] Differences in BAF organization, how strong they are and how often they occur, can be seen as ancestors of the accumulated knowledge of a species. Note that in the animal kingdom no single BAF is aware of the knowledge of the species that is implicit in the variety of behavioural forms and their inter-BAF organization.

It cannot be doubted that many features which the biological perspective has elaborated sound so familiar – in a double sense – that it is tempting to apply them immediately to the human species. And is it not the case that after all humans, to a certain extent still are mammals? This is the point where it becomes important to launch a hypothesis on how the human species differs from other species. The standard argument usually refers to two closely linked features: humans have cognitive abilities not found in other species, and they can use them to develop as tool-making animals. To appreciate the linkage: Cognitive model-building is just a certain kind of tool, and tool-making presuppose anticipation, i.e. cognitive model-building.

It is this rupture in evolution that characterizes the step from a BAF to a family within human society.[4] It remains true that inside and outside organization, families and societies always come in a package; but both organizational forms now are radically different.

Imitation, what was called copying before, now is not only restricted to repetition due to visual or other sensual perceptions, it is mediated by spoken and written language. An information environment filled with well defined signs opens up and links the species. With the use of language memory that survives individual lifetimes can be built up. Moreover this memory can be transmitted and shared by the families of a society, a necessary prerequisite for the transformation of random variation.

Now choice can suddenly use memory to distinguish between possible anticipated futures, the past is reflected as possible future past. There clearly remains an element of uncertainty, but choice nevertheless is directed and not random. Producing more variation by admitting risky choices of family mechanisms therefore is a choice of a society confronted with fast–changing environments. More traditional societies with little scope for variation hinge on imitation and can flourish only in rather stable environments.

The family, in the perspective of this social layer, is characterized as a group of interacting individuals that convene to the more or less formally constituted norms of a society, but to a certain extent also make and break these norms.

A major reason for the success of the human species as measured by biological standards, i.e. by population growth, has been the application of its anticipatory powers to exploit nature. At least since the revolution in agriculture, some 7000 years BC , growth rates of other living systems have been systematically manipulated to increase growth rates of societies. And there is no doubt that exploitation of nature always was accompanied by 'exploitation of man by man', as the classics dubbed it. But note that there is an immediate difficulty implied with this notion: If you increase a population growth rate by reducing another population growth rate, then you necessarily are talking about different populations: society consists of classes.

If this type of exploitation actually exists, then family organization will reflect class relations too. Families belonging to one type of class will be organized differently from families belonging to another class. As is the case with other exploited populations in nature, the exploiting class will try to strike an optimal balance: do not let the growth rate of the exploited decrease too much, but take away their growth if they grow above a certain rate. Early British capitalism indeed promised to have implemented a stable political system that enabled economic mechanisms regulating such an exploitation regime.[5] Families of workers evidently were very different from feudal families. More recently, Göran Therborn (2004) has written an important book outlining the differences in family mechanisms, which are determined by political economy.

But while many differences between family types surely can be observed and categorized, a few basic similarities inherited from BAFs might also prove to be essential for a proper understanding of families: There is a rather fundamental and more or less sudden increase in utility, call it lust, that accompanies sexual intercourse. Though biologists still are not sure about the origin and advantages of sex – and recently would describe its coincidence with lust rather as a side effect[6] – anticipated lust as an incentive certainly has experienced a boost with the emergence of the human species. No other animal has developed a comparable culture of sexual intercourse.

Exploitation, in turn, does not stop with the simple act of taking away somebody else's outputs to enhance one's own growth process. As soon as there is a developed information sphere, strategic behaviour becomes an option. It signifies the third layer of the concept of family – the ideological level. Strategic behaviour means that choices are made by taking into account that other decision makers will base their decisions on elements they take from the information sphere, from pieces of communication and information that can be posted there. It is thus possible to exploit desires that exist in the information sphere, i.e. use the actions they induce their carriers to perform, actions that reduce their growth potential, and actions the consequences of which can contribute to the growth of the exploiter.[7]

The coincidence of sexual lust and procreation has always been a central source of ideological exploitation; in particular its systematic application via family organization is evident. With the evolution of the capitalist mode of production the very specific ideological form of the bourgeois family, propagated as a family model for all classes, acquired an unprecedented importance for the maintenance of this mode of production. The ruling ideology thus promoted the vision of a family mechanism that combined monogamy with a strict power monopoly of the father, i.e. patriarchy.[8] While the latter was meant to reflect a kind of naturally given law that also was to be found in the power structures in capitalist factories, the former was meant to subordinate reproductive functions to this given power structure. As patriarch within his family even the poorest working man could imagine to resemble his boss. And with monogamy, a clear-cut functional divide of reproductive work was implied too. As far as the sexual desires of the patriarch exceeded the boundaries of his monogamous relation he could break this rule as often as his wealth permitted it. Sexual desires of wives were not simply ignored in this family model, female emotions were thought to be 'naturally' channelled towards child rearing and housekeeping. The excess of sexual energy, of lust, thus was regulated along gender–specific roles.

Though this ideological vision of the bourgeois family never was really lived in families of all classes of a society, its influence cannot be denied. Only after periods when the capitalist mode of production was called into question by upheavals and revolutions did this ideological form become less important.

With the arrival of the 20th century, with World War I, the October revolution and its consequences, the evolution of production systems and ideological warfare, the actual social forms of families – at least in Europe – diverged from the old ideological form of the bourgeois family. The search for a new ideological form started.

A BRAVE NEW COMPROMISE AND ITS WATERLOO

World War II had a devastating influence on European societies, including not only the loss of about half of their capital stocks, but also a loss of orientation of micro-units. In some of the core countries of European culture genocide of unimaginable dimensions had taken place; economic, political and military hegemony had shifted away to the USA and to the Soviet Union. It is not surprising that the new ideological family model of Western European populations had to be imported from North America. Families in the movies produced in the USA were young, happy and market-oriented: a rebirth of a modernized bourgeois family model seemed to be at the doorsteps. Walt Rostow propagated the arrival of the age of high mass consumption in the USA, and that all countries of the world would sooner or later end up in this stage – including the appropriate American family model (compare Rostow, 1960).

The United States had not been directly hit by the war; its most impressive experience of a crisis had been the great depression of the 1930s. And the remedy for this crisis had been an economic policy, Roosevelt's New Deal, which in the end produced a new ideological family model too. The new ideology was surprisingly simple: it was a model of people's capitalism. In the ideological vision every individual is split into parts that belong to different classes, e.g. partly worker, partly capitalist and partly rentier. This fits well with the ideas of contemporary Fordism, which held that the maintenance of the circular flow between members of the society should play a major role for a firm's wage policy as well as for the states' incomes policy.

Homogeneous families consisting of highly heterogeneous individual members were just the households needed for that model.[9] Every individual earns a wage that corresponds to its marginal productivity that in turn is evaluated via labour markets that ensure full employment at equilibrium wages. No need to worry about variety necessary for selection, variety in that vision is just an in-built property of individuals: You earn what you are, as you are what you earn! This brave new libertarian compromise was the promise of the 1950s.

But once again reality deviated rather sharply from this vision. It is useful to distinguish between rebellions against this family model that were initiated by family members themselves, and destructive forces that were the consequences of processes taking place outside the families.

A typical rebellion from below came from the disappointed aspirations of young pupils and students who found that equal opportunities for education – and thus entrance into the world of young and happy couples that populated the family vision of the movies – were not provided by the existing education infrastructure. The pupil movement in Italy as well as the student rebellions in France, Germany and the USA in the late 1960s were just the tip of the iceberg of deep cultural re-orientation.

What was pivotal for the lasting impact of that cultural break was the fact that its carriers were largely in a certain phase of their personal development, which always has to be considered as particularly open for a change of lifestyle. Between the ages of 16 to 25 young people experience their formative years: they leave their old families, where they played the roles of children, and start to form ideas about their possible new families, where they will play the roles of adults. With public educational infrastructure failing, and the parent generations ideal types, i.e. a renaissance of the bourgeois family type, found completely inadequate, it is understandable that communication started to focus on exchanges within the same generation. Inter-generational understanding collapsed, the generation gap widened.

The emergent family types were largely driven by more or less individually driven redesigns. The so-called patchwork families in the Western societies of the last quarter of the century thus are not to be considered as failing attempts to achieve a different family model, they actually are a new type of family model.

One of the most significant impacts of redesign of individual life profiles comes from the multi-faceted group of the women's movement. How strong this influence on European families was is shown in Figures 9.1, 9.2, and 9.3. Women (i) started to reverse the trend to have their first child earlier; they (ii) are continuing a long-run trend of rather sharply falling fertility rates; and (iii) their participation in labour markets is approaching the levels of male participation rates. Taking these eclectically chosen indices together, they show that by the end of the century women in Western societies by and large were able to render the patriarch family model obsolete. And some of these trends – like fertility rates falling world–wide – have started to spread.[10]

Figure 9.1: Age of the Mother at the Birth of the First Child in European Countries

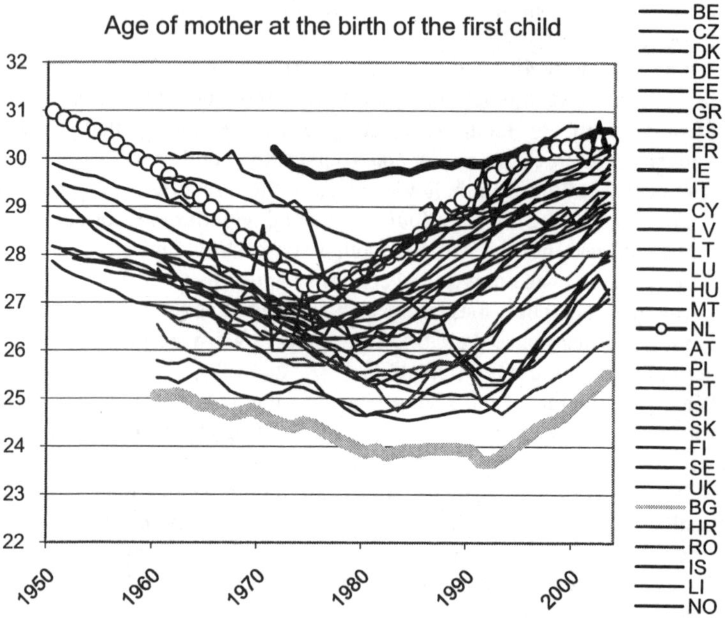

What still is an open question for both genders, is how to square sex with family. The core characteristic of family relations in BAFs, namely (re-) production of the species, is fading away as sexual lust nowadays can be experienced without the burden of subsequent child rearing. Cooperation between woman and man thus is not necessarily forced to be stable over a longer time period, curiosity concerning new and perhaps more exciting partners can be included in lifestyle. The marriage markets once directed and used by patriarchs now have turned into troubled waters with unpredictable dynamics. Divorce rates show a clear trend upwards.

On the other hand global economic developments themselves were starting to demand a different type of family model. Firms had grown so much, with transnational corporations taking the lead, that patriarchy as an overarching governance style was beginning to look ridiculous. It became pointless to motivate patriarch family fathers by comparing them to small shopkeepers who escaped bankruptcy only by subsidies and tax exemptions – they were not heroes any more.

Figure 9.2: Fertility Rates in European Countries

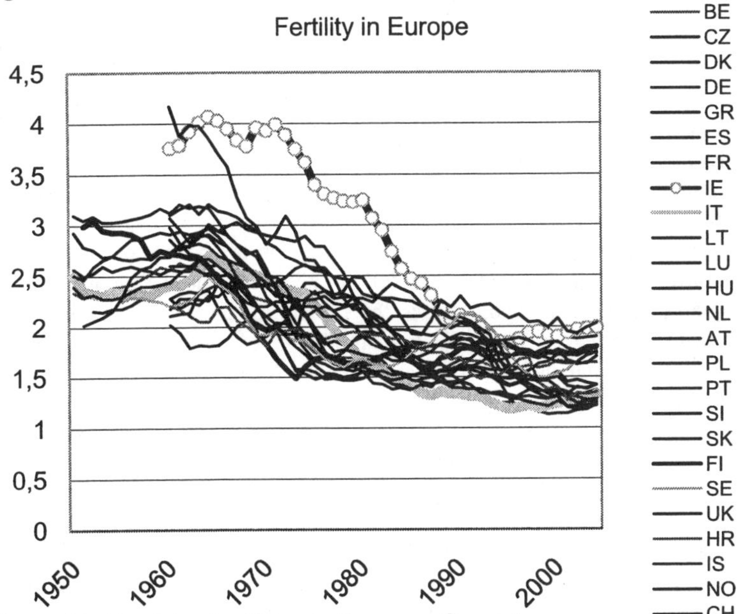

Figure 9.3: Participation Rates in European Countries

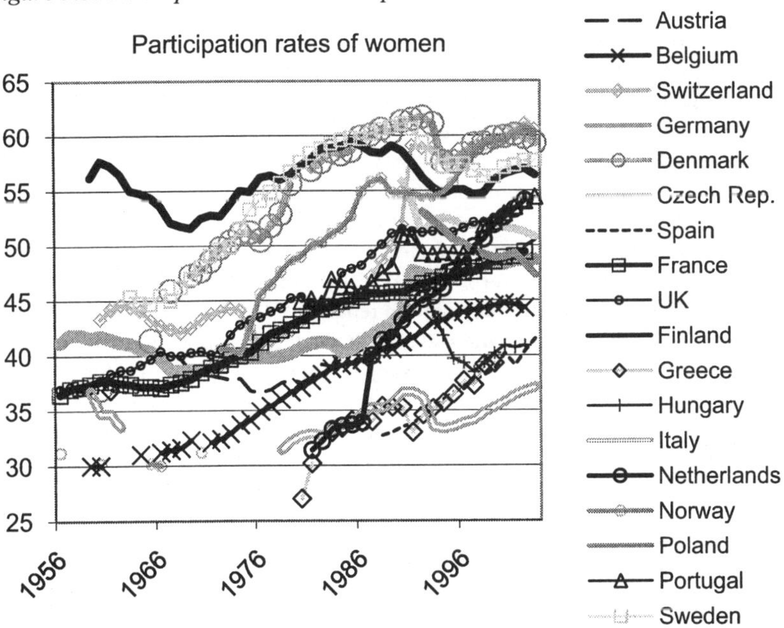

Furthermore, due to advanced IT, control spans and the development of sophisticated control and monitoring networks were possible and simple command hierarchies as exemplified in patriarchy quickly became outdated. Male workers had to offer abilities that did not match those taught by the old gender role; these abilities could not be ascribed to any of the roles present in the old type of family. As a consequence this behaviour, diverse and flexible as it often is, had to be learned on the job and in turn worked as a feedback into the working of families.

Tremendous increases in labour productivity and large shifts of whole production lines across continents and economic sectors resulted in low and unstable employment in Western countries. It is familiar now that at least one person of working age in a family is not fully employed. Stagnating wages often force all members of families to accept non-permanent part-time jobs, sometimes jobs on the black market, to keep the family income on an acceptable level. This again makes the possibility of having children look extremely unattractive. There would be no time to care for them.

Better paid, and usually more permanent, jobs in larger companies are increasingly combined with the obligations for employees to travel a lot, and spend long time periods away from their families, A lot of entrepreneurial propaganda calls for more 'mobility' of the workforce. When such a job is accepted the rest of the family usually is deprived of the two–thirds of lifetime that an employee usually spends outside the firm. So while alienated mobile employees dwell as singles in foreign cities – a new phenomenon of transitory family-free people heavily exploited by employers – the remaining family torso at home has to struggle with increased labour intensity in household work. Families in these social strata therefore often are in a state of permanent emergency.

The conservative political backlash that started in the 1980s had many severe consequences for families. Many of them can be summarized under the header of a deteriorating infrastructure: education, health, transport, social security and other state–financed services were considerably reduced. The reaction on the side of families usually was necessarily passive, there was no scope for defence, substitution by private businesses was either non-existing or too expensive. All the consequences of this lack of infrastructure are not always visible in the short–run; but at least in the mid–run they do pop up as deficiencies that are extremely hard to repair.[11]

Finally banking and credit systems have to be mentioned. In the boom a well developed financial system makes the major part of its profits in using the difference between the interest rates for household savings and firm credits. The chronic low level of the interest structure for the past 20 years signals that relative to the large amount of capital looking for profitable enterprises the opportunities are rather meagre. Private household credit was served in ample quantities and even for risky private businesses some credit was available. To date this situation has not altered too much – but catastrophe might be pending.[12] In case of visible signs of a banking crisis, i.e. a marked interest hike due to the discovery of bad loans, a cascade of bankruptcies, firms and households, might be initiated. In particular in Europe more than 70 per cent of employment is employment in small and medium–sized–enterprises, which are the first to be hit by such a crisis. The majority of European families thus are highly vulnerable to a financial crisis – it is not in sight right now, but it can hit over night. Family members thus often (rightly) have a subconscious feeling that they live on a volcano, again an incentive towards maximum consumption in the present and neglect of long-run concerns for the species.

This brief list of exogenous influences on the wide variety of family types in Europe today in no way is complete – just a few essential aspects are covered.

Indeed this variety of forms calls into question the usefulness of the concept of a family at all. Perhaps one should rather talk of the ideological aftermath of what was once called a family (IAF) – if not the death of the family is to be announced, at least the death of the bourgeois family is granted.

CONCLUSION: SOME SPOTLIGHTS ON MICROECONOMIC POLICY DESIGN

As implicitly already shown one of the main features of global political economy in the last century was the growing dominance of the ideological perspective relative to socioeconomics and biological processes. But this does not mean that the latter two are not to be entertained at a sufficiently high level that makes it possible to keep their importance invisible at the ideological level. ICT did speed up ideological processes enormously – information happens almost instantaneously on this globe, and it shapes actions of individuals in a most profound way. Today actual observation and own interpretation of processes is the exception; the use of ready-made, often centrally mediated interpretations is the rule.

For families, even in the form of IAF, their biological function of preventing a too rapid decrease of species members remains important. As global fertility rate developments show we must be ready for a dramatically changing mix of family types in the not too distant future. While demographers usually underestimate the importance of political economy – their forecasts of half-century developments look extremely naïve – economists have to admit that policy reaction to the dramatic evolution of demo-economics is extremely slow indeed.

Since important decisions in political economy are increasingly taken on a continental level, the institutional voice for this type of design should be established at the level of the European Union. Besides its political implementation it needs scientific consulting; and it evidently overarches several academic disciplines – including economics.

One of the more important reasons for the existence of the current blind spot in economics is that the traditional divide into micro- and macroeconomics has left no space for such a hybrid topic. Evolutionary economics actually would be an almost ideal arena for looking at the design of these new deals between biological and social reproduction. Given the current dominance of the ideological level such a design could probably even be implemented.

NOTES

1. It is interesting that Darwin was very aware of the severe critique which his hypothesis meant for the church. As several biographers of his life show the fear of being prosecuted by the clergy might have even induced him to delay the publication of his scientific discoveries.
2. Compare Hanappi (1994, pp. 43-53) for a more detailed treatment of the notion of a copy.
3. Compare Hanappi and Hanappi-Egger (2004) for a simulation model that shows the inverse relationship between variety and change of speed of the environment. The faster environmental change appears, the more variety is optimal for a species.
4. For reasons of consistency the use of the term 'society' for non-human animal populations is improper use of language – at least in a scientific discourse.
5. It was, of course, Malthus (1820), in particular as interpreted by Richard Day (1999), who formulated this early evolutionary economic model.
6. 'Again and again in recent years evolutionary biologists have found themselves returning to the theme of parasites ... Parasites are touted as the prime movers in the evolution of sex' (Ridley, 1993, p. 66).
7. In Hanappi-Egger (2004) the working of the ideological level is used for a proper definition of gender roles.
8. In his empirical survey Therborn distinguishes three areas of the patriarch's power: with respect to his wife, with respect to the marriage of his children and with respect to fertility. It is revealing that the *ideological* form of the patriarchy (as presented by Therborn) presents control of *biological* (re-)production by the father as the universal *social* model for families in capitalism. The most abstract form of power, ideology, uses the most archaic relations, biology, to prescribe modes of behaviour as universal rules for the particular presence. Socio-biology is just a more fashionable tune on the same instrument.
9. Note that the proof of the welfare–maximizing properties of such a model is the core of the normative part of the so-called neo-classical synthesis that Paul Samuelson made popular in the fifties and sixties at practically every economics department in Western universities.
10. As Longman (2004) nicely describes, television and movies play a central role in spreading visions of family life.
11. As these lines are written riots of unemployed youngsters in the banlieu of Paris and many other French cities show how a misguided economic policy – in particular labour market and education policy – after some time can produce surprising and dramatic results.

12. The measures contained in Basel 2 can be interpreted as safeguards against such a crisis, but on closer inspection it is evident that they might as well fire back and fuel the crisis once it started.

REFERENCES

Day R. (1999), *Complex Economic Dynamics*, MIT Press, Cambridge (MA).

Hanappi H. (1994), *Evolutionary Economics*, Avebury Ashgate Publishers, Aldershot.

Hanappi H. and Hanappi-Egger E. (2004), 'New Combinations. Taking Schumpeter's concept serious', *International Schumpeter Society*, bi-annual Conference 2004, Bocconi University (Milano, Italy), 2004.

Hanappi-Egger E. (2004), 'On the role of gender and diversity in modern organization theory', *Annual Conference of the EAEPE*, in Maastricht, November 2003.

Longman Ph. (2004), *The Empty Cradle. How falling birthrates threaten world prosperity and what to do about it*, Basic Books, New York.

Malthus T. (1820), *Principles of Political Economy*, John Murray, London.

Ridley M. (1993), *The Red Queen. Sex and the evolution of human nature*, Penguin Books, New York.

Rostow W. (1960), *The Stages of Economic Growth*, Cambridge University Press, London.

Therborn G. (2004), *Between Sex and Power: Family in the World, 1900–2000*, London.

10. Small Businesses: The Solution For What and For Whom?

Elisabeth Sundin

SMALL BUSINESSES AND ENTREPRENEURS – EXPANDING AND LOVED

'Small businesses in a large-scale production society' was the subtitle of the Norwegian investigation into power dealing with small and medium–sized firms (Schelderup 1980). It was published more than 20 years ago but could also be used as the title of this chapter which deals with Sweden today – and perhaps even in the future. Figures and facts presented below are Swedish although the phenomenon is not delimited to Sweden. A study made somewhere would probably give – if not the same – similar results.

One point of departure for the chapter is the great importance and positive impact which is now ascribed to small and medium–sized businesses (SMBs) in every public arena. Politicians from all parties stress the importance of small and medium–sized businesses. Further, small businesses and entrepreneurship have become an established area of research. Professorships in this subject can be found throughout Sweden and special courses in entrepreneurship are given at every university and seat of tertiary education.[1] Small business owners and people starting new businesses in particular are seen as the heroes of our times. But what is a small business? What is an entrepreneur? And why is it that small businesses in particular are worthy of support and considered to be so positive, not just for the sake of owners and managers but for whole of the country?

Advantages of Small Businesses

The answers, or rather the ideas behind the answers, to the last question involve both a societal, an organizational and an individual level. It is often said that small businesses occupy a large number, about a third, of those in work today. Further, the fact is stressed that small businesses constitute a support group for big businesses by acting as suppliers and that they provide some of the flexibility that the big organizations are considered lacking.

Small businesses are said to be innovative and regenerative. It is within them new products and services are developed, tried out and tested relatively easily and quickly on the market, as SMBs are less bureaucratic than the big ones. Due to their small size, the key actors are close to the market and can react to the wishes of the customers and consumers. In them and through them, new ideas can be tested. They are the lubricant of the economy. The latter also means that small businesses provide a good environment for the employees.

Small firms, perhaps especially the very smallest, the ones that only employ their owner, so–called micro-firms or solo businesses, are considered to be the natural choice for anyone who wants to be his own man, or her own woman, who does not want to have a boss, who wants to make his/her own decisions and for whom independence is the very essence of their enterprising spirit and driving force. It is individuals expressing such views who are considered to be the classic entrepreneur.[2]

Despite the great changes brought about by new technology, globalisation, new political regimes and so on, the rhetoric concerning small businesses seems to endure and to be comparatively similar to that of 20 years ago. This is evident from the survey of small business politics in a number of countries, carried out by Anders Lundström and Lois Stevenson (2001, 2002) as well as the work edited by Zọltan J. Acs (1999) about the importance of small firms. In addition, SMBs provide disadvantaged groups for the labour market, such as women and ethnic minorities, with the opportunity to make use of their skills.

The positive potential of the small business is also being emphasized in current Swedish debate. One point often made is that absence due to illness and burn-out are strongly related to the unreasonable working conditions within organizations today.[3] The big organizations are said to be bureaucratic and do not allow individuals to develop and act. Responsibility is not followed by authority and reward. The gap between the leaders and the led can be huge, both in absolute terms and symbolically. This creates such great frustration that employees are taken ill. It is argued that this unsatisfactory state of affairs is avoided in small organizations where there is proximity between the leader and the led.

Another current argument for new and small organizations stems from the problems facing the Swedish public health and care system. The question of financing is problematic and the difficulties of recruiting are widely reported. Many see that in several ways the solution is to have a number of small, alternative performers, instead of one monopoly producer in every local and regional authority. It is also argued that more firms will increase the competition for workers and in this way raise the salaries and people's willingness to look for work in the health and care sector.

On the grounds of what has been said above, it can be claimed that the future belongs to small businesses and entrepreneurs. I claim that this is the case only on a very superficial level. Before I go into how and why I make this claim I must devote a few lines to the difference between entrepreneurs and small business owners. This is a distinction which is only too seldom made.

Owners of Small Firms and Entrepreneurs

The term small firm owner is often used as a synonym to entrepreneur. This confusion is made not only on the part of laymen and debaters, but also by decision makers and in policy documents (Lundström and Stevenson 2002). According to the Swedish National Encyclopaedia (Nationalencyklopedin 1992), an entrepreneur is 'a person who by concrete action creates a new business activity'. However, not all small firm owners are entrepreneurs and not all entrepreneurs are small business owners.

The entrepreneurship discourse often includes a dimension of growth. In a political context the desire for growth is often said to emanates from the innovation of small businesses with regard to both process and product (see for example Wennekers and Thurik 1999). It is in this way that Henrekson (2001), for example, states that there is a positive connection between economic growth on the macroeconomic level and a rise in number of new enterprises.

It is probably the case that most small firms have never been managed by entrepreneurs according to the definition given in the encyclopaedia. It is most likely that the majority of small businesses have been set up to provide the person running them with the means of livelihood and possibility to practise their trade. 'Bread and butter business' is often, and not without an element of contempt, the headline when the livelihood aspect of these firms is stressed. 'Solo entrepreneurs' or 'micro businesses' are often used when the growth aspect is considered to be the most prominent. These terms are linked to the research carried out particularly with an emphasis on the individual incitements and contextual factors which underlie the starting up of new enterprises and its changes over time and place.

In this context, the number of possible references is many. I shall limit myself to giving an account of the arguments presented by Dieter Bögenhold (1989, 1999) as these are closely related to the observations and arguments presented and discussed in this article. Bögenhold stresses that the understanding of the business owner's reasons for starting and developing the business and the readiness to stay on the market must be connected to the position of the individual on the labour market. Those with the best business prospects are naturally those who have a privileged position on the labour market and a strong desire to be their own boss. Individuals with weak position on the labour market and no strong desire to own their businesses have the worst position. These are the people who gladly close their businesses if they get a regular job. Bögenhold summarizes the different alternatives in a matrix which has one axis 'desire to be own boss' and the other, 'labour market position'. Both axes are divided into three levels – small, neutral and great, respectively weak, neutral and good. I will come back to this '9-field matrix' later.

Bögenhold's observations are supported by other researchers who note that there are varying reasons for individuals starting their own businesses. Research no longer assumes that everyone with their own business can be categorized as an entrepreneur, full of enthusiasm about being their own boss. In particular, research with a gender or multicultural perspective on running an enterprise has emphasized this lack of homogeneity (Sundin and Holmquist 1989; Sundin 2002; Khosravi 1999).

WHAT TREND?

I argue that some of the classic advantages of the small organizations have never existed to the extent that 'the friends of small businesses'[4] are claiming. I also argue that the small business advantages that really existed have been challenged by fundamental changes. In the rest of this chapter I shall qualify this statement, which, in a small business context, is heretical.

In the following section the increasing number of small businesses will be highlighted. This is a trend which is often pointed out.[5] I claim however that this is *not* a sign of small businesses having a strong position on the market, but rather the complete opposite – a weakened position on the market. This is a trend which seems to have reached a point of no return. Is this of any importance – and if so, for whom? The aim of the chapter is to describe and discuss these claims and questions.

SWEDEN – THE HOMELAND OF SMALL BUSINESS

Sweden's economy is often described as being extremely dependent on a small number of big, dominant companies. From many perspectives, this is true. But Sweden can also be characterized as a real small business country. According to current methods of presenting the figures, there are about 665 000 businesses in Sweden. Of these, slightly more than 1100 or 0.2 per cent are large, that is to say have more than 200 employees. Almost 70 per cent are solo-entrepreneurs with no employees at all. The big firms however are directly responsible for a third of Sweden's total work opportunities while 15 per cent of those on the labour market are self employed.

The development of new businesses always creates big headlines. A large number of new businesses starting up are considered as positive and a low number as negative. During the last ten years, the number of new businesses has varied from just over 22 000 in 1993 to almost 38 000 in the year 2000 (SOS 2002, table 1). New businesses have resulted in 47 000 more firms on the market in the year 2000 than there were in 1990. The greatest increase was in businesses without any employees, that is to say solo-businesses, which rose in number by 22 000 in ten years. According to ITPS,[6] the typical *new* business is a one-man firm in the field of 'Finance and other business activities' located in the Stockholm region. The firm has a turnover of less than 30 000 Swedish crowns (3000 Euro) and employs 1.7 people, of whom 0.8 has a full-time employment. The owner is a Swedish male aged 39 with upper secondary education. Before starting the business, he had been working in the very branch in which he has now set up a business.

Table 10.1: Number and Share of Newly Established Businesses in 2001 Divided by Branch and the Share of the Business Type (SOS 2002).

Type of industry	Number of newly started business	Share of newstarters	Newstarters share
Industry	5 751	15	5.4
Manufacturing and similar	2 469	7	4.6
Construction	3 282	9	6.2
Services	29 819	85	7.9
Trade, restaurant, hotel	6 971	19	5.1
Transport and communication	1 473	4	4.8
Finance, business services	13 763	39	10.0
Education, health care, medical care/nursing and other services	7 611	20	10.8
Total (number of businesses)	35 570	100	

Almost 85 per cent of the new companies established in the year 2000 were in the service sector. Consequently, 15 per cent of the new businesses were established in the industry as is shown in Table 10.1.

As implied in the section above, there are different types of businesses – those of an entrepreneurial nature as well as those without. Researchers have tried to classify new firms according to that and to other dimensions. In this context, I choose to refer to Herman Schmid (1999) as he clearly observes the connection between the labour market and business enterprise. For one group of individuals starting a business can be seen as a pure labour market strategy – self-employment – that is employing yourself while waiting to be employed by somebody else. A second completely different category comprises professionals choosing to sell their competence on the market under their own management. In the last mentioned category there are both craftsmen like carpenters and professionals in the stricter sense of the word, such as lawyers. Schmid has also distinguished the classic entrepreneur in his classifications. As a fourth group, he introduces the firm owner who is rather a leader than an entrepreneur and strongly inclined towards creating social relations and networking for the benefit of the business. This group is often excluded from discussions on entrepreneurship as not being regarded as 'genuine' entrepreneurs. The fact that they have a great impact in modern economy is however evident, and is one of the conclusions which can be drawn from my portrayal of the situation (see also Hjort 2001).

NEW AND OLD QUESTIONS

Information about the situation and types of businesses and new enterprises provide the background upon which the discussion in this chapter is based. The main question is how recent development in small business initiatives should be interpreted. What type of business owner and new business owner do we have today? What is their future? What is the relationship between small and large organizations or, to put it another way, how free are these free businesses? Together, these questions and answers contribute to the discussion on why SMBs are so positive and why they are considered so worthy of support. The conclusions we draw will depend on the point of view, the theoretical angle, from which we choose to interpret the observations. There is a political dimension to the interpretations.

In the following, I shall illustrate and clarify the questions using public statistics as well as my own and others' experience. The questions I ask cannot easily be answered partly because the statistics were not produced with these questions in mind. When there are questions of dependence, the owner-managers' willingness to answer is not very high. Small business owners and the 'friends of small businesses' prefer to stress the freedom of the small enterprise. Neither is there any desire among the large(r) organizations to emphasize dependence and power in relationship between small and big organizations. The relations are not always unambiguous. Relationships can be used and interpreted differently and can also change with time and place. This will be clear from below.

Due to its tentative nature, I shall limit myself to only a few sectors. The manufacturing firms will be discussed as they still are the 'businesses in our hearts'. The building and construction sector has a long tradition of owner-managers moving from being an employee to working as their own boss. The greatest numbers of new enterprises are to be found within the two service sectors which comprise 'finance and business activities' and 'education, health care and nursing and other social and personal services'. This is worth some reflection. Traditionally, the biggest sectors where we find small businesses are retail and farming. Little attention is paid to the latter in a small business context, which is my reason for including them.

DIFFERENT SECTORS WITH SIMILAR CONDITIONS?[7]

Manufacturing Firms – Classic and Hard Pressed

The manufacturing businesses are still, as I mentioned above, 'the businesses in our hearts'. This can be seen in many ways. One is that the Gnosjö region, which by Swedish standards has an unusually high number of small and medium-sized manufacturing firms, is constantly upheld as the norm by other regions. Delegations from other parts of the country have been visiting the region for decades. The way firms work together in Gnosjö in networks is considered as a model and the lively spirit of new enterprise is renowned (Berggren et al.1999; Johannisson 2000).

Although several small manufacturing firms produce for the consumer market most of them are suppliers to big companies. The position of the small suppliers in relation to their big customers has become weakened in recent decades. Among the reasons mentioned are the information technology and the globalization of the Swedish industry most important. Information technology makes distance less important. Orders can, literally, go straight from the purchaser's decision maker into the producers' machines. The close cooperation with or entry into international business constellations by many of the big Swedish companies has weakened the relative position of the small Swedish suppliers. They have to compete with international suppliers often much bigger than the Swedish ones and closely connected to the purchasers in a variety of ways. The 'small businesses in our hearts' are feeling the pinch in our modern economy. The situation raises the question – will the small independent organization never come back?

The Building and Construction Sector – Employees and Self-Employed

The building and construction branch is dominated by small firms. The absolute majority has none, or only a few, employees. One individual out of ten working in this sector is self-employed. Only slightly more than 15 per cent came from a different branch to building and construction. One hundred firms employ more than 100 persons.

The branch is extremely dependent on the economic situation on the national level and has sometimes been used as a regulator for the national economy. During previous recessions the big companies in the branch have made many of their employees redundant, but have allowed them to carry on as self-employed. Such strategies can also be detected in figures from later years.

The small firm owners in the building and constructing sector shall not, however, be victimized. In a report from the Department of Trade (Ds 2003:27) dealing with the so-called combinationists (kombinatörer) that is business owners who combine self-employment in a sector with employment in the same sector or somewhere else, combinationists from the building industry stand out as an extreme. They have a high rate of survival and often claim that they are happy to combine. These people, more than any others, want to carry on combining and have the least desire of all the groups registered to go over to full time self-employment. Thus, the combinationists continue to be employed and to be dependent on their employers. The strategies used raises some fundamental questions covering self-employment and entrepreneurship. Can the combinationists in the building and construction industry be seen as representing a sort of freedom within a framework of security while those going over to a pure form of self-employment lose security without achieving freedom?

Service Sectors With a Large Number of New Enterprises

Almost 40 per cent of the new businesses that were set up in the year 2001 were within the sector known as 'Finance and business services' comprising 10 per cent of all the businesses in the sector. From a new enterprise perspective this is therefore a very dynamic sector.

The sector is not dominated by a few large companies although there are some international companies in this sector nowadays. The fast turnover in the branch and the lively spirit of new enterprises can in part be assumed to be related to the slump in the IT-related sectors. There are comparatively many of the new start-ups, more than 40 per cent, who went from being employed in the same branch to setting up on their own. More than 10 per cent of the new starters state that they did it because they were out of work or feared being made redundant. The impression given by statistics is of individuals self-employed in a state of flux waiting for the markets to stabilize. This impression is strengthened by the fact that one in ten of the combinationists in the branch would rather be just employed. This figure is higher than in any other sector.

'Education, health and nursing and other social and personal services' has the highest number of new enterprises in recent years, 10 per cent. This sector, or rather sectors, was until lately totally dominated by the public sector. The deregulation of the public sector during the past decade to a great extent affected education, care and health care. 'The authorities on the local and regional level have during recent years increased the buying of work and services from external suppliers dramatically' is one of the headings in the SCB report (2001) *Statistiska bilder av privatiseringen av välfärdstjänster* (Statistical pictures of the privatisation of welfare services). Education, health and care are thus an expanding market created by the changing executive strategies of the big public organizations for executing their obligations. What is very noticeable, I maintain, is the speed with which a number of big private players have established themselves on the new market. What the eye sees when we take a walk through many of Sweden's towns is not the sign for the local independent free school, 'The Alternative', but rather, the international 'Kunskapsskolan' (School of Knowledge). The privately owned joint-stock companies are growing most quickly. Some of them have been good at marketing and active in political debate. As has been made evident, the big organizations seem quickly to have taken advantage of the new situation. But they are not alone. One indication as to how the position of small firms has developed is the information on those individuals continuing with their work for the public sector as self-employed by means of so-called hiving off. SCB, Statistics Sweden, observes and states that hiving off within child care is modest, that within compulsory schools it occurs 'only in a few local authorities' and that in upper secondary schools, adult education and municipal music schools it 'occurs very seldom'. However, hiving off is common within the care sector (30 communities of almost 400) and health and medical care (in half of the counties). Seventeen per cent of those who have left a position in the public health and medical care sector have done so in order to start their own business together with some colleagues. The absolute majority leaving the public sector became employed by someone else.

My conclusion is that it is above all big firms which are able to take advantage of the new market for welfare services. This does not mean that there is no room for small firms though. There can be certain niches which, for different reasons, are left vacant by the big firms. There can be room for innovative thinking. My colleagues and I have seen this for example in our studies of around 300 firms owned by nurses[8] and in our studies of firms trying to establish themselves as suppliers of services to a Swedish community (Tillmar 2004). The small businesses we encountered, however, complained that almost without exception the logic within the entire sector is 'to think big'. The question is whether these firms are working in conditions that make the term 'small businesses in a large-scale production society' adequate?

The Retail Trade – Our (Second Largest) Small Business Sector[9]

The retail trade in Sweden employs more than 200 000 people, spread over almost 65 000 places of work. It is therefore a sector characterized by small units and this is how it always has been. The retail business turns towards final consumers and their recurrent needs. It is often a matter of everyday commodities, that is to say, the buyer and seller meet daily. Consequently the geographical spread of the retail business corresponds by and large with the population. This has loosened up to some extent as certain change has taken place over recent decades. External establishments and centres, especially in the form of shopping centres near towns and cities and densely populated areas, have increased in number at the expense of the shops in the suburbs and sparsely populated areas in particular. Retail trade in the town centres seems to have been more successful (Ranhagen 2002; *Supermarket* 2000, No. 9).

The physical distribution of the retail trade gets political attention at the local level. The aspect which I am going to take up here, the dominance of the big organizations, receives less attention. Presumably, consumers, local authority representatives and others responsible for the range of goods and their availability do not consider this to be an evident, serious problem.

Nowadays, a walk along the shopping streets in one Swedish town is very much like a walk in another. By and large, you find the same shops everywhere. It is most obvious when they have the same name. They also have the same products, the same decoration and, something the eye cannot see, the same system of accounting. The formal position can vary. Some shops have a unique name for their premises but have a sign in the window or a notice, to say that they belong to an organization in co-operation. The latter vary in size and market positioning. Some of them have been formed by owners of retail firms. Because of stiff competition on the market their decision was to enter into a co-operation in order to obtain the advantages of economics of scale. For the customer it is often impossible to know whether the shop is publicly owned, in Sweden or abroad, or if the owner is standing in front of him/her. In the case of the latter it is often a franchisee.

Franchising is a dominating concept in various branches and sectors, but is especially common in the retail business. Franchise concepts vary widely. Within some chains, or concepts, quite substantial capital investment is required on the part of the franchisee, whereas others make fewer demands on this score. The relationship between the franchisor and the franchisee is governed by contract. In general, the franchisor provides the business concept, the logotype, the equipment, furnishing and fittings and allows the franchisee to use them. Despite the contract being very tight with regard to both the form and content of the business, the franchisee is the legal owner of the business and is registered as a free-standing company. In function, the relationship is often very close to that of employer–employee but without the regulations concerning the relationships on the labour market.

The forerunners of this trend, which I have attributed the retail business, have been the grocery shops. Today, there is hardly one single grocery and provisions merchant who is wholly independent. The vast majority belong to one of the few blocs dominating the Swedish market. This oligopoly is considered to be one of the reasons for the high Swedish food prices when seen in an international context. The increasing competition, which is expected, comes from big international companies such as the German firm, Lidl.

At a closer lock the small firm dominance in the statistics may be a chimera. Maybe small shops cannot be seen as representatives of a small business sector but instead as the strategy of the big conglomerations to present themselves as small? Is there room for anyone wanting to set up a completely independent shop? Is the era of 'the shop in our hearts' a thing of the past?

Farming – Our Biggest Small Business Sector

Farming businesses are not part of small business politics and are not as a rule taken into account by researchers in the field of SMB. However, for several reasons I consider them interesting in this context. The first one is that they are so many. Secondly, farmers have sometimes been used as the very symbol of entrepreneurship – as a way of life and a will to be independent working on their own (Höjrup 1983; Sundin and Holmquist 1989). Thirdly, these firms are in the process of diversifying and establishing themselves in the 'experience branch' both with products such as the 'Butiken på landet' (Countryside Store) concept and with activities such as farm tourism.

Agricultural business, found in current statistics as 'Agricultural business and services to agriculture' (Jordbruksföretag och serviceföretag till jordbruk) are the biggest single group of businesses. The firms and the places of work are almost the same in number, that is to say, the business is concentrated on one farm which may serve as an indication of the size of the business. Not all the owners of farming businesses work in the business, but nearly 35 000 of them do. The number of owners is greater than the number of employees (Statistisk Årsbok 2002, table 304).

The farming sector is a small business sector dominated by many small firms. Does this mean that the farmer is the typical independent small business owner? I would claim that this question cannot be answered unconditionally in the affirmative, because in the sector some very large and very dominant players are involved. These big Swedish organizations were founded and are formally owned by many individual owners, but this does not guarantee that there is a small business character or a widespread independence. The major organizations within the agricultural sector take a variety of forms such as 'The Federation of Swedish Farmers' (LRF, Lantbrukarnas Riksförbund, information from their homepage, www.lrf.se). LRF is almost all-embracing with its more than 150 000 members from 80 000 firms. Its area of influence is vastly diversified and covers purchasing, distribution, production and sales through its business organizations. In addition, there are connected service organizations which explicit provids financing, advice, insurance and other business services. It is no exaggeration to claim that the entire life of an LRF member can be in the hands of the organization. This brings along many advantages for the individual small farm but also a situation by no means characterized by the classic freedom and independence of the life of the owner-manager. The big organization demands loyalty and the rules to be followed. Alternatives, as in the case of the small business owner in Jämtland who some 20 years ago tried to start a competing dairy, Hammerdals Mejeri, were fought against with the resolute use of economic means. The insurgent had to leave the market (see for example articles in Östersunds-Posten from 29 September 1981 to 20 June 1988). LRF and its different organizations now work together, in a variety of different legal forms, with foreign organizations and firms. Consequently the conclusion is that the agricultural sector is dominated by a few large organizations working in the international arena rather than by many small businesses.

SMALL BUSINESSES: THE SOLUTION OF WHAT AND FOR WHOM?

The heading above is the same as the one given to the whole chapter. I shall try to problemize the two questions, using particularly Bögenhold's and Schmid's classifications as well as the development of the five different sectors presented above. Current research into small and medium-sized firms uses the small firm and its owner as point of departure. Central are the incentives, the motives and the owner's situation. I am convinced that we can come further in our understanding, if we instead take our point of departure in the incentives, the motives and the situation of the *big* organizations. It is these big organizations that create the conditions for the small organizations determining which of the small businesses to survive on the market. As is stated in Ds 2003:27, this is, 'because the increasing number of new business and the increasing proportion of small firms is in part a reflection of the fact that the bigger firms are choosing to outsource production and buy instead of employing people directly themselves'. I would like to tighten up the significance of the quote and propose that the questions about the connection do not only apply to new firms but to all firms and that the reservation 'in part' can be discarded.

Two of the sectors chosen, *Building and construction* and *Finance and business activities*, have been experiencing unstable markets resulting in a reduction of the number of employees in the big organizations and an increased use of small firms as suppliers – in many cases firms run by former employees. The larger companies are creating conditions for survival and flexibility for themselves by transferring uncertainty onto the small firms. In some cases, it is a question of purely adapting volume, that is to say, flexibility in numbers. In others, it is a question of specializing and outsourcing everything not considered to directly be part of the core business. This can create a market for a professional craftsman or woman.

Both sectors comprise all of Bögenhold's nine cells, that is to say people with competitive skills and knowledge as well as those lacking unique competences and people with a strong desire to be their own boss as well as those preferring to have a regular job. Consequently, in accordance with Schmid's terminology, both cases of pure self-employment and professional businessmen are found in these sectors. What is what and what are the quantitative and qualitative balance between them, must be decided from case to case. Statistics can hide many different strategies.

Manufacturing and *Retail* are both mature sectors, where the actions and expectations of the big companies can only be met by those small-firm owners that can act as leaders in established networks. Social competence on the part of the business owners is absolutely essential. This would also seem to be applicable to *agriculture*. What is required of the successful company in these sectors is the ability to negotiate and to adapt rather than entrepreneurship and new ideas. A good education and competence, coupled with the desire to take responsibility and manage, are more suitable than a strong desire to be independent.

Education, health and nursing and other social and personal services are sectors firmly anchored in the Swedish public sector. Changes taken place over the past ten years have made these sectors new markets for private actors – large and small. In general, the individuals working in these sectors in both private and public organizations are well qualified. They are professionals and semi-professionals whether they are employees or self-employed. The profession and the task are seen to be more important than organizational structure and ownership by those who work in the sector. It is especially when employees feel that they cannot practice their profession adequately to their own satisfaction that they want to change the organizational context. Very few individuals express a genuine desire to start a business just for the sake of being self-employed. Those who take this step have a great deal of professional expertise, but differing attitudes to enterprising (Lindgren 2002; Sundin 1997; Tillmar 2005).

What are the consequences, if any and for whom, of the development I have sketched? If it is true that small firms established by entrepreneurs are prerequisite for a healthy economy, then what has been described is negative. There seems to be little room for that type of business in an economy dominated by big organizations. If, on the other hand, it is the case that a modern economy needs a managing entrepreneur, then the conclusions are less certain and require more analysis. It is not clear how power relationships between the organizations and actors involved develops. It seems as if there is a large and growing flora of organized collaboration gaining ground and whose role we cannot yet determine.

To keep to current groupings based on established statistics as I did above, can result in us missing what is new and innovative in the economy. Perhaps new sectors and branches that we have not yet discerned are on their way up? Perhaps we do not see what is new in what already is established? There are perhaps a large number of small retailers serving a local market and filling a niche left empty by the big organizations? And perhaps there is a multitude of small, alternative carers, advisers and so on. One grouping, which may prove to be inadequate and obsolete for an understanding of present day and future enterprises and labour market behaviour, is that which exists between being a self-employed and being an employee. The experience of many individuals testifies to the fact that this line is problematic in practice. It has been discussed in the public debate, for example when putting into practice the franchising concept, in unions like the Union of Care Workers and by authorities as in Ds 2003:27 dealing with the conditions for combinationists. In research, there still seems to be quite a clear line between the so-called labour market researchers and entrepreneurship researchers. This should be changed. Starting a business can often be considered as labour market behaviour.

It is important to bear in mind that many small businesses and a vital growth in the number of new enterprises is not in itself a sign of anything. It can be a sign that many individuals can and want to start their own businesses – but it can also be a sign that there are serious problems in the economy, that large organizations are unstable and that the labour market is stagnant. Small organizations in themselves are not the solution to anything either. Everything depends on what the small businesses are, who starts them and who runs them as well as under what conditions they work. Perhaps the development of organizations, especially SMBs, cannot be discussed as one single trend – but instead as several parallel trends. We must continue to investigate, reconnoitre, and discuss. The future of entrepreneurship and small organizations is an important question both for achieving and for maintaining a vital economy and a vital democracy.

NOTES

1. See for example information from ESBRI, The Institute for Entrepreneurship and Small Businesses, whose function is to act as a link between researchers and the general public. Research and education news is published regularly on their home page and in their information sheet, *Entré*. See also the anthology *Images of Entrepreneurship and Small Business* edited by Bengt Johannisson and Hans Landström; and Landström (1999) *Entreprenörskapets rötter*.
2. These so–called advantages of the small business were explicitly introduced in the English Bolton Report which was published in 1971 and which was then followed in Sweden by research, investigations and proposals. A similar pattern and initiatives can also be observed in other countries (Andersson 1983; Lundström and Stevenson 2001, 2002).
3. In the chapter, 'organization' and 'firm' are used synonymously.
4. As far as I know, the expression 'småföretagens vänner' (friends of small businesses) was coined by Dick Ramström who, when he became professor of business economics in Umeå in northern Sweden, started teaching and researching into small and medium–sized firms. He was a pioneer in the field. Some of the early work by Ramström and his colleagues, is collected in the anthologies *Mindre företag – problem och villkor* (Smaller firms – problems and conditions) 1971 and *Små företag – stora problem* (Small firms – big problems) 1975. Dick Ramström later continued research in this field, for example in the book *Soloföretag* (Solo firms) 2000.
5. Pettersson (2000) is an example of this line of argument as also reported in a paper from the Department of Trade (Näringsdepartementet, Ds 2003 (27)).
6. ITPS, Swedish Institute for Growth Policy Studies, is the authority whose responsibility includes keeping statistics over new businesses. In the list of references the material from ITPS is to be found under SOS S2002:008 and S2003:005.
7. Unless otherwise stated, the information in this section is taken from SOS S2002:008, *Nyföretagandet i Sverige 2000 and 2001* (2002) ITPS and *SCB Basfakta 2002. Tabeller ur företagsregistret.* SCB, table 3. Företag (Firms) (FÖ) and anställda (employees) (AN) given

according to business sector and size 2001 and table 6. Arbetsställen (Places of work) (AE) and anställda (employees) (AN) given according to business sector and size 2000.

8. VIAM is the name of a company set up by the Union of Nurses (Vårdförbundet) to help members start up on their own. A study is being carried out by VIAM. So far, reports have been published by Ellinge and Löfstrand (2002), Persson (2005), Blomqvist (2005) and Sundin (2006).
9. The claim made in the heading, that retail is our second largest small business sector, can be discussed and depends on which level of retailing the estimation is based on. According to my way of seeing things, the biggest is agriculture. The second largest group given by statistics, 'other business services', is so lacking in homogeneity that I choose to give retailing the second position.

REFERENCES

Acs, Zoltan J. (ed) (1999), *Are Small Firms Important? Their Role and Impact*, Boston, Mass: Kluwer Academic Publ.

Andersson, Rune (1983), 'Småföretagspolitik i olika länder', in Rolf Lundin, Mats Glader and Elisabeth Sundin (eds), *Små företag i brännpunkten – En bok om företagande, industripolitik och kunskapsutveckling* (engl.: *Focus on sme:s. A book on entrepreneurship, economic policy and knowledgebases in the fields*), Malmö: Liber förlag.

Berggren, Christian, Brulin, Göran and Lise-Lott Gustafsson (1999), *From Italy to Gnosjö – concerning the importance of social capital for dynamic industrial regions*, Stockholm: Swedish Council for Work Life Research.

Blomqvist, Fredrik (2005), 'Karaktäristika och förutsättningar för företag och företagande inom hälso- och sjukvårdssektorn – en studie av Viamföretag' (engl.: 'SME:s and entrepreneurship in the health and care-sector – organisationens joining VIAM – a company established by the union of nurses'), FSF 2005:4, Örebro: FSF.

Bögenhold, Dieter (1989), 'Die Berufspassage in das Unternehmertum. Theoretische und empirische Befunde zum sozialen Process von Firmengründingen', *Zeitschrift für Soziologie*, 18 (4).

Bögenhold, Dieter (1999), 'Germany – the need to differentiate', in D. Fogden and L. Magnusson (eds), *Entrepreneurship in the European Employment Strategy*, Brussels: ETUI.

Bolton, J.E. (1971), *Report on the Committee of Inquiry on Small Firms*, London: Allen & Unwin.

Ds (2003: 27), *Företags- och anställningsformer i förändring* (engl.: *Employer-employee-relations and self-employment in transition*), Regeringskansliet, Näringsdepartementet (engl.: Ministry of Industry and Commerce), Stockholm.

Ellinge, Anders and Peter Löfstrand (2002), *VIAM visar vården vägen – Vårdförbundets väg ur Babels hus*, Jönköping: Internationella handelshögskolan i Jönköping.

Entrepreneurship and Small Business Research Institute, Stockholm: ESBRI.

Henrekson, Magnus (2001), 'Institutionella förutsättningar för entreprenörskap och företagstillväxt' (engl.: 'Entrepreneurship and growth in an institutional perspective'), in Per Davidsson, Frederik Delmar and Johan Wiklund (eds), *Tillväxtföretagen i Sverige* (engl.: *High growth companies in Sweden*), Stockholm:

SNS förlag.

Hjort, Daniel (2001), 'Rewriting Entrepreneurship – enterprise discourse and entrepreneurship in the case of re-organising', Doktorsavhandling, Ekonomihögskolan, Växjö: Växjö University Press.

Höjrup, Tomas (1983), *Det glemte folk. Livsformer og centraldirigering* (engl.: *The forgotten people. Life forms and centralistic decisions*), Institutet for Europeisk folkelivsforskning och Statens Byggeforskningsinstitut, Köpenhamn.

Johannisson, Bengt and Hans Landström (1999), *Images of Entrepreneurship and Small Business – Emergent Swedish Contributions to Academic Research*, Lund: Studentlitteratur.

Johannisson B. (2000), 'Networking and entrepreneurial growth', in Donald L. Sexton and Hans Landström (eds), *The Blackwell Handbook of Entrepreneurship*, Oxford: Blackwell.

Khosravi, Shamram (1999), 'Displacement and Entrepreneurship – Iranian Small Businesses in Stockholm', *Journal of Ethnic and Migration Studies*, 2 (3), 493–508.

Landström, Hans (1999), *Entreprenörskapets rötter* (engl.: *The roots of entrepreneurship*), Malmö: Liber.

Lindgren, Monica (2002), 'Kvinnor och friskolor – kvinnliga entreprenörer och nya livsformer' (engl.: 'Women and free-schools – female entrepreneurs and new life-forms'), in Carin Holmquist and Elisabeth Sundin (eds), *Företagerskan – Om kvinnor och entreprenörskap* (engl.: *Women as owner-managers. On women and entrepreneurship*), Stockholm: SNS förlag.

LRF, Lantbrukarnas Riksförbund (2003), The Federation of Swedish Farmers, Home-page www.lrf.se. May 2003.

Lundström, Anders and Lois Stevenson (2001), *Entrepreneurship Policy for the Future*, FSF 2001:3, Örebro: FSF.

Lundström, Anders and Lois Stevenson (2002), *On the Road to Entrepreneurship – Volume 1 of the Entrepreneurship Policy for the Future Series*, FSF 2002:2, Örebro: FSF.

Nationalencyklopedin (1992).

Östersunds-Posten. 29/9 1981–20/6 1988.

Persson, Alma (2005), *VIAM – Företag och företagare inom hälso- och sjukvårdssektorn* (engl.: *Firms and small-firm owners in the healthcare-sector joining VIAM – a company created by the union of nurses*), FSF 2005:3, Örebro: FSF.

Pettersson, Karl-Henrik (2000), *Det nya företaget – Om den nya ekonomin i ett företagsperspektiv* (engl.: *The new organization – Reflection on the new economy from an organizational perspective*), Göteborg: Groveda.

Ramström, D. (ed) (1971), *Mindre företag – problem och villkor* (engl.: *Small firms – problems and conditions*), Studier i företagsekonomi, Umeå: Umeå University.

Ramström, Dick (ed) (1975), *Små företag – stora problem* (engl.: *Small firms – big problems*), Stockholm: Norstedts förlag.

Ramström, Dick and Eva-Britt Hult (2000), *Soloföretag* (*Self-employed*), FSF 2000:1, Örebro: FSF.

Ranhagen, Mikael (2002), *Hur påverkas butiksstrukturen av ökad konkurrens – en analys av stormarknadsetableringer* (engl.: *Suburbian shopping-districts and shops in city-centres*), Forskningsrapport No. 73, Stockholm: Handelns Utredningsinstitut, HUI.

Schelderup, Liv (1980), *Småforetak i et stordriftssamfunn* (engl.: *Small firms in a society dominated by big organizations*), Bergen.

Schmid, H. (1999), 'Monitoring the European employment strategy. Entrepreneurship in Denmark', in David Fogden and Lars Magnusson (eds) *Entrepreneurship in the European Employement Strategy*, Brussels: ETUI.

SCB, Statistiska Centralbyrån (2001), Statistiska bilder av privatiseringen av välfärdstjänster (engl.: Privatization of welfare-services in figures. Statistics Sweden), Örebro: SCB.

SCB, Statistiska Centralbyrån (2002), Basfakta 2002, Tabeller ur företagsregistret (engl.: Tables from Statistics Sweden).

SOS, Sveriges Officiella Statistik (2002), *Nyföretagandet i Sverige 2000 och 2001* (engl.: *New established firms in Sweden*), S2002:008,

Statistisk Årsbok (2002) (Annual Book of Statistics) , Table 304.

Sundin, Elisabeth (1997), 'Om makt och kön – i spåren av offentliga organisationers omvandling' (engl.: 'Power and gender in the transition of the public sector and its organizations'), in Elisabeth Sundin (ed), *Om makt och kön – i spåren av offentliga organisationers omvandling SOU 1997:8* (engl.: *SOU=Governmental Official Reports*), Stockholm: Fritzes.

Sundin, Elisabeth (2002), Företagandets manliga prägling (engl.: The male lable of entreprenеruship), in Carin Holmquist and Elisabeth Sundin (eds), *Företagerskan – Om kvinnor och entreprenörskap*, Stockholm: SNS förlag.

Sundin, Elisabeth (2006), 'Unions in the Era of New Public Management – The strategies of the Union of Swedish Nurses (Vårdförbundet)', Paper at the 22nd EGOS Conference in Bergen 6–8 July.

Sundin, Elisabeth and Holmquist, Carin (eds) (1989), *Kvinnor som företagare – osynlighet, mångfald, anpassning – en studie* (engl.: *Women as small firm owners – invisible, diverse and adaptive*), Malmö: Liber.

Supermarket (2000), No. 9, p. 9.

Tillmar, Malin (2004), *Är det möjligt? Om villkor för småföretagande inom vård- och omsorgssektorn* (engl.: *Is it possible? On the conditions for small firms in the health- and care-sector*), Stockholm: NUTEK.

Tillmar, Malin (2005), 'Våffer gör di på detta viset? Villkor för småföretagande inom omsorgen ur ett institutionellt perspektiv' (engl.: 'Why do they do that? Conditions for small firms in the health- and care-sector from an institutional perspective'), *Kommunal Politik och Ekonomi,* 9 (3).

Wennekers, Sander and Roy Thurik (1999), 'Linking entrepreneurship and economic growths', *Small Business Economics*, 15, 27–55.

11. Building on the Micro–Meso–Macro Evolutionary Framework: The Stakes for the Analysis of Clusters of Innovation

Olivier Brette and Caroline Mehier

INTRODUCTION

Recently Kurt Dopfer, John Foster and Jason Potts (2004), thereafter DFP, have developed an analytical framework for evolutionary economics based on a three-level architecture namely the micro, meso and macro levels. The originality of this framework lies in the fact that the authors use the 'micro–meso–macro' distinction in an unfamiliar way which is less classificatory or taxonomic than ontological and analytical. Their approach does indeed not focus on the identification of various classes of economic phenomena but rather on the nature of the relationships between the several analytical levels at which an evolving economic system can be apprehended. According to DFP the main feature of the micro–meso–macro perspective is that it views the social world as a complex and structured open system in which changes occur at the meso level as a result of emergent processes. On this basis the micro–meso–macro perspective claims to provide a unifying framework that can encompass all evolutionary approaches based on the idea that 'economic evolution is a growth of knowledge process'.

Following the argument we will show that Thorstein Veblen's evolutionary economics can be interpreted through the micro–meso–macro lenses. Furthermore it will be argued that such a reappraisal of Veblen's thought can provide many relevant insights to analyse the growth of knowledge process in socioeconomic systems and notably the location of the accumulation of knowledge. Generally speaking the development of the 'New Growth Theory' (or 'Endogenous Growth Theory') and the 'New Economic Geography' has revived the interest of mainstream economists for the agglomeration of economic activities and in particular for the clustering of innovative activities. It is now commonly admitted that these processes of agglomeration and clustering rest on external economies (or externalities) which give rise to cumulative geographical effects. However economic geographers, namely the geographers who are concerned with the spatial characteristics of economic activities, have criticized the method adopted by mainstream economists to analyse these processes. We suggest that the DFP–Veblen micro–meso–macro framework which we will develop further on corresponds to the approach of economic geographers and could provide an appropriate frame to expand a fruitful interdisciplinary dialogue between institutional and evolutionary economists and economic geographers.

The chapter is divided into four sections including the present introduction. Section 2 is primarily ontological and methodological. It considers to what extent Veblen's evolutionary economics can be interpreted as a micro–meso–macro framework and how Veblen's insights can enrich the DFP frame. Section 3 emphasizes some benefits of the DFP–Veblen framework by considering its implications for the analysis of the location of economic activities. We will show that this approach matches the recent so-called 'institutional turn' within economic geography. Accordingly the DFP–Veblen framework could lay the foundations for an evolutionary and institutional economic geography which could concern both non-mainstream economists and economic geographers. In order to highlight the fruitfulness of this approach, we will address the issue of the propensity of innovative activities to agglomerate locally. In this respect we will give some methodological and programmatic insights to analyse the trajectory of the clusters of innovation, conceived as spatial institutional forms of innovation which continually evolve. Section 4 draws some conclusions.

BUILDING ON THE MICRO–MESO–MACRO APPROACH: A DFP–VEBLEN FRAMEWORK FOR EVOLUTIONARY ECONOMICS

Veblen's evolutionary economics can be viewed as a typical case of micro–meso–macro analysis.[1] As will be shown further on, most of Veblen's ontological and methodological principles fit very adequately with those underlying the DFP framework. Besides, interpreting rules in terms of habits enables us to point to the micro–meso–macro architecture of Veblen's economics. We claim that Veblen's theory of habituation could significantly strengthen the behavioural, cognitive and institutional foundations of the DFP frame. Finally we will develop on the main analytical principles in order to deal with the meso trajectory of a new habit emerging, diffusing and maintaining itself, within the DFP–Veblen framework. This three-phase trajectory indeed underlies the growth of knowledge process which takes place in every economic system.

The Ontological and Methodological Foundations of Veblen's and DFP's Evolutionary Economics: A Comparative Analysis

The DFP framework stems from an ontological rejection of both 'historicism' as Karl Popper defines it and 'algebraicism' in the sense given by DFP. Historicism refers to the belief that the course of history is governed by universal and necessary laws such as Karl Marx's historical materialism. Algebraicism relates to the preconception that a genuinely scientific approach of society must be based on mathematical formalism. As Mark Blaug (1999) emphasizes, this unconditional priority given to formalism has been the major distinctive feature of mainstream (orthodox) economics since the 1950s. But this formal requirement has also had many important consequences upon the very content of economic theories, notably upon their behavioural foundations (Dow 2000, pp. 160–61, 165–6). In a general way it has turned mainstream economics into a combination of formal microeconomic propositions in idealized static states, from which macroeconomic consequences have been deduced. Algebraicism thus implies 'a micro–macro division of analysis' and a methodological, if not ontological, reductionism according to which 'the sum of micro is macro, and the decomposition of macro is micro' (DFP 2004, p. 264).

Historicism and algebraicism are also significantly rejected by Veblen on the basis of his evolutionary or 'post-Darwinian' preconceptions and their core postulate of 'cumulative causation'. Given this postulate, evolutionary science aims at theorizing 'a genetic process of evolution … conceived in terms of blind mechanical forces alone, without the help of imputed teleological bias or personalised initiative' (Veblen [1914] 1990, p. 328). As a result Veblen rejects all forms of teleological imputation, including those inherent to historicism and algebraicism. Historicism indeed involves the external imputation of a trend conceived as ineluctable in the course of events (for example the advent of a society without classes). As for algebraicism, it rests on strong *ad hoc* hypotheses, such as the representative agent, aiming at controlling analytically the aggregate consequences of individual interactions.

As DFP emphasize, introducing a meso perspective allows a break with the ontological and methodological principles underlying historicism and algebraicism (or reductionism). It thus allows to view the economic system as an open and complex system of rules which continually evolves. This system more specifically consists of the set of economic rules present in society, namely those rules 'that relate to the production and consumption of goods and services'. The economic system is embedded in a broader environment of rule-systems. As a result of this embeddedness it must be seen as an open complex system the transformation of which cannot be explained only as the outcome of rational actions. Accordingly DFP (2004, p. 266) underline that in a meso perspective the economic agent should be viewed as 'a rule-using and rule-making animal'. Finally the authors assert that the driving force of economic evolution (namely of the growth of knowledge) lies in the process of origination, adoption, adaptation and diffusion of new generic rules into the economic system.

In the main, Veblen supports all these insights. First he ontologically and methodologically opposes all closed-system approaches such as neoclassical economics as well as Herbert Spencer's theory of social evolution based on the alternative 'system of status' (that is compulsory cooperation) *versus* 'system of contract' (that is voluntary cooperation).[2] By and large Veblen's open-system approach rests on his adhesion to the Darwinian postulate of 'cumulative causation'. This postulate involves 'the principle of determinacy' according to which 'every event has a cause' so that 'there can be no first and "uncaused cause"' not even human intentionality and motives (Hodgson 2004a, pp. 54–62). Imposing arbitrary boundaries on the system studied is thus ontologically unfounded and may cause important methodological shortcomings in the analysis. Second Veblen supports the principle of embeddedness according to which economic phenomena cannot be grasped outside of their cultural context. Given that a human being is a social animal whose behaviour is governed by a plurality of motives, it is impossible to understand his economic activity without acknowledging his non economic relations and the reverse is also true. Indeed '[t]he individual is but a single agent in each case; and he enters into each successive action as a whole, although the specific end sought in a given action may be sought avowedly on the basis of a particular interest; as e.g., the economic, aesthetic, sexual, humanitarian, devotional interests' (Veblen [1919] 1990, p. 77). Third, in part as a result of the previous insights, society is to be viewed as a complex system the evolution of which involves emergent processes. According to Veblen ([1904] 1975, p. 374), 'the cultural scheme is, after all, a single one, comprising many interlocking elements, no one of which can be greatly disturbed without disturbing the working of all the rest'. It is thus impossible to understand the nature and the evolution of society by studying its various elements independently of one another. Furthermore it has been shown elsewhere that Veblen analyses the major institutional changes which occur in society as emergent effects in the contemporary sense of this concept (Brette 2003b; 2004a, pp. 282–304). Four, as DFP, Veblen views the economic agent as 'a rule-using and rule-making animal'. He argues that human behaviour is mainly governed by instincts and habits. In his view, habits (namely rules) allow the adaptation of the general motives for human action (instincts) to the specific circumstances of each situation. It is to be stressed that this representation of human behaviour is not in opposition with the acknowledgement of conscious and deliberate actions. Veblen asserts on the contrary that the ability to make and use habits is the *sine qua non* of a purposeful and active human being.[3] Five, Veblen argues, as DFP, that the economic evolution of society consists of an accumulation of knowledge process, which is closely connected with the origination, adoption, adaptation and diffusion of new generic rules that he names institutions. Before considering more precisely how Veblen analyses this growth of knowledge process, let us shed light on the micro–meso–macro architecture of his analytical framework.

Interpreting Rules as Habits: Towards a DFP–Veblen Micro–Meso–Macro Framework

DFP's analysis is centred on the idea that 'an economic system' is 'a set of meso units, where each meso consists of a rule and its population of actualizations'. The distinction which is suggested between the 'rule' and 'its population of actualizations' refers to 'the bimodality of each meso unit' (DFP 2004, pp. 263, 270). This point is significantly developed by Dopfer (2004). In his view, economic rules encompass all 'deductive schemes that allow economic operations to take place' such as techniques, legal rules, strategies, and so on. Besides, he stresses that each rule may have many actualizations since there may exist many carriers of the same rule (Dopfer 2004, pp. 22–3, 41).

We want to highlight that DFP's view of meso units is consistent with Veblen's view of institutions as habits of thought which are shared by many individuals. DFP's distinction between a 'rule' and its 'population of actualizations' indeed corresponds to Veblen's view of habit as an acquired 'propensity to behave [namely to act or think] in a particular way in a particular class of situations' (Hodgson 2004a, p. 169; 2004b).[4] In fact it is only by defining habits as propensities or dispositions, and not as behaviours as such, that we can understand why the same habit may have several actualizations.[5] Acknowledging that many rules are habits in Veblen's sense does not only enable us to establish a parallel between DFP's and Veblen's views. It more fundamentally allows us to strengthen the behavioural, cognitive and institutional foundations of the micro–meso–macro framework for evolutionary economics.[6] It permits us to explain better how individuals make and use rules, how these rules are transmitted among individuals and how they generalize and become institutionalized. In brief, relating the concept of rule to the notion of habit provides firmer foundations to understand the interactions between individuals and structures (Kilpinen 1998, pp. 40–1; Hodgson 2004a, pp. 186–8; 2004b; Brette 2004a, pp. 305–8), which is essential in the perspective of analysing the growth of knowledge process in economic systems.

Since we identify rules to habits, Veblen's analytical framework can be viewed as a micro–meso–macro framework in which micro relates to individual habits of action and thought, meso to institutions and 'institutional logics', and macro to the 'cultural complex' of society. As DFP (2004, pp. 266–7) emphasize, '[t]he rules that matter for understanding economic systems are those that are generic' because they are the ones which provide 'the connective structure of common knowledge that an economic system is made of'. This idea is consistent with Veblen's view of institutions as factors that are essential in the structuring of social relationships, both in a synchronic and diachronic perspective (Brette 2004a, pp. 255–61). To the extent that they are mental frames shared by many individuals in a society at a given time, institutions are vital to interpersonal communication and coordination. Moreover since habits are socially transmissible, institutions confer a relative stability in time to the organization of society. This is all the more true as, in every society, institutions are dependent on one another. First we can generally encompass several institutions in a same set, which Veblen named an 'institutional logic'. It can be defined as a general way of thinking in which lie several institutions consistent with one another.[7] In fact Veblen's notion of institutional logic is very close to Dopfer's (2004, p. 41) concept of 'rule pool' namely 'a pool composed of different rules with the same genus – i.e. fundamental content'. Second all the institutions and institutional logics present in a society at a given time form a structured whole, which Veblen sometimes names the 'cultural complex' of society (Brette 2004a, pp. 262–5). Dealing with the cultural complex of society is the concern of evolutionary macroeconomics in DFP's view. Veblen is particularly interested in theorizing the nature and evolution of cultural complexes, both their 'deep structure', that is 'how the generic rules themselves fit together', and their 'surface structure', that is 'how deep structure manifests itself' (DFP 2004, pp. 270–71).

Let us now expose the main analytical principles to deal with the meso trajectories underlying the growth of knowledge process which takes place in society, within the DFP–Veblen framework.

Some General Insights to Analyse Meso Trajectories Within the DFP–Veblen Framework

According to DFP a 'meso trajectory' can be divided into three phases: the origination, the diffusion and the retention of a novel rule in an economic system. Furthermore each of these phases involves both micro and macro processes.

In DFP's view every meso trajectory starts with an agent developing a new idea/rule into the micro-organizational sphere. In Veblen's analysis the phase of origination (*meso 1*) also begins with an individual producing a new piece of knowledge. In his view this creative process can respond to several motives. Veblen distinguishes three main instinctive proclivities in the making of knowledge: the 'idle curiosity' from which scientific knowledge notably derives, the 'sense of workmanship' which supports the growth of technological knowledge and the instincts of rivalry, including profit seeking, from which stems 'pragmatic knowledge' including business principles (that is the arts of bargaining, salesmanship, and so on) (Brette 2004a, pp. 31–67). Besides, new knowledge is going to be embodied within new individual habits of action and thought. As the case may be, this process of habituation can be more or less deliberate and purposeful. According to DFP the phase *meso 1* will have macro consequences in so far as the novel rule is unsuited to the prevailing order. In other words the novel rule may initiate a macro 'de-coordination process'. In Veblen's view this process of disrupting and questioning the macro order will become effective only if the new habits become mass adopted (phase *meso 2*). In the phase of origination Veblen focuses on the processes of downward causation rather than upward causation. According to him the most important effects are those which the prevailing cultural complex exerts on the rate and character of the knowledge gains.[8]

In DFP's view the phase of diffusion (*meso 2*) is characterized from a micro standpoint by the adoption of the new idea/rule and its adaptation to different local environments. This is a phase of learning and experimentation for the followers who contest the novel situation induced by the emergence of the new rule (for example a monopoly position on a market) or try to adapt the new rule to other contexts (for example in related markets). The 'path to full adoption' ends in 'a process of normalization of behaviours about the new rule' (DFP 2004, p. 275). In Veblen's terms the phase *meso 2* typically corresponds to a process of 'institutionalization' namely a process of generalization of the new habit among a given population. From a micro viewpoint this phase consists of the transmission of the habits of action and thought embodying the new knowledge. Once habits are 'settled' and 'common to the generality of men' (Veblen [1919] 1990, p. 239), they can be viewed as 'institutions' and thus as 'repositories of social knowledge' (Hodgson 2004a, p. 181). Furthermore Veblen argues that the phase of diffusion leads to diversification in the actualizations of the rule, namely to variety in the behaviours stemming from the same habit and to the emergence of related habits leading *in fine* to the formation of an institutional logic. As

DFP, Veblen emphasizes that the phase *meso 2* involves a process of 'de-coordination' then 're-coordination' at the macro level. In his view this process of de-structuring and re-structuring of the cultural complex of society is based on positive feedback between micro agents and macro structures, whose cornerstone lies in the social transmission of habits at the meso level.

In DFP's analysis the phase *meso 3* is characterized by 'the retention of the rule and its population (the meso) as an on-going process'. The authors strongly stress that 'this is achieved through maintenance in the micro and replication in the macro and in both cases refers to a meta-stable distribution of normalized or institutionalized activities'. As DFP, Veblen emphasizes that from a micro standpoint the normalization of behaviours, which is based on shared habits of action and thought, consists only in 'meta-stability' as human beings keep on creating. From a macro viewpoint the phase *meso 3* relates, in Veblen's analysis, to a situation in which the cultural complex of society has become relatively coherent and stable. In such a state a certain institutional logic has succeeded in becoming predominant and in subordinating all the other institutional logics of the cultural complex (coherence) and this balance of power between the different institutional logics tends to maintain itself in time (stability) (Brette 2004a, pp. 271–4). However this 'meta-stability' does not involve a pause in the evolution of the economic system, given the creativity of human beings. In particular the predominant institutional logic keeps on developing incrementally. In fact the very 'meta-stability' of the system may be supported through the increasing elaboration and refinement over time of the prevailing institutional logic, for example through its embodiment in law. But it also happens that the cumulative nature of these incremental variations leads to question radically the deep structure of the cultural complex (Brette 2004a, pp. 300–4).[9] In the main the 'meta-stability' which characterizes the phase of retention of a meso trajectory, both in DFP's and Veblen's analyses, should be interpreted in terms of lock-in and not in terms of neoclassical equilibrium. We finally fall back here on an essential point of evolutionary ontology and methodology. Evolutionary economics indeed implies an irreversible conception of time, which breaks with the Newtonian mechanistic framework from which neoclassical economists draw their own concept of linear and ahistorical causality (Dopfer 1986). In this respect evolutionary economics is quite consistent with Darwin, who put forward the history of species against Newton's equilibrant dynamics of mechanical forces (Hodgson 2004a, pp. 91–2).

ANALYSING THE LOCATION OF INNOVATIVE ACTIVITIES WITHIN THE DFP–VEBLEN MICRO–MESO–MACRO FRAMEWORK

This section focuses on one of the areas of investigation in which the DFP–Veblen framework could be fruitfully applied, namely the location of economic activities. Starting from a brief survey of the evolution of economic geography since the mid-1970s, we will show that the 'institutional turn' which this discipline has recently experienced has paved the way for the development of synergies with evolutionary and institutional economics. In this respect the DFP–Veblen framework previously exposed could be appropriate to the development of an economic geography that would be both evolutionary and institutional. We will highlight the characteristics and the explanatory potential of this approach by addressing the question of the clustering of innovative activities. In this perspective we will give some insights to analyse the dynamics of clusters as the meso trajectory of spatial institutional forms of innovation.

For an Evolutionary and Institutional Economic Geography

In his contribution to *The Social Science Encyclopaedia*, Trevor Barnes (1996, p. 217) stresses that economic geography was born in the late nineteenth century as 'a sub-discipline within human geography concerned with describing and explaining the production, distribution, exchange and consumption of goods and services within an explicitly spatial economy'. While commonly using a historicism-type approach highlighting the uniqueness of each region in the period between the World Wars, economic geography experienced in the mid-1950s a methodological revolution which was quite similar to and partly inspired by the formalist revolution in economics. Economic geography then turned into 'spatial science' or 'regional science', increasingly resorting to sophisticated quantitative techniques and formal modelling. However, from the mid-1970s, this approach came under the attack of a group of radical geographers inspired by Karl Marx's theses, who criticized it for its neglect of the social context in which the location of economic activities occurs. Consequently 'spatial science' was progressively displaced by an alternative approach which was much less formalized and more empirically focused. Since then this approach has imposed itself as the mainstream paradigm in economic geography, even though it has been partly criticized and developed in several ways (Barnes 1996). Nonetheless the formalised 'spatial science' has not vanished from the academic scene. It has significantly benefited from a revival of interest in the location of economic activities by some prominent mainstream economists such as Paul Krugman, Robert Barro, Xavier Sala-i-Martin, and so on. But most contemporary economic geographers have found little interest in this (so-called) 'New Economic Geography' or 'geographical economics'. As the economic geographer Ron Martin (1999) indeed emphasizes, 'it represents a reworking of regional science and urban economics models, precisely the sort of approaches that geographers discarded years ago'.

Far from formal modelling economic geography has developed, as we said, in different ways since the mid-1970s. Economic geographers have in particular been increasingly interested in explaining how the institutional structures both influence and are themselves modified by the localization of economic activities – see among others Martin (1999), Philo and Parr (2000), Martin and Sunley (2001)[10] and Wood and Valler (2001). This 'institutional turn' within economic geography has attracted the interest of some geographers for the 'original institutional economics' the major inspiration of which has been Thorstein Veblen (McLeod 2001, pp. 1149–51; Cumbers, McKinnon and McMaster 2003). In this respect Roger Hayter (2004) has recently offered a well-informed reading of the 'original institutional economics' literature and has outlined 'a framework that explicitly connects the tradition of dissenting [i.e. original] institutional economics with economic geography'. In his paper Hayter identifies and discusses the major principles of the 'social economy' depicted by institutional economists, namely 'embeddedness', 'evolution' and 'difference', and relates them to the works of the economic geographers who have endorsed the 'institutional turn'. Finally Hayter's analysis is all the more interesting as it does not only highlight the significance for economic geography of the works of institutional economists proper, but also abundantly refers to contemporary evolutionary economists such as Richard Nelson, Christopher Freeman, Giovanni Dosi, Gerald Silverberg, and so on. In a general way the 'institutional turn' in economic geography thus offers an important opportunity to expand a fruitful interdisciplinary dialogue between economic geographers and the economists who do not share the ontological and methodological principles underlying 'geographical economics', namely institutional and evolutionary economists. We think that the DFP–Veblen framework could provide an appropriate frame to develop such exchanges about the location of economic activities and notably the clustering of innovative activities.

In a similar way a comprehensive proposal to develop an evolutionary economic geography has been recently outlined by Ron Boschma and Koen Frenken (2005). Even if we think highly of their project as a whole, we have some reservations about the framework they propose. Boschma and Frenken distinguish three main approaches in economic geography which they relate to three different approaches in economics: the Neoclassical Economic

Geography (NEG) notably including the 'New Economic Geography' developed by mainstream economists, the Institutional Economic Geography (IEG) which the authors mainly associate to the 'original institutional economics' and the Evolutionary Economic Geography (EEG), namely the use of 'core concepts and methodologies from evolutionary economics in the context of economic geography'. Then Boschma and Frenken try to identify the main similarities and differences between these three approaches. They argue that NEG and IEG fundamentally differ in two respects. First neoclassical economic geographers usually resort to mathematical models which 'start from a "neutral space" and aim at explaining how agglomeration can occur from this', whereas 'institutional economic geographers dismiss a priori the use of formal modelling and econometric specifications derived from these'. Second 'the two approaches differ in their behavioural assumptions underlying explanations of economic phenomena', the former depicting individuals as utility-maximising agents, the latter as rule-guided beings. Besides, they assert that EEG shares with NEG the appeal for mathematical modelling, while it agrees with the behavioural foundations of IEG namely bounded rationality and rule/routine-guiding. Finally they claim that EEG is a fundamentally dynamic approach, whereas IEG is mainly static, being based on comparative analyses.

Our first disagreement with Boschma and Frenken (2005) lies in a quite different reading of institutional, evolutionary and mainstream economics. Firstly we think that there is a difference in nature between evolutionary and institutional economists on the one hand and mainstream economists on the other regarding formal modelling. As Geoffrey Hodgson (2002, p. xvii) indeed rightly argues, 'institutional and evolutionary economists did not entirely reject mathematics as a tool, but they were critical of the tendency of the mainstream to become immersed in mathematical technique for its own sake'. The fact that Nelson and Winter (1982, pp. 46–8) acknowledge and combine two different ways of theorizing, namely 'appreciative theorizing' and 'formal modelling', opposes the absolute and unconditional appeal of mainstream economists for formalism. Secondly we disagree with the idea that the institutional approach is mainly a static approach. In this respect Boschma and Frenken's thesis is all the more surprising as the very title of their paper paraphrases the famous article of Veblen ([1919] 1990, pp. 56–81), 'Why Is Economics Not an Evolutionary Science?', which precisely aimed at laying the foundations for an economics that would be both institutional and evolutionary.

Furthermore we do not support two methodological principles put forward by Boschma and Frenken (2005) which have strong consequences on the analysis of meso trajectories. Firstly they put forward that 'EEG has theoretical reasons to assume that firms operate in a neutral space' (p. 16). In our view this approach is inconsistent with the evolutionary principle of path dependence as it has been developed by Veblen, Paul David (1985) and Kenneth Arrow (2000). According to this principle, 'each new situation is a variation of what has gone before it and embodies as causal factors all that has been effected by what went before' (Veblen [1919] 1990, p. 242). This view, which stems from the Darwinian postulate of 'cumulative causation', leads to the dismissal of the very notion of 'neutral place', that is 'an initially uniform world' without any local specificity. It implies on the contrary that every place is a 'real place' with specific characteristics which result from the historical, institutional, technological and geographical evolution. As Ron Martin (1999, p. 80) emphasizes, path dependence has 'a place-dependent character'. The inheritance of local characteristics notably involves the existence (or the lack) of externalities specific to the place. In particular 'the institutional forms of knowledge production-diffusion [proper to the place considered] are essential in the emergence and management of externalities' (Feldman and Massard 2002, p. 6). Secondly Boschma and Frenken argue that institutional approaches give an excessive weight to the macro context, leading to an over-socialized account of economic behaviour. As we said previously this criticism must be questioned in the case of Veblen's evolutionary and institutional economics. His conception of institutions in terms of habits does not indeed oppose the acknowledging of purposeful and heterogeneous human behaviours. In so far as institutions are viewed as acquired propensities to act or think in a particular way under certain circumstances, they can be variously actualized by different individuals, namely by different 'carriers' of the same habit. Consequently we disagree with Boschma and Frenken's (2005, p. 14) assertion according to which 'from an evolutionary perspective, to take institutions as explanatory variables in economic analysis is illogical'. On the contrary we should take institutions as explanatory variables, to the extent that we consider that they do not entirely constrain individual behaviour and that they themselves must be explained, notably as a result of individual actions. As Veblen ([1919] 1990, p. 243) states:

> The growth and mutations of the institutional fabric are an outcome of the conduct of the individual members of the group, since it is out of the experience of the individuals, through the habituation of individuals, that institutions arise; and it is in this same experience that these institutions act to direct and define the aims and end of conduct.

Some Guidelines to Analyse Clusters of Innovation Within the DFP–Veblen Framework

In the last decades the spatial clustering of economic activities has increasingly attracted the interest of social scientists in economics, geography and management.[11] As a result we can find in the literature so many different approaches of clusters that Martin and Sunley (2003, p. 10) argue that the very concept has become 'chaotic' 'in the sense of conflating and equating quite different types, processes and spatial scales of economic localization under a single, all-embracing universalistic notion'. In fact, as Jacobs and de Man (1996, p. 425) assert, 'there is not one correct definition of the cluster concept ... different dimensions are of interest'. Built on various selected dimensions, the analyses of clusters offered in the literature thus witness the diversity of the types of clusters.[12] However these typologies, in their taxonomic perspective, do not sufficiently take into account the dynamics of clusters. Generally speaking we still know little, both theoretically and empirically, about how clusters develop and evolve. Accordingly the researches about their life cycle and their evolutionary trajectory need to be expanded (Malmberg and Maskell 2002; Audretsch and Feldman 2003; Nooteboom 2005).[13]

We propose to focus here on the clusters of innovative activities and to conceptualize them as spatial institutional forms of innovation which continually evolve. The cluster of innovation is an institutional form of innovation, in the sense that it can be viewed as an acquired propensity, namely a habit, to agglomerate economic activities in a specific (real) place in order to face the problems inherent to the complexity and uncertainty of innovative activities. Moreover, in accordance with our micro–meso–macro perspective, we are especially interested in the evolution of this institutional form. We will thus successively analyse the different phases of the meso trajectory of clusters of innovation, namely the phases of origination, diffusion and retention. Understanding this meso trajectory demands shedding light on the micro and macro processes which are implied in each of these phases and which shape the way according to which the propensity to cluster will be actualized.[14] However our present aim is not to give a detailed and accomplished analysis of the meso trajectory of clusters of innovation, but some methodological and programmatic insights in order to illustrate the heuristic potential of the DFP–Veblen framework. Accordingly we will only emphasize the 'upward and downward causations' (Hodgson 2004a) which link the micro, meso and macro levels and which play a crucial role in the directing of the meso trajectory of clusters.

Our approach is based on three main hypotheses. Firstly we suppose that two vital kinds of externalities[15] may give rise to spatial agglomeration processes: the pecuniary externalities and the knowledge externalities. Pecuniary externalities are a joint-product of market interactions. They relate to the positive effects which the agglomeration of economic agents exerts on the cost structure of firms, for example on the costs of infrastructure, transaction, hiring, and so on. They arise 'if the inflow of new firms enlarges the local market through the additional demand they generate' (Fujita and Thisse 2002, p. 8). Knowledge externalities are the product of non-market interactions. They relate to the knowledge spillovers, namely the non-market transfers of knowledge, which allow an increase in the innovative performance of the firms which are located in the same area. They arise 'if the inflow of new firms increases the efficiency of local firms because they enhance the productivity of labour through a social learning process' (Fujita and Thisse 2002, p. 8). Secondly we assume that each of these types of externalities is more or less significant depending on the phase of the life cycle of the cluster. Thirdly it is meaningful to suppose that the life cycle of the cluster is itself closely linked to the life cycle of the industries involved. As Audretsch and Feldman (1996, p. 271) indeed emphasize, there is 'considerable evidence suggesting that the propensity for innovative activity to spatially cluster is shaped by the stage of the industry life cycle' (see also Boschma, Neffke and Oort 2005). We will thus assume that the type of externalities (pecuniary or knowledge) giving rise to the agglomeration process depends on the dynamic structure of the industries involved in the cluster, notably whether they tend to diversify or specialize. Even if the various studies on the subject do not reach a consensus,[16] we will try to formulate some assumptions concerning each phase of the meso trajectory of the cluster life cycle.

Phase *Meso 1*: Origination of Clusters of Innovation

Generally speaking, we suppose that the location of innovative activities depends on two kinds of factors: the factors internal to the organization, which relate to its innovation strategy, and the environment in which the organization stands, namely the external factors. We assume that any cluster of innovation originates in the adequacy between an innovation strategy peculiar to a firm and a context favourable to the implementation of this strategy.[17] The essential feature in the origination phase of the cluster is thus that a firm identifies and takes advantage of the opportunity to locate its innovative activities in a place where some resources match its own innovation strategy.

The notion of 'real place' is central from the very first phase of development of the cluster. Firms are not isolated actors but evolve in an environment which may act (or not) as an incubator for their innovative activities. For instance Audretsch and Feldman (1996, p. 254) have shown that 'certain types of knowledge sources, such as university research tend to lead to a clustering of innovative activity in the introduction stage of the life cycle'. Besides, local actors, be they public authorities or other firms, may 'provide technical, financial and networking services which the region's enterprises often cannot afford individually' (Saxenian 1990, pp. 96–7). Finally the power of attraction of a particular area largely depends on the 'region's past success with innovation' (Audretsch and Feldman 2003).

It is to be stressed that however important the role played by the environment in the origination of clusters, what is vital is the adequacy between this environment and the specific strategy of firms aiming at taking advantage of particular externalities in terms of costs and/or knowledge. In other words '[w]hat is critical [in the origination of any cluster] is that conditions in the region simultaneously provided opportunities and pushed individuals towards opportunity exploitation' (Feldman, Francis and Bercovitz 2005, p. 138).

Phase *Meso 2*: Diffusion of the Propensity to Cluster

This phase is characterized by the fact that some other firms grow aware of the opportunity to follow the localization strategy of the prime mover firm. It is precisely at this point that the cluster properly forms. But contrary to Pouder and St John (1996) who claim that the strategy formulation within the cluster becomes homogenous, we suggest that the diffusion of the propensity to agglomerate does not imply that firms reproduce the same strategy as that of the prime mover. The adoption of the localization strategy goes along with its adaptation by the following firms. In other words, the propensity to agglomerate is actualized differently depending on the carrier of the habit and its own motives. For instance, Marjolein Caniëls and Henny Romijn (2005, p. 503) distinguish four 'different advantages that clusters generate for innovation at the firm level': the 'spontaneous costs advantages' which are linked to favourable market conditions in terms of demand pull, the 'facilitated costs advantages' through local collaborations, the 'spontaneous spillovers' in the form of the non-market diffusion of technological knowledge and skills, and the 'facilitated spillovers' which relate to the transfers of knowledge and skills induced by local collaborations. These different motives for agglomeration can operate in various ways in the localization strategies of firms.

The beginning of the phase *meso 2* is characterized by industrial diversity in the local environment (early stage of the cluster life cycle) and by the fact that no product 'dominant design' has still emerged in the industry considered (early stage of the industry life cycle).[18] Under these conditions, the firms which settle their innovative activities in the area must try to take advantage of spillovers by getting closer to useful sources of knowledge. The diversity in the local industrial environment indeed favours radical innovations (Boschma, Neffke and Oort 2005). Besides, since '[d]uring the early stages of the industry life cycle, tacit knowledge should play a relatively more important role in generating innovative activity' (Audretsch and Feldman 1996, p. 259), firms need to come closer so that tacit knowledge could be transmitted through face-to-face contacts. During the later stages of the phase *meso 2*, the cluster often tends to specialize from an industrial point of view, as a 'dominant design' gradually emerges (Paci and Usai 1999). As Corinne Autant-Bernard and Nadine Massard (2005, p. 18) have shown from an empirical analysis based on individual French data, this 'specialisation would favour pecuniary externalities originating from the proximity to other firms'. The main motives for joining the cluster then relate to cost-cutting strategies.

Generally speaking, the clustering process induces important consequences at the macro level, namely a movement towards de-structuring and re-structuring of the industrial sector as well as of the market. Many actors actually try to shape this movement. Political powers, be they regional or national, generally attempt to influence the movement either by supporting it, restraining it or giving it a specific direction. Policies implemented can take the form of direct public financing (subsidies for example), building of infrastructures and indirect financial supports (for instance through the financing of public research centres). It is to be stressed that the content of these policies often generates conflicts between political actors. In this respect, the DFP–Veblen framework does not 'take regions for granted as coherent spaces' but acknowledges 'possible intraregional divisions and tensions' (Cumbers, McKinnon and McMaster 2003, p. 329). We consider that regions are generally the seat of several institutional logics competing with one another. As Hayter (2004, p. 107) indeed emphasizes, 'regions define territories where there are *both* common values, processes of valuation and regulations, modes of thought, and distinct grooves to local life and/or where there are clashes of values over how the available territory is to be used and what the conventions and regulations should be'.

Phase *Meso 3*: Retention of Clusters of Innovation

At the early stage of this phase, the propensity to agglomerate has been actualized by a significant number of firms. The cluster then reaches a critical stage when the advantages of agglomeration start to decrease while the costs of agglomeration grow heavier and heavier due to various effects of congestion (Swann, Prevezer and Stout 1998). At this point many analyses consider that the cluster enters an inevitable phase of decline (see for instance Pouder and St John 1996). Unlike these authors we think that the cluster may follow different trajectories depending on both external and internal factors.

On the one hand, the fact that the DFP–Veblen framework is based on an open-system approach allows us to acknowledge the impact of external factors on the dynamics of clusters. Accordingly it enables us to take into account the part which factors such as industrial and territorial policies, intra-corporate knowledge transfers (between the subsidiaries of multinational companies notably),[19] inter-regional relationships (Martin and Sunley 2003) and globalization[20] may play in the revival of clusters. On the other hand, the cluster may enter a new phase of development as a result of factors that are inherent to its own dynamics. While the 'propensity for innovative activity to geographically cluster would be expected to ... decline as the industry evolves over the life cycle towards maturity' (Audretsch and Feldman 1996, p. 259), we can suppose that other forces of agglomeration may take over (Caniëls and Romijn 2005), thus allowing the cluster to regenerate. In particular the clustering of innovative activities in a given sector can give rise to a new process of agglomeration in related sectors. Once it has reached the mature stage of its life cycle, it indeed happens that the cluster tends to diversify in terms of knowledge accumulated, actors implied and industries involved, thanks notably to the innovation strategies of suppliers. Audretsch (2005, p. 31) himself points out that 'diversity across complementary economic activities sharing a common knowledge base is more conducive to innovation, and therefore economic growth and global competitiveness, than is specialization'. Consequently the cluster of innovation may enter a new life cycle namely follow a new meso trajectory.

CONCLUSION

Our chapter aimed at showing that the micro–meso–macro framework developed by Kurt Dopfer, John Foster and Jason Potts (2004) could benefit from certain insights which Veblen put forward a century ago. In this respect we have notably suggested to consider what DFP name 'rules' as 'habits' in Veblen's sense, namely as acquired propensities to act or think in a particular way under certain circumstances, which can be variously actualized depending on their carrier. Accordingly we have laid the foundations of a DFP–Veblen micro–meso–macro framework for evolutionary economics, which better accounts for the interactions between individuals and structures. We have then applied this framework to the study of the location of economic activities. We think that the DFP–Veblen framework could be appropriate to the building of an economic geography which would be both evolutionary and institutional, and which could concern both non-mainstream economists and economic geographers. According to the economic geographer, Ron Martin (1999, p. 83), it is to be regretted that '[f]or the vast majority of economists, there are just two levels at which economic processes operate and at which theoretical exposition is needed: the micro-level of individual households and firms, and the macro-level of nation states'. We share this viewpoint and consequently suggest developing an evolutionary and institutional economic geography which would be centred on the meso trajectories and which would consider both micro and macro processes in their relations to these trajectories. It is to be stressed that such an approach avoids the shortcomings inherent to two kinds of analyses, the ones which underestimate or take for granted the role of institutions in the localization of economic activities, namely 'geographical economics', and the ones which look into the sole institutions for the entire explanation of the economic geographical phenomena, namely 'soft institutionalism' (see McLeod 2001).

In order to highlight the benefits which could be expected from the DFP–Veblen framework, we have suggested some methodological and programmatic guidelines to reconsider the issue of the clustering of innovative activities. We have conceptualized the clusters of innovation as spatial institutional forms of innovation, analysed the three phases of their meso trajectories (that is the origination, diffusion and retention), and outlined the micro and macro processes implied in each of these phases. This way of contemplating the clustering of innovative activities offers the great advantage of providing a structured and including frame to grasp the various evolutionary features of the phenomenon. Nevertheless the analysis of clusters of innovation which we have developed is still embryonic and deserves to be widely enriched in both theoretical and empirical ways. We need to specify more precisely the micro and macro processes which influence the manner according to which the meso propensity to cluster is actualized. We should also clarify the relative significance of the various motives for agglomeration in the different phases of the cluster life cycle, according to the prevailing characteristics of the industry involved. In so far as it integrates both the costs of access to external knowledge (Andersson and Karlsson 2004; Andersson and Ejermo 2005) and the functional dimensions of knowledge (Iammarino and McCann 2005), the notion of accessibility to knowledge could be a fruitful way to deal simultaneously with pecuniary and knowledge externalities (Massard and Mehier 2008). Finally the political implications of our analysis to promote regional development and innovation remain to be drawn.

NOTES

1. Our interpretation of Veblen's thought mainly rests on Brette (2004a).
2. Following Sheila C. Dow (2002, p. 137) we define closed-system approaches as being all theoretical systems in which 'the boundaries ... are predetermined, as are the full range of

constituent variables and the structure of their interrelationships'. Algebraicism, and thus neoclassical economics, falls into closed-system approaches because of the reason previously mentioned, namely it rests on *ad hoc* hypotheses aiming at controlling analytically the aggregate consequences of individual interactions. Herbert Spencer's theory of social development also falls into this category since it is based on a dualist typology of societies, which is supposed to be exhaustive and definitive (Veblen [1919] 1990, pp. 387–408; Brette 2004a, pp. 185–93).

3. For an extensive analysis of Veblen's theory of human behaviour, see Hodgson (2004a, pp. 153–75; 2004b) and Brette (2004a, pp. 205–78).
4. Veblen's conception of habit notably derives from the pragmatist philosophy and psychology of Charles Sanders Peirce and William James (Hodgson 2004b; Brette 2004a, pp. 243–51).
5. Contrary to Veblen, mainstream economists such as Gary S. Becker commonly view habits as repeated behaviours (Hodgson 2004b).
6. Dopfer (2004, p. 37) himself suggests that 'individual routines can be associated with the notion of habit'. But our stance is fairly more comprehensive since we argue that many individual and social rules can be viewed as habits.
7. For example Veblen ([1914] 1990) refers to the 'logic of workmanship' (pp. 54, 61), the 'logic of the price system' or 'pecuniary logic' (pp. 190, 226), the 'logic of the machine process' (pp. 241, 310, 318, 322, 338) or the 'matter-of-fact logic' (p. 306).
8. For an extensive analysis of Veblen's theses regarding the accumulation of technological knowledge, see Brette (2003a; 2004b).
9. This process significantly illustrates the endogenous character of Veblen's theory of institutional change (Brette 2003b).
10. The paper of Martin and Sunley (2001) is a reply, well-founded in our view, to Amin and Thrift (2000).
11. See notably Porter (1990, 1998a, 1998b), Arthur (1990), Baptista (1997), Rosenfield (1997), Roeland and den Hertog (1999), Swann, Prevezer and Stout (1998). For a review of theoretical approaches of clusters in economics, see Belussi (2004).
12. Clusters can vary in terms of size, state of development, resource and competence bases, power distribution, type of ties, and so on; see for example the typologies of Markusen (1996) and Iammarino and McCann (2005).
13. Even if Pouder and St John (1996) have proposed a theory of the life cycle of clusters, their approach is only based on the costs/advantages of the agglomeration effects. Besides, Swann, Prevezer and Stout (1998) only relate the life cycle of clusters to the life cycle of the technologies developed.
14. Actually the interest of developing a comprehensive approach of clusters which would take into account and link together the micro, meso and macro levels of analysis, has often been argued; see for instance Bergman and Feser (1999).
15. On the notion of externality, see notably Marshall (1920), Arrow (1962), Romer (1986, 1990) – cf. the so-called MAR externalities – and Jacobs (1969, 1984).
16. One can refer to the formal approach of Pouder and St John (1996) who suggest that the strength of economies and diseconomies of agglomeration varies with the age of clusters, to the work of Bianchi, Miller and Bertini (1997) on the cluster life cycle and to the econometric study of Paci and Usai (1999).
17. Following Caniëls and Romijn (2005, p. 498), we suppose that firms are 'the key loci of decision making in processes of innovation and learning'.
18. For a brief but recent survey on the industry life cycle hypothesis, see Nelson and Winter (2002, pp. 35–6).
19. See Almeida (1996), Frost (2001), Gorg and Strobl (2001) and Cantwell and Iammarino (2003).
20. According to Håkanson (2005), globalization can favour clustering in three different ways. By enlarging the volume of demand that can be addressed to (and from) a single location, it can dramatically increase the scope for specialization and division of labour. It can also

increase the flows of inward foreign direct investment to some regions. Finally it can promote skilled immigration on an increasing scale.

REFERENCES

Almeida, P. (1996), 'Knowledge sourcing by foreign multinationals: patent citation analysis in the U.S. semiconductor industry', *Strategic Management Journal*, 17, Special Issue: Knowledge and the Firm, Winter, 155–65.

Amin, A. and N. Thrift (2000), 'What kind of economic theory for what kind of economic geography?', *Antipode*, 32 (1), 4–9.

Andersson, M. and O. Ejermo (2005), 'How does accessibility to knowledge sources affect the innovativeness of corporations? Evidence from Sweden', *The Annals of Regional Science*, 39 (4), 741–65.

Andersson, M. and C. Karlsson (2004), 'The role of accessibility for the performance of regional innovation systems', *Working Paper Series in Economics and Institutions of Innovation*, Paper No. 09, The Royal Institute of Technology, Centre of Excellence for Science and Innovation Studies, August.

Arrow, K.J. (1962), 'The economic implications of learning by doing', *Review of Economic Studies*, 29 (3), 155–73.

Arrow, K.J. (2000), 'Increasing returns: historiographic issues and path dependence', *European Journal of the History of Economic Thought*, 7 (2), 171–9.

Arthur, W.B. (1990), '"Silicon Valley" locational clusters: when do increasing returns imply monopoly?', *Mathematical Social Science*, 19 (3), 235–51.

Audretsch, D.B. (2005), 'Entrepreneurship, cluster formation and the strategic management of places', Paper for the APEC Symposium on *Industrial Clustering for SMEs*, Taipei, 7–9 March.

Audretsch, D.B. and M.P. Feldman (1996), 'Innovative clusters and the industry life-cycle', *Review of Industrial Organization*, 11 (2), 253–73.

Audretsch, D.B. and M.P. Feldman (2003), 'Knowledge spillovers and the geography of innovation', in J.V. Henderson and J. Thisse (eds), *Handbook of Urban and Regional Economics*, Vol. 4, Amsterdam: North Holland Publishing.

Autant-Bernard, C. and N. Massard (2005), 'Pecuniary and knowledge externalities as agglomeration forces: empirical evidence from individual French data', Paper for the *Knowledge and Regional Economic Development* Conference, Barcelona (Spain), June 9–11.

Baptista, R. (1997), *An Empirical Study of Innovation, Entry and Diffusion in Industrial Clusters*, Ph.D. Thesis, University of London, London Business School.

Barnes, T.J. (1996), 'Economic geography', in A. and J. Kuper (eds), *The Social Science Encyclopedia*, 2nd edition, London, UK and New York, US: Routledge.

Belussi, F. (2004), 'In search of a useful theory of spatial clustering', Paper for the 4th Congress on *Proximity Economics: Proximity, Networks and Co-ordination*, Marseille (France), 17–18 June.

Bergman, E.M. and E.J. Feser (1999), *Industrial and Regional Clusters: Concepts and Comparative Applications*, Web Book in Regional Science, Regional Research Institute, West Virginia University.

Bianchi, P., L.M. Miller and S. Bertini (1997), 'The Italian SME experience and possible lessons for emerging countries', *NOMISMA Working Paper*, United

Nations Industrial Development Organization (UNIDO).
Blaug, M. (1999), 'The formalist revolution or what happened to orthodox economics after World War II?', in R.E. Backhouse and J. Creedy (eds), *From Classical Economics to the Theory of the Firm: Essays in Honour of D.P. O'Brien*, Cheltenham, UK and Northampton, MA, USA: Edward Elgar.
Boschma, R.A. and K. Frenken (2005), 'Why is economic geography not an evolutionary science? Towards an evolutionary economic geography', *Papers in Evolutionary Economic Geography*, #05.01, Urban and Regional Research Centre, Utrecht University.
Boschma, R.A., F. Neffke and F. Oort (2005), 'Externalities and the industry life cycle: the changing influence of spillovers in UK counties (1841–1971)', Paper for the 5th Spring School in *Economic Geography*, Cagliari (Italia), 22–24 May.
Brette, O. (2003a), 'L'accumulation des connaissances technologiques dans la pensée de Thorstein Veblen: ressources pour l'analyse évolutionniste contemporaine', *Économie Appliquée*, 56 (4), 7–38.
Brette, O. (2003b), 'Thorstein Veblen's theory of institutional change: beyond technological determinism', *European Journal of the History of Economic Thought*, 10 (3), 455–77.
Brette, O. (2004a), *Un Réexamen de l'Economie 'Evolutionniste' de Thorstein Veblen. Théorie de la Connaissance, Comportements Humains et Dynamique des Institutions*, Ph.D. Thesis, University of Lyon 2.
Brette, O. (2004b), 'Connaissances technologiques, institutions et droits de propriété dans la pensée de Thorstein Veblen', *Cahiers d'Économie Politique*, 48, 111–45.
Caniëls, M.J.C. and H.A. Romijn (2005), 'What drives innovativeness in industrial clusters? Transcending the debate', *Cambridge Journal of Economics*, 29 (4), 497–515.
Cantwell, J.A. and S. Iammarino (2003), *Multinational Corporations and European Regional Systems of Innovation*, London, UK and New York, US: Routledge.
Cumbers, A., D. McKinnon and R. McMaster (2003), 'Institutions, power and space. Assessing the limits to institutionalism in economic geography', *European Urban and Regional Studies*, 10 (4), 325–42.
David, P.A. (1985), 'Clio and the economics of QWERTY', *American Economic Review*, 75 (2), 332–37.
Dopfer, K. (1986), 'Causality and consciousness in economics: concepts of change in orthodox and heterodox economics', reprinted in W.J. Samuels and M.R. Tool (eds) (1989), *The Methodology of Economic Thought*, 2nd edition revised, New Brunswick, US and London, UK: Transaction Publishers.
Dopfer, K. (2004), 'Evolutionary economics: a theoretical framework', in K. Dopfer (ed.), *The Evolutionary Foundations of Economics*, Cambridge: Cambridge University Press.
Dopfer, K., J. Foster and J. Potts (2004), 'Micro-meso-macro', *Journal of Evolutionary Economics*, 14 (3), 263–79.
Dow, S.C. (2000), 'Prospects for the progress of heterodox economics', *Journal of the History of Economic Thought*, 22 (2), 157–70.
Dow, S.C. (2002), 'Methodological pluralism and pluralism of method', in G.M. Hodgson (ed.), *A Modern Reader in Institutional and Evolutionary Economics: Key Concepts*, Cheltenham, UK and Northampton, MA, USA: Edward Elgar.
Feldman, M.P., J. Francis and J. Bercovitz (2005), 'Creating a cluster while building a firm: entrepreneurs and the formation of industrial clusters', *Regional Studies*, 39 (1), 129–41.

Feldman, M.P. and N. Massard (2002), 'Location, location, location. Institutions and systems in the geography of innovation', in M.P. Feldman and N. Massard (eds), *Institutions and Systems in the Geography of Innovation*, Boston, US and London, UK: Kluwer Academic Publishers.

Frost, T.S. (2001), 'The geographical sources of foreign subsidiaries' innovations', *Strategic Management Journal*, 22(2), 101–23.

Fujita, M. and J.-F. Thisse (2002), *Economics of Agglomeration: Cities, Industrial Location and Regional Growth*, Cambridge: Cambridge University Press.

Gorg, H. and E. Strobl (2001), 'Multinational companies and productivity spillovers: a meta-analysis', *The Economic Journal*, 111 (475), 723–39.

Håkanson, L. (2005), 'Epistemic communities and cluster dynamics: on the role of knowledge in industrial districts', *Industry and Innovation*, 12 (4), 433–63.

Hayter, R. (2004), 'Economic geography as dissenting institutionalism: the embeddedness, evolution and differentiation of regions', *Geografiska Annaler*, 86 B (2), 95–115.

Hodgson, G.M. (2002), 'Introduction', in G.M. Hodgson (ed.), *A Modern Reader in Institutional and Evolutionary Economics: Key Concepts*, Cheltenham, UK and Northampton, MA, USA: Edward Elgar.

Hodgson, G.M. (2004a), *The Evolution of Institutional Economics: Agency, Structure and Darwinism in American Institutionalism*, London, UK and New York, US: Routledge.

Hodgson, G.M. (2004b), 'Reclaiming habit for institutional economics', *Journal of Economic Psychology*, 25 (5), 651–60.

Iammarino, S. and P. McCann (2005), 'Firm location, innovation and technology: stylised constructs and illusory policies?', Paper for the 4th European Meeting on *Applied Evolutionary Economics* (EMAEE), Utrecht (Netherlands), 18–21 May.

Jacobs, J. (1969), *The Economy of Cities*, New York: Random House.

Jacobs, J. (1984), *Cities and the Wealth of Nations. Principles of Economic Life*, New York: Random House.

Jacobs, D. and A.-P. de Man (1996), 'Clusters, industrial policy and firm strategy: a menu approach', *Technology Analysis and Strategic Management*, 8 (4), 425–37.

Kilpinen, E. (1998), 'The pragmatic foundations of the institutionalistic method: Veblen's preconceptions and their relation to Peirce and Dewey', in S. Fayazmanesh and M.R. Tool (eds), *Institutionalist Method and Value: Essays in Honour of Paul Dale Bush*, Vol. 1, Cheltenham, UK and Lyme, US: Edward Elgar.

Malmberg, A. and P. Maskell (2002), 'The elusive concept of localization economies: towards a knowledge-based theory of spatial clustering', *Environment and Planning*, A 34 (3), 429–49.

Markusen, A. (1996), 'Sticky places in slippery places: a typology of industrial districts', *Economic Geography*, 72 (3), 293–313.

Marshall, A. (1920), *Principles of Economics*, 8th Edition, London: Macmillan and Co.

Martin, R. (1999), 'The new "geographical turn" in economics: some critical reflections', *Cambridge Journal of Economics*, 23 (1), 65–91.

Martin, R. and P. Sunley (2001), 'Rethinking the "economic" in economic geography: broadening our vision or losing our focus?', *Antipode*, 33 (2), 148–61.

Martin, R. and P. Sunley (2003), 'Deconstructing clusters: chaotic concept or policy panacea?', *Journal of Economic Geography*, 3 (1), 5–35.

Massard, N. and C. Mehier (2008), 'Proximity, accessibility to knowledge and innovation', *Regional Studies*, forthcoming.

McLeod, G. (2001), 'Beyond soft institutionalism: accumulation, regulation, and their geographical fixes', *Environment and Planning*, A 33 (7), 1145–67.

Nelson, R.R. and S.G. Winter (1982), *An Evolutionary Theory of Economic Change*, Cambridge: Harvard University Press.

Nelson, R.R. and S.G. Winter (2002), 'Evolutionary theorizing in economics', *Journal of Economic Perspectives*, 16 (2), 23–46.

Nooteboom, B. (2005), 'Innovation, learning and cluster dynamics', *Centre for Economic Research Discussion Paper*, No. 2005-44, Centre for Economic Research, Tilburg University.

Paci, R. and S. Usai (1999), 'The role of specialisation and diversity externalities in the agglomeration of innovative activities', *Working Paper CRENoS*, Paper No. 199915, Centre for North South Economic Research, University of Cagliari and Sassari.

Philo, C. and H. Parr (2000), 'Institutional geographies: introductory remarks', *Geoforum*, 31 (4), 513–21.

Porter, M.E. (1990), *The Competitive Advantage of Nations*, New York: Free Press.

Porter, M.E. (1998a), *On Competition*, Boston: Harvard Business School Press.

Porter, M.E. (1998b), 'Clusters and the new economics of competition', *Harvard Business Review*, November–December, 77–90.

Pouder, R. and C.H. St John (1996), 'Hot spots and blind spots: geographical clusters of firms and innovation', *Academy of Management Review*, 21 (4), 1192–225.

Roeland, T. and P. Den Hertog (1999), 'Cluster analysis and cluster-based policy making in OECD countries: an introduction to the theme', in OECD, *Boosting Innovation: The Cluster Approach*, Paris: OECD Proceedings.

Romer, P.M. (1986), 'Increasing returns and long run growth', *Journal of Political Economy*, 94 (5), 1002–37.

Romer, P.M. (1990), 'Endogenous technological change', *Journal of Political Economy*, 98 (5), S71–S102.

Rosenfield, S.A. (1997), 'Bringing business clusters into the mainstream of economic development', *European Planning Studies*, 5 (1), 3–23.

Saxenian, A.L. (1990), 'Regional networks and the resurgence of Silicon Valley', *California Management Review*, 33 (1), 89–112.

Swann, P., M. Prevezer and D. Stout (eds) (1998), *The Dynamics of Industrial Clusters: International Comparisons in Computing and Biotechnology*, Oxford: Oxford University Press.

Veblen, T.B. (1904), *The Theory of Business Enterprise*, Clifton: A.M. Kelley, 1975.

Veblen, T.B. (1914), *The Instinct of Workmanship and the State of the Industrial Arts*, New Brunswick, US and London, UK: Transaction Publishers, 1990.

Veblen, T.B. (1919), *The Place of Science in Modern Civilization and Other Essays*, New Brunswick, US and London, UK: Transaction Publishers, 1990.

Wood, A. and D. Valler (2001), 'Turn again? Rethinking institutions and the governance of local and regional economies', *Environment and Planning*, A 33 (7), 1139–44.

12. The New Economy, Innovation Policies, and the Role of Organised Labour

Frank Gerlach

INTRODUCTION

It is often argued that innovation and innovation policy is not in the focus of trade unions. Trade union policy includes a policy for better distribution of income for the employees, a policy for better social security, a policy against dismissals and, last but not least, a policy for better working conditions. Only the last aspect is connected to the innovation process.

THE POLICY OF THE TRADE UNIONS IN THE PAST

The ironical remark, that unions were fighting for a stoker in the engine driven by electricity, demonstrates how some trade unions have been judged in the past. If there is a grain of truth in this verdict regarding some trade unions, this has never been true for the German trade unions. Trade unions and members of the works councils, who are normally members of the trade unions, have been engaged in innovation processes in enterprises and in branches of the economy for some time. They always knew that a good innovation process might be the basis for better salaries and better working conditions. They knew that the development of the productive forces could also have negative consequences, but in their opinion a fight against this development would be ineffective and, in the long run, not good for the labour force, the workers, at all. Therefore their intention was to gain influence on the direction and the conception of innovation processes in the enterprises and in society. This happened on the basis of a concept of innovation that included social and cultural dimensions, and should not be reduced in a technocratic sense to technological issues only. In fact, innovation was understood as a potential for a democratic and human development of society. In this process the integration of the potential of the employees was essential for a continual improvement of the process of production. As was said, without the integration and participation of the employees, a succesful innovation process in the enterprises can not be achieved. This was the philosophy of the programme 'Humanisierung der Arbeit', which was launched by the social-liberal government in the 1970s. The trade unions were integrated in the development of the concept and the realisation of the programme. But to sum up, the energy of the trade unions and the works councils was concentrated on the aspects of the process of production and on a strategy for better working conditions which could also raise the level of productivity.

CHANGE OF STRATEGY

In the 1980s and much more in the 1990s, the strategy of the trade unions and the works councils proved to be too restricted. New challenges forced the trade unions to review their strategy in regard of innovations. These challenges are strongly connected with the process of globalisation and the rise of the New Economy. The German system of innovation was driven into a sort of crisis, as it showed its weakness in the wake of new developments, exemplified by the IT and biotechnological paradigms. The strength of the German model could be seen in its ability to adopt to incremental changes. Typical examples are the car industry and mechanical engineering industry. In these industries innovation follows certain technological pathways. But the realisation of fundamental innovations is more difficult in Germany than in other countries; very often in this context the United States or some Scandinavian countries are cited. The crisis of mobile phone production in Germany is a good example: what is possible in Finland, seems to be difficult in Germany.

As a consequence of this weakness it is often said that Germany has lost its former strong position in some branches, for instance in the pharmaceutical industry in the world market. To avoid some misunderstanding, Germany still has a strong position in the world market, which the surplus of the trade balance shows clearly. But the basis for a strong position in the markets has become more narrow, and this is not a good outlook for the future. The reports about the technological performance of Germany, edited by the Federal Government of Germany (Bundesministerium fürBildung und Forschung 2004) demonstrate the facts, that give evidence to this assessment. The trade unions had to deal with the weak points of the German innovation systems – for instance an insufficient transfer of new knowledge from the universities into the economy or weak knowledge management inside the firms. Furthermore there is another crucial point, which urges the trade unions to interfere more and more in questions of innovation in a more offensive way. The principle of shareholder value, which is followed increasingly by parts of management, is a direct challenge to a good process of innovation, that is sustainable in social, economic and ecological dimensions. That is: if the principal agent in the firm, the management, is oriented increasingly to a short-term shareholder value approach, which neglects more or less directly the interests of the employees, and is failing more and more to manage the process of innovation in the sense of sustainability, then there is a strong need for the employees and their representatives to interfere, to develop alternatives. At least there is a much stronger need for this than in the past and the German system of co-determination provides some instruments for the employees and the trade unions to interfere in the process of innovation.

Indeed, as a consequence of the developments outlined briefly – the shareholder–value and the difficulties for management in the face of scientific and technological revolutions – the trade unions needed a wider concept of innovation policy, which should neithr be restricted to innovation in the production process nor be only reactive in facing management strategies. Let me call it a sort of innovation policy in advance. I will provide two examples of this. First, if you are confronted with the policy of Siemens in the production of mobile phones then the result will most probably be cost cutting, especially cutting the wages. Every expert knows that this is not a good strategy in the production of mobile phones. The share of wages in this sector is under 10 per cent. The real problems of Siemens are to be found in other dimensions, especially in coordinating the innovation and the production process very close to the demands of the markets. Nokia has shown that even in countries with high wage level production of mobile phones is possible, if you find good solutions to combine innovation, production and flexibility in the market. Second, the German Telecom plans 32 000 lay–offs. One reason is that their clients increasingly use the services of small web firms to phone more cheaply with the aid of the internet. The change in communication, which is the result of the internet, has been unexpected for many German managers. We have the impression that Scandiavian enterprises are reacting faster in developing new strategies.

A NEED FOR AN INNOVATION OFFENSIVE

An offensive in the field of innovation policy is therefore important for Germany. This should be a long run–strategy. But we should not change or throw away the core elements of our social and economic system. As Hall and Soskice (2001) underlined in their book *The Varieties of Capitalism*, there are different paths of capitalism possible. Germany needs its human capital at the highest level to preserve its standard of living. This is our main resource. But it can only be reached by a very good education system, good research and innovation in central new fields of science and economy, and a continuous modernisation process in the so-called old economy.

To underline it: it is not at all necessary in this reform process of modernisation and more innovation in Germany to have a fundamental change in the social-economic structures. On the contrary, the German system of codetermination and participation is a strength in the long run. Participation and codetermination can support the innovation process in enterprises, in the branches and in the regions. Empirical research (Klotz 2003) has shown that there are many examples that the impulse for modernization of the production process in the enterprises came from works councils or the workers themselves. This is one of the strengths of the German system. And in view of innovation failures and false management strategies increasingly a sort of co-management by the works councils and the trade unions is necessary. We are aware that the workers, the works councils and the trade unions can make only proposals. Their realisation is only possible on the basis of strong trade unions and strong works councils and employees, which are strong enough to get through sometimes massive conflicts. On behalf of trade unions there is no other way open. They have to react earlier, they have to act before the milk is spilled. A good example of this policy is the offensive for modernisation which has been put on the agenda by the IG Metall district North Rhine-Westfalia. Its headline is 'Besser statt billiger' (in English: better instead of cheaper). The underlying philosophy of this offensive is that the German economy cannot reach competitiveness in the world markets on the basis of cheap labour. This is not possible. What we need is more speed in innovation and modernisation. Works councils and the trade unions should interfere more in the enterprises, should show where the weak points are in the production and in the pipeline of new products, demand more qualifications and a better organisation of the process of production, for instance with more autonomous group work. Detlev Wetzel, the head of the IG Metall district North Rhine-Westfalia states: 'A precondition of success are good qualified employees, better products and services. We afford a policy that is promoting innovation. We are against a policy which is rewarding bad management at the cost of the employees.'

To sum up: a more offensive use of the possibilities for codetermination in the field company policy and more participation at the work–place is a good path to speed up the innovation process. But there is also a danger. Michael

Schumann, a well-known German industrial sociologist, is right when he says that enterprise policy stabilises the economy from the aspect of individual capital. In this sense the trade unions and the works councils are part of the market competition. There are dangers, but one should not overestimate these risks and we do not have an alternative. Furthermore, very often such a policy of modernisation and innovation is combined with an industrial or a regional policy. We have good examples that the German trade unions try to promote the process of modernisation and innovation in sectors of the economy in the interest of the employees. This sort of industrial policy has been established for example in the foundry sector, forge sector and in the shipbuilding industry. One major instrument on this level is more cooperation or networking – a way of coordination beyond the markets.

INNOVATION AND SOCIAL COHESION

But there is yet another danger: social cohesion. In nearly all modern capitalist states the gap between haves and have-nots is widening. Unemployment has risen and a new underclass has emerged. There is a consensus among scientists as regards this aspect. We can see the consequences of this development for instance in France or in some districts of the big cities in Germany. It is often argued that in the New Economy, and as a consequence of the innovation process, only more qualified labour is required. Jobs which require low skills are not created to the extent needed. Is there a contradiction between innovation process and social cohesion? This is often argued, and prima faci with good evidence. But is it right, too? A recently finished project by the Hans-Böckler–Foundation throws more light on this question. The main question of the project was the relationship between innovation policy and social cohesion. Fifteen case studies in the European Union were undertaken in this project. The result is clear: if the promotion of social cohesion is integrated in the aims of innovation policy, then high learning and high networking can be the result. By this means a better innovation process can be reached. The authors of the study recommend consequently the integration of measures in order to promote social cohesion in the instruments of innovation policy. Successful innovation policy is also cohesive innovation policy. This study goes so far, but further research is necessary to analyse the complicated relation between innovation and social cohesion. And also further measures in the field of social policy are needed in order to solve the dangerous problems which are a result of high unemployment. What is one to do? The successful strategy of the Scandinavian countries shows that a good education system and a good qualifications policy can increase flexibility in innovation processes.

Following an OECD ranking, Sweden is in first place as regards investment in the knowledge society. The concept of a learning economy is not a phrase but this implicates enormous efforts and investment in the fields of education, qualification and further training. The innovation process has to integrate the development of competences. This is not only a task at the level of the whole economy but at the enterprise and the branch level as well.

TRADE UNIONS – A PRINCIPAL AGENT IN THE FIELD OF INNOVATION?

In their own interest the trade unions should be a principal agent for a good combination of innovation and social cohesion. Therefore qualifications and development of competences at the level of the firm and the branch is one major aim of the innovation policy of the trade unions in Germany. If the innovation process coincides with a division of society into winners and losers, this would be connected with negative consequences for the innovation process itself. And in the long run it would be crucial for the trade unions themselves; it would weaken the trade union organization. A good example is the Finnish case (Sengenberger 2005). Finland was in a deep depression and they succeeded by their own means and by an offensive in innovation to solve their problems. From rubber boat to mobile phone, from board production to biological technology, this could be the slogan for an advertisement for Finland. One important prerequisite for this success – and this is seldom mentioned – was that Finland had a good, or let me say one of the best, social dialogue with strong and independent trade unions in the world. So in this society the acceptance of a very strong change in the field of economy and social structure could be reached. Finland also has achieved a good regulation of innovation and education policy – the results of the Pisa research show this.

A new deal for a new economy – indeed this is necessary. In this context there is also the need for new institutional arrangements. There is also a need for a widening of trade union policies in the field of innovation at the levels of enterprise, branch and national economy. The German system of codetermination is an excellent prerequisite for these challenges of the future. But there are also dangerous currents. A view into the past shows that strong trade unions made possible the new deal in the United States. The policy of President Roosevelt was based on a political coalition between different groups in society of which the trade unions were an important part.

If the trade unions are going to lose further members and strength, then such a path of innovation policy, including social cohesion, could not be followed. In spite of the crisis in which the trade unions nowadays doubtlessly are, we are not at all pessimistic for the future. 'The times they are changing' – Bob Dylan was right. There are more and more voices on the scientific as well as on the political level who warn of a derailment of modernisation as a result of uncontrolled globalisation (Habermas). There is resistance. And this conference is also a good sign that the dominance of the neoclassical approach is becoming weaker. And there are also the first signs that the trade unions in Germany may reach a turn around. As a result of their policy as regards innovations (I mean the campaign 'better instead of cheaper') the number of trade union members in these enterprises in which this campaign was visible, has increased. To become stronger as trade unions in the new economy – in which they are traditionally weak – was also an important aim of their innovation policy. If they can prove their competence in this sense they will become more attractive for the new type of highly qualified employees, which are characteristic of the New Economy. A good example is the Siemens case, where IG Metall could gain ground in the context of conflicts. Therefore, when there are risks there are also chances. As regards the trade unions it was my intention to stress the chances of a new innovation policy.

REFERENCES

Bundesministerium für Bildung und Forschung (2004), *Bericht zur technologischen Leistungsfähigkeit Deutschlands 2004*, Berlin.

Hall, Peter and David Soskice (eds) (2001), *Varieties of Capitalism. The Institutional Foundations of Comparative Advantage*, Oxford.

Klotz, Ulrich (2003), *Die Innovation der Innovatonspolitik*, Frankfurt/Main.

Guth, Michael, Susanne Jakobs, Petra Kodré, Claudia Mühlenfeld and Roman Noetzel (2005), *Erfolgsdeterminanten für eine sozialintegrative regionale Innovationspolitik.* Forschungsbericht.

Sengenberger, Werner (2005), 'Innovationsorietierte Wirtschaftspolitik und soziale Kohäsion – Das Beispiel Finnland', *WSI Mitteilungen*, 3/2005, Düsseldorf.

13. Social Innovation Between Local and Global

Frank Moulaert and Jacques Nussbaumer

INTRODUCTION

The concept of social innovation is not new. Benjamin Franklin evoked social innovation as small modifications within the social organisation of communities (Mumford 2002). At the beginning of the twentieth century, Max Weber showed the power and force of rationalisation (i.e. having behaviour and processes follow rationalities) in the workings of the capitalist system. He questioned the relationship between social order and innovation. He affirmed amongst other things that changes at the level of living conditions are not the only determinants of social change. According to him, the possibility that individuals can introduce a new behavioural variant, often considered as deviant, can have a decisive influence. If this kind of behaviour spreads, it becomes normal usage within the established order (Weber, [1971] 1995, p. 26). As early as 1893 Emile Durkheim shed light on the importance of social regulation in the development of the division of labour which accompanies technical change. Technical change only has a meaning within the context of innovation or renovation of the social order within which it finds its relevance (see Weber, [1971] 1995, p. 26).

In the 1930s, Joseph Schumpeter put forward the idea of social innovation as structural change within the organisation of society, or within the network of organisational forms of enterprise (Schumpeter, 1932). In reality Schumpeter's theory of innovation went far beyond the economic logic and called on an ensemble of sociologies (cultural, artistic, economic, political...) which he sought to integrate into a comprehensive social theory allowing for the analysis of both development and innovation (Becker et al., 2002).

Each of these authors represents a specific reading of social innovation; Franklin refers to 'one-off' innovation in a concrete context; Weber and Durkheim refer to transformations of social relations, or of social organisation within society or political and economic communities;

Schumpeter refers to the relationship between development and innovation where economic innovation of a strong technological character is considered of prime importance among other types of innovation, and the entrepreneur is viewed as a leader who, despite facing a multitude of contradictions, introduces innovation into the modes of organisation of corporations. Almost all of them highlight the importance of social innovations within a diversity of institutions (such as those in public administration, world politics, enterprise, local communities).

From the 1970s onwards, social innovation has made a comeback. Its impact has worked through two movements. The first of these is the debate held in France in the 1970s around the journal, *Autrement*. This journal offers a reading of social innovation as much structural – in tune with the spirit of the time – as specific and localised (Chambon and Devefey 1982). Well-known figures such as Pierre Rosanvallon, Jacques Fournier and Jacques Attali, participated in this debate. A second movement started at the end of the 1980s, and beginning of the 90s, and continues to this day. It is wider than the French movement of the 1970s with its emphasis not only on the work of theoreticians but also of practitioners. This second movement, to which we will return in more detail in later sections, offers an interesting point of entry to the social economic debate on social innovation. As in the work of Schumpeter, social innovation reveals itself through the innovative entrepreneur, who transforms social relations within his/her enterprise – or any organisation, be it to improve its operation, or to transform it into a social enterprise or an enterprise with a social rationale. And following the re-reading of Benjamin Franklin, who viewed social innovations as solutions for concrete life problems (Mumford 2002), and of the founding fathers of sociology, who identified themselves as creative thinkers about a new society and its forms, social innovation can be rediscovered at the heart of the artistic dynamic; a dynamic where art re-invents itself as sociology as indicated in the 'Sociologist as an Artist' approach that underlines the importance of sociology as the science of innovation in society (Du Bois and Wright 2004). Note that Schumpeter and Weber are cited again and again to legitimise the social transformation of enterprise or organisational structures; finally, 'the return of social innovation' is also manifested by the use of the concept as an alternative to the logic of the market, and to the generalised privatisation movement that affects most systems of economic allocation. This alternative is expressed in terms of solidarity and reciprocity (Liénard 2003; Nyssens 2000). Starting from this conception of social innovation, we will develop our analysis.

In the next section, we try to identify simultaneously both the foundationial ideas ('idées porteuses') and the hegemonic practices which at first inhibited social innovation, and then in a dialectical way provoked its return: the privatisation of public space, the alienation of labour relations (wage–labour relation, deskilling of work and labour), the homogenising consequences of the capitalist economy and of large-scale production on culture, the rationalisation of the knowledge society (which reduces knowledge to an ensemble of information arising from, or preliminary to, purely rational creation processes), and the processes promoting mass consumption, including those that are typical of the knowledge economy (Moulaert and Gonzalez 2006). The third section examines the scientific analysis of this rediscovered social innovation concept: what are the problematics to be addressed? What questions arise? Which disciplines are concerned? What are the opportunities for a scientific approach to social innovation which is more integrated and oriented towards social action?

TENDENCIES TOWARDS 'PRIVATISED' DEVELOPMENT AND THE CHALLENGE FOR SOCIAL INNOVATION

Since the major oil crisis of the 1970s and the ensuing climate of job shortages in Western Europe or of hidden unemployment in the Anglo-Saxon world, economic restructuring strategies and socio-economic regeneration policies have increasingly turned for inspiration to neo-liberal recipes of economic recovery (Moulaert and Vandenbroucke, 1983). The failure of the liberalism of the end of the 19th and beginning of the 20th centuries seems to have been completely forgotten; yet this liberalism has been identified as one of the greatest factors responsible for the excess in supply, the climate of deflation and the collapse of the financial system in the 1920s/30s. Those who warn of the risks of a 'return to the past' – as for example the Euro–Memorandum Group (2004) – are considered as prophets of doom.

It is true that Keynesian economic policy took over from liberalism after the 1930s in the USA and after the war in Europe, and lasted until the mid 1970s. But after the coming of the 1973 oil crisis, the previous golden years of full employment and a high level of wellbeing amongst the majority of the population have been viewed as a specific epoch, an historical accident of market distortion and considered as constituting a major factor of the economic crises in western societies today. According to the neo-liberals, only a return to a free market economy and a free flow of investment at the global scale can counteract these perceived economic weaknesses (Choudry, 2003). That the liberal policy of a century ago provoked massive human misery for both the poor and the rich of the time, seems no longer to be part of the collective memory. Rereading the history of capitalism is a low priority for contemporary analysts of orthodox economic policy. However, through this memory exercise, political economic analysts could have understood, as did Polanyi in his analysis of the capitalist economy, that an economic system exists only by the grace of the institutions that both regulate and reproduce it (Polanyi [1944] 1983). Thus, while the emergence of the capitalist economy can only occur thanks to the initiative of the nation state (Polanyi [1944] 1983), the development of the market always comes from the creation or the adaptation of institutions that allow integration of that market into society. At the risk of provoking a crisis, these institutions seek to equilibrate social relations within economic development (Boyer, 1987).

Positioning itself outside this understanding of the history of development, contemporary liberalism is expressed not only through deregulation of capital flows on the world scale, through the free trade in goods and, more recently, in a large scala of services, but also through the deconstruction of the social protection system. Attesting to this deconstruction is the reduction in public expenditure allocated to the maintenance of social wellbeing. This includes the dismantling of the welfare state in certain western countries as well as a reduction in the tax rate in the majority of them, which then impinges on the good and efficient functioning of social protection services (EuroMemorandum, 2003, 2004). Thus liberalism expresses itself as one among many re-emerging fundamentalisms – religious, political and bureaucratic. Together they form the ideological bases of political regimes that are intolerant and authoritarian and that operate repressive social and security policies. In this respect, for example, are the ideological political practices in certain Islamic states but also the repressive tendencies observable in the USA and other countries in the western world. It is important to point out nevertheless that the term 'neo-liberalism' conceals an economic and political practice which does not correspond to its own discourse. Dominant practice among authors and actors of this ideology is far from constituting true 'liberalisation' for all economic agents; on the contrary, it promotes the consolidation and extension of the power of monopolies at the global level as revealed in the 'founding' as well as the contemporary literature, and the development, in the name of market logic, of conflicting power relations (social, commercial and economic) at all spatial levels of the economy. At the global level, trade negotiations to a large extent mirror the power relations between states (Dicken, 1994). At the local level, industrial restructuring movements, linked to both the concentration and the rationalisation of production, have exerted an unsettling influence on numerous regional economies, and provoked important social movements at the same time (Moulaert et al., 2000).

The establishment of global markets which mainly benefit multinational companies, is based on the creation of institutions that limit the freedom of action of small–scale economic agents, however ingenious, who are situated both outside the market logic (in a social or 'solidary' economy) or inside it (less globalised small and medium–sized enterprises, and social enterprises operating within the market) (see for example Tremblay et al., 2002). Numerous examples illustrate the truth of this: recent movements towards concentration in the financial world have accelerated the decline of local and regional banks; the development of quality control favours chemical purity at the expense of organic quality of agricultural and textile products, so excluding a considerable number of predominantly smaller size ecological producers from the market; or again the spectacular rise of multinational hypermarkets has strangled – except in those countries with strict control over location – small traditional town centre businesses and so dealt a mortal blow to the social fabric of medium–sized cities and 'urban villages' within big cities. Remarkably, these so-called liberalisation movements have eliminated large numbers of enterprises, as much in developed as in developing economies, and especially in the sphere of traditional activities. In this way these movements have annihilated those technological and artisan traditions integral to community life.

Privatisation as a Strategy of Market Liberalisation

The liberalism discourse legitimises a privatisation, presented by orthodox theory as beneficial to all, which in practice is very uneven in its effects on different layers of society. According to the neo-liberal tenet, privatisation reduces the influence of the state on the economy and in so doing, by introducing deregulation and returning public resources to the private sector, frees the engine of economic development from state–imposed constraints and so allows private enterprise to develop enormously. But in reality privatisation is heavily dependent on the financial power of those who acquire any public capital released onto the market. Several consequences of this generalised privatisation movement can be observed. First of all, it is the most powerful financiers who have the greatest opportunities to acquire those parts of the state and public sector put up for sale (on the role of institutional investors see Chesnais, 2004). Of course there are small–size economic agents who obtain their share – for example, in the privatisation of personal and services to enterprises – but in the main the profitable activities subjected to the market dynamics are taken up by the big, often international players. Secondly, for these major global actors, privatisation is only one instrument to implement a strategy of concentration in the economic sectors which they seek to control. In this way, 'liberalisation' leads to a homogenisation of the economy dominated by a few large sectors with an oligopolistic market structure. Thirdly, these same actors strive to transform the regulatory system of the market to favour a strong financial and economic concentration that pure liberalism, centred on competition and ruling out inefficiencies due to market concentration, is meant to combat. This transformation requires in part an instrumentalisation of the political world to the advantage of large enterprises and financial groups. Thus it is contradictory to the ideology and theory put forward by neo-liberalism. In this way, there is a reinforcement of a dominant economic practice that does not favour small–scale economic initiatives either with or without a market logic. This practice also overlooks the diversity of national and regional economies, their institutions and their particular market structures. For example, large–scale privatisation ignores or seeks to eliminate the reality of national economies where the role of the state and the third sector is very important. These economies are often more diversified, more creative, more just (with a more equal access to capital) and possess a respect for creativity and for development from the bottom up (Favreau and Lévesque, 1999; Gibson-Graham, 2003).

Social Innovation as the Answer

The official discourse of (neo-)liberalism imposes a model of development based on a narrow human ontology, or even an economistic ontology. By linking all economic thought to instrumental rationality and strategic market relations, neoliberal discourse promotes a vision that reflects mainly the aspirations of certain interest groups benefiting from financial concentration in various sectors of the economy and high returns on financial assets themselves. Although this phenomenon is perceptible in the first place at the global market scale, it has overwhelming consequences for local economic structures. The strategic and political choices of the Bush administration show the truth of this: the refusal to ratify the Kyoto Protocol, the willingness to apply in a linear way WTO and GATS agreements which would destroy local potentiality in many countries; the employment of a strategy of reverse distribution (tax exemptions for high income households, privatisation of pension systems). In parallel this discourse implies a denigration of alternative approaches in the name of economic and financial orthodoxy. Within the milieus of this orthodoxy, these approaches are considered to be inefficient, inefficacious and above all as acting as brakes on economic development through the workings of the market.

The discourse accompanying liberal strategies also expresses a willingness to minimise the efficacy of the state and public services by portraying them as malfunctioning, and presents traditional social security systems as a disincentive to be active in the job-market. We should note however that none of these observations made by neo-liberal analysts is based on cost–benefit analysis or corresponds to an identifiable existing societal reality. The justification for neo-liberal policies remains at the level of ideological discourse and of privatisation activity with no scientific foundation (for an analysis concerning the US, see Galbraith, 1998).

It is within this malaise about both the state and collective and citizen initiative that we must situate the rise or the renaissance of the social economy, of initiatives based on solidarity, of a rapprochement between the social and the artistic; in short, it is within this context that a return to social innovation must be placed. This return manifests itself in many forms and in diverse social and political arenas.

What then constitutes the strength, the force of the concept of social innovation? First of all, the concept offers a constructive response to the economistic and technologistic vision of economic development dreamed up and implemented by the protagonists of neo-liberalism; it supports an ontology of cooperation and diversity (human, cultural, economic…) and of solutions to the problems of human development. It sits as much at the level of ideological discourse as at the level of scientific analysis, and social scientific analysis in particular.

Secondly, the concept of social innovation mirrors the main concerns of actors on the ground, i.e. those groups deprived of the possibility of fulfilling their elementary needs because of the privatisation of their living spaces and socio-political movements, and public and private economic agents increasingly feel hamstrung by the contradictory consequences of the discourse and the practices of neo-liberalism. The concept of social innovation seeks to reconstruct social bonds – whether outside the market or in relation with it.

Thirdly, throughout the history of the social sciences, social innovation has been championed by those advocating institutional changes in society, be it in the form of new institutions as in modern bureaucracy and democracy, or as a function of the real demands and needs expressed at different epochs in history (see Moulaert and Ailenei, 2005). A contemporary interpretation of this phenomenon makes a renewed wave of social innovation feasible as a reaction to the exaggerated individualism of the privatisation movement, as explained previously (Lipietz, 2001; Bouchard et al. 2000). Social innovation therefore can be seen today as a structural reaction to the unequal deprivation of resources resulting from privatisation practices and processes, and consists essentially of forms of governance based on solidarity and reciprocity – as opposed to individualism and private appropriation.

In the next section, we present a reading of the interpretation of social innovation within contemporary social and human science. This reading will then lead on to show the diversity of the dimensions of social innovation, as found in the literature of both theory and practice.

SOCIAL INNOVATION IN CONTEMPORARY SCIENTIFIC LITERATURE

We have distinguished five spheres of thought or approaches where the idea of social innovation is used or analysed. We try to identify the various meanings given to social innovation and to organise these according to the different dimensions revealed in the 'founding' as well as the contemporary literature (for a detailed presentation, see Hillier et al., 2004).

The first sphere is that of the *management sciences*. In this context, we focus on those opportunities for improving social capital which would allow improved functioning of organisations in the economy, paying particular attention to the positive effects of social innovation in the not-for-profit sector (Manoury, 2002, op. Cit.). Damanpour (1991) makes a distinction between the effects of the 'determinants' and the 'moderators' of organisational innovation. He uses this to test the relevance of several theories of innovation on an understanding of organisational innovation today. The Stanford Social Innovation Review focuses as much on dimensions of social innovation within the various areas of society as on the role of leadership, the organisation of the charitable sector, or more generally, the not-for-profit sector.

The second sphere of thought arises from a *multi-disciplinary approach* which examines the complex relationship between the business sector and social and environmental progress, the latter mainly supported by scholars in various disciplines within social science (see Moulaert and Nussbaumer, 2008). Several institutional initiatives support this approach. One example is the International Association for Business and Society that also sponsors the journal *Business and Society*. The IABS covers a research domain including various aspects of the interface between management and the social political dynamics of society (corporate social responsibility and performance, emerging social issues for business, business ethics, environmental affairs, and so on; see their website http://www.iabs.net). Another well-known institution, this time teaching and researching in this intersection between business and society, is the Center for Social Innovation at Stanford Business School, focused on various dimensions of social innovation within a variety of domains in society (http://www.gsb.stanford.edu/csi/; and Moulaert and Nussbaumer, 2008).

The third approach belongs to the field of the *sciences of the arts and creativity*. It shows the role of social innovation in intellectual and social creation. Michael Mumford (1992), an author central to this way of thought, defines social innovation as follows:

> The generation and implementation of new ideas about how people should organise interpersonal activities, or social interactions, to meet one or more common goals. As within other forms of innovation, the production resulting from innovation may vary with regard to their breadth and impact. (p. 253)

For Mumford, author of several articles on social innovation within the sphere of creativity and arts, there exists a range from large impact innovations, like those of Martin Luther King, Henry Ford or Karl Marx to more specific and localised innovations such as the introduction of new procedures to improve working cooperation, the introduction of new social practices within a group or the development of new business practices (p. 253). In his overview of the literature of social innovation, Mumford suggests three main lines within social innovation research which have led him to formulate significant hypotheses. He then tests these with reference to the social innovations put forward by Benjamin Franklin.

The fourth approach concerns *social innovation in territorial development.* Jacquiers (1991), Moulaert et al. (1990, 2002), Fontan et al. (2001, 2003) stress inherent problems in local development strategies within the context of European cities: the dispersion of skills among the various sectors of urban and local development policy (social, cultural, environmental, commercial…), the lack of integration between the various spatial levels and, above all, the neglect of the social and economic needs of marginalised groups within urban society. To overcome these hurdles, Moulaert et al. (2002) proposed the development of neighbourhoods, following the Integrated Area Development approach which seeks to integrate spheres of socio-economic development and the principal actors involved according to the structuring principle of social innovation. This principle establishes a strong link between the satisfaction of human needs and innovation within the social relations of governance. In particular, it underlines the need to foster social and political integration of groups and individuals and the key-role of access to the resources required for the satisfaction of human needs; this would involve participation in decision-making processes within structures that are often perceived as alienating or even oppressing (Martinelli, et al., 2005). This positioning, although applied here to territorial dynamics, is near enough to the analysis made to that developed in the debates led by the journal *Autrement* as cited previously.

The fifth approach is that of *political governance* and *public management.* The recent, but prolific, literature questions the relationship between governance and government, and examines the hypothesis of a possible reinvention of relations between the state and civil society. The challenge is to create a mode of relationship that can guarantee democratic public management without minimising the role of the state as both a major actor and the ultimate guarantee of social harmony (Swyngedouw, 2005; Novy and

Leubolt, 2005).

Social Innovation: A Multi-Dimensional Concept

The literature cited so far within the five different but closely related approaches opens up a number of avenues of exploration; these stress specific features according to their own traditions and origins but also offer complementary tools for the analysis of social innovation, as shown by Hillier et al. (2005).

Work in business and management science underlines the interaction between organisational restructuring dynamics on the one hand, and creative learning on the other. Communication, adaptation, creativity and learning within organisations all come together, become reality, at the intersections between changing social structures and the innovative behaviour of both individual and collective actors. Applied to not-for-profit organisations, the goals of economic innovation broaden to include social emancipation, concern for the environment, shared creativity etc.

In this way, social innovation as applied to change in human organisations chimes with the second approach in exploring the possible links between commercial success and social and environmental progress. Research on ethical entrepreneurship makes use of a vast area of social innovation research which examines themes such as self-managed work, ecological production, influence of large corporations on the international (trade) policy of 'their' own countries or on the economic and trade policy of international organisations.

The third domain, bearing on arts and creativity, reflects interest in being less constrained by the structural or organisational thinking of the business world. It links organisational innovation to individual charisma and initiative within social innovation; moreover it takes account of the learning process highlighted in case studies of social innovation and even in historical studies capable of inspiring or provoking social innovation at both the micro and macro level of society.

The fourth domain with the most territorial approach is also perhaps the most structural: it stresses the importance of the structure of society as a catalyst, but also as a package of constraints on social innovation within any given territorial level, regional, local or micro-local (neighbourhood). Nevertheless, by recognising constraints at the international and national level of the structure of society, this approach is less open to types of action conducive to overcoming obstacles to the integration of new ideas than is the organisational innovation approach or the creativity approach stimulated by leadership and/or charismatic individuals; both these latter approaches are considered prime movers in the bypassing of structural harnesses and institutional rigidities (Mumford, 2002, p. 255).

The fifth domain insists on the need to redefine relations between state, public sector and civil society in order to re-dynamise democracy in a world society and an economy much more complex and unequal than those of the 1960s and 70s.

Integration of the varied dimensions of social innovation as developed in the different approaches cited here appears the obvious way forward: it seems logical to explore the links between creative ideas and innovative action, and to analyse organisational changes combined with individual initiatives, including leadership. It is also analytically relevant to show the role of learning within the dynamics of social innovation, the dialectics between history and contemporary change or even the need to transform the dynamics of governance at several levels of society, whether private or public.

Table 13.1 summarises the variety of dimensions of social innovation, indicated by this review of contemporary literature. By combining the structural and organisational dimensions, plus the dimension of the satisfaction of human needs – this last taking priority over a purely economic result (see Polly Toynbee in *The Guardian* 9 April 2004) – social innovation should integrate the articulation between the different structural levels of society – multi-level governance matters! – to the benefit of social progress at the regional and local level (through reorientation of agendas, of institutions and of responsibilities).

SOCIAL INNOVATION AS A PLATFORM FOR HUMAN DEVELOPMENT

In this section we present first of all, the features of social innovation that constitute a reaction to the dynamics of privatisation as outlined in Section 2. The confrontation between social innovation and the neo-liberal discourse and practice has the advantage of repositioning the debate on social innovation within the context of contemporary social and political struggle; it shows the necessity of establishing the idea of social innovation with reference to identifiable needs. Starting from this confrontation, and utilising elements from the theoretical overview of the preceding section, we outline a framework of human development based on the diverse dimensions of social innovation. To achieve this, we adopt, while changing it slightly, Schumpeter's view which links development to innovation by recognising that development trajectories and organisation do not allow anticipation or prediction of the nature of varying types of radical innovation (Schumpeter, 1932 and Becker et al., 2002).

Table 13.1: Dimensions of Social Innovation in Different Scientific Disciplines

Dimensions of social innovation Disciplinary approaches	Role of the specia agents: leadership, creative individuals.	Role of path dependency and of the structural constraints.	How to overcome the tensions between normativity and reality?	Aim of the initiative	Change in the organisation of the initiative
Management and organisational science	The innovative actors in the organization are empowered within the organisation	Awareness of *path dependency* in relation to the business culture and its organization.	Tangibility of objectives Regularisation of the relationships between the organisational elites and the rest of the organisation Learning dynamics	Improve the coherence of an organisation in order to achieve its objectives (financial profits, ethical work, ecological products)	Build a space for the exchange of information and ideas 'Horizontalise' the decision-making and communication systems
Relationships between economy, society and environment (including social responsibility)		Tension between the mainstream and the ethical entrepreneurship (represented by the tension between professional organisations)	Interfaces between business and society Ethical forums	Integrate the social and ecologic aims within the mainstreams agendas of businesses.	Stress on the human relations dimension of work
Art and creative sciences	Particular attention attributed to individually created initiatives	Historical inspiration for contemporary social innovation (grand examples, practical experiences)	The role of information and its assimilation by the creative community. The discovery of constraints and solutions Revision and interactive refinement of the proposed solutions.	Social innovation	Quality of work and social relations
Territorial approach (Integrated Area Development)	Increased focus on the role of the community and its social agents	Substantial importance of the historical reproduction of institutional capital	Through multi-level governance and the creation of networks of cooperation between community agents	Satisfaction of human needs…	… in accordance to changes in the governance relations
Governance and public administration	Civil society movements lobbying for democracy	Bypassing bureaucratic rigidities	Simplifying structures – regular evaluation of restructuring actions	Efficient, transparent, democratic administration	De-hierarchising bureaucracies – network communication

Privatisation Versus Social Innovation

Table 13.2 summarises the characteristics of social innovation and of privatisation. The comparison starts from the shared concern of the two 'strategic concepts': to change the visions and the strategic choices in order to enable a better integrated and more harmonious society.

Table 13.2: Privatization Versus Social Innovation

Dimensions	Social Innovation	Privatisation
Ontology – strategic behaviour	Cooperation as a function of multidimensional development	Individual action with occasional cooperation aiming for private economic benefits
Societal structure	Equilibrium between social, cultural, economic and political forces	Dominance by economic forces, especially 'monopoly capital'
Main economic dynamics	Economy of diversity	Financial concentration, privileging HVA sectors
Economic institutions	Mixed economy: market, public sector, third sector (institutionally supported)	Economic regulation limited to the protection of large scale private property
Regulation at the global scale	Promotion of fair trade based on redistributive value chains	WTO, GATS (with a negative impact on small–scale initiatives)
Main economic forces	Redistribution of income and wealth guaranteeing existential quality	Destruction of non – or lowly – competitive capital Growing inequality of income and wealth 'Deprivation' of small-scale capitals (including SMEs)
Arenas of struggle and emancipation	Patchwork of cultures of resistance and innovation – arts as an instrument of socio-political struggle	Privatisation of public spaces, financial, political, social and cultural – paralysis of social resistance and spontaneous culture

We must remember in this context, that the two concepts under consideration, social innovation and privatisation, should be perceived as structuring concepts of the processes of innovation articulated through identifiable strategies and not as autonomous structural transformations, historically produced or the unique outcomes of conjunctures of social change. This does not mean that we shut our eyes to the structural and societal dimension – the explanation of these depends on structural and institutional characteristics, or also on the visions of society embodied in these strategies – but that these only indirectly reflect the processes of alienation and the constraints of social change strategies. In particular, it is within the characteristic 'arenas of struggle and emancipation' in Table 13.2 that there is an implicit link to structural constraints on development. These constraints represent primarily: society as structured in classes and with conflicting interest groups; social movements based on a social critique of alternative strategies; as well as the complexity of social institutions which often tend to resist strategies of social change.

Social Innovation: A Structuring Principle of Human Development

Social innovation processes respond to the need to surmount alienation mechanisms (to follow up on a social critique, see Martinelli et al., 2005), to fill gaps in socio-political institutions and to surmount market failure in the satisfaction of human needs – the identification of these mechanisms and gaps is reminiscent of what Eve Chiapello (1998) calls the 'artist critique' of a system (in this case, capitalism). These processes are always in defined contexts; by taking into account the historical trajectory, the territorial and institutional framework, the availability of human and financial resources and of institutional capital, 'path dependency' becomes very clear. Nevertheless, it is also necessary to explore the 'world of the possible' and the opportunities required for the emergence of social innovation. Some consequences of this contextual line of thinking are immediately obvious:

- the specific character of each social innovation strategy;
- the realistic mobilisation of existing resources;
- the influence of historic heritage which often means a reinterpretation or reappropriation of an old idea or practice rather than the emergence of a really new one;
- novel ideas and practices in this sense consisting of updating the old. This makes us think there is a need for development of a plurality of sociologies (of the economy, of knowledge, of the arts, of political life) in order to promote a deeper understanding of the development of society as a whole (Schumpeter, 1932; Becker et al., 2002); such sociologies, according to Du Bois and Wright (2001), could stimulate specific innovations and even structural ones;
- the operationalising of innovation norms according to their potential ability to overcome constraints.

However, the dependency of social innovations on context, development trajectory, powerful institutions etc. does not mean that they are predictable. On this point we agree with Schumpeter (1932) in affirming that structure can certainly explain the context in which novel ideas are actually put into practice; that the role of the innovator, whether individual or collective, is strategic but that the analysis of the interaction between the two does not allow for prediction of the exact nature of these 'novel working ideas' (and of the radical ones in particular); that this goes for innovation in all parts of society (the economy, civil society, the artistic world, the political world). Does this mean that theorisation about innovation, and especially about social innovation, is consigned to the realm of the impossible? We believe that predictability is not a determining criterion in the construction of a theory, especially in the social sciences (Hodgson, 2001); rather the objective of theoretical analysis is the development of conceptual frameworks that, in dialogue with historical and institutional reality, would allow for an understanding of both past and present processes with the overall purpose of updating innovation strategies and policies (Moulaert and Nussbaumer, 2005).

TOWARDS AN EPISTEMOLOGY OF SOCIAL INNOVATION?

The dynamics of social innovation are complex. We have seen in the previous sections that social innovation responds to social needs that are the products of alienation of rights and desires, and to critiques – artistic or social – which demonstrate a strong desire for creation or for change, to paraphrase Chiapello. Many needs and critiques are adopted and carried forward by social movements belonging to a wide variety of social spheres. Analysed from this point of view, social innovation can respond to the ultimate aims of the satisfaction of fundamental needs (shelter, food, social interaction), or of more cultural needs (education, the arts, socially organised communication); but equally it can encompass transformation in social relations (for example, from patriarchy to egalitarian cooperation), including relations of political governance in the wider sense of the term (i.e. governance of the diverse communities of ideals or interests to which human beings belong).

Furthermore, reaction to a process of alienation or the emergence of a resistance or opposition movement can be viewed as a response to a particular discourse or to 'the spirit of the time' or can be translated into action (e.g. establishing a social enterprise in a situation where certain economic functions are no longer guaranteed) or into an intellectual exercise (e.g developing the capacity of social innovation discourse to formulate a response to privatisation). Furthermore, social innovation can manifest itself at several spatial scales of society – international, national, regional, local. It does not necessarily depend on the dynamics of change within an organisation in need of transformation and can express itself through the mediation of a variety of existing structures, whether public or private. Finally, it will always be implemented in relation to and in conjunction with the local historical and institutional context. This does not mean it would have no influence on historical trends or the character of institutions. As a result, within the analysis of innovative transformation of what is, we regularly witness the reproduction of tension between social innovation as a norm to pursue, and innovation as it occurs and is accomplished in real contexts. Thus the analytical and normative dimensions feed reciprocally from each other and return continually to epistemological questions on the role of reflexive thought in social science (Smart, 1996). For social innovation, this reflexivity concerns first of all the risk of projecting the ethical norms of the researcher onto the analytic framework of the innovative experiences. This risk is increased when the researcher also occupies a strategic role or is even a charismatic leader within those experiences of social innovation subject to analysis.

Faced with such complexity, what could be the role of social innovation analysis within the social sciences and the humanities? By way of conclusion, we make a plea for a 'pre-theorising' exercise and share some concerns about the absence of a coherent epistemology of social innovation. The starting point of our plea is not only the complexity of the material and ideological reality of the world of social innovation but also the existence of multiple and diverse theories (shown in the short survey within this chapter) which deal poorly with the epistemological dimensions of their analyses.

Therefore our plea favours a 'sociology of knowledge' approach, addressing epistemological questions in the analysis of social innovation. We put forward two arguments in support of this view. First, a large part of scientific thought on social innovation arises either from political challenges within society – and demonstrates a cyclical nature in response to great movements of social change (see Lipietz, 2001; Laville and Delfau, 2000; Moulaert and Ailenei, 2005), or from practical challenges relating to specific needs. This approach through 'sociology of knowledge' would allow the reconstruction of the social context, the social and political discourse which is typical of the environment leading to the emergence of these innovations; it would allow the discovery of analytical convergences and divergences about social innovation both over time and in many and varied milieus. Our second argument reinforces the first; although the epistemology of social innovation analysis is in a very preliminary stage, a profitable way of moving forward would be to reconstruct the world visions, the ontologies so to speak, expounded by the analysts of social innovation. Once again, 'the sociology of knowledge' approach to this reconstruction and comparative analysis of world views seems the natural, obvious one.

Table 13.1 outlines a useful tool for developing a first exercise in the analysis of social innovation through the sociology of knowledge. Five dimensions of innovation are listed alongside five areas of contemporary research. These dimensions allow the reconstruction of the ontology of social innovation as it is implicitly or explicitly carried out within the literature cited. Moreover, the same dimensions, once translated into more structural terms, could guide the analysis, the strategies and the visions of scientific communities. In this way, a more coherent way of thinking about the orientations, the direction of theoretical analysis of contemporary social innovation, could be established. It would then become possible to demonstrate how this analysis relates to strategies applied in communities open to social innovation.

REFERENCES

Becker M.C., Esslinger H.U., Hedtke U. and Knudsen Th. (2002), *Schumpeter's unknown article Development. A missing link between Schumpeter's theories of economic development, business cycles and democracy*, Odense, University of Southern Denmark, Dep. of Marketing, unpublished document.

Bouchard M., Bourque G. and Levesque B. (2000), 'L'évaluation de l'économie sociale dans la perspective des nouvelles formes de régulation socio-économique de l'intérêt général', *Cahiers du CRISES*, Collection Working Papers, 0013.

Boyer R. (1987), *La Théorie de la Régulation: une analyse critique*, Paris, La Découverte.

Chambon J.-L., David A. and Devevey J.-M. (1982), *Les innovations sociales*, Paris, PUF.

Chesnais F. ED. (2004), *La finance mondialisée: racines sociales et politiques, configuration, conséquences*, Paris, La Découverte.

Chiapello E. (1998), *Artistes versus managers*, Paris, Métailié.

Choudry A. (2003), 'Neoliberal Globalization: Cancun and Beyond, Burlington, Action for Social and Ecological Justice', *Green Paper 4*.

Damanpour F. (1991), 'Organizational Innovation: A meta-analysis of the effects of determinants and moderations'. *Academy of Management Journal*, 34, 555–90.

Dicken, P. (1994), 'The Roepke Lecture in Economic Geography. Global-Local Tensions. Firms and States in the Global Space Economy', *Economic Geography*, 70(2), 101–28.

Du Bois W. and Wright R.D. (2001), *Applying Sociology. Making a Better World*, Boston, Allyn and Bacon.

Durkheim E. (1991) [1893], *De la division du travail social*, Paris, PUF.

EuroMemorandum Group (2003), *Full Employment, Welfare and a Strong Public Sector – Democratic Challenges in a Wider Union*, Brussels

EuroMemorandum Group (2004), *Beyond Lisbon. Economic and social policy orientations and constitutional cornerstones for the European Social Model*, Brussels.

European Commision (2001), *Green Paper on Governance*, Brussels, European Commission.

Favreau L. and Levesque B. (1999), *Développement Economique Communautaire. Economie Sociale et Intervention*, Sainte-Foye, Presses Universitaires du Québec.

Fontan J.-M., Klein J.-L. and Levesque B. (2003), *Reconversion économique et développement territorial : le rôle de la société civile*, Québec, Presses de l'Université du Québec.

Fontan J.M., Klein J.L. and Tremblay D.G. (2001), Mobilisation communautaire et gouvernance locale: le technopôle Angus', *Politique et Sociétés*, 20(2–3), 69–88.

Galbraith J.K. (1998), *Created Unequal: The Crisis in American Pay*, New York, The Free Press.

Gibson-Graham J.K. (2003), 'An ethics of the local', *Rethinking Marxism*, 15(1), 49–74.

Hillier J., Moulaert F., Nussbaumer J. (2004), 'Trois essais sur le rôle de l'innovation sociale dans le développement territorial', *Géographie, Economie, Société*, 6, 19–42.

Hodgson G. M. (2001), *How Economics Forgot History: The Problem of Historical Specificity in Social Science*, London and New York, Routledge.

Jacquier C. (1991), *Voyage dans dix quartiers européens en crise*, Paris, L'Harmattan.

Jacquier C. (1995), *Les approches integres de developpement urbain en Europe, Centre de Recherche sur les mutations territoriales et les politiques des villes*, Grenoble.

Laville J.L. and Delfau G. (2000), *Aux sources de l'économie solidaire*, Daumont, Editions Thierry Quinqueton.

Levesque B., Malo M.-C. and Girard J.-P. (1999), 'L'ancienne et la nouvelle économie sociale', in Defourny J., Develtere P. and Fonteneau B. (ed), *L'économie sociale au Nord et au Sud*, Paris – Bruxelles, Editions De Boeck & Larcier, 195–216.

Lipietz A. (2001), *Pour le tiers secteur. L'économie sociale et solidaire: pourquoi, comment*, Paris, La Découverte.

Manoury L. (2002), *L'entrepreneur social et l'enjeu de sa professionalisation, Aix-en-Provence*, Université Coopérative Européenne.

Martinelli F., Moulaert F., Swyngedouw E. and Gonzalez S. (2005), 'Towards a conceptualization of social innovation in community development', *Urban Studies*, 11(42), 1969–990.

Moulaert F. (2000, 2002), *Globalisation and Integrated Area Development in European Cities*, Oxford, Oxford University Press.

Moulaert F. and Ailenei O. (2005), 'Social economy, économie solidaire and third sector: history, practice and analysis', *Urban Studies*, 11(42), 2037–53.

Moulaert F. and Gonzalez S. (2006), 'Is there Life beyond the Knowledge Based-Society?' *Towards a Decelerated Approach to Learning, Creativity and Enjoyment in Europe*, Brussels, EUROCADRES Website.

Moulaert F. and Nussbaumer J. (2005), 'The social region. Beyond the territorial dynamics of the learning economy', *European Urban and Regional Studies*, 12(1), 81–100 .

Moulaert, F. and Nussbaumer, J. (2008), *La Logique Sociale du Développement Territorial*, Sainte–Foye: Presses de l'Université du Québec.

Moulaert F. and Vandenbroucke F. (1983), 'Bestrijding van de werkloosheid : de bijdrage van de post-Keynesiaanse economen', in Van Ryckeghem W. (ed) *Macro-Economics and Policy*, Alphen a/d Rijn, Kluwer.

Moulaert F., Alaez Aller R., Cooke Ph.., Courlet Cl., Häusserman H. and Da Rosa Pires A. (1990), 'Integrated Area Development and Efficacy of Local Action', *Feasibility study for the European Commission*, Brussels, DG V.

Mouzelis N. (1997), *Conceptualising complexity on the sociocultural and educationnal levels*, Athens, paper presented to the EAEPE conference.

Mumford M.D. (2002), 'Social innovation : ten cases from Benjamin Franklin.', *Creativity Research Journal*, 14(2), 253–66.

Novy A. and Leubolt B. (2005), 'Participatory budgeting in Porto Alegre. The dialectics of state and non-state forms of social innovation', *Urban Studies*, 42(11), 2023–36.

Nyssens M. (2000), 'Les approches économiques du tiers secteur', *Sociologie du travail*, 42, 551–65.

Polanyi K. (1983) [1944], *La grande transformation*, Paris, Gallimard.

Smart B. (1996), 'Postmodern Social Theory', in Turner B.S. (ed), *The Blackwell Companion to Social Theory*, Oxford, Blackwell, pp. 396–428.

Schumpeter J. (1932), *Entwicklung*, Texte original à consulter sur le site web. Avec traduction en Anglais www.schumpeter.info.

Schumpeter J. (1942), *Capitalism, Socialism and Democracy*, London: Allan and Unwin.

Swyngedouw E. (2005), 'Let the people govern ? Civil society, governmentality and governance-beyond-the-state', *Urban Studies*, 42(11), 1991–2006.

Tremblay M., Tremblay P.A. and Tremblay S. (réd) (2002), *Développement local, économie sociale et démocratie*, Sainte-Foye, Presses Universitaires du Québec.

Weber M. (1995) [1971], *Economie et Société*, Tome 2, Paris [Plon] Pocket.

PART THREE

An Economics For A New Economy?

14. A New Economics of Complementarity, Increasing Returns and Planning Horizons

Frederic B. Jennings

INTRODUCTION

The twin mantras of orthodox economics are substitution and decreasing returns suppositions. Substitution allows convexity, subadditivity, negative feedbacks and, therefore, equilibrium models and decomposition of wholes. Substitution sets limits upon the spreading effects of action, such that externalities can be ignored beyond the bounds of attention. Consequences are damped and die out; they do not amplify outward forever on path-dependent tracks. Stability is the rule and disequilibrium the exception. Neoclassical theory – as a massive investment in sunk cost – does not work without substitution and independence assumptions. As Krupp (1982, p. 390) put it: 'Axioms of independence ... lead directly to the laws of substitution... Independence means that the behavior of the elementary unit can be described without reference to the behavior of other units.'

Substitution, however, relies not only on independence but also on increasing costs of production, on which the whole argument rests. The justification for rising cost derives from Hicks's (1939, pp. 82–5) amazing 'getaway', where he asserted decreasing returns, on no foundation at all, in the face of a general belief in increasing returns and falling costs of production. Hicks (1977, pp. v-viii) later retracted this statement, though in Chicago it is still taut doctrine (Reder 1982, pp. 17–19). The post-Marshallian crisis in economics – started by Clapham (1922) – made a claim for increasing returns as stated definitively by Pigou (1927, p. 197): 'cases of increasing costs ... do not occur'. There is no justification for rising cost in production technology, yet economists seem to adhere to the premise like grim death at times. So tenacious is the assumption – despite its lack of foundation – that denial likely is the reason for its long endurance. Axiomatic conditions are only asserted and thus not open to challenge, if embedded in the 'hard core' of a social research programme; as Blaug (1976, pp. 156–7), quoting Lakatos, said: 'all scientific research programmes may be characterized by their "hard core"... The "hard core" is irrefutable by "the methodological decision of its protagonists" '. The proof of a paradigm lies in the pudding, namely, in its adoption and use (Rescher 1979, p. 102).

Substitution, decreasing returns and independence assumptions are joined – and not to be torn asunder – in the hard core of mainstream models, shaping all economic concerns. So what is the problem with this? Substitution, decreasing returns and independence should be contrasted to an alternative frame of complementarity, increasing returns and total interdependence, if just to plumb the opportunity costs of what we economists do. Complementarity implies a concert – instead of a conflict – of interests among consumers and other agents, such that our fortunes are more aligned than opposed (as substitution describes them). Increasing returns say unit costs fall with new output and never rise, save for factor rigidity. Interdependence suggests economy is akin to ecology, in which everything interacts complexly with no bound to effects. So what we have framed is a controversy on how the world truly works: substitution or complementarity, rising or falling cost, and segmentation or interdependence. Which answer is more realistic, and how might we frame it?

The aim of this chapter is to make a case for complementarity as a general form of interdependence, showing cooperation as optimal and competition as inefficient. The interdependence of economic causality in a systems approach is outlined in the next section, then the case for increasing returns is argued in the section to follow. An introduction of planning horizons and 'horizon effects' shall lead to a claim that complementarity is more important than substitution in the chapter's penultimate section. Then the conclusions will be summarized and implications explored. The nature of economic constructions in a complementary universe shall be unfamiliar and disturbing to an orthodox theorist. There are reasons why economists entered an Age of Denial after accepting the Hicksian Getaway, as an economics of increasing returns and complementarity is quite different from mainstream models. The notion of planning horizons serves to reconcile these sundry approaches, in a 'horizonal' economics whose elements shall be sketched.

THE PROBLEM OF INTERDEPENDENCE

The full interdependence of economic causality is so obvious that its stolid avoidance by economists is a surprise. Substitution is the primary form of relation known to economists: scarcity and tradeoffs seem endemic in economics. Certainly all are repeatedly encountered in daily life: we have but one chance to live and one track to run, at the opportunity cost of everything else we could do. And the immediate truths of our existence cycle through an awareness of all we cannot attain. There are 'tradeoffs in everything' that none of us can avoid.

But is that the whole story? In ecological theory, it is known that every act tends to ripple outward into everything else in indeterminate ways. Systems theory (Bertalanffy 1968) was developed to address such problems, and the main resistance to its allure originates in economics. Substitution assumptions serve to excuse economists from attending to interactions surrounding us, and our rigid devotion to instant outcomes steers us away from broader views. The interdependence of economic causality is not just substitution; the complementarity of phenomena ought to be seen as well.

The notion of interdependence – or the composition rule – around which all of this centres in economics is the industry model. How economists aggregate from individual agents to 'markets' is through industry groups of firms selling substitute products. So is a bias against systems set into place at the outset. As substitution is the defining characteristic – if not the standard – of aggregation in this setting, complementarity gains no purchase on our attention at all. Linearity also emerges from arithmomorphic constructions, as Georgescu-Roegen (1967, pp. 50–61; 1971, pp. 105–10) notes. Such suppositions may be methodologically 'convenient', but they involve very high cost if they guide decisions awry. A more flexible model is needed than 'industry' aggregation.

A way to frame interfirm interdependence stems from Chamberlin, where every individual firm interacts diversely with others. Chamberlin (1933, 1957) never addressed the issue of complementarity in his schema, and did not even embrace increasing returns as a general phenomenon, though the 'tangency point' in monopolistic competition had declining costs. But Chamberlin saw the firm as a unique individual agent in a world of qualitative variation and diversity. In this situation, there is no 'industry' of identical outputs; Chamberlin's early attempt to 'group' producers into a quasi-market of similar but not identical firms was so inconsistent with his signal approach it should be considered an error. But how we emerge from individual sales to their aggregation is a problem in need of solution for any interdependent domain.

Let us make the realistic assumption that every firm is special, and is sensitive to everything else occurring in the economy. In this situation, our representations start with individual choice, and then incorporate feedbacks through a rule of composition. Substitution is such a rule, but it confines economics to narrowly-focused short-term models selecting a single end of a larger spectrum including complementarity. In this sense, substitution is only one half of the story (if that); the role of complementarity has been too long ignored by economists.

Systems theory, according to Senge (1990, pp. 79–80), has three basic components: positive vs. negative feedback and delays in time. In economics, negative feedback covers substitution through its damping of causal effects, such that consequences dissipate as they extend through space and time. Positive feedback, cumulative causation and complementarity, on the other hand, do not attenuate but amplify as they spread, to bring a path-dependent trace of factual outcomes in which history matters and nothing ends or reverses. This scenario – often attributed to increasing returns – shall also emanate from adopting complementary interdependence. Myrdal (1978) and Kaldor (1972, 1975) embraced this story.

But how we integrate these phenomena is still unresolved. Many approaches address such issues, including complexity theory, ecological economics, institutionalism and management theory. Yet none of these systems of thought distil to a unified theory of interdependence. So we are left with a question of how to analyse 'seamless wholes' without any joints to guide a carver (Georgescu-Roegen 1971, p. 66). Transportation network contexts serve as system examples, so will help us see the problem (Jennings 2006).

Figure 14.1

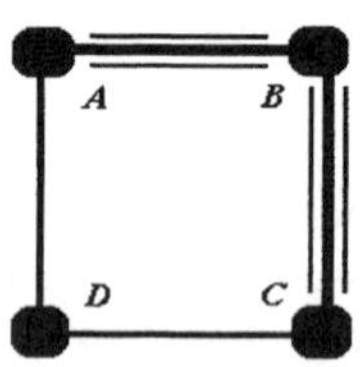

The simplest transportation network can be imagined thus: four routes linking four towns in a square as shown in Figure 14.1, where routes AB and BC are considered in terms of their relationship. Are AB and BC substitutes or complements? It turns out they are both: they are rivals for traffic going between B and D, and they are complements for travel between A and C. In any transportation network, combinations of substitution and complementarity are the rule and not a special exception: AB links to all other routes in complex systems of feedback which do not decompose.

But this is the very same problem encountered in generalised Chamberlinian models of firms in product space. Take the case of beer vs. wine as rivalrous substitute goods, and throw in chips and cheese as complements, when choosing an afternoon drink. Consumption patterns tend to sort into beer and chips (as complements) vs. wine and cheese (an alternative pair), although when hosting a party vs. some other entertainment these are all complementary goods. Substitutes are rivals in an 'either–or' relation, whereas complements shift together. For substitutes, sales, profits and growth are opposed; they have a conflict of interest. Complements share a concert of interest, as their fortunes are joined. The general case – in all economic contexts – is a nondecomposable mix of substitution and complementarity in our relations.

The interdependence of profit effects can be formalized thus, as the difference between own-profit and joint-profit maximization for any particular entity within a group I of firms. The own-profit maximizing price is:

$$P_j^* = M_j^* \cdot E_j^* \tag{14.1}$$

where $M_j^* \equiv MR_j^* = MC_j^* > 0$ and $E_j^* \equiv \epsilon_j^*/(\epsilon_j^* + 1) > 1$ for demand elasticity $\epsilon_j^* \equiv dlnQ/dlnP < -1$. The joint-profit maximizing price is:

$$P_j' = P_j^* + S_I \tag{14.2}$$

where the 'feedback term' S_I is a combinatorial Ω of the following components for all $i \neq j$:

$$S_I \equiv \Omega \; s_{i \neq j} \tag{14.3}$$

where

$$s_{i \neq j} \equiv (Q_{i \neq j}/Q_j) \cdot (M_{i \neq j}^* - P_{i \neq j}^*) \cdot [\epsilon_{ij} \,/\, (\epsilon_j \; + 1)]$$ (14.4)[1]

Now, when most $s_{i \neq j} > 0$ because $\epsilon_{ij} > 0$, such that $S_I > 0$, then the relation of good j to the rest of group I for $i = 1, \ldots, n$ is one of net substitution: the impact of collusion (or cooperation) is to raise P_j' above P_j^*: this is the orthodox story. But when net interdependence is such that $S_I < 0$, showing complementarity in group I with respect to product j (as most $\epsilon_{ij} < 0$), then it is cooperation – not competition – that reduces price, so assuring efficiency. The welfare results of industrial organization are turned on their head in the presence of complementary interdependence: here cooperation is efficient and competition is not.

Think of this in the broader realm of human social affairs. The question is whether relations suffer rivalry or alignment in their general aims and endeavours. Standard theory in economics uses substitution assumptions, so is premised on a claim that our interests are opposed: whatever you get is denied to me. Yet does substitution reflect the full reality of our relations? When you become better off, is my own well-being impaired? Or rather would our fates be joined, so when you thrive so do I? If joys expand or retract together, most scarcity is self-imposed: for rivalrous struggle among complements, competition creates shortages where they do not exist.

This is the harm of competition among complementary goods, which is closely analogous to the collusive failures of substitution: each brings serious social losses stemming from undue restriction of output. The optimal organizational outcome may be irresolvable: once we admit to a nondecomposable mix of substitution and complementarity, we encounter a conflict among contradictory institutions. Should we encourage individual rights, selfish gain, acquisitive values and disaggregated endeavours in economics, or should we focus on group priorities, social concerns, ethics and generosity? Competition and cooperation are incompatible systems with regard to their economic incentives: competition rewards behavior antisocial to cooperation.

So recognizing complementarity opens some meaningful issues on the role of competition in impeding cooperation, or in causing scarcities it should deter. If complementarity is 'far more important' than substitution, as Kaldor (1975, p. 348) opined, then maybe our economy is suboptimal and inefficient. Are we taking a poison to cure? The case for complementarity – and against substitution in economics – seems so unlikely that the initial reaction is often denial. The scope of the error implied is incredible: what is the evidence for it? The driving force for complementarity comes from increasing returns.

THE CASE FOR INCREASING RETURNS

Kaldor's (1972, 1975) case for increasing returns is simply asserted against a vital longstanding commitment to rising cost. Mainstream economists simply ignored (though some acknowledged) his argument, which is cited in other circles as an important departure from orthodoxy, built on a Keynesian frame. But there is more to this story. A brief sketch is offered below of the basis for rising cost, which has never been more than asserted – without foundation – in orthodox circles. The fact decreasing returns endures suggests an issue Michael Polanyi (1958, pp. 78–9) raised against Popper (1934, pp. 278–9) on the self-policing of science to guard against error. It also reveals the path dependence of irreversible outcomes and its sway over economics.

The origin of increasing returns, says Kaldor (1972, pp. 1240–42), is in Adam Smith (1776), who called chapter 3 in his *Wealth of Nations* 'The

Division of Labour is Limited by the Extent of the Market'. But then Smith, according to Kaldor, became preoccupied in the next chapter with 'how values and prices ... are determined. ... As a result, the existence of increasing returns and its consequences for the whole framework of economic theory have been completely neglected'. As Kaldor remarked, 'without a major act of demolition – without destroying the basic conceptual framework – it is impossible to make any real progress'. How could such a well-trained discipline, in an academic competitive framework calling for research and publication to avoid these slip-ups, ever allow an error of such importance to go unchecked?

Marshall's supply curves sloped downward, though in the short run – due to rigidities – such costs could rise, so offsetting these scale effects. It was not till Clapham (1922), two years before Marshall's death, opened these 'empty boxes' that the debate began. The defining moment of this series of papers was when Pigou, as successor to Marshall, wrote on cost (1927) and supply (1928) endorsing increasing returns, stating that rising costs are not 'admissible' as economic conditions. Next Allyn Young (1928) – Chamberlin's thesis advisor – reviewed the impact of falling cost on economics, and Chamberlin (1933) then developed the implications of product diversity. Keynes set forth the macroeconomic connections as well, although he did not assume increasing returns. The point is that the whole thrust of argument during the 1930s stood on increasing returns to output.

Then along came Hicks. What Hicks said is one of the most outrageous statements in the whole history of economic controversy. He won a Nobel Prize for this work, for which he later voiced some 'mixed feelings' (Hicks 1977, pp. v–vii). Hicks (1939, pp. 82–5) simply asserted decreasing returns – against twenty years of debate – because if he didn't 'the basis on which economic laws can be constructed is ... shorn away'. Seeking instead to 'save ... the threatened wreckage ... of general equilibrium theory', he added that: 'At least, this getaway seems well worth trying' despite that 'we are taking a dangerous step'. But he closed this singular passage with the curt dismissal that: 'Personally, however, I doubt if most of the problems we shall have to exclude for this reason are capable of much useful analysis by the methods of economic theory.'

In spite of Hicks's (1977, pp. v–vii) own later retraction of the Hicksian Getaway as 'nonsense' built on an 'indefensible trick' (conflating actions with outcomes, so removing time), by then economists were committed to rising cost and equilibrium models. Samuelson (1947), Arrow and Debreu (1954) and many others staked and built their reputations on the Hicksian frame, and were not about to reject it. The rigid doctrine taught in Chicago was founded on Hicks's schema, as the basis for 'the authority of neo-classical price theory in general', from which any departures in Chicago's graduate programme 'are penalized as evincing failure to absorb training' (Reder 1982, pp. 17–19). The Hicksian Getaway offers such a good illustration of path dependence in its own denial thereof, the irony would be amusing were it not so tragically costly in its impact upon our world.

The case for decreasing returns was strengthened in 1951 when George Stigler – a denizen of the Chicago School – put forth this perspective on Adam Smith's endorsement of falling cost, in a paper entitled "The Division of Labor is Limited by the Extent of the Market'. Here again, substitution of factors is simply asserted without defence, where the 'distinct operations' of firms are assumed to be 'independent'. Stigler (1951, pp. 140–44) reviews this 'important' detail, saying: 'Actually, many processes will be rival... Other processes will be complementary ... If, on balance, the functions are rival, then usually the firm will increase its rate of output of the final product when it abandons a function; and I think that this is generally the case'. Stigler's claim may be contrasted with that of Nelson (1981, pp. 1053–5), who remarks that: 'If factors are complements, growth is superadditive ... The growth of one input augments the marginal contribution of others. Where complementarity is important, it makes little sense to try to divide up the credit for growth, treating the factors as if they were not complements. ...[It is like] dividing up the credit for a good cake to various inputs.'

Hicks said in 1977 that the excision of time and history from his analysis in 1939 was its fatal flaw. In 1959, Armen Alchian published a paper on 'Costs and Outputs' sketching a way to incorporate time into production theory. Alchian posed the total cost of any production run as a function of volume (V), output rate (X), run length (m) and a planning period (T), such that $C = C(V, X, m, T)$. Alchian offered nine propositions on the first and second partial derivatives of this function: cost (C) depends on how production runs structure volume by speed vs. time. Higher output rates (X) for a given volume (V_0) increase its cost, whereas taking more time (through m or T) reduces its cost of production. The core of the argument over returns to scale is about the sign of d^2C/dV^2 and how that increase in V is achieved: through raising X or by lengthening m. The key to Alchian's story is that increasing X for a given V_0 involves shortening m, inviting a further simplification.

That revision had the aim of 'rescuing the orthodox cost function' with a decisive verification that 'the classical analysis is consistent and correct' (Hirshleifer 1962, pp. 237–8). Assuming $V = m_0X$, so removing time from his analysis, Hirshleifer claimed that Alchian's frame made the marginal cost with respect to output rate X over run length m_0 turn upward, thereby upholding 'the powerful logic of the law of diminishing returns' (Hirshleifer 1962, p. 235). Alchian (1968, pp. 319–20) later accepted this view in his essay on 'Cost' for the *International Encyclopedia of the Social Sciences*, stating conclusively that diminishing returns was 'a general and universally valid law'. So economics, in 40 short years, turned from Pigou's (1928, pp. 252–3) outright dismissal of decreasing returns, where 'the law of increasing supply price ... is excluded completely' to Alchian's (1968, pp. 319–20) 'general and universally valid law ... of increasing marginal costs [which] reflects the well-known law of diminishing marginal returns with respect to rate of output'.

Walter Oi (1967, pp. 590 and 594) addressed these arguments, showing like conclusions from the Alchian–Hirshleifer framework (both of which papers 'appeal to learning, experience and economies which derive from not having to rush production plans') and Hicksian dynamics (à la 1939), declaring that if the former writers 'had adopted a Hicksian inter-temporal production function and [Oi's] two theorems ... all nine [of Alchian's] propositions are seen to be logical consequences'. Oi concluded thus: 'To sum up, a dynamic theory of production along the lines of Hicks provides us with an essentially neoclassical explanation for progress functions. ... To attribute productivity gains to technical progress or learning is, I feel, to rob neoclassical theory of its just due.' In consequence, substitution and decreasing returns simply obviated the need for any special learning assumptions; such were already in the Hicksian frame (which Hicks has since called 'nonsense').

In my PhD dissertation (Jennings 1985, ch. 5), I examined Hirshleifer's argument, to reveal it as a non sequitur from Alchian's nine propositions, which took no stand on scale effects. Indeed, Alchian's schema accommodates falling costs, so Hirshleifer's claim makes stronger assumptions than Alchian ever posed or intended, whose rising costs stem from shortening m and not from widening X. So Hirshleifer's (1962, p. 253) findings – subsequently endorsed by Alchian – about 'the essentials of the problem of economies of scale: marginal costs are a rising function of rate of production [and] a declining function of scheduled volume of production' are just plain wrong. 'The upshot of this grievous mistake is that any incorporation of learning by doing and technical change into cost and price theory has been deferred. The point lies in fifty long years during which we have painted a 'well-behaved' world, forestalling development of our conceptions in the direction of proper behavioral science' (Jennings 1985, pp. 99–101).

There is no case for decreasing returns, simply asserted by Hicks with 'The Hicksian Getaway' and again by Alchian after 'The Hirshleifer Rescue'! The alternate thread – that of increasing returns and complementarity – is in need of further review, with technical change and learning included, once the 'indefensible trick' underlying the Hicksian Getaway is exposed. Time and positive feedbacks should be added to the negative feedbacks supposed throughout economics in the form of substitution assumptions (Senge 1990, pp. 79–80), if we are to emerge from the Age of Denial opened by Hicks. A critical step in this direction is to incorporate planning horizons in their relation to cost, through the equations $Q \equiv V/(m+T)$ and $H_t \equiv m + T$ as the time horizon of output.[2] The time horizon (H_t) is related to planning horizons (H) through the fact of interdependence: for real decisions, the way you extend your projections in time is by apprehending effects in social and physical space, since that is where reactions emerge in the form of feedback constraints. So time horizons are reflective of full awareness and knowledge, and they extend or retract in response to our understanding of causal relations. Indeed, 'horizon effects' – ordinal changes in planning horizons – serve as an entropic measure of organizational learning applied to economics in Boulding's (1956) and Georgescu-Roegen's (1971) sense (Jennings 2005).

PLANNING HORIZONS AND COMPLEMENTARITY

A conversion of Alchian's nine propositions into horizonal terms shall lead to the following conclusions: for marginal cost $M(Q,H)$, dM/dQ can have any sign but dM/dH is always negative. Furthermore, for larger outputs, dM/dQ is constrained from above in accord with Alchian's postulates (Jennings 1985, ch. 5). Consequently, we can state some propositions on pricing effects:

$$P^*(Q,H) = M^*(Q,H) \cdot E^*(Q,H) \text{ for } M^* > 0 \text{ and } E^* > 1 \tag{14.5}$$

$$\text{with } dM^*/dH < 0 \text{ and } d^2M^*/dH^2 > 0 \tag{14.6}$$

$$\text{and } dE^*/dH < 0 \text{ and } d^2E^*/dH^2 > 0 \tag{14.7}$$

$$\text{so } dP^*/dH < 0 \text{ and } d^2P^*/dH^2 > 0 \tag{14.8}$$

$$\text{and } dg^*/dH > 0 \text{ and } d^2g^*/dH^2 < 0 \text{ for } g^* \equiv dlnQ/dt \tag{14.9}$$

In sum, all prices respond to horizon effects, so the fixed horizons in neoclassical theory also repress some meaningful lessons for us. Substitution assumptions simply obscure recognition of interdependence, and therewith the need for rational bounds on knowledge of ongoing impact. Traditional theories suppose substitution, neglecting complementarity and time, making independence and decomposition into rigid dogma at the expense of realistic construction.

To paraphrase Senge (1990, pp. 79–80), interdependence – systems theory – entails three elements: substitution, complementarity and (horizonal) time. Building on one without the rest truncates applicability. Assuming horizons are fixed and placing complementarity out of frame blocks awareness of both. Wherever relations are complementary – or horizon effects occur – representing them as substitution will lead decisions astray, yet with no indication of error; we never observe opportunity costs save through a theoretical lens. Substitution is not the essence of economic connection: complementarity is, and horizon effects show why. There are two realms of interdependence: substitution/complementarity, as already noted above, and the social linkage of planning horizons through horizon effects. So what are planning horizons?

Every decision is made among imagined projections of outcomes: suppressing cognition (Georgescu-Roegen 1967, p. 104) and treating choice as selection of outcomes direct is what Hicks (1977, pp. v–vii) saw 'was non-sense. It does deliberate violence to the order in which the real world (in any real world) events occur.' Planning horizons serve as a proxy for the range of these projections: though they cannot be calibrated precisely, ordinal shifts are enough; we call them 'horizon effects'. But these horizonal changes spread like contagion across social groups: if you are in my decision environment, our horizons interact through learning, emotions, signalling and/or role model effects. In virtually all cases, interhorizonal linkages are reinforcing and not counterbalancing; interhorizonal complementarity is the general rule:[3]

$$dH^*_{i\neq j}/dH^*_j > 0 \text{ for all } i,j = 1,\dots,n \text{ in any group } I \tag{14.11}$$

Information and knowledge spread across society as 'public goods', stretching our horizons outward in novel patterns of growth or collapse. Horizon effects are contagious; horizons extend or retract together.

What are the implications of this? Interhorizonal complementarity alters our relations of interdependence with horizon effects: the balance of substitution and complementarity in any economic context – transportation or otherwise – shifts with a change in planning horizons in a predictable way:

$$dS_I/dH_j < 0 \tag{14.12}$$

An increase in H^*_j yields – through contagious effects on neighbours' $H^*_{i\neq j}s$ – a shift of S_I away from substitution in favour of complementarity. For any $i \neq j$ element of S_I, namely $s_{i\neq j} \equiv (Q_{i\neq j}/Q_j)\cdot(M^*_{i\neq j} - P^*_{i\neq j})\cdot[\epsilon^*_{ij}/(\epsilon^*_j + 1)]$,[4] extension of H^*_j will likely reduce the magnitude of both $Q_{i\neq j}/Q_j > 0$ (as a weighting scalar) and $|(M^*_{i\neq j} - P^*_{i\neq j}) < 0|$ while increasing own-elasticity

$|\epsilon_j^* < -1|$ and thus the negative magnitude of $|(\epsilon_j^* + 1) < 0|$; also cross-elasticity (ϵ_{ij}^*) is shifted away from substitution ($\epsilon_{ij}^* > 0$) toward complementarity ($\epsilon_{ij}^* < 0$), such that $d\epsilon_{ij}^*/dH_j < 0$ as well. So regardless of the sign of S_I (as a combinatorial Ω of $s_{i \neq j}$ across any group I around member j), $dS_I/dH_j < 0$. A mutual lengthening of horizons shifts our interdependence away from substitution ($S_I > 0$) toward more complementarity ($S_I < 0$) in our relations, in all economic contexts.

In this sense, horizon effects mimic complementarity and increasing returns in their economic connections and welfare results. Such is true even in the presence of rising cost/decreasing returns to additional output, though we have shown why increasing returns should displace standard dogma on cost. Kaldor (1975, p. 348) regarded falling costs as sufficient to make complementarity in our relations 'far more important' than substitution assumptions. But even under decreasing returns, interhorizonal complementarity yields the same result: longer horizons make complementarity more important than substitution, thus shifting efficiency attributes from competition to cooperation. In sum, when horizonal lengthening is seen in development terms, social systems ought to evolve from rivalry into collaboration as a means to foster economic growth and social welfare improvement. Dogmatic allegiance to competition and its efficiency attributes stands on substitution assumptions; standard theory on neoclassical lines simply has no relevance to a complementary setting: indeed, its central propositions are wrongly applied therein.

Only if substitution and decreasing returns can be upheld do orthodox standards survive. Facing a lack of foundation for either rings in a new economics emphasizing complementarity in ecology and education, as our purest and best examples of positive feedback systems. Even a glance at these two settings shows how damaging competition has been to their resilience. An information economy offers another related demonstration of failure rising from opposition due to rivalrous strife, where open source sharing contributes to output and growth. The scarcity implications of information networks show a reversal from mainstream models and dogma: 'In the networked economy, the more plentiful things become, the more valuable they become. … In a networked economy, value is derived from plenitude, the concept of abundance' (Matthew 2001, p. 2 of 7). As Elsner (2004, p. 1032) put it: 'The "new" economy, thus, has entered a stage of informational abundance which bears little resemblance to the conventional mainstream economic assumption of scarcity'. If so, worth no longer rises from exclusivity in network contexts; ubiquity often augments value rather than the other way round. This is the nature of complementarity; it turns over a lot of economists' most cherished doctrines.

CONCLUSIONS AND IMPLICATIONS: THE CASE FOR COMPLEMENTARITY AND ECONOMIC COOPERATION

Kaldor (1972, pp. 1240–42; 1975, p. 347) remarked that Adam Smith got distracted by 'values and prices' at the expense of increasing returns, and called for 'a major act of demolition ... to make any real progress' in advancing economics out of a developmental 'cul-de-sac'. He made a case for complementarity out of increasing returns, based on a Keynesian model of macroeconomic growth and decline. The introduction of planning horizons – as an ordinal index of 'bounded rationality' in Simon's (1982) sense – shows complementarities suffusing economics whether returns are increasing or not. The institutional implications of venturing out of an 'industry' grouping into an aggregation technique – or composition rule (Krupp 1963) – based on S_I as a measure of interdependence (within any group with respect to one member) remain unresolved: the mix of feedbacks (substitution and complementarity) yields an imbroglio where rivalry and collusion improve value in different domains. With positive and negative feedback closely intertwined, the mere assertion of substitution cannot be the basis of an efficiency case favouring competition. Complementarity opens a claim for optimal cooperation.

The indeterminacy of framing an institutional answer to a complex system of feedback characterized by interdependencies of both substitution and complementarity means another representation of the problem is needed. This is where horizon effects supply a novel insight: that the balance of interactive feedbacks – substitution and complementarity – is affected in every case by horizonal length. A shift of planning horizons – for better or worse, longer or shorter – will lead to a lower or higher respective S_I, and therewith a change in relations. Shorter horizons also imply inefficiency in an economy: clearer foresight through broader horizons brings social welfare improvement. There are two implications of this that can now be explored.

First, as social horizons extend, enhancing complementarity, our reward system must evolve from rivalry into cooperation to support development. Competition in the presence of complementary interdependence simply does not work; cooperation is our route to efficiency in this setting. Consequently, if longer horizons spread complementarity and reduce substitution in human affairs, social cultures ought to reward and not discourage cooperation, and grow beyond their addiction to overconsumption due to commercial goads. Sociologists, psychologists, social theorists and even economists see such trends with concern. But competition is still described as economists' standard of optimality in neoclassical theory and elsewhere.

The second implication arises as an extension of the first. The case was made that longer horizons serve as a welfare standard, in that every human decision needs to adjust to its impact on others in advance of its implementation, at least sooner rather than later. Economists should frame this as a matter of ethical conscience, where prospective externalities are internalized into imagined projections. This is why horizonal lengthening carries a moral lifeline into the centre of economics. Substitution and independence saved economists from morality (Lux 1990, pp. 87–9); here, a new 'horizonal economics' is ethical to the core. But this significance simply is the context of the point.

If planning horizons serve as a welfare standard – or as an ordinal index of negative organizational entropy in dynamic complex systems (Jennings 2005) – then the economic policy question is how we induce their extension. In learning communities and information networks, substitution cedes to complementary interactivity, even for fixed horizons. The implication is that cooperation – not competition – ought to be used to encourage longer horizons through its impact on knowledge. Competition impedes this process: individual P^*s exceed joint $P's$, because $S_I < 0$ reflects a concert of value achieved through cooperation. If so, competition is keeping our (private and social) horizons short. This is the failure of competition in complementary settings: its singular impropriety appears in negative horizon effects, so is invisible to perception through a neoclassical lens.

At this point, one turns to evidence. As Rescher (1979, p. 102) says: 'Someplace along the line of justification there must be provision for a corrective contact with the bedrock of an uncooperative and largely unmanipulable reality – a brute force independent of the whims of our theorizing. … The proof of the theoretical pudding must, in the final analysis, lie in the applicative eating.' Symptoms surround and truly assault us of our myopic concerns, in an advancing cultural and ecological crisis savagely undermining our very existence on this planet. Short horizons so encumber us, we hardly see them at all, but take them for granted as part of the human condition. As some wise soul once said: 'Fish discover water last' (McGregor 1960, p. 317).

The case for a new economics centred on complementarity, not substitution (save for myopic concerns), is strong. Even without horizon effects, static conceptions show increasing returns as a universal case, in line with the claims of Pigou (1927, 1928) and Kaldor (1972, 1975). If so, then complementarity trumps substitution, making cooperation more efficient than competition. Adding contagious horizon effects strengthens the claim for complementarity: planning horizons steer economic events and influence social behaviour. What this says is surprising: that economic analysis has selectively emphasized tradeoffs and scarcity at the expense of concerts of interest, and has divided us through rivalrous struggles shortening our horizons and truncating ecological conscience and social awareness. The immaturity of economic culture is often noted by anthropologists, sociologists and psychologists in their research (Kohn 1986). It is mostly economists who are blind to all our myopic concerns. Embracing complementarity in our relations of interdependence shall open doors to an ethical economics of cooperation, social cohesion and ecological health. This is the promise of a new 'horizonal' economics.

NOTES

1. $S_I = \sum s_{i \neq j}$ only with all $s_{i \neq j}$ terms *independent*, which is here ruled out by assumption.
2. I am indebted to a former colleague, Robert G. Wolf, for this suggestion.
3. One can imagine jealous reactions to a friend's success as an example of interhorizonal substitution in its short-term effects. But in time, envy is selected out due to its irrationality, especially in open markets.
4. As shown in equation (14.3) above.

REFERENCES

Alchian, Armen A. (1959), 'Costs and Outputs', in M. Abramovitz (ed.), *The Allocation of Economic Resources*, Stanford University Press, Stanford CA, 23-40.

—— (1968), 'Cost', in the *International Encyclopedia of the Social Sciences*, Vol. 3, Macmillan and Free Press, New York, 404–15, reprinted as ch. 12 of *Alchian's Economic Forces at Work*, Liberty Press (1977), Indianapolis IN, 301–23.

Arrow, Kenneth J. and Debreu, Gerard (1954), 'Existence of an Equilibrium for a Competitive Economy', *Econometrica*, 22, 265–90.

Bertalanffy, Ludwig von (1968), *General System Theory: Foundations, Development, Applications*, Braziller, New York.

Blaug, Mark (1976), 'Kuhn versus Lakatos or Paradigms versus Research Programmes in the History of Economics', in Spiro J. Latsis (ed.), *Method and Appraisal in Economics*, Cambridge University Press, Cambridge, England, 149–80.

Boulding, Kenneth E. (1956), *The Image: Knowledge in Life and Society*, University of Michigan Press, Ann Arbor.

Chamberlin, Edward H. (1933), *The Theory of Monopolistic Competition: A Reorientation of the Theory of Value*, 8th ed, Harvard University Press, Cambridge.

—— (1957), *Towards a More General Theory of Value*, Oxford University Press, New York.

Clapham, John H. (1922), 'Of Empty Economic Boxes', *Economic Journal*, 32 (128), 560–63.

Elsner, Wolfram (2004), 'The "New" Economy: Complexity, Coordination and a Hybrid Governance Approach', *International Journal of Social Economics*, 31 (11/12), 1029–49.

Georgescu-Roegen, Nicholas (1967), *Analytical Economics: Issues and Problems*, Harvard University Press, Cambridge.

—— (1971), *The Entropy Law and the Economic Process*, Harvard University Press,

Cambridge.

Hicks, John R. (1939), *Value and Capital*, 2nd ed. (1942), Oxford University Press, Oxford.

—— (1977), 'Preface (and Survey)', in his *Economic Perspectives: Further Essays on Money and Growth*, Oxford University Press, Oxford.

Hirshleifer, Jack (1962), 'The Firm's Cost Function: A Successful Reconstruction?' in *Journal of Business*, 35 (3), 235–55.

Jennings, Frederic B., Jr. (1985), *Public Policy, Planning Horizons and Organizational Breakdown: A Post-Mortem on British Canals and Their Failure*, Stanford University Ph.D. Dissertation, Stanford, California.

—— (2005), 'Planning Horizons as an Ordinal Entropic Measure of Organization', presented at a Conference on *Complexity, Science and Society* at the University of Liverpool, Liverpool, England, September.

—— (2006), 'A Horizonal Challenge to Orthodox Theory: Competition and Cooperation in Transportation Networks', in Michael Pickhardt and Jordi Sarda Pons (eds.), INFER Research Perspectives, Volume 1: *Perspectives on Competition in Transportation*, LIT Verlag, Berlin, 207–19.

Kaldor, Nicholas (1972), 'The Irrelevance of Equilibrium Economics,' *Economic Journal*, 82 (327), 1237–55.

—— (1973), 'Equilibrium Theory and Growth Theory', in Michael Boskin (ed.), *Economics and Human Welfare: Essays in Honor of Tibor Scitovsky, Academic Press*, New York (1979), 243–91.

—— (1975), 'What is Wrong with Economic Theory,' *Quarterly Journal of Economics*, 89 (3), 347–57.

Kohn, Alfie (1986), *No Contest: The Case Against Competition*, Houghton Mifflin, Boston.

Krupp, Sherman R. (1963), 'Analytic Economics and the Logic of External Effects', *American Economic Review*, Papers and Proceedings, 53 (2), 221–26.

—— (1982), 'Axioms of Economics and the Claim to Efficiency', in *Journal of Economic Issues* (1968), 2 (3), 273–82; reprinted in Warren J. Samuels (ed.), *The Methodology of Economic Thought: Critical Papers from the Journal of Economic Issues*, Transaction Books, New Brunswick, NJ.

Lux, Kenneth (1990), *Adam Smith's Mistake: How a Moral Philosopher Invented Economics and Ended Morality*, Shambhala Publications, Boston.

Matthew, Angus (2001), 'The New Economy – Truth or Fallacy?' in Pool: *Business and Marketing Strategy* (13), www.poolonline.com/archive/issue13/iss13fea4.html

McGregor, Douglas (1971), 'Theory X and Theory Y', ch. 16 in D.S. Pugh (ed.), *Organization Theory*, Penguin, New York, 358–74.

Myrdal, Gunnar (1978), 'Institutional Economics', *Journal of Economic Issues*, 12 (4), 771–83.

Nelson, Richard R. (1981), 'Research on Productivity Growth and Productivity Differences: Dead Ends and New Departures', *Journal of Economic Literature*, 19 (3), 1029–64.

Oi, Walter Y. (1967), 'The Neoclassical Foundations of Progress Functions,' *Economic Journal*, 77 (3), 579–94.

Pigou, Alfred C. (1927), 'The Laws of Diminishing and Increasing Cost,' *Economic Journal*, 37 (146), 188–97.

—— (1928), 'An Analysis of Supply,' *Economic Journal*, 38 (150), 238–57.

Polanyi, Michael (1958), *Personal Knowledge: Toward a Post-Critical Philosophy*, University of Chicago Press, Chicago.

Popper, Karl (1954), *Logik der Forschung*, published in English as The Logic of Scientific Discovery, Basic Books (1959), New York.

Reder, Melvin W. (1982), 'Chicago Economics: Permanence and Change', *Journal of Economic Literature*, 20 (1), 1–38.

Rescher, Nicholas (1979), *Cognitive Systematization: A Systems-Theoretic Approach to a Coherentist Theory of Knowledge*, Rowman and Littlefield, Totowa, NJ.

Samuelson, Paul (1947), *Foundations of Economic Analysis*, Harvard University Press, Cambridge, MA.

Senge, Peter M. (1990), *The Fifth Discipline: The Art and Practice of the Learning Organization*, Doubleday-Currency, New York.

Simon, Herbert A. (1982), *Models of Bounded Rationality*, Volumes 1–3, MIT Press (1982–97), Cambridge, MA.

Smith, Adam (1776), *An Inquiry into the Nature and Causes of the Wealth of Nations*, Modern Library (1937), New York.

Stigler, George J. (1951), 'The Division of Labor is Limited by the Extent of the Market', *Journal of Political Economy*, 59, 185–93; also ch. 10 in William Breit and Harold M. Hochman (eds), *Readings in Microeconomics*, 2nd ed, Holt, Rinehart and Winston, New York (1971), 140–48.

Young, Allyn A. (1928), 'Increasing Returns and Economic Progress', *Economic Journal*, 38 (152), 527–42.

15. Taking Economics to Bed: About the Pitfalls and Possibilities of Cultural Economics

Robbert Maseland

INTRODUCTION

In the slipstream of the resurgence of institutional economics, the interest in the role of culture in the economy has increased in recent years as well. For decades, economics has attempted to move away from 'soft issues' like norms, values, beliefs and culture, leaving those to the (other) social sciences. In recent years, however, the awareness has grown among many economists that without including these issues in analysis, it is impossible to come up with satisfactory answers to questions such as why there are vast differences in economic performance between societies. The idea of embeddedness has taken hold. The process has been helped by the new institutionalists' explicitly conciliatory stance towards neoclassicism, which has facilitated the acceptance of a focus on institutions, norms and values in economic theory. But the interest for culture has not been limited to new institutionalist theory only. Also, a new literature has sprung up that seeks to relate economic performance to cultural characteristics empirically.

The growing popularity of culture in economics can be illustrated by the mushrooming pile of publications devoted to the topic. Examples include Franke et al. (1991), Dieckman (1996), Granato et al. (1996), all regressing economic growth on cultural variables. Others have related culture to central bank independence and price stability (de Jong 2002), innovation (Shane 1993), and entrepreneurship, redistribution and national savings (Guiso et al. 2006). If one takes a slightly broader view of culture, Barro and McCleary (2003), McCleary and Barro (2006), and Guiso et al. (2003) established relationships between religion and economic outcomes, while others have focused on the influence of trust and per capita growth (Knack and Keefer 1997). Still another literature has focused on cultural explanations of economic development (Tabellini 2005), most notably in East Asia (Dore 1990; Harrisson 1992; Brook and Luong 1997; Barr 1999). Apart from this mostly quantitative literature, works such as those of Clark (1988), Landes (1998) and Harrison and Huntington (2000) have adopted an economic historical approach to the question what accounted for the economic rise of Europe and North America relative to the rest of the world, arguing that culture has played a decisive role. That these examples are part of a wider and longer-standing trend can be derived from DiMaggio (1994, 29–30), who showed that references in ECONLIT to the keyword 'culture' increased steadily between 1981 and 1992.

In contrast to its popularity, however, there has been remarkably little in the way of meaningful theoretical development with regard to cultural embeddedness in economics (Williamson 2000). That culture – like institutions – matters has been increasingly accepted, but how and why exactly has hardly been subject to analytical contemplation in the recent works. Put differently, while most of the works mentioned in the above make it sufficiently clear that persistent differences exist between societies, few of them enter the discussion about what it means to call such differences cultural and why we should do so. In fact, this touches upon a deeper neglect in the literature. Even though many people seem to have an idea of what it refers to, 'culture' is a concept still in want of clear definition within economics. The definitions that are in use, such as 'the collective programming of the mind that distinguishes the members of one group or category of people from another' (Hofstede 2001, p. 9); or the 'intergenerational transmission of knowledge, values, and other factors that influence behaviour' (North 1990, p. 37) are hardly a product of thorough conceptual reflection and discussion. As such, they leave too many questions open about the boundaries and origins of culture. In practice, they are usually narrowed down to the extent of being replaced by operationalisations such as religion, individualism, risk aversion or, at most, a general set of values. Such operationalisations bring with them the problems that it is not clear why these issues would represent culture, even in the vague definitions provided, nor why it has any added value to speak of culture instead of confronting these issues directly. But most seriously, without a clear delineation of culture, it is next to impossible to develop an elaborate theory of relations between culture and the economic.

In this chapter, I will attempt to provide a discussion of culture and its relation to the economy. A starting point is the observation that the idea of a relation between culture and the economy is made up of two sub-ideas. First, culture and economy are thought of as two different, separate things. Secondly, they are thought of as not just different, but also connected in some way. While the discussion so far has focused on arguments and propositions about the connection between culture and the economy, the questions how and why culture and economy would be separate spheres in the first place precedes and predetermines this interrelation. In order to be able to say something meaningful about the relation between culture and economy, therefore, we need first to establish why we have come to think of the two as separate issues and on what basis we separate them. For this reason, the first part of this chapter is devoted to the history of thought about culture and economy. It traces the gradual emergence of the cultural and the economic as two separate spheres of society, eventually resulting in an economic science that, until recently, came to see culture as lying outside its domain.

It is only after we have established the origins and lines of their separation that we can start discussing any relations between culture and economy. This is what is done in the second part of the chapter, in which I discuss the potential avenues along which culture can be re-injected into economics. Based upon this discussion, a third section suggests some directions for a research agenda of a new cultural economics. The chapter ends with a conclusion.

ECONOMICS AS CULTURELESS SCIENCE

Before discussing the possibilities of integrating culture in economics, it is worthwhile asking why culture has not been part of economics already. After all, economics is a science devoted to the understanding of human behaviour, of which culture would presumably be considered an important aspect. However, the fact of the matter is that culture has stood squarely outside the economic debate, at least after the fall of the older institutionalist schools. For the reasons behind this omission, one needs to go back to the history of the concept of culture, and the emergence of economics as a discipline.

Before we start out doing so, a few caveats are in order. Given the potential scope of a project discussing culture and economy, a paper such as this can only be rather superficial, going throughout history with very great steps. More particularly, the history presented here only deals with those ideas about culture that are most directly and obviously relevant to economics, leaving aside many of the nuances of the concept's evolution. Also, it is not concerned with culture in the sense of art, literature and the like, but with that something else also called culture, which has commonly been identified with factors such as values, religion, beliefs etc.[1]

In an illuminating article about the history of the concept of culture, Gyorgy Markus (1993) argues that culture as a concept is a distinctive characteristic of modernity. It reflects the modern idea that society and our behaviour are not entirely natural and preordained, but are – in part – the outcomes of a human-made evolutionary process. Thus, the idea of culture itself can be seen as culturally specific. It not only refers to outcomes of human-made evolution, but is also subject to it itself, in the sense that the meaning of 'culture' has also continued to evolve further since its original introduction.

From Individual Cultivation to Societal Progress

The term culture stems from the Latin cultura, a derivative from colere: to grow, to cultivate. Already in ancient times, it had come to be used as a metaphor, referring not only to cultivation of agricultural land, but also to the 'cultivation of the soul', i.e. to education. During the middle ages, with its focus on religious worship rather than human development, this meaning of the term disappeared. By the time it returned in the Renaissance, its metaphorical meaning had replaced the agricultural one as the dominant understanding of culture.

From this point on, the concept culture underwent two significant transformations. First, whereas culture at first referred to a process of cultivation of one's development, from the seventeenth century onwards it began to connote the results of this process rather than the process itself (Markus 1993, p. 9). With it, culture acquired the character of a concept of opposition. Culture became a 'thing', which people possessed or not. The educated did; the vulgar did not.

Also, something which could be called the socialisation of culture took place. Instead of referring to (the product of) individual education, in the late sixteenth and early seventeenth centuries, culture began to be applied to societies as a whole. Thus, the idea of there being more and less cultured societies came into view, advocated by authors such as Montaigne and Pufendorf (ibid., p. 10).

By the end of the seventeenth century, these two developments had resulted in a culture concept which referred to the results of the moral development of a society. Such a concept already bore many similarities to the concept of culture as it is understood nowadays. However, there were important differences as well. A most crucial one for our purposes is the point that in this understanding, culture was a dichotomous affair. A society either 'had' culture, or it had not. Culture had a meaning much closer to our current understanding of the term civilised; it was a concept imbued with moral and aesthetic notions. One could either be and act 'civilised' and 'cultured', or behave in a vulgar, barbaric, or savage manner. As such, it referred to a normative standard rather than something that could enter our thinking as an explanatory variable.

A first change towards a more descriptive rather than prescriptive interpretation of culture occurred in the eighteenth century. Especially in Britain – most notably in Scotland – a new view of history had emerged, centring around the idea of progress. Scottish authors, who were simultaneously confronted with new images and information about 'less cultivated' colonies and with their own peripheral position within Britain, developed the idea that history could be seen as societies evolving progressively, in stages. David Hume ([1757] 1976), for example, developed this idea of progression with regard to the history of religion. The idea of progress had been informed by the so-called Querelle des Anciens et Modernes, i.e. the struggle between those who continued to hold classical culture as the normative standard, and those who began challenge the prescriptive relevance of ancient culture for modern times. As a consequence of the Querelle, the idea of a universal, trans-historical human nature and ideal society began to make place for a more pluralistic view in which different societies were seen in their own historical context (Baars 1988). History thus came to be classified in distinctive periods; the idea of progress subsequently added an evolutionary structure to this classification.

The idea of culture fitted neatly within these ideas. The dichotomy between culture and barbaric vulgarity, mentioned earlier, now made place for a gradual, historical dimension. A cultural pluralism emerged, although – in contrast to current understandings – it only accounted for differences of degree, not of kind. In this evolutionary idea of progress, the prescriptive character of the culture concept did not so much disappear as was 'disguised' as description. The content and desirability of culture were still universal, but it was recognised that different societies were at different stages in their development towards such culture. It is in this context that an author like Adam Smith wrote his theories about what nowadays might be seen as 'culture and economy'. Smith's advocacy of the market economy fitted the idea of the progressive evolution of societies as a whole, not making any distinction between cultural, moral evolution and economic processes yet. *The Wealth of Nations* was not so much a book discussing merely production and trade decisions as a call for an entire social order, brought about through the morally cultivating effect of commerce. In Smith's view, a society of free individuals engaging in commercial relations with each other would be both orderly and prosperous. Commerce created a society which was civilised, because it was a necessary condition for arts and moral development (Smith [1763] 1983, p. 137) and commercial relations bred liberty and virtues. Such a liberal society, with its moral and material prosperity, was perceived to be the most advanced stage of history, in which commerce was the structuring element. Culture or civilisation equalled the market society, which through commercial development would eventually emerge in every society, however savage it was at the time.

From Universal Progress to ParticularNature

If we look at the above conception of culture, it might be noted that at this point (late-eighteenth century), culture meant something almost opposite to how it is commonly understood in social science nowadays. To someone like Adam Smith, culture was the endpoint of universal progress, something which developed societies had more of. In twentieth century social science, by contrast, culture tended to refer to something particularistic and of more relevance to less developed societies.

This latter interpretation has it roots in another important development originating in late-eighteenth-century Germany, where culture came to be opposed to civilisation. The former denoted self-actualisation and the unfolding of humans' full potential, whereas the latter referred to alien, artificial behaviour and rules that are morally corrupting. Becoming 'cultured' in this interpretation was not a process of increasing artificial social structures and self-control at the expense of one's natural identity. Becoming cultured, in the interpretation of universal progress, was a process of becoming what one really is, actualising one's essence (Hau 2000, pp. 24–5).

Gradually, the idea began to emerge in the nineteenth century that this self-actualisation culture referred to and applied to different 'selfs' for different societies. Whereas in historical stages-theories, societies only differed on the level of universal cultivation, now differences between societies acquired two dimensions. First, there was the difference between the cultured and the savage; secondly, among the 'developed' societies, various societies were cultured differently.[2]

In economics, such ideas can be encountered in their most explicit form in the works of an author like Wilhelm Roscher, and some of his followers in the German Historical School (e.g. Gustav Schmoller). Roscher, in particular, envisioned a programme of national economics, which ought to analyse the historical laws of economic progress, development and cultivation of the specific ethical characteristics of a people. He sought a 'simple description of; firstly, the economic character and needs of a nation (Volk), secondly the laws and institutions created to fulfil the former and finally the degree of success they have had. In other words, a simultaneous description of the anatomy and physiology of economics' (Roscher [1854] 1918, p. 77, §26). Roscher believed that all history portrayed a cyclical structure; each society goes through a period of growth, maturity and decay. However, each people follows its own path, and its own period of maturity. Thus, on the one hand there is a universal historical law of progress (and decay), but on the other hand, this universal laws applies differently to different societies on the basis of their national characters. In addition to an understanding of culture as cultivated moral quality, in works of people like Roscher an understanding of culture as the particular, inherent characteristics of a people was born.

These two dimensions (i.e. differences of degree and of kind) of culture eventually came to drift apart. The idea of a universal path of development was maintained. Naturally, what people considered to be part of such a universal state of 'culturedness' was informed significantly by ideas, values and meanings derived from their own social context. The achievements of the own society were thus translated into the norm for all societies. Modernity, for example, though clearly modelled on the experiences of Western Europe and North America, was a fate that would eventually be shared by the whole of humankind, being the endpoint of all development. In this context, culture in the meaning of 'general knowledge' or (knowledge and appreciation of) arts and literature also entered the scene. However, apart from in this arts and literature context, in this understanding of culture the term itself began to make place for terms like civilisation, modernity and developedness.

The word culture thus came to denote the differential dimension mainly. Moreover, since modernisation was considered to be a universal, homogenising process, cultural differences existed only where there had not been development as yet. Culture – the particular, the specifically own – therefore became the deviation from the mould of modernisation. From cultivation it turned into tradition, becoming the opposite of the idea of modern development. Development indicated progress and change; culture, which only still existed where development had not taken place, began to imply stability, tradition and changelessness. Development was a process that was the same everywhere; culture entailed the specific deviations from it. And perhaps most crucially, where civilisation was modelled after the own, culture was a term reserved for the other. The educated West was modern, whereas the unenlightened peoples of the world – including, perhaps, the poor and less educated mob in the core societies – had these irrational habits and remnants of the past called culture.

Until the day of today, culture is often considered a topic especially relevant in the context of developing nations, or 'Eastern' societies like Japan or the Asian Newly Industrialised Economies. A search in the ECONLIT database shows that any reference to culture and economics is about 1.8 times more likely to also refer to development than other searches, and even 2.7 times more likely to contain the search term Asia. For any incorporation of culture into the economic model, this association with 'the other' is problematic, since it informed the demarcation of the social sciences.

Culture vs. Economy

For the study of relations between culture and economics, these developments had important consequences. The emergence of a dominant understanding of culture as specific behaviour, norms, values and meanings that are inherent to a society and set it apart from others coincided with a reinterpretation of the subject of economics as a consequence of the Methodenstreit. Under the influence of authors like Menger and later on Robbins (1932), economics eventually came to focus on the universally applicable behavioural structure of economic rationality. Without delving into the details of this process, what is of interest here is that this redefinition of the economic subject was much opposed to the newly dominant understanding of culture. In fact, the structure of rationality that economics sought to analyse had much in common with that other, now discarded meaning of culture: culturedness.

Rational behaviour, i.e. adhering to principles of modern, efficient conduct such as that of educated people, referred to that part of our behaviour that had become cultured. Particularistic, undeveloped culture was much the opposite of these universal cultured principles. It referred to actions and situations in which the behavioural structures of cultured behaviour did not yet apply fully; those segments and aspects of society that were not developed (cultured), and not yet rational and civilised. Culture had no place in economics.[3] Other social sciences were needed to study these phenomena. When it came to analysis of Western societies, the study of deviations from the structure of economic rationality came to be the subject of a new sub-discipline called economic sociology, to which economists not adhering to the separation of social sciences were expelled.[4] Economic sociology went on to study the irrational traditions, customs and beliefs that the economic model could not account for. When it came to non-Western societies, otherness or deviation from the norm was almost everything there was. Lack of development equalled an abundance of culture and traditions, after all. Therefore, different disciplines such as economic anthropology came about, investigating other societies in their totality as cultural phenomena.[5] The invention of economic sociology and economic anthropology sealed the fate of culture, removing it from economics proper once and for all. In the new constellation, culture came to stand for the particularity of a case, and as such was the opposite of what economics, dealing with the universal structure of behaviour, was about.[6] In so far as culture still had a place in economics, it was in development economics; the economics dealing with the less developed, cultural countries. Modernisation theory, for example, called for cultural modernisation as well. Culture entered as a set of obstacles for economic rational progress, and tradition as something to get rid of in order to develop and reap the benefits of modernisation (e.g. Hoselitz 1954; Nash 1964; McClelland 1961).[7] Although occasionally you would find cultural elements that were compatible with rationality and development (Eisenstadt 1968; Levy Jr 1962), culture basically was a problem.

The currently observable project seeking to bring culture and economics back together starts out from this division. This is obvious in approaches such as Coleman's, treating culture as 'norms that mandate action that is not in one's own interest or proscribe behaviour that is' (DiMaggio 1994, p. 29). It almost goes without saying, then, that this antagonistic state of affairs poses real problems for an integration of culture and economics, since to do so meaningfully would require going back on conceptions and definitions of economics as well as ideas of culture.

BRINGING CULTURE INTO ECONOMICS

The idea of economics as the science devoted to the study of rational choice under scarcity, as argued, meant that culture lay outside its realm. Given this background, it is interesting to look at the ways in which culture has been re-introduced in economics.

Saying that culture has come to lie outside the scope of economics is not the same as saying that the economic model is completely incompatible with the concept of culture. In the basic model of economically rational choice, goals and preferences (deemed unlimited) are confronted with means or constraints, bringing about scarcity. If we hold on to such a model, there are three main openings through which one could potentially bring in culture. First, culture could enter as (source of) preferences. Secondly, it could be invoked as (a source of) constraints. Thirdly, it has been invoked as complementary deviation from the model.

Culture as Preferences

The first opening is through preferences. Neoclassical economics, while studying choice on the basis of individual preferences, has always explicitly left the formation of preferences outside its analysis. Rather than that, neoclassical theory dealt with individual choices, given certain preferences. If we take culture 'as the basis for individual preferences (goals) and beliefs' (Sun Ki-Chai 1997, p. 45), then, we are able to fill in substantially the formal models of neoclassicism. This is the line–at least implicitly and indirectly–taken by the many recent empirical studies into culture and the economy on basis of large-scale, cross-country survey data, such as de Jong (2002), Shane (1993) or Barro and McCleary (2003). The argument in such studies runs that, for example, if people are risk-averse, they will choose risk-reducing social arrangements such as bank credit, whereas risk-loving people will opt for stock markets to finance their investments.

This line of research does not alter the neoclassical model, but applies its abstract predictions over choice to concrete, substantial decisions. Although such research is conducive to answer many specific questions, such as why stock markets are more developed in society A, it is not that interesting theoretically. Merely filling in the preferences within the neoclassical model does not amount to any theoretical insights, nor does it make clear what would be the difference between culture and other sources of preference, so that to speak of 'culture' instead of 'preference' has no genuine added value. In a sense, the approach is similar to market research; we can predict which 'product' people will choose, on basis of their preferences we studied. Only when combined with an elaborate theory about the nature, emergence and development of cultural preferences, could such work fundamentally contribute to our understanding of the economy. Unfortunately, such a theory is hardly available in the data-sets of Hofstede, Inglehart, or Schwartz underlying most of this work. That is not to say that this work is entirely devoid of theory; but a theory about the origins and development of cultural values is absent. For this reason, this line of work fails to have a wider relevance than to the specific, empirical cases it addresses.

Culture as Constraints

A second route to impute culture into economics is via the other given in the rational choice model: constraints. This is the way culture is approached in new institutional economics, which treats culture as a constraint for institutional development.

The core idea of new institutional economics is that institutions, the 'rules of the game' as they are defined, 'define and limit the set of choices of individuals' (North 1990, p. 4), posing the constraints for individual choices. Because they channel human behaviour and reduce possible courses of action, institutions have a dampening effect on uncertainty and transaction costs. A main problem with this line of argument is that institutions are basically rules that are human-made and do not exist prior to society. In other words, they need not be as they are, and because of that, they are not constraints in the neoclassical sense of the term. Institutions can only constrain if people are bound by them, not when there are contingent agreements that can be altered.

The solution of this problem, given by many new institutional economists, is to argue that there are limits to institutional change, posed by the fact that their adaptation is constrained by other factors – such as culture. The whole system can be seen as consisting of several levels, each level providing the context in which decisions at a lower level must be made. Note, however, that allocations at each level are established in a way very similar to neoclassical reasoning. Agents, having certain preferences, are confronted with relative prices and decide upon an allocation on basis of that confrontation. If an institutional structure is to change, therefore, 'the sources of change are changing relative prices or preferences' (North 1990, p. 83).

This argument can be found with authors such as North, claiming that institutions do not change very rapidly or profoundly (North 1990, p. 83) because formal institutional structures are set by underlying informal institutions and by culture. Changes in formal rules that go beyond the informal institutions of a society are unlikely to be effective because, due to enforcement costs, efficacy requires people believing formal rules to be just (North 1992, p. 478). Stability, then, 'is accomplished by a complex set of constraints that include formal rules nested in a hierarchy, where each level is more costly to change than the previous one' (North, 1990, p. 83). Therefore, even revolutions and discontinuous changes tend to portray a high level of continuity, in spite of possible initial appearances. The reason for this is that 'formal rules change, but the informal constraints do not' (North 1990, p. 91). Culture, in this argument, is fairly stable and its development occurs outside the conscious intervention of individuals. It is the ultimate source of scarcity; without its stability, institutions would not provide constraints, because they could be changed at will. Because institutional development is checked by culture, it changes only incrementally. This idea is captured in the term embeddedness.[8]

The idea of changes taking place in various levels with each lower level being embedded in slower changing higher levels has also been adopted and worked out by other authors, such as Lal (1998) and Williamson (2000). Both of them, minor differences notwithstanding, distinguish several levels of human behaviour, from specific allocation on to legislation, culture, and levels like evolutionary biological constraints and material natural constraints, each higher level setting the limits for adaptations inside the level beneath it. As in North's work, to the pure idea of embeddedness the idea is added that higher levels typically change more slowly. The explanation differs somewhat, however. Lal explains it as slower and faster working equilibrating forces; in his view culture could be perceived as equilibrium, since both can be described as a state 'where self-seeking agents learn nothing new so that their behaviour is routinised' (Lal 1998, p. 7). If one is prepared to see institutions and culture as social equilibria,

> there are a number of different processes with their respective equilibria that could explain social outcomes. They can be distinguished by the period of time over

> which the equilibrating forces work. The quickest working is the market process of supply and demand, which leads to a market equilibrium. The second fastest are the processes leading to an equilibrium regarding material beliefs, which determine the organisational framework within which the market process operates (or, as in controlled economies, does not operate). Changing signals from the environment can alter such material equilibria within the lifetime of a generation. Slower moving are the cultural equilibria associated with cosmological beliefs. These would seem to require at least a generation or two to alter. Finally, there is the evolutionary equilibrium associated with the 'selfish gene', which is the slowest moving of all and for all practical purposes can be ignored in our investigations, except for its legacy on our minds. (Lal 1998, pp. 11–12)[9]

Williamson (2000) puts forth a similar idea, which he exposes graphically in the following model of institutional changes (Table 15.1).

Table 15.1: Economics of Institutions According to Williamson[10]

Level	Frequency	Purpose
Embeddedness: Informal institutions, customs, traditions, norms, religion	10^2 to 10^3	Often noncalculative; spontaneous
Institutional Environment: formal rules of the game – esp. property (polity, judiciary, bureaucracy)	10 to 10^2	Get the institutional environment right. 1st order economising
Governance: play of the game – esp. contract (aligning governance structures with transactions)	1 to 10	Get the governance structures right. 2nd order economising
Resource allocation and employment (prices and quantities; incentive alignment)	Continuous	Get the marginal conditions right. 3rd order economising

What does this mean for the place of culture in economics? Frankly, very little. Although culture is important in being the source of ultimate constraints, the theory says little about what culture is and even less about how it develops. As North (1990, p.87) argues, 'cultural evolutionary theory is in its infancy and is not of much immediate value in analyzing changing specific informal constraints, except for one important point: the persistence of cultural traits in the face of changes in relative prices, formal rules, or political status makes informal constraints change at a different rate than formal rules' (North 1990, p. 87). From this point of view, North's definition of culture as intergenerational transmission of factors that influence behaviour (ibid., p. 37) is not surprising; culture in this theory comes into play as a source of constraining factors, but is not analysed, or even defined directly. The question, however, is whether it makes sense to be concerned with culture at all instead of focusing on informal institutions and knowledge

directly. What is more, given the absence of a substantive definition of culture, it is by no means clear what the difference between informal institutions, knowledge and culture would be; yet, all these concepts are used separately (e.g. North 1990). Culture, in new institutional economics, seems to serve as a stop-gap to maintain the choice-under-scarcity model. Apart from that, it attracts or warrants very little interest.

Problems with Culture as Constraint

Although the inclusion of culture in the new institutional model of the economy is perhaps promising, it begs many of the more interesting questions. Like in the culture-as-preferences approach, a substantive theory about what culture is and how it evolves is lacking. To their credit, most of the authors involved acknowledge this. North, for example, argues that 'cultural evolutionary theory is in its infancy and is not of much immediate value in analyzing changing specific informal constraints' (North 1990, p. 87). Williamson (2000) calls for more research on the level of embeddedness; economic sociologists Smelser and Swedberg do the same (1994, p. 18). If one is to assess the theory, for this reason, the question should perhaps not be whether new institutional economics is currently providing meaningful insights about the role of culture in economy, but whether it can be reasonable expected to do so in the future. In this respect, there are two obstacles that the theory needs to confront.

First, it should be noted that the idea of culture as source of constraints depends on the evolution of culture as unintended, incremental process. If culture were subject to conscious, rational design, it would not be serving as source of constraints because it could be changed at will by the actors bound by it. Culture, in other words, develops following mechanisms and processes unknown to economic actors; they fail to see or predict the effect of their actions on their cultural environment. When cultural evolution is a process that cannot be known by economic actors, however, it cannot be grasped by theoretical models of economists either. After all, economists are also actors. The idea of culture as source of constraints thus depends on the vision of cultural evolution as a black box, insensitive to conscious design. The model precludes the development of a substantive theory about culture and cultural evolution.

In fact, the only substantive statement about cultural evolution in this line of thinking is that culture evolves slowly and incrementally. It is in this respect, however, that the culture-as-constraint approach treads on thin ice. Anthropological studies have argued for a long time that culture ought to be approached as a dynamic, complex web of meanings spun and re-spun by people in daily life, instead of as a static set of traditions (e.g. Geertz 1973).

Many studies have shown that cultural change is possible, and occurring everywhere. Post-colonial theorists have argued that much of what nowadays is viewed as the static cultural heritage of less developed societies can often be traced back to colonial policies. A seminal study by Anderson (1984) analysed the way in which national identity has been created in various societies. With regard to the culture of non-Western countries, Said ([1978] 1995), moreover, has made a very strong case that the very idea this category of societies steeped in static, unalterable traditions and culture is inextricably related to colonialism.

In contrast to all this, institutional economics in so far as it turned towards culture has tended to approach national cultures as static, or at least very slowly adapting givens. Arguments for this proposition are mostly lacking. In Williamson (2000) it is not very clear where the differences in adaptive speed come from, or how the specific timetable is derived. Moreover, Lal (1998), although mimicking much of Williamson's argument, comes up with entirely different time-frames. In his view, the forces working towards market equilibria adapt constantly, whereas equilibrating forces of material beliefs work within the lifetime of a generation, and deeper-rooted cosmological beliefs exhibit equilibria that take at least two generations to change. Again, arguments beyond intuitive appeal for these time-frames are lacking.

Secondly, invoking culture as a source of constraints for institutional development invites the question why we are not dealing with institutions directly. This concern is aggravated by the lack of substantive theory and definitions of culture. The way North delineates culture is illuminating in this respect. Culture – the intergenerational transmission of factors that influence behaviour (North 1990, p. 37) – comes into play as a source of constraining factors, but is not analysed, or even defined directly. Culture is addressed as a black box resulting in constraints for institutional change. However, if we are not ready to define and theorise culture beyond its impact on institutions, invoking culture becomes merely a more complex way of assuming that institutions change only incrementally. In short, the role ascribed to culture in new institutional economics is as yet both quite fundamental and marginal. It is a necessary prerequisite for the theory to hold, but apart from this purpose, little attention is paid to it. Theoretically, it has not evolved into a theory about culture and its evolution yet. Consequentially, the danger exists for culture to serve mainly as a stop-gap needed to maintain the choice-under-constraints model. For an addition of culture to economic thinking through the route of constraints to deliver a fundamental contribution to our understanding of the economy, more theorisation is required.

Culture as Complementary Deviation from the Model

Looking at the ways in which culture enters in institutional theory and value survey-based work, it is clear that in both cases culture is in fact invoked as deviation from the model. Although not as explicit as in approaches such as that of Coleman, culture serves as the rest category invoked to save the structural rational-choice model from unfriendly empirical observations. It is not theorised itself; it is a category of external factors that we do not need to explain, and are invoked to explain everything that the economic model is unable to. This state of affairs more or less follows logically from the way in which culture and economy have separated and come to be defined. With culture being 'that which is not economic' any meaningful comprehensive framework is out of the question. To try to find relations between culture and economy defined thus is not likely to bring meaningful results in the future.

A more promising route for cultural economics lies on a higher level of reflection. Note that we started out our historical overview with the observation that the idea of there being something called culture was itself specific to our time and place. Now, instead of trying to establish relations between culture and economy that are inevitably pre-determined by the way we have defined the two relative to each other in the first place, we can question the reasons and impact of the way in which we use categories like 'culture' and 'economic'. In that case, we can investigate the influence of the cultural construct 'culture' on the cultural construct 'economy'. Our thinking about culture and economy then becomes the object of inquiry, rather than culture and economy – whatever these may be – themselves. The questions we need to answer then are why, with the definition of culture as problematic as it is, are we all still using the term? What is implied by using it? What are the consequences of invoking culture in economic analysis?

If we take this line, a first observation is that in thinking about culture and economy, culture always seems to be invoked as something given and fundamentally irrational. It is inherent to a society and in the end unexplainable itself. Societies simply have certain cultural characteristics, and it is impossible to make any scientific statements about the culture they are born in. It just is. To paraphrase Weber, the moral irrationality of the world extends to a 'cultural irrationality'. Culture cannot and need not be explained itself; it just enters as an exogenous factor in our models of the world.

This black-box character of culture follows from our conception of it, rather than being a characteristic of a clear-defined set of phenomena called culture. Culture is the category defined by society as the things that are constant and fundamental to its identity. These attributes are constitutive of culture. Consider cultural norms for example; what distinguishes a norm from an action is precisely the idea that it is not specific to a certain moment and place, but continuously repeated over time in a society. Similarly, the difference between a value and a specific opinion is that a value is deemed to be rooted in society and its history. Culture, in this respect, refers to those aspects of our society we consider as intrinsic to its identity and stable. When we stop considering these as stable, they stop being thought of as our culture. Culture serves as the structuring principle, binding past and present with an unchangeable historical identity, against which evolution and economic change can be understood.

If we look at it in this way, the fact that culture serves the role of being the deviation from the economic model becomes more interesting. Now, the question is not 'is it analytically valuable to invoke culture in this way?' (to which the answer would be rather obviously 'no'); the question is 'what is the impact of the fact that society creates separate spheres for culture and the economic?'

For one thing, the effect is that different spheres are subject to different principles and mechanisms. The statement that culture is deep-rooted and stable, for example, gets to be seen in a different light. This statement is in fact in a way correct, but only by definition – culture is deep-rooted and stable because that which we do not think of as deep-rooted and stable, we do not call culture. It is part of our conception of culture that those things we categorise as culture are thought to evolve very slowly over people's heads, and to be intrinsic to a particular people's identity. By contrast, what we consider as belonging to 'the economic', we deem susceptible to universal principles of economic behaviour. Aspects like allocation and production can be altered quite easily, but such development happens according to certain mechanisms that govern the economic realm of our society – opportunism and rational self-interest.

It is quite likely, then, that society's categorisation of actions and phenomena as cultural or economic has an impact on the evolution and performance of social structures. Statements like 'culture is stable' or 'economic behaviour is rational in structure' are revealed as self-validating. Arguing that certain institutions are cultural has the effect of freezing them, because it adds a veneer of anciennity and untouchability. People will stay away from trying to adapt them, because they are not subject to political but sociological debate. In this way, the very fact that people consider something to be 'cultural' makes it harder to change. Similarly, the fact that people categorise other spheres as 'economic' invites differently structured behaviour in that sphere. Opportunism and rational self-interest are more likely to dominate actions.

All this does not mean that statements about culture and economy and their interrelation are not true. Culture indeed cannot change – by definition.

What can change, however, is which phenomena and actions we consider to be cultural, and which we classify as economic in nature. However, because culture is deemed unchanging, stable and given, it changes by rewriting history. When looked upon from a distance, the purportedly 'Judo-Christian culture' of Europe, for example, does not refer to the same values and beliefs nowadays as it did in Victorian times. Yet, then, as now, the very idea of such a culture implies the thinking of a long-standing continuity in 'Judo-Christian' identity. In the process of cultural change, the history in which our identities are rooted has changed alongside. Similarly, beliefs about cultural identity in most Western countries nowadays refer to national culture, which is taken to go back centuries if not longer. However, two centuries ago, and in some places considerably more recently still, the cultural identity people attributed to themselves was almost certainly not positioned at the national level. However, these prior generations took their culture to be historically rooted as well. The changes in culture that took place in the meantime thus have replaced one history with another, precisely because the very essence of culture is the idea that it is rooted and intrinsic to one's historical identity. Culture can change, in contrast with new institutional economics; but it will take its historical, unchangeable character with it.

In that sense, the system described by Williamson is misleading. The 'embeddedness' level, with its alleged duration of change, is not a pre-given category. Structures we denote as culture could just as well be categorised as politic, making them subject to discursive debate. It is because we do not do so that they become static and unalterable. Therefore, Williamson's system should not be read as a model of pre-given reality, but as a reflexive description of how we constitute society in our thoughts and actions.

THE POLITICAL ECONOMY OF EMBEDDING: TOWARDS A RESEARCH AGENDA

The underlying argument in the above is that embeddedness, culture and the economic should not be considered as a priori determined categories, but as social constructions in need of explanation. Any possible embeddedness of the economy in institutions and culture always refers to a set of structural social relations, between the economic and the social and cultural. These relations are contingent upon time, place, and the way in which society has defined the various categories. The extent to which society has created separate spheres of the economic, social and cultural, is then revealed as not only a characteristic of institutions, but as a fundamental social structure itself. The insight with which we begun our story – that the idea of culture is specific to modern society – is illustrative of this. The conceptions of culture and economy and their interrelation set the patterns and structures according to which social action is shaped; it is one of the basic 'rules of the game'. As it is a contingent social structure, it needs to be investigated as such.

The question we need to ask, therefore, is not so much whether the economic is actually embedded in the social and cultural or not. After all, that in itself does not tell us very much; the answers and mechanisms behind them might very well differ from case to case, so that abstract, universal theories about it do not apply. Rather than to succumb to such temptations, one should address the questions why and how embeddedness in a particular case is constructed, i.e. which areas of social environment are classified as economic, which to culture, and what their interrelation is. Moreover, one should ask what the implications of such a constructed embeddedness or constructed absence of embeddedness are. In other words, why do some societies create separate social spheres for the economic and the cultural, while others explicitly bring the two together? How do they do so? These are the questions an investigation into embeddedness should address.

These questions are important because of the effect embedding has. As argued, to maintain that some structures are 'cultural', has the effect of freezing the status quo. As culture, they are not subject to debate, because they are not susceptible to change and people cannot be held accountable for it. Culture is a given. This means that to position certain structures in the realm of culture has strong political effects. It effectively depoliticises institutions.

For example, in the current debate about immigration and integration in the Netherlands, frequent mention is made of a historical culture of tolerance and gender equality the Dutch would posses. This classification has less to do with historical accuracy – gender equality in the Netherlands is, if it exists at all, a matter of the last few decades – than with a desire to position these values as fundamental and beyond questioning, and immigrants as norm-breaking outsiders. As a result, it has strong political effects, directing political discourse about integration and strengthening the position of 'the native Dutch' (whoever that may be) in the debate. Similarly, debates like the one about 'Asian Values' and 'Asian Democracy' in Southeast Asia served for a large part only to legitimate and support the position of (semi-) authoritarian leaders (Kim Dae-Jung 1994; Maseland and Peil 2008). If collectivism and preferences for social order and hierarchy are part of one's culture, questioning or opposing the government is not likely. Even if you would like a different form personally, the message is that authoritarian regimes are culturally determined, so that any action to have them otherwise is deemed futile.

In this situation, to reflexively ask questions about the how and why of embeddedness construction is not only illuminating, but also serves an important political, emancipatory function. Insight into the way certain institutions have been essentialised, and why, discloses debate about the desirability of these institutions vis-à-vis their potential alternatives. It opens the door for a more thoughtful theory about institutional development and the role culture plays in it. To present culture as pre-given facts that cannot or can hardly be changed, as most of the new cultural economists seem to do, is problematic not only for reproducing the very ideas a cultural economics seeks to investigate, but also for harnessing and legitimising a political status quo in this process of reproduction. Awareness of and reflection upon such pitfalls is a must for a new cultural economics to be of any value. Rather than confirming essentialism, a cultural economics should focus on the political effects of embedding, and the motivations behind it. Only thus can it make an important contribution to the improvement of social theory and social practice.

CONCLUSION

In this chapter, I have discussed the problems of and possibilities for a new cultural economics. First of all, it has been argued that there are historical and conceptual reasons why culture has not been part of the economic lexicon already, and that these reasons continue to hamper integration today.

Subsequently, I have sketched three main avenues along which culture could in principle be aligned with economics, of which only one – culture as a complementary deviation of the economic model – is theoretically promising. While viewing culture as (a source of) preferences may be able to solve many specific empirical questions, it reproduces the opposition between culture and economy and does not directly contribute to the development of theory. The same goes with the avenue of culture as constraint, which has been common in new institutional economics. The proposition that culture is a given constraint prohibits any theoretical argument about the relation between our actions and cultural evolution. After all, culture can only be a constraint if we do not know how to influence it. On top of that, it should be noted that convincing arguments about why there should be something like culture in our social environment, static and inherent to society's identity, are lacking.

Cultural economics, therefore, should be aware of the fact that economics has constructed culture as the complementary deviation from the economic model. Culture serves in many ways as opposite of the economic in the way societies are constituted. This function of culture as it appears to economists follows from the historical origins of the concept and the way the social sciences have drifted apart. Culture, in this constellation, has always referred to the marginal other, whether the agents in (post-)colonial societies or the poor and deviating in the own society. Whereas economics was concerned with behaviour according to the norm, non-rational culture began to represent the deviation from it, becoming the subject of sociology and anthropology. As culture refers to parts of the society that we do not deem susceptible to economic mechanisms of change and development, it is a complementary deviation from the economic model, describing a set of aspects of society that do not follow economic principles.

The content of this set is not pre-determined, however. The classification of some structures as culture and others as economic is essentially a political process. It is in this context that seeing culture as a complementary deviation from the economic model becomes interesting. Instead of building on constructions like culture and economy, a meaningful cultural economics should question them reflexively. New institutionalist ideas about the static character of culture and its relations with the economy should be perceived as reflective of the way society is constructed socially, rather than as models of a pre-given reality. The way in which and reasons why an economy is being embedded is the main question. To address such questions, awareness of the politically laden character of conceptualisations of culture and the economic is necessary.

All in all, a new cultural economics ought to be primarily concerned with embeddedness as a question, not as a model for answering questions. This also implies that it should not consider the definitions of 'the economic' and 'the cultural' – and the demarcations of the social sciences accordingly – as a priori. On the contrary, these definitions and demarcations should be object of critical investigation. In the end, a meaningful theory about culture and economy requires not only a consideration of definitions of culture. It also requires a reconsideration of our definition of economics.

NOTES

1. It should be noted, though, that part of the discussion presented here might shed some doubts about the validity of this distinction.
2. A parallel with the discussion about various 'capitalisms', emerging after the demise of the socialist model might be observed.
3. Swedberg (1994, p. 72) cites Durkheim in this respect, arguing that 'l'économie politique classique a créé un monde économique qui n'existe pas, un *Güterwelt*, un monde isolé qui demeure à jamais identique à lui-même et au sein duquel les conflits entre des forces purement individuelles sont régis par de lois économiques immuables'. A century later, the same point would be made by Bourdieu (1998), indicating its continued relevance. The point was perhaps most explicitly made by one of the founding fathers of modern neoclassical economics, Vilfredo Pareto, who argued that a distinction ought to be made between strictly economic

behaviour, being the outcome of 'a series of logical reasonings', and behaviour determined by what he called 'custom' (Pareto [1906] 1972, pp. 29–30; Bourdieu 2005, p. 209).

4. Most notably, Max Weber, whose started out holding a chair in economics but went into history as a founding father of sociology. Bond (2005) makes a strong case that Schumpeter was largely responsible for Weber's expulsion from economics, which is rather ironic given the fact that Schumpeter himself would eventually suffer more or less the same fate. In similar processes, authors such as Marcel Mauss and later on Karl Polanyi were banished to economic anthropology and history.
5. Again, expelling authors that had thought of themselves as analysts of economic phenomena in general towards a separate discipline (e.g. Mauss [1925] 1970).
6. With non-economists dealing with such marginal aspects of behaviour, the meaning of their analyses was restricted to 'compléter les analyses déjà existantes des économistes' (Swedberg 1994, p. 33). Bourdieu (2005, p. 210) argues that this 'distinction (is) still present today in the minds of economists, who leave the curiosa or failings of economic operations to sociologists'.
7. This situation can be said to have been informed by a kind of ethnocentrism describing the civilised, economically rational way of doing things as universal, while other ways of doing things were reduced to non-rational, norm-breaking culture (Bourdieu 2005, p. 5). Economics, as a result, has always found itself betwixt and between, claiming to be a positive science– describing and analysing an aspect of behaviour – while often being accused of being normative. The reason is that while economics might possibly be 'positive' when it comes to analysing economically rational behaviour, it is normative in focusing on this type of behaviour as universal standard.
8. The concept of embeddedness can be traced back to Polanyi (1944), and has been widely used in institutional economics, although it is still felt by many that it 'remains in need of greater specification' (Smelser and Swedberg, 1994, p. 18). Indeed, there seem to be some possibly important theoretical differences between the ways in which it is understood by, for example, Granovetter (1985), Williamson (2000), or North (1990). Amusingly enough, North (1990) actually uses the term 'imbeddedness' rather than 'embeddedness', whereas in later writings about new institutional economics, it is the word 'embedded' that generally came to be used. This in itself goes some way in illustrating the idea of path-dependency and the reproduction of recognised meanings.
9. As indicated, Lal (1998) argues that various levels should be seen as social equilibria; subsequently, he argues that there are differences in the pace of adjustment between various levels, because of differences in the equilibrating forces. However, apart from being tautological when explaining slow change with slow processes, this argument suffers from an apparent misunderstanding of the meaning of slow equilibrating forces. If such forces work slowly, the result is not that the equilibrium is more stable; the result is that states of disequilibrium will last longer, to the extent that equilibrium will never be reached. If that is the case, the view of culture as social equilibrium is not tenable, and the theory would predict cultural instability rather than stability.
10. Taken from Williamson (2000, p. 597).

REFERENCES

Baars, P. (1988), *Anachronisme en Historisch Besef*, Den Haag: Nijgh en van Ditmar Universitair.

Barr, M.D. (1999), 'Lee Kuan Yew: race, culture and genes', *Journal of Contemporary Asia*, 29 (2), 145–66.

Barro, R. and R. McCleary (2003), 'Religion and economic growth across countries', *American Sociological Review*, 68 (5), 760–81.

Bond, N. (2005), 'Eliminating the "social" from "Sozialökonomik"', Paper presented at the meeting of the *European Society for the History of Economic Thought*, Stirling, June 2005.

Bourdieu, P. (1998), 'L'essence de néolibéralisme', *Le Monde Diplomatique*, March 1998, 3.

Bourdieu, P. (2005), *The Social Structures of the Economy*, Cambridge: Polity Press.

Brook, T. and H. Luong (1997), *Culture and Economy: the shaping of capitalism in Eastern Asia*, University of Michigan Press.

Clark, G. (1988), 'Economists in search of culture: the unspeakable in pursuit of the inedible?', *Historical Methods*, 21, 161–64.

Dieckmann, O. (1996), 'Cultural determinants of economic growth: theory and evidence', *Journal of Cultural Economics*, 20, 297–320.

DiMaggio, P. (1994), 'Culture and Economy', in Smelser, N. and R. Swedberg (eds), *Handbook of Economic Sociology*, 27–57.

Dore, R. (1990), 'Reflections on Culture and Social Change', in Gereffi, G. and D.L. Wyman (eds), *Manufacturing Miracles*, Princeton: Princeton University Press, 353-367.

Eisenstadt, S.N. (1968), 'Review article: some new looks at the problem of relations between traditional societies and modernization', *Economic Development and Cultural Change*, 16 (3), 436–50.

Franke R.H., G. Hofstede and M.H. Bond (1991), 'Cultural roots of economic performance: a research note', *Strategic Management Journal*, 12, 165–73.

Geertz, C. (1973), 'Thick Description: Toward an interpretive theory of culture', in *The Interpretation of Cultures*, New York: Basic Books, 3–30.

Giddens, A. (1974), *Max Weber over politiek en sociologie* [transl. H.O. van den Berg], Meppel: Boom.

Granato, J., R. Inglehart and D. Leblang (1996), 'The effect of cultural values on economic development: theory, hypotheses, and some empirical tests', *American Journal of Political Science*, 40, 607–631.

Granovetter, M. (1985), 'Economic action and social structure: the problem of embeddedness', *American Journal of Sociology*, 91, 481–510.

Guiso, L, P. Sapienza, and L. Zingales (2003), 'People's opium? Religion and economic attitudes', *Journal of Monetary Economics*, 50, 225–82.

Guiso, L, P. Sapienza, and L. Zingales (2006), 'Does culture affect economic outcomes?', *Journal of Economic Perspectives*, 20 (2), 23–48.

Harrison, Lawrence. E and Samuel P. Huntington (2000), (eds) *Culture Matters: How Values Shape Human Progress*, New York: Basic Books, 29–43.

Harrisson, L. (1992), *Who Prospers? How Cultural Values Shape Economic and Political Success*, New York: Harper Collins, Basic Books.

Hau, C. (2000), *Necessary Fictions: Philippine Literature and the Nation 1946-1980*, Manila: Ateneo de Manila University Press.

Hofstede, G. (2001), *Culture's Consequences* (second edition), Beverly Hills: Sage.

Hoselitz, B.F. (1954), 'Problems of Adapting and Communicating Modern Techniques to Less Developed Areas', *Economic Development and Cultural Change*, 2 (4), 249–268.

Hume, D. [1757] (1976), *The Natural History of Religion*, (ed. J.V. Price) Oxford: Clarendon.

Jong, E. de (2002), 'Why are price stability and statutory independence of central banks negatively correlated? The role of culture', *European Journal of Political Economy*, 18, 675–94.

Kim Dae Jung (1994), 'Is culture destiny? The myth of Asia's anti-democratic values', *Foreign Affairs*, 73 (6) (November/December), 189–94.

Knack, S. and P. Keefer (1997), 'Does social capital have an economic pay-off? A cross-country investigation', *Quarterly Journal of Economics*, 112 (4), 1251–88.
Lal, D. (1998), *Unintended Consequences; The Impact of Factor Endowments, Culture, and Politics on Long Run Economic Performance*, Cambridge, MA: MIT Press.
Landes (1998), *The Wealth and Poverty of Nations: Why are Some so Rich and Some so Poor?*, London: Little, Brown and Co.
Levy Jr, M.J. (1962), 'Some aspects of "individualism" and the problem of modernization in China and Japan', *Economic Development and Cultural Change*, 10 (3), 225–40.
Markus, G. (1993), 'Culture: the making and the make-up of a concept (an essay in historical semantics)', *Dialectical Anthropology*, 18, 3–29.
Maseland, R. and J. Peil (2008), 'Assessing the new Washington pluralism from the perspective of the Maylasian model', *Third World Quarterly*, 1175–88.
Mauss, M. [1925] (1970), *The Gift: Forms and Functions of Exchange in Archaic Societies* (translated by Ian Cunnison), London: Routledge and Kegan Paul.
McLeary, R. and R. Barro (2006), 'Religion and Economy', *Journal of Economic Perspectives*, 20 (2), 49–72.
Nash, M. (1964), 'Social prerequisites to economic growth in Latin America and Southeast Asia', *Economic Development and Cultural Change*, 12 (3), 225–42.
North, D. (1990), *Institutions, Institutional Change and Economic Performance*, Cambridge: Cambridge University Press.
North, D. (1992), 'Institutions, ideology and economic performance', *CATO Journal*, 11, Winter 1992, 477–99.
Pareto, V. [1906] (1972), *Manual of Political Economy*, London: Macmillan.
Polanyi, K. (1944), *The Great Transformation*, New York: Octagon Books.
Robbins, L. (1932), *An Essay on the Nature and Significance of Economic Science*, London: Macmillan.
Roscher, W. [1854] (1918), *Grundlagen der Nationalökonomie*, Stuttgart and Berlin: Gotta'sche Buchhandlung Nachfolger.
Said, E. [1978] (1995), *Orientalism*, London: Penguin.
Shane, S.A. (1993), 'Cultural influences on national rates of innovation', *Journal of Business Venturing*, 8, 59–73.
Smelser, N. and R. Swedberg (eds) (1994), *Handbook of Economic Sociology*, Princeton: Princeton University Press.
Smith, A. [1763] (1983), *Lectures on Rhetoric and Belles Lettres* (ed. by J.C. Bryce), Oxford: Oxford University Press.
Sun Ki Chai (1997), 'Rational Choice and Culture: Clashing Perspectives or Complementary Modes of Analysis?' in Richard Ellis and Michael Thompson (eds), *Culture Matters*, Boulder: CO: Westview Press, 45–56.
Swedberg, R. (1994), *Une histoire de la sociologie économique* (translated by I. This), Paris: Desclée de Brouwer.
Tabellini, G. (2005), *Culture and Institutions. Economic Development in the Regions of Europe*, Memo. IGIER, Bocconi University.
Williamson, O. (2000), 'The new institutional economics: taking stock, looking ahead', *Journal of Economic Literature*, XXXVIII, 595–613.

16. Almost Everything You Would Like to Know About Technology and Growth and You Will Never Be Told By Neo-Schumpeterians

George Liagouras

INTRODUCTION

The second oil crisis put an end to the hegemony of Keynesian economics. Then, the 1980s have been characterised by the domination of short-termist and ultra-liberal versions of supply-side economics. Since the end of the 1980s, we have been witnessing a shift within supply-side economics from short-run to long-run concerns and from neo-liberal policy recommendations to more pragmatic ones. The latter focuses on the key role of public investments in technology for enhancing long-run growth and structural competitiveness in a globalized economy. As a result, an overwhelming literature has been developed on the questions of technical change, innovation and competitiveness. This was the neo-Schumpeterian turn in modern, mainstream and non-mainstream, economics.

This chapter is a critical assessment of the above turn, and more exactly of its non-mainstream – and according to the author, more interesting version, i.e. evolutionary economics. It is argued that neo-Schumpeterian dominance, far from resolving the impasses left by short-term supply-side economics, it is also responsible for the economic and social impasses accumulated until now, namely the slow growth and the increasing social exclusion. It is also suggested that it is now time to explore the possibility of a new virtuous cycle between supply and demand dynamics.

The argument is developed in two parts. The first part analyses the history of the debate between supply- and demand-led approaches of growth by focusing on the 'demand-pull versus technology push' controversy from

Schmookler (1966) to current debates. The second part overviews four recent contributions seeking to explore a synthesis between Schumpeter and Keynes and proposes an agenda for a socially responsible economic research in this vein.

THE ARCHAEOLOGY OF THE SUPPLY-SIDE POWER: THE 'DEMAND-PULL VERSUS TECHNOLOGY-PUSH' CONTROVERSY

This part starts from the debate about Schmokler's book, continues with a critical assessment of non-mainstream neo-Schumpeterian approaches and finish with a brief review of the existing empirical evidence on the question.

Schmookler, or not Schmookler? Rewriting the History from the Standpoint of the Losers

In the 1940s and 1950s, the dominant response to the question: 'What are the driving forces behind technological innovation?' was 'scientific discoveries'. In the 1960s, the influential book of Jacob Schmookler (1966), 'Invention and Economic Growth', undermined the scientific determinism of the previous decades. Schmookler, using time series and cross-sectional data, showed that the invention activity of firms is positively correlated with the growth of demand. In his own words, 'the amount of invention is governed by the extent of the market' (Schmookler 1966, p. 104).

Schmookler's scientific endeavour was to go beyond the static framework of neoclassical theory and to empirically study the long-run dynamics of economic development by endogenizing technical change. As he noted, 'except for a few economists, largely those of a heterodox stripe preoccupied with problems of economic development, like Marx, Veblen, Schumpeter, and Kuznets, technological change was generally ignored until the last decade or so' (Schmookler 1966, pp. 3, 4). Significantly enough, his book was dedicated to Simon Kuznets. And, even though the message of the book was akin to the Keynesian discourse of this period, Schmookler's leitmotif, 'the amount of invention is governed by the extent of the market', sounds like a replication of Adam Smith's famous insight that 'the division of labour is limited by the extent of market'.

Furthermore, Schmookler argued that in order to seriously study the economic development we need to endogenize not only technology but also 'wants'. He remarked however that modern consumer theories (including K. Lankaster's approach) were not relevant for such a purpose. Such theories, 'brings us no closer to effective analysis of new products that are created because utility functions have changed, whether because of changes in people themselves or because of their external circumstances' (ibid. p. 188). Therefore, Schmookler concluded that to apply the framework of consumer theory 'effectively to the rise of new goods, economists may have to link their discipline to others, such as the psychology of motivation, in order to uncover the nature of the link between wants and the goods that satisfy them' (ibid., p. 213).

It is very important to note that most of the criticism was addressed to Schmookler's followers and not to Schmookler himself. The studies that have been inspired by Schmookler's work on innovation have been criticized by technology-push theorists (Mowery and Rosenberg 1979; Dosi 1982) on the following grounds:

- First, concerning the micro level, they shared with neoclassical microeconomics the same simplistic representation of the firm. In other words, they reduced firm and the process of technology creation to a 'black box'. Moreover, the whole argument of demand-pull theorists reproduced neoclassical ideology about demand and consumer sovereignty.
- Second, at the policy level, they proposed only indirect measures seeking to promote demand for innovation, and not direct measures for boosting the scientific and technological potential of national economies.
- Third, even though they had some relevance in explaining incremental technical progress they were totally irrelevant for explaining major technological breakthroughs.
- And fourth, at the macro level, they were not able to come to terms with empirical evidence showing that differences in economic performance of nations are correlated with differences in R&D and not in demand.

Are the above criticisms also valuable for Schmookler's approach? The first point is not really convincing. Schmookler, as argued above, was extremely cautious about the capacity of neoclassical production and consumption theory to deal with dynamic phenomena like economic growth. Still, given that his interest was on economic growth and not on the microeconomic aspects of invention, he consciously left out of his scope questions about how firms innovate or how it matters for industrial organization: 'if we ask not *how* the inventions are made, or which industry makes the invented product, but why inventions directed toward the given effect are invented at all, the answer is demand' (ibid. p. 166). In this way, he missed the chance to conceive growth as the interplay between supply and demand factors, but this is very different from being criticized for adopting the neoclassical approach. It remains, however, that his theory could not give a rationale for supply-side policy measures (i.e. the second point).

The third criticism was already anticipated by Schmookler himself. He argued against the 'naïve interpretation of history sometimes known as technological determinism' (ibid. p. 73), which underestimates the importance of incremental innovations for sustainable growth by considering them as by-products of major technological breakthroughs.

Finally, the view that differences in economic performance are explained by technology and not by demand variables is too reductionist to be accepted. But the question of empirical evidence will be addressed in the next section.

Still, whatever the pertinence of the attack against Schmookler and his followers, it was far from being an historical accident. The obsolescence of the Fordist model of growth and the subsequent fall of Keynesian economics in the late 1970s gave rise progressively to two supply-side schools, the neo-liberals and the neo-Schumpeterians. Consequently, in the sub-field of the economics of technology and innovation a new school has emerged focusing on supply-side factors, and especially on R&D activities, in the study of innovative process (Freeman 1982). The problem with these 'technology-push' theories was that they had many troubles when attempting to integrate economic and social factors in their study of technological innovation.

Revisiting the Triumph of the Neo-Schumpeterian Turn in Technology and Growth Theory

Two solutions have been proposed in order to deal with the above problem. The first solution was to reduce economic institutions to the market, and present the market as a 'selective device' (Dosi 1982) among different technologies/firms. The adoption of biological concepts, like 'natural selection', by Richard Nelson and Sidney Winter (1982) is the best example of the above tendency. Natural selection may have proved an extremely pertinent metaphor for modelling the process of competition in an industry, but its extrapolation to questions of growth (ibid. ch. 9) is irrelevant. [1] It implies the composition fallacy, denounced by Keynes in his 'General Theory'. What seems good for the firm is not necessarily good for the national economy, and what seems good for individual national economies is not necessary good for supranational regions or the world economy. From this standpoint, the extrapolation of industrial dynamics to the national and world level prompts what Krugman (1994) called the 'dangerous obsession' with competitiveness.[2]

So, it is not surprising that Nelson and Winter's model of economic growth misses the significance of effective demand and the cumulative causation between supply and demand factors that we find in the literature going from Keynes to Kaldor and Pasinetti. As Philip Mirowski argued in his – now forgotten – review essay of Nelson's and Winter's book:

> (I)t is also beyond me how anyone could make any cogent statements about economic growth employing a model that allows no linkages between the growth of output and the growth of demand in the aggregate (part 4): the 'demand curve' for output is exogenous and stable for all runs. (Mirowski 1982, p. 762)[3]

The second solution to deal with the inherent tendency of technology-push approaches towards the 'naïve interpretation of history sometimes known as technological determinism' came from the long waves approach of Chris Freeman and Carlota Perez (1988). According to the above authors, after the irruption of a new technological paradigm, the inertia of the existing institutions (including the macroeconomic ones) results in a mismatch which in turn is the main cause for the manifestation of structural crises in the capitalist system. On the contrary, the progressive elaboration of institutional set-ups that are coherent with the new techno-economic paradigm, inaugurates golden eras of stability and expansion for the capitalist system.

The idea of macroeconomic and social institutions as inertial factors can hardly be considered of general value. Very often, institutions, instead of lagging behind technical change, precede it and shape it. For example, today market-led institutions in the world economy cannot be seen as the result of the information revolution. Neo-liberal reforms in national and international level occurred just before the rise of the new techno-economic paradigm, and in a certain sense they have shaped it. Therefore the institutional reforms needed to open a new era of sustainable development will not be an adjustment of the old Fordist institutions to the information revolution, but a response to the impasses accumulated by the market and finance-led institutions during the last decades.

In practice this is also what Perez (2002) presupposes in her path-breaking study on the relationship between financial capital and technological revolutions Nevertheless, even in Perez's personal work (1983, 2002), which is less deterministic, the technology-based version of long waves remains problematic. Ex post one can present the historical evolution of capitalist institutions as the 'one-best way' response to the challenges put forward by technological revolutions. But whatever the difficulties of the above exercise – see for example the differences in the periodization between Freeman and Perez (1988) and Perez (2002) – this is far from being enough to give ex ante solutions to the present problems. For example, even if we accept that Keynesianism was a response to the electricity-based technological paradigm, this is not enough for making ex ante statements about the present macroeconomic imbalances. In the same way, the historical regularities analysed by Perez (2002), are very important to situate the actual omnipotence of financial capital. But at the same time they cannot tell us how to deal with the negative aspects of financial globalization. When the day arrives to deal with it, the long waves' theorists of the future could ex post interpret the whole institutional change as the one-best way response to the rise of ICTs paradigm. But, what is really the issue is to invent and realize such a change in macroeconomic institutions. And putting technology as the prime factor in our analyses diverts us from doing so.

Thus, even though the theoretical framework of long waves is much more relevant than the evolutionary approaches that simply extrapolate industrial dynamics to the macro level, the policy message remains, in the last instance, the same. In the whole neo-Schumpeterian literature (i.e. Freeman and Soete 1994) one can find abundant policy recommendations concerning science, technology and competitiveness and too little reflections about how the interaction between the supply and the demand could lead to a new virtuous cycle of growth and full employment. The problem is that, against the promises for entering the ascendant phase of a new long wave, the most appropriate title for the state of the global economy over the last two decades is not 'Technology and the Wealth of Nations' (Freeman and Foray 1992) but 'Technology, Competitiveness and the Poverty of Nations'.

Furthermore, questions of social exclusion put aside, one would expect that the explosion of studies and policies concerning R&D and technology over the two last decades would have led to a rise in the impact of R&D and technology on output and productivity. In fact, the opposite has been the case. The more we are concerned with R&D, the less productive it becomes! Such a paradox should lead us either to accept that the ICT paradigm is prematurely blocked by internal decreasing returns, or to rethink the role of demand in long-run growth.

Surprisingly enough, a minority of mainstream scholars has proved more sensitive to the importance of demand and active macroeconomic policies. The starting point was the idea that, by promoting (or interrupting) the process of cumulative learning in production, temporary real shocks induce higher (or lower) rates of technological accumulation and subsequently of economic growth in the long run. But, the same can be said about nominal (monetary) shocks in a context of nominal rigidities, or (why not?) demand shocks (Stadler 1990). So, if *temporary* recessions – whatever their cause -

have *permanent* negative effects on growth, then countercyclical policies are legitimated for maximizing economic growth and social welfare.[4]

Thus, at a time when some mainstream scholars (re)discover that aggregate demand management and countercyclical policies in general can have positive consequences on long-run growth, neo-Schumpeterian scholars continue to suppose that in the long run only supply-side variables matter.[5] They offer undoubtedly a very appealing alternative to neo-liberal doctrines by showing that globalization, instead of rendering obsolete the nation-state, asks for aggressive microeconomic (mainly technology) policies seeking to boost domestic innovation systems. There is, however, a simpler question that is consistently left out of their agenda. Is it possible to enter the upswing of the fifth long wave or to 'build the information society for us *all*' by simply exacerbating technological and economic competition at the world level?[6]

Do Dominant Theories in Social Sciences Need to be Verified by Empirical Evidence?

Judging from the suffocating domination of technology-based approaches on the contemporary academic and policy debate, one would suppose that there is an overwhelming empirical evidence in favour of the technology-push hypothesis. But this is far from being the case, as we will see just below.

As already said above, one of the most important criticisms addressed by neo-Schumpeterians to Schmookler and his followers was that the latter were not able to come to terms with empirical evidence showing that differences in economic performance of nations are correlated with differences in R&D. Still, in order to support the technology gap theory one needs to show not only that a technological proxy like R&D is positively correlated with growth rates, but also that demand is not. To the best of our knowledge, the only empirical investigation, which examined together technology and demand variables for explaining why growth rates differ between nations, is that of Fagerberg (1987).

Fagerberg used a sample of 25 industrial countries during the period 1960-83 and estimated two models. In the first one, the independent variables were the actual level of GDP (a proxy for the existing gap between countries), the investment rate (a proxy for the efforts in exploiting the potential for imitation) and the patents applications abroad (a proxy for technology).

In the second model he added international trade as a proxy for the world demand and found that,

> the average growth rate of all countries is determined by the growth of world demand, but that deviations from this average growth rate are determined by the technology gap variables mentioned above. It may be regarded, then, as an extreme 'Keynesian' version of the general technology gap model. (Fagerberg 1987, p. 93)

According to Fagerberg's estimations, 'both models go a long way in explaining the differences in economic growth, ... but in terms of fit the 'Keynesian' is in general the most successful one (ibid., p. 94). Note also that if the proxy for the world demand was the world income and not the world trade, it is very probable that the fit of the 'Keynesian' model to data would be much more successful. For example, for the sub-period 1960-73 the coefficients of world trade are not significant.

Concerning now the Schmooklerian demand-pull hypothesis, the most known empirical studies before the 1990s (i.e. Scherer 1982; Kleinknecht and Verspagen 1990) gave mitigate results. From 1990s up to now the provision of new data at the firm level and the use of time series econometrics seem to give more reason to the demand-pull than to the technology-push hypothesis.

Regarding the existence of new massive data at the firm level, an important step forward has been made thanks to the launching of the Community Innovation Surveys (CIS). As Alfred Kleinknecht comments:

> With the 1992 *Community Innovation Survey*, it became possible to test Schmookler's hypothesis with firm-level data and to include, in addition to demand growth, other factors that influence innovation, thus reducing the chance of finding pseudo-correlations. Cross-section model estimates in Switzerland ... in France and in Netherlands ... confirm the impact of demand on innovation. This finding is robust to alternative model specifications and to alternative measures of demand growth. (Kleinknecht 1998, p. 392)[7]

The exploitation of time series techniques permit separating the long-run from the short-run relationships and testing for direction of the causality. The empirical evidence that has been accumulated up to now is far from rejecting the demand-pull approach.

Let us start from the evolution of the innovative activity over the business cycle. Saint Paul's estimations for 22 OECD countries in the period 1950-88 found little evidence of any pro or counter-cyclical behaviour of R&D expenditures (Saint-Paul 1993). Still, as the author concedes in a later paper, such a neutral result may 'be due to the poor quality of aggregate R&D data' (Aghion and Saint-Paul 1998b, p. 299). The study of Geroski and Walters (1995) is more convincing at this point because it uses more reliable data, namely the number of the major innovations produced in the UK and the number of patents taken out by UK firms in the USA. The two authors find that in the UK patents and innovations moved pro-cyclically over the business cycle during the period 1948-83.[8]

The most known empirical evidence on the long-run relationships between technological innovation and demand, but without causality tests, stems from the papers of Guellec and Ioannidis (1997), Guellec and van Pottelsberghe (1997) and Le Bas (2004). Guellec and Ioannidis (1997) estimate through an Error Correction Model (ECM) the impact of GDP, public finance for private R&D, real long-run interest rates, and industrial structure on the Business Expenditure on R&D (BERD). The data concern 6 and 12 most R&D-intensive OECD countries for the period 1972-96. The long run elasticity of demand for both groups of countries is always positive but its magnitude presents important variations: around unity when the variable of industrial structure and a trend are included in the model, and between 1.7 and 2 when the above terms are not included. Guellec and van Pottelsberghe (1997) estimate two ECMs, which have as dependent variable the BERD financed by enterprises and as main independent variables the added value of enterprises, the part of BERD financed by the State and the financial incentives. Their data set includes 17 OECD countries for the period 1981-96. The long-run elasticities of demand are positive and range from 1.54 to 2.40. Finally, Lebas (2004) uses OECD data about patents and value added (a proxy for demand) for 7 countries and 16 manufacturing sectors for the period 1975-96. He finds that the short-run elasticity of demand is significant and around 0.7, whatever the specification of the ECM, but the long-run elasticity is low and weakly significant.

Finally, as already said, the econometrics of time series permit using causality tests to verify if it is demand variables that lead technology variables or the reverse.

A study by von Tunzelmann and Efendioglu (2001), concerning 18 European countries over the period 1950-95, finds that the long-run impact of GDP on technology variables (Gross Expenditure on R&D, Business Expenditure on R&D, Higher Education Expenditure on R&D, patents per million of population) appears to be greater than the reverse. The authors, however, prevent that 'one should beware of simple conclusions of the Schmookler kind: using a series for total patents, instead of patents per capita, we found that patents appeared to lead GDP' (ibid. p. 56).

Dirk Frantzen (2003) finds the opposite results. He tests through Vector Auto-Regressive (VAR) models the direction of causality between total factor productivity (TFP) and R&D for 22 manufacturing sectors in 14 OECD countries during the period 1972-94. His results 'show that, although there are feedbacks, both on average and in a clear majority of sectors the causation runs mainly from the R&D variables to TFP rather the other way round' (Frantzen 2003, p. 125). The author interprets his findings as showing the dominance of technology-push over demand-pull mechanisms. But a conclusive causality evidence of the 'technology-push versus demand-pull' controversy should require a direct test of the relationships between demand (not productivity) and technology variables.

In sum, the existing empirical evidence does not justify the absolute domination of supply-side theories and policies during the last decades. Note also that the quasi-totality of the above evidence uses R&D expenditure or patents as proxies for technology. To the extent that output or productivity growth depends more on technological diffusion, imitation, spillovers etc. than on technology creation *stricto sensu*,[9] and given that the former are more sensitive to demand than the latter, the econometric tests underestimate the role of demand. The above bias should be even bigger for evidence confined to the manufacturing sector.

BREAK ON THROUGH TO THE OTHER SIDE: SEARCHING FOR A NEW VIRTUOUS CYCLE BETWEEN SUPPLY AND DEMAND DYNAMICS

The chapter has been constructed until now as if there was no bridge between Schumpeter's and Keynes' ideas. Fortunately enough, this is not entirely true. There are *at least* four important contributions in this domain that constitute an excellent starting point for further research.

Four Ways to Render More Complex the Dominant Discourse on Technology and Growth

The first synthesis comes from Alfred Kleinknecht whose analysis combines Schumpeterian long waves theory with effective demand and distributional equity concerns. Kleinknecht develops further the Keynesian vision of investment in physical capital to the investment in intangible capital, and more specifically into R&D. He provides important empirical evidence (Kleinknecht 1998) showing the relevance of the Schmooklerian demand-pull hypothesis 'for major or minor innovations which occur in very large numbers' (Brouwer and Kleinknecht 1999, p. 392, note 2). He can then combine his findings with long waves approaches on the ground that 'while the many "smaller" innovations have a major impact on competitiveness and employment growth, the few "basic" innovations are important as indicators of "paradigm change" in the historical analysis of Kondratieff long waves in economic growth" (ibid).[10]

A second possible synthesis between Schumpeter and Keynes is proposed by Nick von Tunzelmann (2002, 2004). His empirical work with Efendioglu on the direction of causality between demand and investment variables has already been presented above. At a theoretical level Tunzelmann argues, against mainstream and non-mainstream versions of supply-side economics, that appropriate demand policies are necessary for long-run growth. His main argument suggests that a positive demand shock, by inducing more investments in tangible and intangible capital, can have positive consequences on long-run growth. Tunzelmann qualifies his argument by using the heuristics of aggregate demand and supply curves. He convincingly argues that supply-side economics reject the manipulation of aggregate demand as a means to promote long-run growth because they commit the fallacy of considering (aggregate) supply and demand as independent from one another. Once this unrealistic ceteris paribus assumption is removed, it is easy to imagine that a shift of the demand curve upwards can generate an outward (downward) move to the supply curve, expressing the technology-boosting impact of demand to supply. Therefore, the boosting of demand does not result in an inflation jump as advocated by monetarist and rational expectations schools, but mainly in an output increase (von Tunzelmann 2004, pp. 88–90).

This permits Tunzelmann not only to criticize the EU macroeconomic policy and especially the Maastricht criteria for joining the EMU, but also to put in question the very logic of EU innovation policy. As he remarks, the 1995 *Green Paper on Innovation* completely overlooks the role of demand on innovation. Furthermore, the author convincingly argues that the more recent 'Barcelona target' to raise R&D intensity in the EU to around 3 per cent of GDP could have no positive effects on growth unless it is accompanied by appropriate demand measures (Tunzelmann, 2002). The solution, according to him, is the boosting of demand through public investment to productive purposes (infrastructure). He contends, however, that what hinders the development of a hybrid Keynesian–Schumpeterian approach has to do with an 'open economy' version of such a model (von Tunzelmann 2004, p. 100).

The third synthesis is a nice surprise coming from Brussels headquarters (DG 12), which as mentioned above are not very friendly to demand approaches. The starting point of Paraskevas Caracostas and Ugur Muldur (1997) is the evolution of research and innovation policies in the post-war advanced countries. They distinguish between three main periods. The first period (1945-70) is characterised by the maxim 'Science, the endless frontier' and the locomotive role of military applications of basic science. The second period (1970-2000) is no longer science-led but technology-led. The main feature of this period is the pairing of industry and technology in order to promote the competitiveness of firms and economies in an adverse economic environment. The authors estimate that this second period is now over – without however explaining why – and argue that we have entered a new era where the pair innovation–society dominates over the pair technology–industry; this is where the nice title of their book, 'Society, The Endless Frontier', comes from.

On the ground of the above considerations the two authors conclude that the research and innovation policy of EU should be more demand- than technology-led. Apart from the necessary changes in the institutional arrangements they proposed, the two authors are very specific on the new mix of economic policy that is needed:

> Whilst it is true that a measure of 'Keynesianism' reflected in the funding of the large trans-European networks in transport, telecommunications and energy may provide extra growth, the transition to an intangible economy which respects the environment and is favourable to social cohesion and the quality of life is an even more pressing agenda item. This transition could be speeded up further by a 'Pasinettian' policy of promoting new markets and new social activities, a policy which would impact on both the supply and the demand for knowledge-intensive and learning-intensive products, systems and services. (Caracostas and Muldur 1997, p. 143)

This is a very original work, but there are two points needing further clarification. The first point concerns the kind of macroeconomic policy which is appropriate for such a change in paradigm. In another part of their book (p. 67), the authors – perhaps because of their position – seem very diplomatic with the Maastricht Treaty.[11] A second point that needs clarification is the change of paradigm itself. Briefly speaking, such a non-conflicting change seems too good to be true. In another paper (Liagouras, 2005) I have argued that the dominance of finance- and market-led institutions does not permit the satisfaction of societal needs like those advocated by Caracostas and Muldur, and even that the intrusion of markets into the education, communication and aesthetic spheres of the social and individual world is likely to be the main pathology of the post-industrial society. Perhaps I have been too pessimistic, but anyway it seems that there is a controversial point here which deserves further study.

The fourth and last contribution comes from Pascal Petit (2003, 2005). The author bases his studies on the Regulation School's and Kaldor's insights to discover the structural features of the emerging post-Fordist economy. Following his previous work with Boyer (Boyer and Petit 1991), he understands growth regimes as a cumulative causation process between productivity and demand dynamics. Therefore, Fordism is described as the combination of a productivity regime based on process innovation within firms and a wage-led demand regime with undifferentiated wage growth. The candidate growth regime of the post-Fordist era is assumed to combine productivity gains coming mainly from product innovation and cooperation between firms with a demand regime based on differentiated access to profits distribution (workers are participating either as stakeholders or as financial investors, especially through pension funds).

Most importantly, the above change of economic paradigm corresponds to another change concerning the dominant institutional package (or structural form) of each era. Fordism was obviously characterized by the central role of institutions assuring the functioning of the labour market and the organization of work. Contrary to left-wing scholars that consider the notion of work as central to all forms of society, Petit argues that the dominant institutional sphere of the post-Fordist era will be the organization of markets (or in other words, the forms of competition). Such a change has been initiated by the deregulation–privatization movement of the previous decades. Petit suggests that the importance is not in the public or the private property but in the re-regulation of the new markets and the participation of citizens-consumers to the above process of re-regulation[12] as well as to the new productivity gains, mainly associated with network services. Therefore, the future of the above 'hedonic growth regime', based on the satisfaction of the increasingly diversified needs of post-modern individualised societies, depends on two packages of institutional innovations. These should address the growing demand for quality, certification and accountability of new services and the ethical need that all citizens should acquire the required capabilities in order to be able to use these new services. Last, but not least, such a growth regime would relax the 'technology plus competitiveness' imperatives that led to the current zero-sum game in the world economy. The reason is very simple: 'the localised nature of the services under view would avoid an external constraint to be too binding' (Petit 2003, p. 14).

This is a daring and original contribution. However, it poses questions about the appropriate macroeconomic policy that would support the hedonic growth regime, as well as about the long-run stability of profit-driven demand dynamics. Furthermore, the whole analysis seems to presuppose the reduction of the citizen to the consumer in the post-Fordist era, which is rather controversial from both a normative and an analytical point of view.

What Are the Questions? A Partial and Incomplete Agenda for Further Research

Usually the hard core of a research agenda is theoretical propositions. Policy implications are given at the end to complete the theoretical hypotheses. However, in cases where one thinks that there is a hiatus between social and economic problems and economic theorizing, the best way to proceed is to put forward the policy challenges and finish with theoretical suggestions.

A first and more abstract level of policy challenges concerns the rehabilitation of demand in growth thinking. There are two different ways to rehabilitate demand, but both imply that supply and demand, instead of being distinct entities, are in continuous interaction.

The first is to take into account the impact of demand management on long-run growth. There is until now a broad consensus, going from mainstream growth theories to neo-Schumpeterian approaches, that the supply factors are responsible for the long–run growth trend, whereas the demand ones, in the best of cases, are responsible for the fluctuations around the above trend. Note that Schumpeter was one of the first to undervalue Keynes's contribution by suggesting that its applicability is limited 'to a few years at most' (Schumpeter 1952, p. 282). Certainly, in quantitative macroeconomics the distinction between a deterministic trend and the fluctuations around it has been questioned since the beginning of the 1980s. But, curiously enough, the above evolution had not had a serious impact on the consensus dominating contemporary growth theory.

Moreover, it is rather obvious that, especially in a knowledge-based economy, even a temporary recession, by interrupting the cumulative process of social learning, will have permanent negative effects on the long-run dynamics of the economy. And these negative effects will be much more pronounced in the case of long periods of stagnation or slow growth accompanied with increasing social exclusion. Of course, as Aghion and Saint-Paul (1998a, b) argue, developing further the cold shower hypothesis of Schumpeter, crises and recessions have beneficial cathartic consequences on the productive system. But the problem with the cold shower hypothesis concerns its pertinence today. From the coming to power of Reagan and Thatcher up to now, we have witnessed more than 25 years of 'creative' destruction of the world economy. Isn't it now time to think how we will pass to a process of cumulative creation?

In such a process the interplay between demand and supply can be used not only in a defensive way, i.e. to smooth, through countercyclical policies, the fluctuations of the economy. As von Tunzelmann argues, economic policy, by using positive demand shocks, could induce more tangible and intangible investments and thus accelerate the growth process.

The second way to rehabilitate demand is to pass from its volume to its qualitative features. This corresponds to what Caracostas and Muldur call 'a "Pasinettian" policy of promoting new markets and new social activities'. The importance of qualitative characteristics of the demand – which were considered as given by old Keynesians – has also been put forward by the Regulation School in its analysis of the consumption norms of the Fordist era. The works of the same School teach us how difficult it is to match production, re(distribution) and consumption patterns in a coherent growth regime.

Unfortunately, in the present situation we are too far from asking how to match the different systemic patterns of the economy. It is amazing how much the domination of supply-side paradigms has marginalized the reflection and the debate not only about social needs (the way of life people would like to pursue), but also concerning the role of targeted meso-demand policies for innovation. It seems that until recently even the importance of demand stimulation measures (financial incentives to users, public procurements, high-level standards) for creating or promoting markets for new technologies has been underestimated (Watanabe and Tokumasu 2003, Aho 2006).

Supposing that the above underestimation of demand will be corrected in the near future, there will remain two much more difficult problems to deal with. The first one concerns the excessive occupation with manufacturing implied by the 'technology-competitiveness' consensus. Modern advanced economies are supposed to be service economies, but this is far from being reflected in research about innovation and growth dynamics. Especially the growing demand for health, education, leisure, culture, quality of urban life, and personal services is not seriously taken into account, and when this happens, this is only as a potential absorber of new technologies (principally ICT).[13] And here lies the second problem. Most of the above services cannot be produced like industrial goods. As the notions of utility and productivity can hardly be applied to them, their development depends on social conventions about quality and on the capacity of social actors to put under control market forces and bureaucratic apparatuses. Still, the domination of social and political life from a mix of neo-liberalism and technological Colbertism during the last two-and-half decades has contributed to (further) undermine the interest of citizens for public affairs. As a result the need for social accountability is systematically confused with the subordination to market imperatives.

A sceptic could remark that the policy challenges presented above ignore the pressures exercised to national economies by the ongoing globalization process. After all, the suffocating consensus in favour of supply-side policies cannot be explained by conspiracy theories. The underestimation of the services sector, in which the external constraint is not binding, is a first but not entirely satisfactory answer. Manufacturing (also) matters. Thus, the critical question is, which geographical instance will be more capable of tempering the current rational fools' game of competitiveness and thus to re-subordinate the profit imperatives to social welfare. As showed by Pascal Petit (2005), neither the world, nor the supranational, nor the national space, seem to have any chance of doing that in the near future.

By simple act of faith I would like to suggest that supranational entities like the EU are in the long run the better candidates to inaugurate a new virtuous cycle between supply and demand. In fact the external constraint of individual EU members is due rather to their decision to create the Single Market than to the supranatural forces of globalization and technical change. Seen as an economic entity the EU is a rather closed economy. But seen from the standpoint of each member-State, the EU seems more like an arena of cut-throat competition and social drubbing that eventually depresses aggregate demand. Brussels and the big majority of European economists have long been obsessed with competitiveness and the 'cost of non-Europe'. It is perhaps now time to think also of the cost of Europe (as it is) and the need for federal demand policies. This implies not only the reform of the Maastricht Treaty and the status of ECB, but also the elaboration of a new Treaty on socio-developmental policy aiming to temper gradually the social dubbing and give priority to the needs of EU citizens for a better quality of life. The recognition by Brussels and national governments that the fiasco of the Lisbon Strategy was mainly due to the obsession with supply-side policies could constitute an excellent starting point for such a turn in the EU policy agenda. Unfortunately, for the moment this seems not to be the case.[14] Finally, regarding the possible theoretical implications of the above policy challenges, one can see at least two big areas for further research. The first area concerns the role of services in modern economies and especially in the final consumption and in the quality of life. This goes together with the need to revise the economic concepts and measurement standards – output, productivity, growth, etc. we inherited from industrial capitalism. In the latter collective happiness was equated to economic growth (the wealth of nations …), and growth was understood as an accumulation of goods having the form of commodities. In our rising post-industrial societies those two equations tend to be obsolete. We 'produce' far more services than goods. And, above all, our economic performance has no positive impact on our happiness (Oswald 1997; Lane 2000). This 'paradox of happiness', or of 'joyless economy' (Scitovsky 1976), is of primordial interest for colleagues seeking to go beyond the supranatural imperatives of technology, globalization and competitiveness.

The second area of research is to rehabilitate the Kaldorian concept of growth as a virtuous cycle between supply and demand factors and show with all the possible means – qualitative theorizing, field research, models, simulations, econometric tests, etc. – the impasse of supply-side theories and policies in the supranational and world level. In this direction, the prisoner dilemma in which the EU members have been auto-trapped – each country search to be more competitive than the others, but no one has interest to take care of the aggregate demand – could be a very promising object of study.[15]

CONCLUSION: FROM EVOLUTIONARY MICROECONOMICS TO AN EVOLUTIONARY POLITICAL ECONOMY?

It is beyond doubt that the (re)discovering of Schumpeterian dynamics has launched a scientific revolution at the level of microeconomics of technical change and industrial organization. We are very proud today of our evolutionary microeconomics. Still, regarding the macro level the supply-side optimism of Schumpeter risks making us advocates of a perpetual 'creative' destruction process. Ironically enough, neoclassical theorists of the 1950s and 1960s would be right to point out that their static approaches were more successful in growth and employment outcomes and had a social sensibility that is almost absent today.

Finding refuge under the supranatural forces of technical change and globalization cannot be a serious excuse. As Keynes taught us, the ethical and political role of the economist is not to inform the economic units as to how they will get rid off of the crisis, but to put an end to the crisis of the economic system by promoting radical changes of the status quo. Or, to paraphrase Marx, the ethical and political responsibility of economists should not be to interpret the existing world, but to change it. So, what is at stake for the neo-Schumpeterian approaches from now on is to go beyond their evolutionary microeconomics towards an evolutionary political economy.

NOTES

1. For a more general argumentation on the irrelevance of extrapolating biological metaphors from the micro to the macro-historical level, see Freeman (1991).
2. Still, Krugman did not convincingly explain the rise of the competitiveness imperative and of the neo-mercantilist policies. For a penetrating critique of the competitiveness imperative see Petrella (1995).
3. After the seminal book of Nelson and Winter, there have been some efforts to integrate macroeconomic variables in the evolutionary modelling of technical change, but the results have not been very successful. For an account of the above efforts and a more promising model towards this direction, see Llerena and Lorentz (2004).
4. The case for countercyclical fiscal policies has been formalized by Martin and Rogers (1997).
5. Note also that there is now an important convergence between neo-Kaldorians and neo-Schumpeterians. Starting from the late Kaldor's idea that, in an open-economy world, the growth of national economies depends on their international trade performance (Kaldor 1981) other scholars (i.e. León-Ledesma 2002) went further and added variables linked to non-price competitiveness and catching-up (education, innovation efforts, and knowledge spillovers).
6. The only evolutionary text, to my knowledge, that poses sound questions about the global or the macro coherence of the new techno-economic paradigm is written by Foray and Lundvall (1996).

7. For a further study of the Dutch case, see Brouwer and Kleinknecht (1999).
8. Note however that the empirical evidence of Geroski et al. (1997) suggests that there is no significant impact of demand on the persistence of innovative behaviour of firms.
9. See Frantzen (2000) who found that, for OECD countries during the period 1961–91, the impact of the international technological diffusion on the total factor productivity was stronger than this of the domestic R&D.
10. In fact, Kleinknecht (1998) goes much further and argues against the economic orthodoxy that whereas labour market flexibility is advantageous for the growth of employment in the short run, it is detrimental in the long run since it discourages product and process innovation. Unfortunately, this important contribution cannot be analysed within the limits of this brief review essay.
11. In an earlier work Caracostas and Muldur (1995) envisaged as one of the possible solutions to the Solow paradox, the boosting of the effective demand in the world scale (pp. 108, 109).
12. Concerning this central point it seems that there are important similarities between Pascal Petit and Jürgen Habermas. The latter argues that what matters in contemporary societies is not the trade-off between the market and the state, but the capacity of citizens to control both the market and the state, though the debates developed in the public spaces (Habermas 1987).
13. See Moulaert and Conzalez (2003) for a very interesting analysis of the technological and economic determinism that characterizes the EU discourse about the Knowledge-Based Society (KBS). As the two authors comment: 'evolutionary economics is the only discipline that plays a real role in the EC's debate on the KBS. The contributions from the other social science disciplines are not known or not taken into consideration by the EC' (p. 2).
14. The EU is perhaps also the better candidate to lead a process of reform in the international economic order, aiming especially at eliminating the negative aspects of financial globalization. For the impact of the latter on investment and output, a very important issue that has not been treated within the limits of this brief essay, see Landesmann and Stehrer (2004) and Stockhammer (2004).
15. Of course, there are many other myths of the supply-side economics that need to be challenged, i.e. the ICT-based growth of the US in the last decade, the importance of training and lifelong education programmes for fighting unemployment, the technology-based explanations of the rising inequalities by the 'digital divide' doctrine, etc. Regarding the hidden 'Keynesianism' of the American model of growth and employment and the role of the health care, education, housing and pensions within it, see James Galbraith (2003).

REFERENCES

Aghion, P. and G. Saint-Paul (1998a), 'Virtues of bad times. Interaction between productivity growth and economic fluctuations', *Macroeconomic Dynamics*, 2 (2), 322–44.

Aghion, P. and G. Saint-Paul (1998b), 'Uncovering some causal relationships between productivity growth and the structure of economic fluctuations: A tentative survey', *Labour*, 12 (2), 279–303.

Aho, E. (ed.) (2006), 'Creating an Innovating Europe', Luxembourg: Office for the Official Publications of European Communities.

Boyer, R. and P. Petit (1991), 'Technical change, cumulative causation and growth: Accounting for the contemporary productivity puzzle with some post Keynesian theories', in OECD: *Technology and Productivity. The Challenge for Economic Policy*, Paris: OECD Publ.

Brouwer, E. and A. Kleinknecht (1999), 'Keynes-plus? Effective demand and changes in firm-level R&D: an empirical note', *Cambridge Journal of Economics*, 23 (3), 385–91.

Caracostas, P. and U. Muldur (1995), 'Cycles longs, technologie et emploi: Blocages actuels et perspectives', *Science, Technologie, Industrie Revue (OCDE)*, 15, 86–117.

Caracostas, P. and U. Muldur (1997), *Society, The Endless Frontier*, Luxembourg: Office for Official Publications of the European Communities.

Dosi, G. (1982), 'Technological paradigms and technological trajectories', *Research Policy*, 11 (3), 147–62.

Fagerberg, J. (1987), 'A technology gap approach to why growth rates differ', *Research Policy*, 16 (2-4), 87–99.

Foray, D. and B.A. Lundvall (1996), 'The knowledge economy: From the economics of knowledge to the learning economy', in Foray, D. and B.A. Lundvall (eds), *Employment and Growth in the Knowledge-Based Economy*, Paris: OECD Publications.

Frantzen, D. (2000), 'Innovation, international technological diffusion and the changing influence of R&D on productivity', *Cambridge Journal of Economics*, 24, 193–210.

Frantzen, D. (2003), 'The causality between R&D and productivity in manufacturing: an international disaggregate panel study', *International Journal of Applied Economics*, 17 (2), 125–46.

Freeman, C. (1982), *The Economics of Industrial Innovation*, London: Frances Pinter.

Freeman, C. (1991), 'Innovation, changes of techno-economic paradigm and biological analogies in economics', *Revue Economique*, 42 (2), 211–31.

Freeman, C. and D. Foray (1992), *Technology and the Wealth of Nations*, Paris: OECD Publications.

Freeman, C. and C. Perez (1988), 'Structural crises of adjustment: Business cycles and investment behavior', in Dosi, G. et al. (eds), *Technical Change and Economic Theory*, London and New York: Pinter Publishers and Columbia University Press.

Freeman, C. and L. Soete (1994), *Work for All or Mass Unemployment? Computerised Technical Change into the 21st Century*, London: Pinter Publishers.

Galbraith, James K. (2003), 'What is the American model really about? Soft budgets and the Keynesian devolution', *The Poznan University of Economics Review*, 3 (1), 5–21.

Geroski, P. and C.F. Walters (1995), 'Innovative activity over the business cycle', *Economic Journal*, 431, 916–28.

Geroski, P., Van Reenan, J. and C.F. Walters (1997), 'How persistently do firms innovate?', *Research Policy*, 26 (1), 33–48.

Guellec, D. and E. Ioannidis (1997), 'Causes des fluctuations des depenses de R-D. Une analyse quantitative', *Revue Economique de l'OCDE*, 29, 133–51.

Guellec, D. and B. van Pottelsberghe (1997), 'Le soutien des pouvoirs publics stimule-t-elle la R-D privée?', *Revue Economique de l'OCDE*, 29, 103–31.

Habermas, J. (1987), *The Theory of Communicative Action*, 2 volumes, Oxford: Polity Press.

Kaldor, N. (1981), 'The role of increasing returns, technical progress and cumulative causation in the theory of international trade and growth', *Economie Appliquée*, XXXIV (4), 593–617.

Kleinknecht, A. (1998), 'Is labour market flexibility harmful to innovation?', *Cambridge Journal of Economics*, 22 (3), 387–96.

Kleinknecht, A. and B. Verspagen (1990), 'Demand and innovation: Schmookler re-examined', *Research Policy*, 19 (4), 387–94.
Krugman, P. (1994), 'Competitiveness: A dangerous obsession', *Foreign Affairs*, 73 (2), 28–44.
Landsesmann, M. and R. Stehrer (2004), 'Technology diffusion, international competition and effective demand', *Revue d'Economie Industrielle*, 105, 23–46.
Lane, R. (2000), *The Loss of Happiness in the Market Democracies*, Yale: Yale University Press.
Le Bas, C. (2004), 'Demand growth as a determinant of R&D expenditures: A quantitative study at the sectoral level', *Revue d'Economie Industrielle*, 105, 11–22.
León-Ledesma M.A. (2002), 'Accumulation, innovation and catching-up: an extended cumulative growth model', *Cambridge Journal of Economics*, 26 (2), 201–16.
Liagouras, G. (2005), 'The political economy of post-industrial capitalism', *Thesis Eleven*, 81, 20–35.
Llerena, P. and A. Lorentz (2004), 'Co-evolution of macro-dynamics and technological change: an alternative view on growth', *Revue d'Economie Industrielle*, 105, 47–70.
Martin, Ph. And C.A. Roberts (1997), 'Stabilization policy, learning-by-doing, and economic growth', *Oxford Economic Papers*, 49 (2), 152–66.
Mirowski, Ph. (1983), 'An Evolutionary Theory of Economic Change. A review article', *Journal of Economic Issues*, XVII (3), 757–68.
Moulaert, F. and S. Gonzalez (2003), 'Is there life beyond the Knowledge-Based Society?' *Towards a decelerated approach to learning, creativity and enjoyment in Europe*, mimeo, GURU, University of Newcastle upon Tyne.
Mowery, D. and N. Rosenberg (1979), 'The influence of market upon innovation: a critical review of some recent empirical studies', *Research Policy*, 8 (2), 102–53.
Nelson, R.R. and S.G. Winter (1982), *An Evolutionary Theory of Economic Change*, Cambridge, MA: The Belknap Press of Harvard University Press.
Oswald, A.J. (1997), 'Happiness and economic performance', *The Economic Journal*, 107, 1815–31.
Perez, C. (1983), 'Assimilation of new technologies in the economic and social systems', *Futures*, 15 (5), 357–75.
Perez, C. (2002), *Technological Revolutions and Financial Capital. The Dynamics of Bubbles and Golden Ages*, Cheltenham, UK and Northampton, US: Edward Elgar.
Petit, P. (2003), 'On growth regimes in a post-Fordist era', Mimeo, presented at the 2003 EAEPE Conference, November 7-10, Maastricht, Netherlands.
Petit, P. (2005), *Croissance et Richesse des Nations*, Paris: La Découverte (Collection: Repères).
Petrella, R. (1995), 'Critique de la compétitivité', *Futuribles*, 198, 71–80.
Saint-Paul, G. (1993), 'Productivity growth and the structure of the business cycle', *European Economic Review*, 37 (4), 861–90.
Scitovsky, T. (1976), *The Joyless Economy. An Inquiry into Human Satisfaction and Consumer Dissatisfaction*, Oxford: Oxford University Press.
Scherer, F.M. (1982), 'Demand-pull and technological invention: Schmookler revisited', *Journal of Industrial Economics*, XXX (3), 225–37.
Schmookler, J. (1966), *Invention and Economic Growth*, Cambridge, MA: Harvard University Press.
Schumpeter, J. (1952), *Ten Great Economists*, London: Allen and Unwin.
Stadler, G.W. (1990), 'Business cycle models with endogenous technology',

American Economic Review, 80 (4), 763–78.

Stockhammer, E. (2004), 'Financialisation and the slowdown of accumulation', *Cambridge Journal of Economics*, 28 (5), 719–41.

von Tunzelmann, G.N. (2002), 'Comments from the MACROTEC project on the "Barcelona target" to raise R&D intensity in the EU to around 3% of GDP', mimeo, *SPRU*, University of Sussex, Brighton, UK.

von Tunzelmann, G.N. (2004), 'Integrating economic policy and technology policy in EU', *Revue d'Economie Industrielle*, 105, 85–104.

von Tunzelmann, G.N. and U.M. Efendioglu (2001), 'Technology, growth and employment in postwar Europe: short-run dynamics and long-run patterns', in Petit, P. and L. Soete, (eds), *Technology and the Future of the European Employment*, Cheltenham, UK and Northampton, US: Edward Elgar, 46–77.

Watanabe, C. and S. Tokumasu (2003), 'National innovation policies in an IT society: the myth of technology policy focusing on supply sides', *Science and Public Policy*, 30 (2), 70–84.

17. Economics Remains the Same – Or Does It? Challenges of the New Economy

Jorma Sappinen and Kalevi Kyläheiko

INTRODUCTION

According to Shapiro and Varian (1999, p. 2): 'Technology changes. Economic laws do not.' Stiglitz and Walsh (2003, p. 6) seem to agree in stating that 'the same fundamental laws of economics that explained agricultural prices in the eighteenth century can help us to understand how economies function at the dawn of [the] twenty-first century'. Krugman and Wells (2005, p. 533) think along similar lines: 'The principles of economics remain the same as ever, and the issues raised by information goods are not new.' These statements by these prominent economists puzzle us because the New Economy seems to have brought along various phenomena incongruent (in various ways) with standard mainstream economics, at the substantive, methodological and economic-policy levels. The above quotations are all drawn from the pages of textbooks, and perhaps the authors' need to assure students of the importance of learning plain economic theory explains these quite bold, and in our view not quite well-justified, statements.

Along with the rise of the so called New Economy in the 1990s, an increasing number of new types of goods, usually called information goods,[1] appeared to take up an increasing share of the GNP. Information goods often seem to differ from the more traditional (or standard) goods in terms of both production and consumption activities. For example, because of novel sources of economies of scale and scope, information goods appear to have features that would ruin the incentive to produce anything that does not carry monopoly power. For instance, if they were priced according to marginal costs that often come close to zero, no one would be willing to produce them any longer. In addition, since it is not viable to use traditional marginalist principles as a decision rule when pricing, the consumer's willingness to pay becomes the most decisive, or the only, criterion. Its use is difficult and complicated, however, because many information goods are by nature experience goods, i.e. goods you have to experience first in order to know how valuable they are to you.

Our idea is to look at the possible changes that the rise of the New Economy might generate within the fundamental principles of economics used in the received view. Certainly, views on the exact definition of the core principles adopted in the received view differ among economists, but in mainstream microeconomics certain elements seem to be more fundamental in that they are to be found in almost all of the (basic) models economists build when analysing various economic and social phenomena. With a view to capturing these core principles, Hausman (1992) introduced the basic equilibrium model, which includes the most fundamental law-like statements of microeconomics. This basic model could be seen as a reduced and condensed package of the basic causal ideas of microeconomics. It also constitutes the way in which economists are tempted to think when analysing real-world phenomena. Of course, we are fully aware that not all contemporary microeconomic models include all the laws of the basic equilibrium model, and that, in order to do a proper job in analysing real-world economic phenomena, mainstream economists often use various kinds of additional assumptions to supplement these laws. Nevertheless, in order to analyse and appraise the views of the prominent economists quoted above, we need to fix the fundamental economic laws and law-like statements, even if their status is somewhat subject to debate.

No doubt the very concept of the New Economy has also provoked a considerable amount of media hype. Hence, it is easy to understand that serious scholars with the attitude that it is better to analyse before assessing remain cautious about the sustainable importance of the phenomenon, despite (or even because of) the hype.[2] Still, when it comes to the profession of economics, our view is that the reaction has been slow, and that so far surprisingly small amounts of resources have been allocated to the serious study of the basic characteristics of the New Economy and the way in which the potential changes might affect the law-like sentences used in the received view. Perhaps the fact that economic research is often strongly theory driven and slow to react to changes in the real world partly explains the relatively low level of interest among economists. Our aim in this chapter is to analyse the challenges the New Economy presents to microeconomics, especially in terms of whether the more or less fundamental parts and causal mechanisms of the received view are called into question. Our analysis makes a modest attempt to point out which parts, if any, of the received view should be modified in order to improve its explanatory power when accounting for phenomena related to the rise of the New Economy.

CHARACTERISING THE BASIC EQUILIBRIUM MODEL

Basic economic theory is certainly a contestable concept. However, mainstream microeconomics shows considerable uniformity if examined at the textbook level. Although novel economics principles and intermediate microeconomics textbooks are published, and contemporary works are revised constantly, new theoretical and empirical developments do not surface at this level. Hence, the basic theoretical core seems to be intact. We know, of course, that the textbooks give too uniform a picture of the research practice at the frontiers of economics, where one meets theoretical, empirical and methodological challenges to the standard theory (see, for example, Colander et al. 2004 and Davis 2006a). Forecasting whether economics will be theoretically more uniform in the future, and what its theoretical core will comprise, seems to be particularly difficult at present. After the relatively stable period in the development of core microeconomics over many decades, recent times have been quite turbulent, on both the theoretical (e.g., evolutionary game theory, behavioural economics, complexity theory) and the empirical (e.g., experimental economics) level.[3]

However, to be able to consider the (ir)relevance of the challenges of the New Economy we have to establish what we mean by the received view in basic microeconomics. In our opinion, Hausman's equilibrium theory, or the basic equilibrium model, gives a good starting point for discussion. According to Hausman, its fundamental elements are consumer and producer theory, and the assertion that markets quickly reach (stable and unique) equilibrium. In total, the theory comprises seven laws or law-like statements. In the words of Hausman (1992, p. 30), the theory of consumer choice consists of the following three laws or law-like statements:

(1) (*Rationality*) Individuals are rational (they have complete, transitive, and continuous preferences and do not prefer any available (affordable) option to the one they choose).

(2) (*Consumerism*) (a) The objects of every individual *i*'s preferences are bundles of commodities consumed by *i*, (b) there are no interdependencies between the preferences of different individuals, and (c) up to some point of satiation (that is typically unattained), individuals prefer larger commodity bundles to smaller. Bundle *y* is larger than bundle *x* if it contains at least as much of every commodity or service as does *x* and more of some commodity or service. Consumerism implies self-interest.[4]

(3) (*Diminishing marginal rates of substitution*) For all individuals *i* and all commodities or services *x* and *y*, *i* is willing to exchange more of *y* for a unit of *x* as the amount of *y i* has increases relative to the amount of *x i* has.

Consumer-choice theory is used to explain and predict the demand side of markets. In order to work, however, they must also have a supply side, the basic laws of which are summarised in the theory of the firm. Hausman (1992, p. 43) states that the theory of the firm is made up of three laws or law-like statements:

(1) The quantity of output in any production process is an increasing function of each of the inputs to the process, but within the range of the quantities of inputs normally used by the firm, the extent to which any given input *d* increases output, quantities of the other inputs held fixed, is a decreasing function of the quantity of *d* ('diminishing returns').
(2) If in the neighbourhood of the equilibrium point, *all* of the inputs into production are increased or decreased in the same ratio then output will increase or decrease in exactly that ratio ('constant returns to scale').
(3) Firms attempt to maximise net returns or 'profits' ('profit maximisation').

In addition, Hausman (1992, pp. 51–2) considers the assertion that markets clear to be a fundamental constituent of the received view of microeconomics. He admits that not all microeconomics models incorporate all these seven law-like statements, and some may even go directly against some of them. There also seems to be a difference in status when compared to the basic laws of natural science, in the domain of which any questioning of the fundamental laws just for the sake of theoretical exercise would not be considered a sensible thing to do at all.

NEW PHENOMENA OF THE NEW ECONOMY AS CHALLENGERS OF THE RECEIVED VIEW

New Wine in Old Bottles: An Introduction to the Peculiarities of Information Goods

The New Economy has already brought a lot of changes into the real-world sphere. For example, it has made production in many sectors much more efficient due to the adoption of new production and distribution technologies, especially those based on breakthroughs in information and communication technologies (ICT). It has also increased labour and total factor productivity, and hence GNP growth, thus increasing the people's welfare by bringing out new kinds of goods and by making many older ones cheaper, for example.

One way of making things clearer is to make a distinction between microeconomic and macroeconomic changes. DeLong and Summers (2001, p. 3) suggest that the principal effects of the New Economy are more likely to be microeconomic than macroeconomic in nature. In fact, they only find two possible useful macroeconomic consequences: the possibility of lower average unemployment rates, and the chance that firms' enhanced inventory control will diminish the inventory-driven component of business cycles. Both of these clearly reduce the need for traditional interventionist macroeconomic policy using fiscal and monetary policy as instruments.

They also suggest that the microeconomic effects generated by the New Economy will generate structural changes in terms of how the open markets work, which will also call for new kinds of government thinking on the role of competition and technology policy. In brief, DeLong and Summers (2001, p. 5) see issues 'of benefits from the extent of market, of price discrimination and the distribution of economic well-being, of monopoly, and of the interaction of intellectual property with scientific communication and research ... very important and very complicated'.

In an attempt to make sense of the fundamental changes in the microeconomic sphere, DeLong and Froomkin (1999, p. 6) argue that all the 'three pillars' on which the working of a market economy has traditionally rested are being shaken by the changes the New Economy is bringing along with it. These three pillars represent three features of the workings of property rights and exchange. The first of these is excludability, which means that sellers are able to charge buyers for the goods and services they have consumed; the second is rivalry, which means that long-term average costs (of production) are roughly constant (or at least there are no infinite economies of scale); and the third feature is transparency, which means that it has been quite easy for consumers to see and recognise what they need, what is for sale, and how their desires are to be fulfilled. The New Economy is shaking all of these three pillars at the same time.

If there is no excludability the purchase-and-sale relationship between a producer and a consumer vanishes, as does the traditional basis for market exchange. If there were any exchange, it could only be of some other nature, such as some kind of gift exchange based on reciprocity and/or altruism between individuals, otherwise the government would have to arrange the production and distribution of these goods in order to maximise the value of consumers' surplus.

If the marginal cost of a commodity is zero, then, as the standard Pareto-efficiency condition holds, the price should also be zero. If that were the case, however, private profit-maximising firms would be willing to produce such a commodity only if it were a by-product of some other product (giving the necessary returns), and if it could be used as a marketing device for some of the firm's other products, e.g., through generating goodwill among potential customers. It is hard to find any other cases in which a non-rival good could be privately produced.

One of the traditional boosters of the development and extension of market exchange has been commodity transparency. If the consumer knows what he or she wants and is getting when making the purchase, some of the basic requirements for an exchange are fulfilled, as uncertainty related to the decision situation is substantially reduced.[5]

The next step is (i) to bring to light the peculiar characteristics of information goods flooding into the New Economy, (ii) to show how they differ from the more traditional goods, and (iii) to study some of the major implications of these differences. This will enable us to see, among other things, how the three pillars outlined by DeLong and Froomkin really are being challenged. The main peculiarities of information goods compared with normal or standard goods include the following:

(1) The creation of a piece of new knowledge is related to prevalent market- and technology-driven uncertainties. Sharing these risks generates incentives for partnerships, and to some extent results in a network economy, i.e. in an economy in which 'a distinct form of interfirm organization ... works alongside and in combination with markets and hierarchies' (Fischer 2003, p. 345).
(2) The creation of a piece of new knowledge often requires large fixed sunk costs that cannot be covered by reselling (large first-copy costs). Hence, the average total costs are often strongly decreasing.
(3) The new codified knowledge is easy to copy, transfer and imitate, i.e. the marginal costs of transferring and copying come close to zero. This kind of commodity is called non-rival.[6] Non-rival goods, once they are produced, can be distributed to additional consumers without extra cost.
(4) Because of the (almost) zero marginal costs, a piece of knowledge cannot be priced in such terms: the pricing or valuation of a knowledge-based information good requires detailed knowledge about the willingness to pay of potential customers.
(5) A piece of knowledge can be utilised without losing its inherent value, and it can be transferred, even over the whole of mankind, without the loss of its use value. Although there have existed various public goods with this feature of non-excludability for a long time, the number has increased dramatically with the digital revolution. Various digital goods, i.e. 'bit strings, sequences of 0 and 1 that have economic value' (Quah 2003, p. 289), a subset of information goods, are cheap and easy to copy, and while there are ways of making things difficult and troublesome for the copier, the use of such methods involves extra costs and complexity. This, in turn, generates

positive externalities in production and, much more interestingly, also on the demand side. These information-related positive network externalities (i.e. the more users there are, the more valuable a piece of knowledge is) generate increasing marginal returns, and facilitate the shedding of the production-capacity constraints that are so typical of traditional commodity production.
(6) Knowledge is inherently cumulative and path-dependent, meaning that history really matters. Therefore the technological options chosen are not necessarily the optimal ones, as the famous QWERTY example shows.
(7) As for the nature of knowledge, part of the knowledge base is tacit, which in turn means that it is hard to transfer but easy to protect, while another part is more or less codified, thus implying easy transfer but hard appropriation. It should be noted that the existence of this continuum from tacit to codified knowledge has the effect of blurring the clear-cut distinction between excludability and rivalry in talk about the very nature of a piece of knowledge. Many mainstream economists following the lead of Arrow overemphasise its codified nature when interpreting knowledge simply as a non-excludable (and non-rival) public good. Satellite and cable television offers a good counter-example: it is clearly non-rival but excludable, thus generating enough incentives to produce programmes privately. Hence, the production of information goods does not always entail market failure. It is just this phenomenon that makes it very complicated to create workable legal rules for competition and technology policy.
(8) Decreasing average total costs and increasing marginal returns due to network externalities together generate what has been called the first mover's advantage (which can even be strengthened by entering into knowledge-sharing partnership contracts).

We will illustrate this curiosity not with one unique stable equilibrium but with two equilibria of which the first is unstable and the second is stable, which is becoming more and more common, in the following (Figure 17.1, see http://www.inforules.com).

Figure 17.1: Network Externalities and the Crucial Role of the Critical Mass in the Case of Information Goods

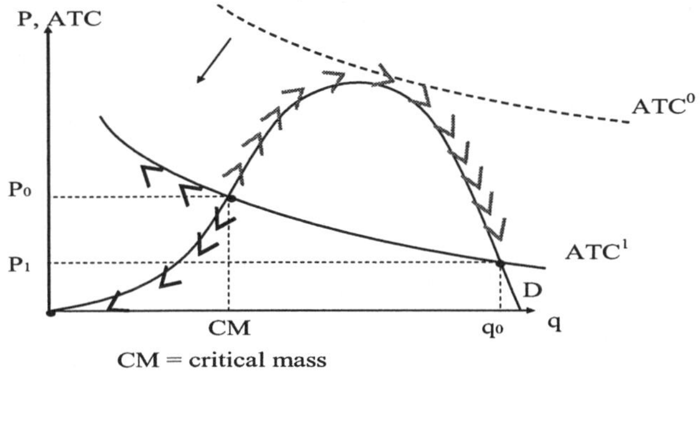

The basic assumptions giving rise to positive network externality are as follows:

(a) The more users there are, the more valuable is the commodity, i.e. the willingness to pay (wtp) is increasing and the demand curve (D) is sloping upwards at first, but there is an upper limit to this. The wtp then begins to decrease, resulting in a downwards-sloping demand curve.

(b) Finally, when there are only customers who are not so interested in the product, (i.e. the wtp approaches 0), the D curve turns down.

(c) Due to large fixed sunk costs there are economies of scale in production, implying a decreasing average total cost curve (ATC), and also decreasing marginal costs.

The logic of network externality can be explained by means of the following telecommunications example. Take a situation in which a potential UMTS licence-owner operator makes a decision on whether to start to provide telecommunications services in a new country dominated by strong native operators already in the markets with relative large market shares. The two equilibria (Figure 17.1) convey the idea of this real-world phenomenon in an interesting way. The following two options are available to a new operator:

(a) The no-entry option: At the high-average-cost level (ATC^0) the newcomer operator cannot start production at all, since it always holds that ATC > WTP (willingness to pay). There is no chance of success.

(b) The loser loses everything or the winner takes it all.

Let us assume now that the net manufacturer makes it financially possible for the operator to shift its ATC curve downwards (from ATC^0 to ATC^1) by subsidising the building up of necessary nets. Cooperation between operators may also make this target feasible as the large sunk costs can be shared. At this stage we can now identify the importance of the critical mass (CM), where ATC^1 = WTP = D, thus resulting in the stable 'winner takes it all' network externality equilibrium characterised by the quantity q^0 and the price P^1. However, if the operator cannot reach the CM he or she is trapped by the devil's dynamics and loses everything she/he has invested in the project.

The main lesson here, according to Shapiro and Varian (1999, pp. 50–1), is the following: in markets in which there is more than one player, only the biggest or fastest is able to survive. Information is costly to produce but cheap to reproduce, which makes the first mover's advantages valuable.

(9) Arrow's dilemma in terms of the valuation of the willingness to pay: if you do not know the value of a piece of information, you are not willing to pay anything for it, and if you know its true value, in fact you already have it and are not willing to pay anything for it either. This is a typical characteristic of all so-called experience goods. According to Shapiro and

Varian (1999, p. 6), the answer is to give away some prototypes to potential customers, and to diversify the product according to the willingness to pay. This raises another special problem typical of an information society, i.e. 'the tension between giving away your information – to let people know what you have to offer – and charging them for it to recover your costs'. In many cases networking helps to overcome these problems of getting customers locked-in: a small sub-contractor may succeed in this by networking with a big partner with a strong brand and the ability to set standards, for instance. However, there are many risks involved in this strategy: we only need to think about the fate of the Apple-using software producers who almost lost the game after betting on the wrong horse.

Sometimes, too, experiential learning of the right value may take a long time and lots of work, since many information goods tend to be non-transparent by nature. For instance, it is not easy to fully understand the real quality of a piece of software, i.e. the usefulness of all its features, its compatibility with other software, and the producer's commitment to its future development.

(10) The main methods of pricing the piece of information are: (i) personalised pricing, i.e. selling to each customer at a different price, (ii) group pricing, i.e. setting different prices for different customer groups, and (iii) versioning, i.e. offering varieties of products and allowing the customers to choose from them according to their needs (revealed through the willingness to pay) (Shapiro and Varian 1999, p. 39).

(11) Since the only way to cover large, fixed sunk costs is to use monopoly power in some form, there is always a built-in and inherent contradiction between the neoclassical anti-trust ideals of (almost) perfect competition and the ability to generate viable first-mover advantage based on competitive equilibrium in an information society. Once again, there is an evident need to rethink the emphases and priorities in the trade-off between traditional competition and technology policies.

While production and distribution technologies have been progressing for a long time, and various technological revolutions have occurred, in our view the changes the New Economy is bringing along are fundamental and cannot be overlooked. They have significant implications for consumer and producer behaviour, and for the working of the market. By way of a simple concluding observation, if we consider the above list of peculiarities from the perspective of the firm, clearly the starting point is that the structure of the market for information goods is likely to be imperfect, and that firms can use various means to exercise their market power. In terms of profit maximisation, it would be silly to take the market price (if that even exists for a novel commodity!) as given.

A Closer Look at Basic Consumer Theory in the New Economy

As mentioned above, according to Hausman the basic law-like statements of consumer-choice theory are rationality, consumerism, and the diminishing marginal rate of substitution. For one thing, the law of the diminishing marginal rate of substitution clearly seems to be intact: the commodities that are typical of the New Economy do not seem be exceptions to this law as it is formulated in the received view.

Then the problems start, however. The rationality assumption of standard microeconomic theory seems to be called into question. Many commodities of the New Economy possess features of experience goods, meaning that only after their purchase and use is the consumer able to learn what he or she really has. What is worse, this process may be slow, and involves a great deal of uncertainty. For example, one may need to learn more computer and other skills in order to be able to use all of the features of a piece of software, and only after this learning does one have the ability to compare the value of that piece of software to the value its competitors will provide. Moreover, these (learning) processes often involve path-dependency and lock-ins, making it hard to switch over to some other commodity once some initial investments have been made. In our view, these transparency-related problems represent a serious challenge to the assumption of the completeness of preferences, according to which a consumer is able, at some point of time, to rank all the possible bundles of commodities he or she can afford at the given prices and income. Certainly this assumption is unrealistic, even in the case of traditional (and more transparent) commodities, because it requires a huge information management and storage capacity when the number of commodities is large (especially when the so-called contingent commodities of the Arrow–Debreu model are included). However, the experienced-good nature of many information goods makes the assumption of completeness of preferences increasingly unrealistic.

The 'law of consumerism' consists of assumptions that the objects of the preferences of an individual are commodities personally consumed, and that there are no interdependencies between the preferences of different individuals. There are several commodities in the New Economy with strong, usually positive, network externalities. The utility an individual gains from using some means of communication, such as fax machines and telephones, and/or software, is dependent on how many users there are of these commodities, and not only on his or her consumption, as is the case with a standard rival commodity such as beer. For example, when choosing between personal computers with different operating systems, one has to consider the preferences of the people with whom one works and interacts (to prevent frequent incompatibilities), and the preferences of computer users in general (to ensure the future development of software and hardware and their maintenance, for example). Thus, it is not only the sheer number of other users that matters, but also who uses the product, i.e. how popular it is among those with whom one frequently interacts.

Reciprocity, i.e. the willingness to reward friendly actions and to punish hostile ones even though the reward or punishment might cause a net reduction in the material payoff of those who reward and punish (Camerer and Fehr 2004, p. 56), may explain phenomena related to the lack of direct compensation for the development of some software in the voluntary communities of programmers (the so-called Open Source movement). In this case, consumers are simultaneously producers, and the development work is a form of gift exchange in which all participants gain if they are playing their part in the whole enterprise. This phenomenon could also be explained in terms of each individual's effort to gain a reputation, and with it in all probability a well-paid job in the future (Quah 2003, pp. 313–4). While both motives may be involved in the decision to participate in this kind of software development, the benefits of creating a good reputation are usually more uncertain and not immediate, while those of producing improved programmes are fairly immediate, if all concerned are doing their part.[7] Moreover, as Quah (2003, p. 316) notes, economists have not so far been able to formulate 'a complete economic equilibrium description of how successful outcomes can emerge from the complex range of individual actions and mass interactions undertaken in Open Source software'. An interesting interpretation of the open-source movement is provided by Bowles (2004, p. 501). He suggests that 'a system of prestige and norms of sharing' will replace market-type interaction, and that in this respect the interaction in this movement resembles the culture of the foraging band of human prehistory.[8]

A Closer Look at the Theory of the Firm and the Functioning of Open Markets in the New Economy

The law of diminishing returns seems be safe from the changes the New Economy is bringing along, if this ceteris paribus law describes a short-run technical regularity. The law of profit maximisation as formulated by Hausman also seems be quite safe. One should nevertheless remember that the degree of profit maximisation by the firms of the New Economy will crucially depend on the extension of the (intellectual) property rights societies will adopt. In the case of information goods this is a subtle normative issue, and the interests of firms and the whole of society may easily strongly conflict. We will not discuss this issue here, however (see Kyläheiko 2005).

The status of the law of constant returns to scale is questioned by the development of the New Economy because increasing returns are the consequence of the non-rival character of commodities, and are most likely to occur in commodity (including knowledge as a commodity!) production, which is highly technology-intensive. The production of various digital goods is the most likely candidate for increasing returns. The bigger the proportion of industries with increasing returns to scale, the further away the economy will be from perfect competition. Some new methods of price comparison and other technologies (such as shopping agents finding the cheapest prices available for a specified item) functioning on the Internet may intensify the price competition in a number of markets by reducing transaction costs. However, it is likely that, in general, market competition in the New Economy will be, in various ways, imperfect. It will not be price competition, but quality competition related to various forms of product differentiation that will rule.

The seventh law-like statement in Hausman's list is that markets clear or that equilibrium is attained. While there are several different concepts of equilibrium, Hausman seems to have in mind traditional equilibrium of markets with perfect competition. The market structure is monopolistic or oligopolistic in many of the growing sectors of the New Economy, and it is possible that there are multiple equilibria. Certainly, economics textbooks have long included models of imperfect competition, but still the model of perfect competition has occupied centre stage, both because in the Walrasian tradition the belief in the working of the price mechanism has been strong and because the assumption of perfect competition is used when deriving influential welfare theorems. It remains to be seen whether models of imperfect competition, with parallel changes in welfare economics, will gain a more prominent position at the textbook level, thus better characterising the features of the New Economy. Moreover, when there are network externalities multiple equilibria may exist even under perfect competition because some portions of the demand curve may slope upwards (see Figure 17.1 above and Economides 2006, p. 100).

CONCLUSIONS

Engelbrecht (2003, p. 60), in his discussion of the New Economy in terms of the 'usefulness' of the tools of mainstream economics, provides what he calls 'a short answer':

> parts of mainstream economics have become less relevant, but so far it is more a question of emphasizing the increased importance of already existing, but

previously less prominent, concepts instead of having to develop a 'new economics' that revokes basic economic laws.

Like Engelbrecht, many prominent mainstream economists (see section 1 above) have found that the phenomena associated with the New Economy do not really challenge the principles of economics. For example, Shapiro and Varian (1999, p. x) state: 'You don't need a brand new economics. You just need to see the really cool stuff.'[9] Simultaneously, however, these economists often maintain that the New Economy is bringing along significant structural changes, using as an example the affluence of novel commodities with features that make them somehow less suitable for market exchange than the more traditional commodities.

Many economists have also expressed the view that some developments in the New Economy have led to the reconsideration of competition policy issues. For example, DeLong and Summers (2001, p. 7) see it as 'Schumpeterian' (while the traditional economy is (was) 'Smithian'), and claim that 'the competitive paradigm cannot be fully appropriate' in this new economic environment. The traditional normative wisdom of microeconomics is usually based on the so-called (two) welfare theorems (on the relationship of competitive equilibrium and Pareto-optimality), and these theorems are derived using the Walrasian framework (the general equilibrium model or the Arrow–Debreu model). If these welfare theorems form the basis of normative thinking, it would, in our view, be natural to assume that economists are consistently committed to the idea that the Walrasian general equilibrium model also describes the workings of the market economy quite well.

In our discussion about the relationship between phenomena of the New Economy and basic equilibrium theory we have suggested that not all the laws of basic equilibrium theory are realistic descriptions of how a large part of the current economy works. We could call these laws the core assumptions of neoclassical (Walrasian type) microeconomics. Neoclassical models always include a host of other unrealistic assumptions, which are not as central as those outlined by Hausman, i.e. they involve various auxiliary assumptions. While all economic theories, including the classical, the neoclassical, the institutional and the evolutionary, involve unrealistic assumptions, it is less serious for the theory in question if the auxiliary assumptions rather than the core ones are unrealistic, because economists are not as committed to them as they are to core assumptions.

The situation among mainstream economists seems to be quite puzzling. On the one hand, they make bold statements that economic laws do not change, and thus they signal their commitment to the core assumptions of neoclassical microeconomics. On the other hand, they point out some major changes brought out by the New Economy, namely phenomena that clearly seem to be incongruent with (or even contradictory to) some laws of microeconomics. How does one explain this curious situation? It could be that, even if (mainstream) economics graduate-level teaching is still dominated by the economic laws Hausman outlines, the leading economists do not really believe in them. The bold statements quoted may be mere rhetoric (which anyone well-informed enough does not really believe), directed mainly to various outsiders such as newcomer students of economics, other social scientists and lay people to assure them about the explanatory capabilities of the discipline. On the other hand, economists might really have adopted a Friedmanian instrumentalist stance towards economic theories, and thereby feel free to make any assumptions as long as they promote the formulation of useful theories or make successful predictions.

At face value, it seems that mainstream economists are not seriously committed to the general equilibrium model (and the assumption of perfect competition) as a description of the working of the economy, even though many of them consider market competition important for economic efficiency. The model of perfect competition incorporates strong abstractions, and consequently it is not descriptively accurate in most (or all) situations.[10] Indeed, mainstream economists seem to be quite flexible in selecting models to analyse economic phenomena, as long as it is an equilibrium model. Often an instrumentalist attitude of sorts appears to rule. Still, if and when economists analysing the information economy (e.g., Shapiro and Varian 1999) make recommendations, or offer 'lessons' as they call them, on how firms should make their strategic decisions, they are at least implicitly committed to the idea that economic theory really says something about causal mechanisms. If you are giving firms recommendations, they should be based on knowledge of causal relationships, e.g., do x (differentiating) to obtain the desired outcome y (more profits). In our view, giving such advice does not make sense if the economists giving it are not committed to the truth and relevancy of their theories.

We have taken a somewhat different line in this chapter to the one held by mainstream economists interested in the New Economy. First, we are interested in the issue of how the changes it has brought might affect our thinking on the laws of economics. In other words, we take the laws outlined by Hausman seriously as descriptions of the working of the real economy. Secondly, we think that there is, at the minimum, a need for discussion on the applicability of these basic laws, and their possible alternatives, in this novel situation generated by the rise of the New Economy. We find bold statements such as 'the economic laws do change' misleading if they are not suitably qualified. The leading economists in question have not specified what they mean by economic laws when making these statements. Due to the long-lasting dominance of the Walrasian paradigm in mainstream economics, we assume that many mainstream economists understand economic laws to be those outlined by Hausman (some of which are included in the competitive general equilibrium model). If it is the case that an increasingly larger number of industries are subject to increasing returns, path-dependency and lock-ins, and network effects, the core assumptions of mainstream economics are increasingly unrealistic descriptions of the current economy (contrary to what Leibowitz (2006, p. 168 and Quah suggest! See endnote 10 below). Although all theories and models are, at least to some degree, unrealistic, the models that allow for and deal with increasing returns, path-dependency and lock-ins, and network effects are, in our view, significantly less unrealistic than traditional mainstream models.

It may well be that any possible shortcomings of the Walrasian paradigm are not immediately evident in its condensed expressions such as the one put forward by Hausman. As Bowles (2004, pp. 9–10) points out, implicit in the paradigm has been the assumption that individual interaction is governed by complete and readily enforceable contracts.[11] While the effects of incomplete contracts have been studied in mainstream economics, quite often phenomena related to them are seen as special cases, not the generic case. If the idea of the non-contractual character of much economic and other social interaction is accepted, this puts more emphasis on the study of norms and power, for example, instead of market exchange in governing human interaction. Moreover, Bowles argues for taking 'generalised increasing returns' seriously. While the issue of returns to scale in production was made explicit, and discussed above, the idea of generalised increasing returns is not limited to production, but 'refers to any situation in which the payoff to taking an action is increasing in the number of people taking the same action' (Bowles, 2004, p. 12). Generalised increasing returns may occur in the sphere of consumption as well as in the institutional sphere of an economy. The implicit assumption in the Walrasian tradition has been that while commodities are scarce, (efficient market) institutions are freely available. This should be put under scrutiny in the development of theories applicable to the New Economy, which underline the importance of strategic behaviour, both towards other actors and towards the institutional environment, resulting (in various ways) in inefficient outcomes if the Walrasian paradigm is taken as the standard. Let us allow Bowles (2004, p. 500) to sum up:

> Direct noncontractual interactions with positive feedbacks arise increasingly in modern economies, as information-intensive team production replaces assembly lines and other technologies and other technologies more readily handled by contract, and as difficult to measure services usurp the pre-eminent role – as both outputs and inputs – once played by measurable quantities like kilowatts of power

and tons of steel.

While developments related to the New Economy will not make all economic laws obsolete, the need for a new kind of economic thinking is, in our view, clear.

NOTES

1. Krugman and Wells (2005, p. 520) define information goods as 'products whose value comes not from their physical characteristics but from the information they embody.'
2. Discussion in the popular press of the revolutionary character of the New Economy has often drifted to excesses, as Stan Leibowitz (2006, 146-9) has illustrated with quotations from the Wall Street Journal. Leibowitz is clearly irritated by the hype, but as a '... neolithic Chicago School economist' he is also irritated by the questioning of the relevance of standard microeconomics found in the article.
3. Davis (2006a) has even argued that economics is currently moving from neoclassical dominance to mainstream pluralism. Note, however, that he (Davis 2006b) has also lately discussed the return of a dominant approach within the discipline, deriving from motives within the profession such as 'the need to speak with a unified voice regarding policy', and 'the need to suppress debate over the character of economics as a science'.
4. An example of a modern piece of research that does not take this law for granted is that conducted by Heinrich et al. (2004), in which the existence of various kinds of 'pro-social' preferences is studied. The assumption of self-interest is questioned by means of game theory and experimental methods.
5. Exchange in the New Economy may also cause problems concerning whether and how much to trust your trading partner when there is usually less personal interaction than has traditionally been the case (Ben-Ner and Putterman, 2003). In a way, the problem of trust is a matter of transparency, albeit the transparency of your trading partner and not of commodities.
6. Note that some non-rival commodities have been with us for a long time, lighthouses (and other pure public goods) being a prime example.
7. The development work may also involve a great deal of intrinsic motivation, in other words the person participating is interested in the programming itself, instead of or in addition to the extrinsic motivation of reputation building.
8. This is just a single example of how interactions between individuals became noncontractual, and are coordinated by means other than markets – in this case, quite successfully. This success may puzzle many economists because they have been used to thinking that market interaction is more efficient than other forms of interaction.
9. Shapiro and Varian (1999, p. x) suggest that economics 'literature on differential pricing, bundling, signaling, licensing, lock-in, or network' belong to this 'cool stuff'.
10. Quah (2003, p. 292) suggests the opposite, however: 'because many observers consider the ideal of zero transaction cost, instantaneously buyer-seller matched, friction-free, transparent, perfect-information markets to be the end result of the new economy in any case, studying what happens at the limit point, i.e., what textbook economics has always assumed in the Arrow-Debreu model, might yield more enduring insight than will studying the hypothesized transition towards it.'
11. Software is a typical New Economy commodity that is not subject to complete contracting. The incompleteness is related to the quality of the piece of software. For example, the buyer is faced with uncertainty about its updating, as well as its compatibility with other software in the future.

REFERENCES

Ben-Ner, Avner and Louis Putterman (2003), 'Trust in the New Economy', in Derek C. Jones (ed.), *New Economy Handbook*, San Diego, US: Elsevier, pp. 1067–95.

Bowles, Samuel (2004), *Microeconomics: Behavior, Institutions and Evolution*, Princeton, US: Princeton University Press.

Camerer, Colin and Ernst Fehr (2004), 'Measuring Social Norms and Preferences Using Experimental Games', in Joseph Heinrich, Robert Boyd, Samuel Bowles, Colin Camerer, Ernst Fehr and Herbert Gintis (eds), *Foundations of Human Sociality, Economic Experiments and Ethnographic evidence from Fifteen Small-Scale Societies*, Oxford University Press, pp. 55–95.

Colander, David, Richard P.F. Holt and J. Barkley Rosser Jr (2004), *The Changing Face of Economics, Conversations with Cutting Edge Economists*, University of Michigan Press.

Davis John B. (2006a), 'The Turn in Economics: Neoclassical Dominance to Mainstream Pluralism?', *Journal of Institutional Economics*, 2 (1), 1–20.

Davis John B. (2006b), 'The Turn in and Return of Orthodoxy in Recent Economics', paper presented in History of Economics Society Conference, June 2006, Grinnell College, Iowa, The United States.

DeLong, J. Bradford and A. Michael Froomkin (1999), 'Speculative Microeconomics for Tomorrow's Economy', http://www.j-bradford-delong.net/Econ_Articles/Econ_Articles.html.

DeLong, J. Bradford and Lawrence H. Summers (2001), 'The "New Economy": Background, Questions and Speculations', http://www.j-bradford-delong.net/Econ_Articles/Econ_Articles.html.

Economides, Nicholas (2006), 'Competition policy in network industries: an introduction', in Dennis W. Jansen (ed.), *The New Economy and Beyond - Past, Present and Future*, Cheltenham, UK and Northampton, MA, US: Edward Elgar, pp. 96–121.

Engelbrecht, Hans-Jurgen (2003) 'Data Issues in the New Economy', in Derek C. Jones (ed.), *New Economy Handbook*, San Diego, US: Elsevier, pp. 57–76.

Fischer, Manfred M. (2003), 'The New Economy and Networking', in Derek C. Jones (ed.), *New Economy Handbook*, San Diego, US: Elsevier, pp. 343–367.

Hausman, Daniel (1992), *The Inexact and Separate Science of Economics*, Cambridge UK: Cambridge University Press.

Heinrich, Joseph, Robert Boyd, Samuel Bowles, Colin Camerer, Ernst Fehr and Herbert Gintis (eds) (2004), *Foundations of Human Sociality, Economic Experiments and Ethnographic Evidence from Fifteen Small-Scale Societies*, Oxford University Press.

Krugman, Paul and Robin Wells (2005), *Microeconomics*, Worth.

Kyläheiko, Kalevi (2005), 'From Comedy of Commons to Tragedy of Anti-Commons', in G. Huber, H. Krämer and H.D. Kurz (eds), *Einkommensverteilung, technischer Fortschritt und struktureller Wandel*, Metropolis Verlag, pp. 191-207.

Quah, Danny (2003), 'Digital Goods and the New Economy', in Derek C. Jones (ed), *New Economy Handbook*, San Diego, US: Elsevier, pp. 289–321.

Shapiro, Carl and Hal R. Varian (1999), *Information Rules, A Strategic Guide to the Network Economy*, Boston, US: Harvard Business School Press.

Stiglitz, Joseph E. and Carl E. Walsh (2003), *Economics*, New York, US: W.W. Norton & Company.

Index